THE ABUSE OF CONSCIENCE

The Abuse of Conscience

A Century of Catholic Moral Theology

Matthew Levering

WILLIAM B. EERDMANS PUBLISHING COMPANY
GRAND RAPIDS, MICHIGAN

Wm. B. Eerdmans Publishing Co.
4035 Park East Court SE, Grand Rapids, Michigan 49546
www.eerdmans.com

27 26 25 24 23 22 21   1 2 3 4 5 6 7

ISBN 978-0-8028-7950-9

Library of Congress Cataloging-in-Publication Data

Names: Levering, Matthew, 1971– author.
Title: The Abuse of Conscience: a century of Catholic moral theology /
    Matthew Levering.
Description: Grand Rapids, Michigan : Wm. B. Eerdmans Publishing Co.,
    [2021] | Includes bibliographical references and index. | Summary: "A sur-
    vey of twentieth-century Catholic moral theology with an overarching
    argument against conscience-centered Christian ethics"—Provided by
    publisher.
Identifiers: LCCN 2021018067 | ISBN 9780802879509 (hardcover)
Subjects: LCSH: Christian ethics—Catholic authors—History—20th century.
    | Conscience—Religious aspects—Catholic Church.
Classification: LCC BJ1249 .L465 2021 | DDC 241—dc23
LC record available at https://lccn.loc.gov/2021018067

Contents

Acknowledgments

Many generous scholars have made corrections to this manuscript and directed me toward relevant sources. Matthew Minerd carefully reviewed the chapters on the moral manuals and Thomism, and his suggestions greatly strengthened these chapters. He also graciously permitted me to use his translation of Benoît-Henri Merkelbach, OP's text. Nick Ogle read the whole manuscript at an early stage and offered encouragement and corrections. Reinhard Hütter, Joshua Steele, and Bill Mattison read parts of the manuscript, resulting in valuable improvements. Jörgen Vijgen helped me to track down important secondary literature without which I would have missed key connections. Melanie Barrett, professor of moral theology here at Mundelein Seminary, gave me some articles that proved to be of great value. Cajetan Cuddy, OP, read the full manuscript at a late stage and offered welcome encouragement. During the COVID-19 lockdown, when even a trip to the post office was a big deal, Emery de Gaál mailed me some needed books from Germany.

An earlier version of my discussion of Servais Pinckaers, OP, in chapter 3 and of my discussion of Bernard Häring, CSsR, in chapter 4 was written in late 2017 for the inaugural Pinckaers Symposium co-organized by Bill Mattison and me and held in May 2018 at Moreau Seminary at the University of Notre Dame. I received helpful feedback from participants in the Pinckaers Symposium, for which I am grateful. A second Pinckaers Symposium in May 2019 provided an opportunity to research conscience in the Bible. Although I did not end up presenting this paper at the Symposium, I appreciate the motivation given to my work on this topic by the Symposium. The first paper has been published as "Pinckaers and Häring on Conscience," *Journal of Moral Theology* 8, Special Issue 2 (2019): 134–65.

After writing these two papers, I had the opportunity to pursue my research further when I received an invitation from Mount Angel Seminary to give their annual Robert J. Dwyer Lecture Series in November 2019. I delivered lectures there with the titles "Conscience and Christ: New Testament Background," "Conscience and the Neoscholastic Manuals," and "Conscience in Twentieth-Century German Thought: Rahner and Ratzinger." I thank my kind hosts at Mount Angel Seminary, including Shawn Keough and Abbot Jeremy Driscoll, OSB; I also thank all the people who asked such helpful and penetrating questions at the lectures. My lectures were still quite undeveloped, but they provided the basis for further intense work on this book during the COVID-19 lockdown of spring 2020.

From the bottom of my heart, I thank James Ernest of Eerdmans for seeing the potential of this book. Jason Paone took time out of his busy schedule as a doctoral student at Catholic University of America to prepare the bibliography and index with his customary skill. Erika Harman, who copyedited the manuscript, and Laurel Draper, project editor at Eerdmans, made many improvements. The book would not have been possible without the generous support of Jim and Molly Perry, who endowed the chair that I hold at Mundelein Seminary. My wife, Joy, helped me in innumerable ways. Her generosity goes far beyond anything that even charity would dictate. God be praised for what Joy has done.

I dedicate this book to a spiritual master whom I am privileged to call a friend, Michael Sherwin, OP. In addition to his erudition and his love for Dave Brubeck's jazz, what is notable about Fr. Michael is his love for people. He has laid up much treasure in heaven through his friendships. Jesus told his disciples, "You are my friends if you do what I command you. . . . I have called you friends, for all that I have heard from my Father I have made known to you" (John 15:14–15). Fr. Michael has embodied for me what it means to be a friend of Jesus.

Introduction

Conscience-Centered Moral Theology

This book is both an intervention in the domain of Catholic moral theology and a short history of, or sourcebook to, twentieth-century developments. Twentieth-century Catholic moral theology was marked throughout by an "abuse of conscience." It gave too expansive a place to conscience in the Christian moral life. By the 1950s, Catholic moral theology was poised to overcome this problem, only to fall even more fully into a *new* version of conscience-centered moral theology after the Second Vatican Council.

This book offers a window into how and why this happened. I provide detailed surveys of twenty-six figures whose perspectives on conscience (and related themes) will help readers to apprehend the main lines of twentieth-century Catholic moral theology. My aim is twofold: to introduce the main paths taken by Catholic moral theology in the twentieth century and to expose the deficiencies of the dominant academic versions of conscience-centered Catholic moral theology. Along the way, I attend to some notable critiques of conscience-centered Catholic moral theology offered by scholars expert in biblical and Thomistic ethics, and I provide background to the Catholic debates by examining influential philosophical and Protestant perspectives.

If one reads this book in order to get a sense for what conscience is, or what its relation to prudence should be, or how Christians should act in cases of doubtful conscience, one will find much food for thought. But the book's intention is not to provide a new account of conscience in its manifold dimensions. Rather, my aim is largely diagnostic. As noted, I seek to explore how conscience-centered moral theology survived after the Council in a new and even more problematic form. For readers seeking a constructive proposal for renewal in moral theology, I have attempted to sketch such a path in my book *Aquinas's Eschatological Ethics and the Virtue of*

Temperance.[1] The present book looks back to the twentieth century and asks how we got to where we are today.

A Failed Revolution

Before describing the four chapters, with their surveys of the twenty-six notable figures, let me offer some further background. Since at least the sixteenth century, Catholic moral theology has been largely centered on conscience, law, obligation, and casuistry. The great exemplar of this conscience-centered approach is the Catholic Church's most honored moralist, Alphonsus de Liguori. He begins his *Theologia Moralis* with an exhaustive treatise on conscience, in which he explores the nature of conscience, the distinction between a doubtful conscience and a probable conscience, and the use of the "probable opinions" of moral authorities with regard to particular moral cases. Drawing upon Aquinas and debating with other post-Tridentine moralists, he warns against both rigorism and laxism. His opening treatise on conscience is followed by an even longer treatise on laws, after which he takes up human acts and sins. He then addresses, in book 3, the precepts of faith and charity, including such topics as what counts as culpable heresy and whether Christians are allowed to have contact with Jews.[2]

To my mind, Alphonsus's approach is insufficient. In the early decades of the twentieth century, many Catholic theologians agreed, and they were moving to reform and enhance Catholic moral theology. Thus in 1961 Gerald Healy, SJ, observed that the cutting edge of Catholic moral theology advocates "a reorganization or a new orientation of the whole treatise [on morals] in such a way as to put the emphasis on virtue, avoiding the minimal-obligation approach, stressing charity and the imitation of Christ. . . . The enrichment of the whole treatise is sought by reintegrating moral theology with dogma and Sacred Scripture."[3] Those calling for the replacement of the conscience-centered moral manuals were on the verge of succeeding. In its 1965 Decree on Priestly Training, *Optatam Totius*, the Second Vatican Council mandated that the teaching of "theological subjects should be renewed through a more vivid contact with the Mystery of Christ and the history of salvation. Special care should be given to the perfecting of moral theology. Its scientific presentation should draw more fully on the teaching of holy Scripture and should throw light upon the exalted vocation of the faithful in Christ."[4]

Optatam Totius spelled the end of the post-Tridentine tradition of conscience-centered morality. Raphael Gallagher, CSsR, comments, "The casuist manual, already being undermined, finally crumbled, blasted under by the reforms of the council."[5] Yet, a *new* conscience-centered morality emerged immediately after the Council, almost as though there had never been a critique of conscience-centered morality!

This new postconciliar morality integrated some relatively superficial discussion of Christ and the Holy Spirit into an even more conscience-centered moral framework, now with an emphasis on responsible freedom and human liberation from structures of oppression rather than an emphasis on law and sin. Gallagher observes that "the inheritors of the manual system," as distinct from its preconciliar and postconciliar Thomist critics, thought "that the tradition represented by the casuist manuals [could] be reformulated in a theologically consistent way."[6] In the event, the centrality of conscience served as the bridge from the manuals to the new Catholic moral theology.

How this happened is a fascinating story. As will become clear, it involved transcendental anthropology, a new view of the radical historicity of human nature, and existentialist and personalist philosophical understandings of authenticity.[7] William Wallace, OP, perceived in 1963 that moral theologians were attempting "to cross-breed existentialism and phenomenology with neo-scholasticism."[8] As we will see in chapter 4, Wallace did not realize how far things had already gone.[9]

In short, after the Second Vatican Council, Catholic moral theology was reconceived but now with "conscience"—understood quite differently—as central as ever. In seeking to offer a window into how this happened, my book's four chapters examine the portraits of conscience found in notable twentieth-century biblical analyses (chapter 1), the moral manuals (chapter 2), Thomistic writings (chapter 3), and German thought (chapter 4). I seek to be scrupulously fair and accurate in my surveys of the twenty-six figures covered in these chapters. My historical argument regarding the postconciliar continuance of conscience-centered morality unfolds primarily in chapter 4. A number of thinkers treated in chapters 1 and 3, such as C. A. Pierce, Richard B. Hays, Michel Labourdette, and Servais Pinckaers, help to show what *should* have happened after the Council and what *did* happen in certain postconciliar circles but which, unfortunately, did not happen in the dominant academic strands of postconciliar Catholic moral theology.[10]

Postconciliar Catholic Moral Theology: A First Glance

To get our bearings, a place to begin is James Keenan, SJ's *A History of Catholic Moral Theology in the Twentieth Century: From Confessing Sins to Liberating Consciences*. The book's title implies that the past century, while marked by a sharp division in purpose, was consistently a century of conscience-centered morality.[11] In my view, Keenan is correct in this judgment.

Of course, Keenan knows that during the 1980s and 1990s Pope John Paul II and moralists such as Servais Pinckaers advanced a biblical and Thomistic moral theology that integrated conscience into the broader framework of the Christian moral life, characterized by existential encounter with Christ and by the new law of the grace of the Holy Spirit.[12] It may seem, therefore, that Keenan exaggerates when he describes postconciliar Catholic moral theology as focused upon "liberating consciences." But in fact it is easy enough to show that Keenan's description is accurate with regard to the dominant strands of morality in preconciliar and postconciliar Catholic academic and popular circles. As a starting point, let me mention three representative examples of postconciliar Catholic moral theology.[13] In her 1991 *In Good Conscience*, Sidney Callahan examines the growing importance of individual decision-makers—such as a person who has control over nuclear weapons or over a virus—and she concludes that casuistic moral theology is needed now more than ever. In her view, the answer to the threats that face us today is the formation and right exercise of conscience. We must "focus our thinking once more on the individual self, self-consciousness, conscience, and individual moral decision making."[14]

Similarly, Anthony Marinelli published a popular book in 1991 titled *Conscience and Catholic Faith: Love and Fidelity*. Marinelli's overarching point is that, "for Christians, conscience is the way that we live our faith on our daily decisions."[15] He treats Christian conscience as "the art of being fully human," and he explains that conscience is formed by "the teaching of Jesus and the church and the values and wisdom of the Christian community" and also by the values and wisdom of all humans, whether Christian or not, who "live in fidelity to their own humanity."[16] He examines erroneous conscience, lax conscience, scrupulous conscience, natural law, the impact of cultural bias, the psychological roots of conscience, original sin, the fundamental option, the seven deadly sins, virtue, and grace. Affirming the absolute centrality of conscience in all dimensions of the moral life, he concludes that "it is fair to say that conscience is not something that one *has* as much as it is something that one *is*."[17]

Lastly, in his 1997 *Moral Discernment*, the Sulpician moral theologian Richard Gula remarks that the response to the question "What should I do?" changed in the twentieth century. Earlier, the answer was "Obey the Church"—and thus obey the moral wisdom of divine revelation, as determined for practical application by the "probable opinions" of learned authorities. Now, says Gula, Catholic moral theology has finally grasped that authorities, no matter how wise, cannot replace individual conscience.[18] Christian conscience is the place of our encounter with the Holy Spirit who guides us. The moral life entails arriving at a "mature conscience," through which we no longer simply do what the church tells us—let alone what the unreflective crowd tells us—but take existential responsibility before God for our judgments, emboldened by the knowledge that we have been true to ourselves.[19]

All three authors inflate conscience in striking ways. In addition to these examples, one might also confirm Keenan's thesis by reference to two edited volumes, one from the immediate postconciliar era, the other much more recent. In 1971 Fordham University Press published a notable compendium of essays titled *Conscience: Its Freedom and Limitations*. Four essays treated freedom of conscience—from theological, philosophical, psychiatric, and legal perspectives, respectively. Eight essays treated conscience and civil order/civil disobedience. Five essays treated conscience and *Humanae Vitae*.[20] Four essays treated conscience and the church, including notable essays by Avery Dulles and Gerald McCool.

In 2015, showing that conscience remains as preeminent as ever, a very similar book appeared—though now written mainly by lay theologians and focused on contemporary issues. Leading moral theologians, along with other specialists (and one archbishop) from around the world, produced a compendium of essays titled *Conscience and Catholicism*. This compendium is less interested in *Humanae Vitae* and more interested in global instantiations of liberation theology. Testifying to the place of conscience in Catholic morality, the coeditors observe, "few notions in Catholic theology today have as much rhetorical power as 'conscience.'"[21] Their goal is to advance a new and better conscience-centered morality. Summing up the volume, they remark, "How can persons be better empowered by engagement with the Christian story to recognize distortions and to 'do the truth in love' in complex situations? With an accent on conscience that connotes an ongoing search rather than premature close, we hope this collection will foster ongoing discernment and further open up a conversation in a global church."[22] They deplore the alleged fact that "the papacies of both John Paul II and Benedict XVI engaged in a decades-long effort to constrain conscience and force compliance with the directives of the hierarchical magisterium of the church."[23]

For further support of Keenan's claim, we might also consider three more studies of Catholic moral theology. First, in his 2013 book *The Development of Moral Theology*—reflecting his many earlier writings of the same nature—Charles Curran finds in Catholic moral theology a "subjective pole" (the fundamental option, virtues such as openness to God and gratitude for divine gifts, prayer, the works of mercy, the liturgy) and an "objective pole" (basic "values" such as love, mercy, and justice; general principles such as respect for life; concrete norms).[24] The purpose of conscience, he proposes, consists in uniting the two poles "in concrete decision making."[25] With regard to conscience, the postconciliar difference consists in replacing the manuals' emphasis on law and on weighted lists of authorities with postconciliar moral theology's personal and communal Spirit-guided discernment of spirits. Instead of consulting casuistic authorities known for their learning in the details of the natural and divine law, Catholic conscience today discerns the spirits by measuring actions by their fruits and by seeking interior peace.[26] Curran argues that when one makes a good decision in conscience, one will experience peace and joy, since one has rightly discerned the Spirit's presence in the particular action, whether or not the decision accords with what the church deems to be natural or divine law.[27]

Second, in his 1998 book *Conscience and Catholicism*, Robert Smith concludes that a conscience-centered Catholic moral theology can rightly proceed if it is Spirit-centered. Smith proposes that local faith communities, faithful to the Spirit's work in believers, will now judge whether claims of conscience are "authentic and inauthentic and whether or not they are at the service of the community."[28] In the local church, believers embody and live out a true "reciprocity of consciences," in which believers learn how to follow Catholic conscience by attending to the wisdom and example of people whom they know, in accord with "local custom, tradition, experience, wisdom, and memory."[29] This understanding of the Catholic moral life remains conscience-centered, with Spirit-filled local churches fueling a moral pluralism within the church.

Third, in his 2014 essay "The Primacy of Conscience, Vatican II, and Pope Francis," David DeCosse rejoices in what he deems to be "the new

openness to the primacy of conscience in the papacy of Pope Francis."[30]
DeCosse recalls that the young Joseph Ratzinger criticized the paragraph
on conscience found in *Gaudium et Spes* §16. He finds that Ratzinger's emphasis on the limitations of conscience neglected the elements that fueled
the renewal of conscience-centered Catholic morality after the Council.
In three areas, Ratzinger missed the mark and sought to undermine postconciliar conscience-centered Catholic moral theology. The three areas
are "conscience as a place of encounter with what is new"; "the complexity
of identifying the moral law in markedly different cultural contexts"; and
the understanding of "synderesis" by association with "Cardinal Newman's
more participatory sense of the faithful intuition of the laity" rather than
with "the defensive role of the hierarchical teaching office in guaranteeing
the unchanging perpetuity" of the moral law.[31]

For DeCosse and many others, the excitement of the present moment
consists in the growing ecclesiastical strength of the dominant academic
postconciliar conscience-centered Catholic moral theology, in which "conscience" is a place of profound encounter with the other, grounded in a
pluralistic sense of historically contextualized human personhood and
in respect for the laity's ability, guided by the Spirit, to get things right
even when this necessitates changing the church's consistent magisterial
teaching.[32]

Conscience and the Biblical-Thomistic Alternative

For most scholars, the preceding remarks will contain no surprises:
of course postconciliar academic Catholic moral theology has been
conscience-centered, focused, as Keenan says, on liberating conscience.
Yet, I confess it was a surprise for me. I was trained in the 1990s within a
Thomistic framework. Conscience was valued, and it clearly had an important place in moral action, within the virtue of prudence. But conscience
was not the center of the moral life.

My understanding of conscience was essentially what is found in the
book *Introduction to Moral Theology: True Happiness and the Virtues*, written by William Mattison. Mattison treats conscience within his discussion
of prudence.[33] Although he treats various cases of conscience—the use of
alcohol in college life, the use of the atomic bomb in World War II, non-
marital sex, and euthanasia—his book is fundamentally about the virtues.
Indeed, my reference to "cases of conscience" may be misleading. "Cases

of prudence" (and thus also of conscience) in light of the human desire for happiness might be a better way of expressing what Mattison has in view. His book begins with happiness and the good life, and then it treats human acts, temperance, prudence, justice, fortitude, faith, hope, and charity, with chapter-length discussions of sin, Christ, and grace. Conscience does not receive its own chapter since he connects it closely with prudence. In his most recent book, *The Sermon on the Mount and Moral Theology: A Virtue Perspective*, Mattison does not mention conscience at all.[34]

Trained within a perspective similar to Mattison's, I gave conscience little explicit attention in my writings on moral theology. I was therefore quite surprised when a leading American bishop told me in 2016 that the most exciting movement in Catholic moral theology today is grounded in a renewed vision of conscience.[35] I had imagined that conscience-centered moral theology was a thing of the past, or at least it was no longer attractive to the church of the present or the future. It became clear that I needed to relearn twentieth-century Catholic moral theology to understand the ongoing centrality of conscience.

When I began to explore twentieth-century moral theology in more detail, I soon discovered the German moral theologian Fritz Tillmann's 1937 popular textbook *The Master Calls*. Tillmann's work influenced the young Bernard Häring and Servais Pinckaers.[36] Tillmann also directed the doctorate of Theodor Steinbüchel, whose volumes on moral philosophy the young Joseph Ratzinger devoured—finding in them "a first-rate introduction to the thought of Heidegger and Jaspers," among others.[37] Tillmann, in short, was an influential man.

The Master Calls begins by emphasizing the call to follow Christ by the grace of the Holy Spirit, in accord with the beatitudes, adoptive sonship, our new creation in baptism, self-sacrificial love, purity, charity, compassion, humility, and the fruits of the Spirit. In an orderly fashion that I do not have the space to replicate here, Tillmann treats divine mercy, the cross, eternal life, God as judge, detachment from worldly things, obedience to the will of God, the Decalogue, acceptance of divine providence, the Sermon on the Mount, conversion to Christ, and the quest for Christian perfection in charity. He then devotes two pages to conscience, remarking that conscience has a "decisive value" due to its opposition to "any contradiction between internal conviction and external conduct."[38] He identifies conscience with the "eye" described by Jesus in his Sermon on the Mount: "The eye is the lamp of the body. So, if your eye is sound, your whole body will be full of light; but if your eye is not sound, your whole body will be full of darkness" (Matt. 6:22–23). Tillmann explains that "the voice of conscience in the disciple of the Lord is drawn into his new life in Christ."[39] Further chapters treat piety, faith, hope, charity, the virtue of religion, prayer, the Mass, vows, duties toward the body (including sexuality), love of neighbor, truthfulness, justice, marriage, and church and state.

Tillmann's book recognizes conscience's importance, as do I. But the biblically grounded Catholic moral theology that he develops is not conscience-centered or conscience-driven. While lacking a discussion of prudence, his book represents a major step toward valuing conscience without giving it a dominant role. However, although Tillmann's book received a second edition in 1948 and an English translation in 1961, it soon disappeared from view. After the Council, Tillmann was lost to history, except in occasional lists of the preconciliar moral theologians who critiqued the moral manuals.[40]

The same thing happened to another striking book, Gérard Gilleman, SJ's *The Primacy of Charity in Moral Theology*.[41] This book appeared in French in a second edition in 1954 and in English in 1959. Gilleman advocates "a charity-centered moral theology."[42] His first part treats Aquinas on the acquired and infused virtues, followed by charity as the form of the virtues. His second part describes knowing, willing, and acting, with emphasis on the "finality" of love and on the relation of divine love and human love. He explores the ways in which the virtues mediate the ends of charity, in light of the interrelation of the virtues. Finally, his third part sets forth a charity-centered moral theology by beginning with Christ and his cruciform love (wholly "for us") and then treating holiness as "filial" and as an imitation of Christ's "mortified life." He urges that the sacrament of the Eucharist and self-surpassing love are the keys to moral life. On this basis, he ties together moral theology and ascetic or mystical theology, and he unites law and love. He treats such topics as fraternal charity, bodily suffering and death, chastity, and justice.

The first sentence of Gilleman's book signals his sharp critique of the moral manuals: "On reading certain of our texts in moral theology, one gathers the impression that there is a notable difference of perspective between their exposition and the Christian revelation of moral life as found in the Gospel and Tradition."[43] Lest anyone be in doubt of his intention, he goes on to sharpen the critique: "The very soul of the moral life expressed in the fundamental law of love . . . does not obviously appear to be reflected in our classical treatises on morals."[44]

The heart of the matter, Gilleman insists, is Christ's love for us, our elevation to share in the life of the Trinity by love, and our adoption into the "divine family" as sons and daughters in the Son, called to live in accord with Christ's new commandment of love.[45] He approvingly cites the title of the third volume of Tillmann's 1934 moral manual: *Die Idee der Nachfolge Christi* (the volume that formed the basis for *The Master Calls*).[46] Unfortunately, Tillmann's moral manual is the exception that proves the rule. Gilleman grants that "all the elements of revelation can be found in our moral manuals," but in the standard manuals these elements are scattered, and so he proposes to reformulate moral teaching by "molding it faithfully on Revelation and true Christian life."[47] He warns that, in the nineteenth century at least, the manuals of moral theology were "far too negative and concerned chiefly with minimal obligations; virtues were passed over in favor of commandments and law."[48]

With regard to the manuals closer to his own day, he grants that the manuals of Dominic Prümmer, Benoît-Henri Merkelbach, and others can be said to have rightly concentrated on the primary task of moral renewal, namely, integrating moral and dogmatic theology. He also makes clear that his own work is not meant to be a manual or to take the place of the manuals. But at the same time, he emphasizes that charity does not receive a significant place in the moral manuals, where it usually receives a small chapter toward the back.[49] In urging a new methodological primacy of charity, he states that "too many present textbooks overstress the objective and individualistic bearings of moral theology; they keep harping, with a casuistic bias, on minimum obligation and sin. . . . They do not formulate morality with sufficient reference to the interior life."[50]

Gilleman draws his perspective from Aquinas. He notes that, while Aquinas certainly does not reduce the life of virtue to charity, Aquinas places charity at the center of the moral life both in Christ and in us. The perfection of the will, and its participation in beatitude, consists in charity. Therefore, rather than advancing a conscience- or obligation-centered morality, it behooves the Catholic Church in its moral theology to return to a charity-centered (and thus grace-centered and Christ-centered) morality. I agree with Gilleman, and I concur with his appreciation for the unity of law and love. This unity makes possible the integration of conscience as an important element within the charitable life.

A final book worth mentioning in this context is Emile Mersch, SJ's 1937 *Morality and the Mystical Body*.[51] For Mersch, Christ is the perfect priest, and Christianity "exalts human nature" by insisting first and foremost that "it cease to belong to itself" and instead exist in self-gift to God.[52] He emphasizes that Christ is not only an individual man but also is the head of his body the church. We are intrinsically incorporated into Christ, and our lives are meant to extend Christ's own love. He opines, "To contribute, in ourselves and in others, to this mystical prolongation of the Incarnation, which is the divinisation of the human race, is our entire duty, and it should constantly preoccupy us."[53]

From this perspective, Mersch contends that Catholic moral theology boils down to "act[ing] as a member of Christ."[54] Our whole moral organism must be transformed, every aspect of our being. Baptism accomplishes this, but we must cooperate and grow in holiness. We do so as "parts and members of one another" in Christ.[55] In detail, he examines charity and obedience. He also reflects upon the sacrifice of the Mass as the greatest prayer, in which all prayer outside the liturgy participates. He promotes the Catholic Action movement, and he examines the spiritual priesthood of the faithful, united to Christ's sacrifice on the cross.[56]

Mersch goes on to reflect upon Christian poverty, in the existential sense of radical detachment from the things of this world and dependence upon God alone. He urges that we must renounce earthly things that threaten to impede our spiritual path. The reality of the mystical body reminds us that all things in fact belong to Christ. The true Christian poverty is love; and love means mutual self-gift. The moral requirements of marital (sexual) purity receive attention in this context.[57] From the perspective of charity, he concludes, the union of all elements of Christian morality can be perceived.

If books like these were being published before the Council, how is it that the dominant strand of postconciliar Catholic moral theology remained so firmly conscience-centered?[58] All Catholics recognize that conscience is an important part of the Christian moral life, but the question is why, in Catholicism, conscience so easily and stubbornly takes over the whole terrain.

I assume that part of the answer consists in the needs of the confessional. Catholics regularly consult conscience in order to know whether to make recourse to the sacrament of reconciliation. Yet, this cannot be the determinative answer, since, after all, today's conscience-centered moral theology assures Catholics that the confessional is very rarely needed, if ever.[59] There must be a deeper reason for the continued grip of conscience-centered morality. Sometimes Pope Paul VI's *Humanae Vitae* (1968) is seen as the trigger for the new conscience-centered Catholic moral theology, but the evidence pushes against this claim, or at least requires substantial broadening of perspective. As we will see, Karl Rahner's breakthrough work began to take shape in the mid-1940s and was completed by the early 1960s, and Josef Fuchs's shift took place well before *Humanae Vitae*. John Gallagher remarks, "The decisive moment in the transition from neo-Thomist to revisionist moral theology has usually been associated with the publication of Paul VI's encyclical *Humanae Vitae* and the theological debate which it engendered."[60] But as Gallagher goes on to say, it was in fact the debates over "existentialist ethics" beginning in the late 1940s, especially in postwar Germany, that fueled the transition.[61]

These debates began among important German Catholic thinkers in response to the explosion of existentialist philosophy, due not least to Martin Heidegger's and Karl Jaspers's popularity in the late 1920s and early 1930s. Promoting a Christian existentialist viewpoint critical of the lack of transcendence in German existentialist philosophy, Erich Przywara, SJ, published *Christliche Existenz* in 1934. In his 1932 masterwork *Analogia Entis*, Przywara notes that Heidegger's *Being and Time* helped him to clarify "the concept of creatureliness," although Przywara was generally critical of Heidegger.[62] Alfred Delp, prior to entering the Jesuits (and a decade before his execution by the Nazis), published a significant engagement with Heidegger, *Tragische Existenz*, in 1935.[63] In the early 1930s, too, Protestants such as Dietrich Bonhoeffer, Rudolf Bultmann, and many others were avidly reading Heidegger or imbibing the excitement surrounding existentialism.

Therefore, in order to understand the ongoing allure of conscience-centered morality for Catholics, it cannot be enough to study the historical highlights of the Catholic doctrine of conscience as found in Scripture, Augustine, Aquinas, Newman, and the Second Vatican Council—although this has helpfully been done by Eberhard Schockenhoff.[64] Historical overviews of the development of the concept of "conscience" from the Greco-Roman philosophers to the modern world have proliferated in recent years,[65] but they cannot pinpoint (nor do they try to do so) why conscience-centered morality retains so much energy today in Catholicism, at a time when so many Catholic moral theologians are having difficulty accounting for basic biblical norms.

Conscience itself, of course, is of great value. As *Gaudium et Spes* says, we experience the interior judgment of conscience as a voice calling us "to love and to do what is good and to avoid evil"; and the interior depths where Christian conscience resounds are a place where the divine law "is made known which is fulfilled in the love of God and of one's neighbor."[66] Likewise, conscience forms a basis for pluralistic communities to seek the common good together. At the same time, as *Gaudium et Spes* goes on to say, conscience can be "by degrees almost blinded through the habit of committing sin."[67] In his *Introducing Moral Theology*, Mattison gives the example of some Southern slaveholders' apparently sincere belief in the goodness of their brutal and oppressive slave system.[68]

As *Gaudium et Spes* teaches, conscience plays an important role when we "act out of conscious and free choice, as moved and drawn in a personal way," in order to choose what is good and to "freely attain [our] full and blessed perfection" in union with God.[69] Yet, for Christians the most central moral framework is found in the cross, the church, and new creation—to draw from the subtitle of Richard B. Hays's *The Moral Vision of the New Testament*.[70] The Catholic moral life consists in a Christ-centered ethics of the inaugurated kingdom of God, in which the Spirit heals and elevates us in charity while also forming us in humility and prudence and enlightening our perception of the natural law.[71] An exaggerated conception of conscience within moral theology is an impediment to proclaiming and practicing the Catholic moral life.

The Plan of the Work

In the four chapters that follow, I introduce the perspectives on conscience of twenty-six figures who will help us to understand what happened in Catholic moral theology in the twentieth century. Most of these figures are Catholics, but a number of Protestant voices also play a role. The first step is to understand how biblical ethics in the twentieth century responded to the primacy of conscience in moral theology. For the biblical testimony to conscience, my first chapter examines the perspectives of the following theologians and exegetes spanning the century: George Tyrrell, Hastings Rashdall, Rudolf Bultmann, C. A. Pierce, Yves Congar, OP, Johannes Stelzenberger, Philippe Delhaye, and Richard B. Hays.

The chapter begins with the insights of the Catholic modernist George Tyrrell, due to his significant influence upon Rashdall's exegetical understanding of Christ and conscience. As we will see, Tyrrell's approach influences later Catholic views of collective conscience. Bultmann provides an existentialist reading of Paul on conscience, one that reflects the movements that I explore in chapter 4.[72] Delhaye's perspective reflects that of the moral manualists, even though Delhaye was aware of the need to integrate Scripture more fully into Catholic moral theology.[73] Congar provides a subtle exegetical critique of conscience-centered Catholic moral theology. From differing vantage points, Pierce and Stelzenberger undertake historical-critical surveys of the New Testament in order to demonstrate that while conscience has a significant place in New Testament morality, it does not have a *central* place. Hays shows that it is quite possible and reasonable to present New Testament ethics without mentioning conscience at all.

Turning to the preconciliar conscience-centered Catholic moral manuals, my second chapter begins by sketching Réginald Garrigou-Lagrange, OP's and Servais Pinckaers, OP's criticisms of the moral manuals, in light of Brian Besong's recent defense of the manuals. Investigating the place and function of conscience, I explore the preconciliar manuals of Austin Fagothey, SJ, Thomas J. Higgins, SJ, Michael Cronin, Antony Koch, and Dominic M. Prümmer, OP.[74] Others have provided fuller introductions to the moral manuals, as, for instance, Johann Theiner's *Die Entwicklung der Moraltheologie zur eigenständigen Disziplin*.[75] In *Time Past, Time Future: An Historical Study of Catholic Moral Theology*, John Gallagher treats a number of moral manualists, whose views he knows well.[76] Similarly, James F. Keenan, SJ's *A History of Catholic Moral Theology in the Twentieth Century* surveys in detail three popular manuals from the first half of the twentieth century: those of Thomas Slater, SJ, Henry Davis, SJ, and Heribert Jone, OFM Cap.[77]

In addition, other scholars have offered recent book-length defenses of the moral manualist tradition. For example, the theologian Julia Fleming defends the seventeenth-century Italian bishop Juan Caramuel as a "probabilist" rather than a "laxist," in the course of mounting a constructive defense of probabilism as a moral stance.[78] The historian Stefania Tutino's *Uncertainty in Post-Reformation Catholicism: A History of Probabilism* proposes that "we need to resurrect probabilism," on the grounds that probabilism "enabled theologians to articulate a moral and especially epistemological space for absorbing change, while safeguarding the normative authority and the hermeneutical force of the eternal and immutable Truth of doctrine."[79] I agree that there will always arise cases of conscience that, from within charity and prudence, will require casuistic reasoning of a kind—although Albert Jonsen and Stephen Toulmin are correct to point out that in classical probabilism a "probable opinion" was "never the opinion of the agent making the decision, but the opinion of 'accepted doctors' based upon sound 'intrinsic reasons'" as applied to a particular case.[80]

My third chapter treats the Thomists who, during the twentieth century, retrieved and analyzed Aquinas's teachings about conscience, prudence, and the Christian moral life. Prior to the late 1920s, Dominican moralists were probabiliorists and wrote moral theology within the conscience-centered framework of the moral manuals. These probabiliorist Thomists sought a more central place for prudence than found in most moral manuals. They understood conscience to be prudence's act of judgment.

My presentation of the groundbreaking Thomists treats five figures (to which can be added the treatments of Congar, Garrigou-Lagrange, and Prümmer offered in the first two chapters): Benoît-Henri Merkelbach, OP, Michel Labourdette, OP, Eric D'Arcy, Reginald G. Doherty, OP, and Servais Pinckaers, OP. Labourdette's work is particularly important for chapter 3 because his critique of conscience-centered moral theology is especially profound and has been neglected in contemporary moral theology, by contrast with the widely known and equally valuable perspective of Pinckaers.[81]

D'Arcy offers an exposition of Aquinas on conscience that extends Aquinas's thought to include a conscience-grounded rationale for religious freedom. This is important because the moral manual tradition, like Aquinas himself, generally supported the oppression or even suppression of other religions. For his part, Doherty analyzes the distinction between the judgment of conscience and the judgment of prudence according to Aquinas, helping us to see precisely why prudence is more central than conscience.[82] Pinckaers locates conscience within the Christian moral life in a manner that gives conscience its due while also definitively showing conscience-centered morality to be inadequate to the New Testament.

Lastly, my fourth chapter examines twentieth-century German philosophical and theological thought about conscience. I survey the viewpoints of the following eight thinkers: Martin Heidegger, Karl Jaspers, Dietrich Bonhoeffer, Karl Barth, Karl Rahner, SJ, Josef Fuchs, SJ, Bernard Häring, CSsR, and Joseph Ratzinger. Heidegger and Jaspers offer post-Christian existentialist philosophical accounts, according to which "conscience" names the domain in which authentic human selfhood is actualized. At the self's deepest core ("conscience"), we actualize our true self in resolute decision. Bonhoeffer and Barth provide Christ-centered existentialist accounts of conscience and the moral life.[83] I show that Rahner and Fuchs were significantly influenced by existentialist ethics, though not along the Christocentric lines taken by Bonhoeffer and Barth.[84] In the 1940s and 1950s, Rahner and Fuchs maintained their allegiance to preconciliar natural law doctrine and to universal moral norms, while emphasizing that there exists a domain in which a person's acts in the presence of God cannot be governed by universal laws. Rahner unfolded the implications of his understanding of human nature, according to which "categories such as nature (or essence) have a reference to 'spirit-person'" and "self-disposal is always necessarily to be seen in terms of 'historicity' . . . and thus should be qualified as 'person in the world.'"[85] As their viewpoints changed and developed during and immediately after the Council, Rahner, Fuchs, and Häring charted what became the dominant new path for conscience-centered Catholic morality.[86]

For his part, Ratzinger emphasizes that conscience recalls us to our creaturehood under God, so that we accept God's law rather than attempting to be our own ruler.[87] He defends conscience on the grounds that without it tyranny would have no check. Even when ineffectual, protests of conscience expose the truth about human dignity. Ratzinger also reconceives Christian synderesis as the locus of God's eternal law and of the principles of faith, held in the church's memory and articulated by the magisterium of the church.

Conscience was hugely popular in eighteenth-, nineteenth-, and early-twentieth-century philosophical ethics. In early twentieth-century biblical theology influenced by religious liberalism, conscience stood at the very center, mirroring and measuring the truth claims of Christ. In the moral manuals, conscience was at the center, though it was under God's law. Later twentieth-century scholars showed that conscience is not central for Paul and the New Testament. The goal of many of these scholars—at least in the Catholic realm—was to unseat the conscience-centered morality of the moral manuals and to replace it with prudence, faith, hope, charity, and the entirety of the Christian moral organism.

Although I will show that the moral manuals were richer than is often supposed, I agree with the preconciliar biblical and Thomistic reformers. To my mind, the path forward today consists in integrating the best biblical and Thomistic insights with an existentialist emphasis on a personal encounter with the Lord Jesus Christ. Conscience will continue to have a significant role, but now within the virtue of prudence.

The current dominance of conscience in Catholic moral theology is anomalous in light of the present-day wider philosophical world. Almost all pre-World War II philosophers gave an important place to conscience (or, in Nietzsche's case, to attacking conscience), but for many decades now, conscience has been out of favor in philosophical circles. The philosopher Douglas Langston lamented in 2001: "Conscience has been ignored. Although we use it to guide our actions and we appeal to freedom of conscience in a variety of situations, in the last twenty-five years little has been written about conscience as a useful analytical concept."[88] Langston points out that the horrors of the twentieth century have made it seem as though conscience is hardly real or at least never much help.[89] He also observes that contemporary virtue ethicists tend to say little about conscience, given that neither Plato nor Aristotle sets forth a doctrine of conscience. Langston calls for an increase in discussion of conscience among virtue ethicists, on the grounds that the formation of conscience and its proper act of judgment serve "the development and cultivation of the virtues."[90] I agree with Langston in this regard, although he does not distinguish clearly enough between conscience and prudence. Conscience should not be the center of ethics, but neither should it be ignored.

What makes conscience-centered moral theology so attractive to Catholics today? Here we must recall that the church's magisterium for almost four centuries prior to Vatican II supported a conscience-centered moral theology—though grounded firmly in biblical norms as interpreted and handed on from the patristic period onward. Thus, even if the ongoing predominance of conscience in a new form is mistaken, it is not entirely surprising. In what follows, my purpose is not to explore magisterial teaching, but rather to examine twentieth-century scholarship in order to discern how Catholic moral theology arrived at its present situation and what are the best paths forward. For "the wisdom of a prudent man is to discern his way" (Prov. 14:8).

Chapter 1

Conscience and the Bible

A central purpose of this chapter is to establish a foundation for the three chapters that follow. For this reason, many of the scholars whom I treat in this chapter on conscience and the Bible are theologians, although biblical scholars are also present. In light of twenty-first-century developments, I will begin by pairing two Englishmen: George Tyrrell, removed from the Jesuit order and excommunicated from the Catholic Church during the modernist crisis of the early 1900s, and the Anglican ethicist Hastings Rashdall, whose 1916 *Conscience and Christ* explores the New Testament view of conscience and owes a debt to Tyrrell. Tyrrell is important due to the expansive meaning and place that he gives to "conscience" and "collective conscience." Rashdall does something similar by arguing that Christ's words and claims must be measured and judged by the standard of Christian conscience.

Next, I examine the approach to conscience taken by the influential German New Testament scholar Rudolf Bultmann. In the first volume of his 1948 *Theology of the New Testament*, Bultmann argues that Paul carves out a space for conscience as a realm of interiority where we can either turn outward in receptivity to transcendent judgment and commandment (thus *constituting* our true self) or turn inward toward a false self-sufficiency. Existentially, the judgment of conscience—directing us toward the transcendent judge and granting us true self-knowledge—is connected strongly with faith. Bultmann's existentialist position has importance not only for study of the New Testament's teachings on conscience but also in the development of German doctrines of conscience, which I survey in chapter 4.[1]

Responding explicitly to Rashdall, the Cambridge scholar C. A. Pierce published a book in 1955 on the meaning of "conscience" according to Scripture, in which he emphasized the limits of conscience's role according to the New Testament. I pair his approach with the 1961 book of the German Catholic moral theologian Johannes Stelzenberger, *Syneidesis im Neuen Testament*. Stelzenberger firmly opposed the moral manuals' emphasis on conscience.[2] Influenced by Christian existentialism, he argues that many New Testament uses of the term *syneidēsis* do not actually refer to "conscience" as we understand it today. As is well known, the Greek word for "conscience" (*syneidēsis*) does not appear in the Gospels but does appear multiple times in Paul's letters, including Romans 13:5—"Therefore one must be subject [to the governing authorities], not only to avoid God's wrath but also for the sake of conscience"—and 1 Corinthians 10:28–29—"If some one says to you, 'This has been offered in sacrifice,' then out of consideration for the man who informed you, and for conscience' sake—I mean his conscience, not yours—do not eat it."

In between my surveys of Pierce and Stelzenberger, I explore the eminent French Catholic theologian Yves Congar's 1958 essay "St. Paul's Casuistry." Congar investigates how Paul adjudicates cases of conscience that contain gray areas and lack a clear moral norm for determining behavior. Congar's essay emphasizes the guiding role of charity and faith, and especially the imitation of Christ. His purpose is to strike a forceful blow against conscience-centered morality. His perspective is similar to what we will find in chapter 3 in the sections on Labourdette and Pinckaers, though he offers more insight than they do into the place of particular casuistic cases within Paul's ministry.

The Belgian Catholic moral theologian Philippe Delhaye, writing in the early 1960s, provides a window into the final years of the moral manualist tradition. He argues that the moral manuals' expansive understanding of conscience has a firm biblical grounding. By way of contrast, I pair his perspective with that of the Reformed biblical scholar Richard B. Hays. In his 1996 book *The Moral Vision of the New Testament*, Hays ignores conscience completely, and it hardly seems a loss.

My conclusion is that the New Testament does not support conscience-centered morality. Nevertheless, the contributions of Tyrrell, Rashdall, Bultmann, and Delhaye underscore how attractive conscience-centered morality can be, and their perspectives continue to be influential today. For Catholics seeking an alternative to contemporary conscience-centered morality, Congar's and Hays's approaches offer the richest insights, but much can be learned as well from Pierce and Stelzenberger.

George Tyrrell

In events that shaped an entire Catholic century, the theologian George Tyrrell—a widely popular author—was dismissed from the Jesuit order in 1906 and excommunicated from the Catholic Church in 1907 for denying the ontological realism, or enduring propositional truth, of dogma. His views would not have surprised anyone in classical "Liberal Protestant" circles, in which the view that dogma is authentic insofar as it expresses the community's religious-ethical experience, and ceases to be authentic when it no longer does so, had long been presumed.

Conscience, understood in a distinctive way, has a central place Tyrrell's religious worldview. In the 1907 encyclical *Pascendi Dominici Gregis*, Tyrrell is in view though not explicitly named. Pope Pius X notes that for Tyrrell the church "is the product of the *collective conscience*, that is to say, of the association of individual consciences which, by virtue of the principle of *vital permanence*, depend all on one first believer, who for Catholics is Christ."[3] Some of the foundations of the dominant strand of postconciliar conscience-centered ethics are laid by Tyrrell's work.

According to Tyrrell, Christ is "the Incarnation of Conscience."[4] Christ is such because he is the perfect expression of the human consciousness of God. Tyrrell asks rhetorically, "By what vehicle does He [God] speak . . . with us? By voices from the clouds or by the gradual evolution of His Mind and Will in the collective spirit of mankind?"[5] For Tyrrell, the answer is the latter: the human collective spirit is the voice of God. In proclaiming the universal brotherhood of love, Christ speaks to the collective spirit of humanity and is recognized by it. The human race thereby comes to appreciate "God immanent in the spirit of man."[6]

Tyrrell goes on to explain that "faith" is evoked by "a certain ideal of conduct" that the human person reveres and to which the human person ultimately entrusts or abandons himself.[7] The divine reveals itself to us "through and in this ideal of conduct, through the sum-total of these experienced suggestions and inspirations."[8] We do not blindly respond to a God who calls us arbitrarily. Rather, through this ethical ideal, arising from the sum total of human experience, the divine manifests itself and its "Will" or "Spirit." We respond to this ethical ideal, known in conscience, by embracing it in faith and love and by learning to name it as divine. Tyrrell observes that "in the measure that one yields oneself to the guidance of Conscience, its direction (and therefore its self-revelation) becomes more abundant, more clear, more delicately discerning"—and as a result "the answering affections of faith, reverence, trust and love are deepened, enriched, and refined."[9] The bottom line is that all Christian doctrine, rooted in a "revelation" that speaks to one's conscience, must be measured by conscience.

Since faith embraces not a body of propositional knowledge but an ethical ideal of life, a person of faith will inquire into why this ideal is right and how it should be understood. In the end, the person of faith will come to see that all truth "must be fundamentally in harmony with the affirmations of Conscience."[10] The person of faith will recognize that moral conscience—the ethical ideal—is the Creator and "the governing principle of all," and that the unfolding of history and the sum total of human experience are none other than the progressive revelation of "Conscience" or the "Divine Will."[11]

According to Tyrrell, therefore, true authority in the church is nothing other than "the imperativeness of the collective conscience."[12] Again, this is because of the nature of "revelation" in its true form. Earlier times understood revelation "rationally or rationalistically (as delivered in suggested speech or concepts)," in accord with the worship of a philosophical God.[13] But to more mature religious thought—namely, to "the religion of Conscience"—it is apparent that revelation comes about in interior spiritual experience as an encounter with the ethical ideal. The object of faith "is the Power that reveals itself in the workings of my Conscience," as manifested in the expression of conscience found "in the life, words and actions of Jesus Christ, or of the Church of His servants and saints."[14] What our own conscience reveals is what Christ and the church reveal or should reveal; in this sense "faith is . . . a loyalty, a trust directed towards my own Conscience" (and thereby toward Christ and the church also, when the latter is not abusing its power).[15] As the Liberal Protestant theologian Ernst Troeltsch remarked in 1913, "The demands of Christianity are . . . purely spiritual, sensed only by the conscience."[16] It follows that, as Pope Pius X characterizes this view, "For the Church to trace out and prescribe for the citizen [including any Catholic] any line of action, on any pretext whatsoever, is to be guilty of an abuse of authority, against which one is bound to protest with all one's might."[17]

We will find continuities between Tyrrell's general approach and Hastings Rashdall's position regarding biblical ethics and conscience. Let me now turn to Rashdall's argument.

Hastings Rashdall

In the midst of World War I, Hastings Rashdall published *Conscience and Christ*. If necessary, he argues, we should follow conscience over the Christ of the Gospels. However, it is possible to ascertain that Christ is the ethical ideal, and so, Rashdall argues, Christians need not depart from a biblically grounded faith. Rashdall praises Tyrrell for accurately expressing "the right relation between the three great authorities—Conscience, Christ, the Church."[18]

Rashdall begins by asking whether Jesus has a reasonable claim to be at the center of a modern person's worldview. What if, as scholars such as Albert Schweitzer hold, Jesus was merely a Jewish eschatological prophet who assumed that the end of the world was imminent and who was quickly proven wrong? In answer, Rashdall first suggests that "the extent to which Jesus shared the eschatological ideas of His time has been exaggerated, and . . . some of the more definite eschatological sayings are probably distorted or coloured by the ideas of His immediate disciples or of the early Church" (73). But Rashdall also argues that even if scholars are right about Jesus's false apocalyptic hopes, this should not dissuade Christians from perceiving God's self-revelation uniquely in the teachings and life of Jesus. Even if Jesus accepted "traditional ideas on the subject which were in point of fact mistakes," still God could "have made His fullest revelation of Himself in one conscience, one character, one life"—that of Jesus (74). Indeed, says Rashdall, it would be "absurd to reject or to disparage the ethical ideal of Jesus a priori because He entertained eschatological hopes which we cannot share" (72).[19]

Rashdall's solution consists in setting up conscience (or "moral consciousness") as the testing ground for whether Christ's moral teaching is true. This gives conscience a preeminent place, above Christ. Rashdall remarks in this regard, "If we once allow the self-evidencing truth of His moral teaching to occupy a prominent place in the argument for His Divinity, we are trusting to the validity of our own moral consciousness; and when we have done this, we can no longer profess ourselves willing to accept any and every moral precept of Christ, without any criticism of its contents" (28). We are not called to follow Christ by the path of blind faith or blind obedience. Although it is reasonable for individuals to defer to people whose views have been found to be accurate by the broader community, if our private judgment were to be found regularly in conflict with Christ's moral teaching, then this would undermine the credibility of faith in Christ. If Christ's moral teaching failed to persuade "the community generally"—that is to say, *if* the "whole community, including its best and wisest," disagreed with Christ's moral teaching—then we would have to hold that Christ's voice should not "prevail against the voice of such a collective Conscience" (30).

When assessing whether God has revealed himself in Christ, therefore, Rashdall appeals first and foremost to "collective Conscience." According to Rashdall, Christ does not require arbitrary obedience but "always addresses Himself to Conscience" and always "assumes that His hearers, too, have some of that power of judging about questions of right and wrong which He possessed Himself in a supreme degree" (33).[20] Rashdall is confident that Christ's moral teaching will meet the test, since his moral teaching and example are nothing less than "the highest moral ideal known to Humanity" (281). More than all other moral teachers, Christ recognized that morality is fundamentally found in the truth that "Love is the fulfilling of the Law" and that God is "the common Father of Humanity whose nature is best expressed by the word Love" (281).

Rashdall is well aware that Jesus was a Jewish teacher influenced by the Judaism of his day, not only eschatologically but also with regard to his moral teaching. He denies that Jesus ever "encouraged the non-observance of [Mosaic] precepts obviously and fairly deducible from the commands of Scripture: or that He ever explicitly drew a distinction between ceremonial precepts which were not, and moral precepts which were, of eternal obligation" (99). Nevertheless, says Rashdall, Jesus managed to transcend his culture. Rashdall argues that "by a sort of instinct of spiritual insight the mind of Jesus fastened upon the spiritual and ethical import of the Jewish Scriptures, and ignored all the rest" (100). Jesus undermined strict Sabbath laws, did away with the ethical significance of clean and unclean foods, and (in the Sermon on the Mount) spiritualized and deepened the meaning of Old Testament moral precepts. His moral teaching always flowed from "the principle of human Brotherhood, in its fullest possible extent," conjoined with "the Fatherhood of God" (113).[21]

Although he considers the Pharisees and their followers to have fallen into legalism, Rashdall still finds much to praise in Jewish morality of biblical times. For example, he considers that "there can be little doubt about the superiority of the Jews on the side of sexual Morality," both with respect to the rejection of polygamy and with respect to "the great principle which confines sexual relations to lawful marriage" and rejects the "darker vices" of sexual immorality (80–81).[22] However, had Jesus set forth a code of laws of his own, this would have been a grave error in Rashdall's view.

He states, "The attempt to guide our conduct by such a code would put a stop to all social progress, and would be fatal to the moral life itself, which at its highest implies that men should be continually acting upon their own judgement, using their own moral and intellectual faculties, basing their lives upon their own sense of right and wrong" (166). The church's understanding of the moral life can be expected to grow and develop over time, as befits a living organism.

Indeed, for Rashdall, the progressive development of the ethical ideal is the purpose of the church. He observes that in their detailed elaboration, "the principles [of morality] require infinite expansion, application, development, in accordance with the growing experience of the race, and the altered needs and circumstances of successive ages. To effect this development is . . . the work of the Church of Christ—that religious community which should be the highest organized expression of the enlightened Christian consciousness of the time" (166–67). Flowing from the fundamental moral principle of the brotherhood of man and the Fatherhood of God, the church—as "the enlightened Christian consciousness"—will express as a unified body the progress made by individual consciences "in accordance with the growing experience of the race, and the altered needs and circumstances of successive ages."[23] In so doing, the church's collective Conscience will bear witness to the fact that "no one has ever taught" the central truth of morality "with the same clearness, consistency, and force as Jesus or illustrated it so forcibly by the whole of the life and character" (221). To be sure, there has been and will be "enormous development" in our understanding of the details of the moral life, but the "principle of universal love as the supreme and all-important ethical command" as "taught by none so penetratingly as by Him" will stand firm (221; cf. 165).

This view of Christ as the preeminent ethical teacher and exemplar (though not necessarily in the details of his teachings) makes conscience—and above all the upward-tending collective Conscience, which turns out to be the purpose for the church's existence—the supreme guide for Christianity. Vast development in collective Conscience is expected, but Christ as the definitive ethical ideal will stand firm.

Rudolf Bultmann

Tyrrell shows what an influential place conscience received in early twentieth-century efforts to reimagine Catholicism; and Rashdall incorporates this perspective into biblical scholarship by urging that Jesus proposed his ethical ideal to our consciences, calling upon conscience to confirm the truth of his ethical ideal. Continuing this expansive view of conscience, the influential German Protestant biblical scholar Rudolf Bultmann argues that Pauline conscience involves the actualization of the true self, in response to God's call. According to Bultmann, the kingdom consists in a radical existential decision *here and now* in the face of the proclamation (the "kerygma"[24]) of the action of God in Christ to free us from sin. In this decision, conscience plays a central role in discerning our fundamental stance: either inward-turning or turning toward God.

During the period 1923–27, when he and Martin Heidegger were professors together at the University of Marburg and when Heidegger's *Being and Time* was being prepared, Bultmann was profoundly influenced by Heidegger's existentialism. Unlike Heidegger, however, Bultmann retained the act of God at the center of all things, even as he sought to demythologize the Scriptures.[25]

In 1948 Bultmann published the first volume of his two-volume *Theology of the New Testament*. This volume contains a significant section titled "Mind and Conscience," which I will examine here. Bultmann begins this section by discussing various Pauline references to *nous*. The mind (*nous*) can perceive God's existence and nature, but God far exceeds the mind's grasp. The mind includes powers of contemplation and judgment, and also of intention and volition. In Bultmann's view, Pauline *nous* is a person's "real" self, the "self that hears God's will speaking through the Law, agrees with it, and adopts it as its own."[26] This "real" self hears God's commandment and orients itself by God's commandment. The "real" self is opposed interiorly by the sinful and rebellious self (turned inward upon itself), the *sarx*.

According to Bultmann, Romans 7:13–25 serves as the key to understanding the Pauline meaning of *nous*. On the one hand, *nous* is open to either good or bad paths. On the other hand, *nous* inclines toward good. Human nature inclines toward good, but humans must make the good our own. We must "actualize [our] human will for 'good' by willing what the Law requires."[27] The problem is that fallen *nous*, despite inclining toward the good, can reject the good. Our *nous* may even now be turning away from God's commandment, since *nous* does not have to fulfill its inclination toward the good. In this sense, our *nous* is depraved or "base" (Rom. 1:28).

Building upon Romans 1, Bultmann goes on to say that knowledge of God is insufficient for a good *nous*. We must not only know but also acknowledge God. Existentially, we must choose to be *for* God, and we must do so despite the fact that our depraved *nous* may lead us astray in judging what is good. Our *nous* may be hardened, veiled, and blinded. Bultmann cites 2 Corinthians 4:4, "the god of this world [Satan] has blinded the minds of the unbelievers." We need to beg God to take our wills (and minds) captive for Christ (2 Cor. 10:5). Paul calls us to repent, to exchange our earthly, carnal attitude for a heavenly, spiritual one, in which we no longer pride ourselves on our own strength or merits. We must turn ourselves over to "the will of God, what is good and acceptable and perfect" (Rom. 12:2). Paul urges us to test ourselves (2 Cor. 13:5). Bultmann concludes that our self or *nous* must make "itself the object of its own judging."[28]

Next, Bultmann turns to the various Pauline meanings of *krinein*, "to judge." He links it with various terms for "consider," "ponder," "understand," and "know." In this light, he interprets *syneidēsis* (conscience) as "knowledge shared with one's self."[29] He holds that Paul takes *syneidēsis* to mean awareness or consciousness of having done wrong; *syneidēsis* is self-knowledge.

Bultmann contrasts the negative "objectivized self," or the self turned in upon itself, with the "real" self, or fulfilled and actualized *nous* that hears and obeys God's commandment. In *syneidēsis*, a person recognizes "his conduct as his own."[30] Perceiving the intention or stance of our *nous* (whether inward-turning or turned toward God), *syneidēsis* or conscience judges this intention. Conscience applies a knowledge of the standard of good and evil—the requirements of the law, known even to the gentiles (Rom. 2:14–16)—to particular actions that we either intend to do or have done.

Bultmann considers 1 Corinthians 8 and 10 to offer an example of what he means by conscience. Conscience can forbid or command certain intended actions. Conscience can condemn us when we do forbidden actions or fail to do the actions that we should have done. As a faculty of judging, conscience can also judge our actions and testify to our fidelity or sincerity. 2 Corinthians 4:2 suggests that our conscience can also testify to the truthfulness of another person whose intentions and actions we know well.

According to Bultmann, then, Pauline conscience is a "knowledge of the demand that is incumbent upon man."[31] Yet, conscience can go wrong in specifying what this demand involves. In 1 Corinthians 8 and 10, Paul portrays erroneous conscience and makes clear that even an erroneous judgment of conscience has binding force. Thus, we must never compel someone to undertake actions that are against his or her conscience. By affirming the judgment of conscience, we affirm the transcendent *demand* upon us. We thereby affirm that we are accountable to God's commandment. This is why even erroneous conscience binds; were we to reject conscience's judgment, we would be rejecting the moral authority of the transcendent sphere, rather than merely rejecting some ethical ideas.

In sum, conscience is the transcendent demand whose existence we interiorly recognize. We may perhaps misunderstand the content of this demand, but conscience assures us that we stand under an authoritative, transcendent commandment and are obligated to obey it. Existentially, our task is to achieve our "real" self by acknowledging and obeying God's judgment or command, rather than allowing ourselves to be ruled by merely human judgments (including our own). We constitute ourselves rightly by obedience to the judgment of conscience.

Bultmann warns that the wrong path is taken when, instead of obeying God, we seek to conform ourselves to a merely human authority. When we do this, we have failed in conscience, because we have denied the existence and authority of the transcendent demand upon us. So long as we hold ourselves accountable to God's judgment, no merely human judgment will worry us.

Bultmann goes on to connect "faith" with conscience.[32] For both faith and conscience, obedience to God's commandment or God's verdict is the heart of the matter. In both cases, we are dealing with "the self's knowledge of itself"—a knowledge that arises not from turning inward but from turning toward the God who commands and judges.[33] It is in obeying God that the actualization of our "real" self takes place. This obedience, in which we turn from the darkness and sin of inward-turning sufficiency (our false self), comes about through God's gift of his Spirit in our "heart," our interior self. This deepest self is our conscience.

C. A. Pierce

In his 1955 *Conscience in the New Testament*, C. A. Pierce is writing specifically against the viewpoint of Hastings Rashdall and others who share his opinions. Pierce aims to show what the New Testament actually teaches about conscience. He offers a sharp exegetical pushback against the exaggeration of conscience's place in the moral life.

Pierce observes that *syneidēsis*, in Hellenistic thinkers prior to Paul, constitutes "an element of human nature as such," present in every human as a witness against evildoing.[34] Conscience bears a reference to God as the creator or orderer of human nature. Conscience knows and judges a person's past acts—although these acts may of course be ongoing. It causes spiritual pain and remorse in the person who has done wrong. Pierce notes that "*conscience* was taken by the N. T. from Greek popular thought."[35]

In Pierce's view, Paul's use of "conscience" in Romans 13:5 is normative for Paul's perspective. Romans 13:5 states, "Therefore one must be subject, not only to avoid God's wrath but also for the sake of conscience." Those who rise up against what God has appointed in the order of human society will experience the "wrath" of God through not only the ministers of the state exercising justice but also an interior condemnatory judge: conscience. This is what Paul understands conscience to be: an interior judge of past actions.

In 1 Corinthians 10:27–29, Paul instructs believers, "If one of the unbelievers invites you to dinner and you are disposed to go, eat whatever is set before you without raising any question on the ground of conscience. (But if some one says to you, 'This has been offered in sacrifice,' then out of consideration for the man who informed you, and for conscience' sake—I mean his conscience, not yours—do not eat it.)" In Pierce's interpretation, this passage shows Paul's view that conscience can be fallible because it is "to some extent conditioned by habit and environment."[36]

Pierce reviews other passages that mention conscience, including Romans 9:1, where Paul underscores the depth of his sorrow for the Jewish people by remarking, "I am not lying; my conscience bears me witness in the Holy Spirit," and Romans 2:14–15, where the "Gentiles who have not the law" have a "conscience" that "bears witness." He argues that these two passages confirm that conscience's role is to judge past actions and to bear witness to whether we have deviated from truth and goodness.

In 2 Corinthians 1:12, Paul speaks of "the testimony of our [Paul's] conscience that we have behaved . . . with holiness and sincerity, not by earthly wisdom but by the grace of God." This passage refers to the witnessing function of conscience. Pierce hypothesizes that Paul has been engaged in a debate with the Corinthians over their appeal to the authority of "conscience," with the result that Paul is asserting his authority as an apostle by appealing to his own conscience. Notably, Pierce goes on to deny that the uses of *syneidēsis* in 2 Corinthians 4:2 and 5:11—where Paul twice appeals to the "consciences" of his hearers—are rightly translated as "conscience." Instead, Paul is appealing to the *knowledge* that his hearers have of his conduct.[37]

Pierce considers that 1 Corinthians 4:4, "I am not aware of anything against myself, but I am not thereby acquitted" (RSV), should in fact be translated: "I have nothing on my conscience, yet am I not hereby justified" (*ouden gar emautō synoida, all' ouk en toutō dedikaiōmai*).[38] Conscience can err due to "inaccurate knowledge of the quality of the act, habit, environment, imperfect awareness of Christ as judge, and of the standard which he embodies and by which he must judge; and insufficient quickening of the inner man by the indwelling of the Holy Spirit."[39] Even if a person has a clear conscience, the person may be objectively in a state of guilt. This is one reason why conscience alone is not enough for the Christian moral life.

Turning to the Pauline books that many scholars think were not written by Paul, Pierce discusses 1 Timothy 4:2's description of "liars whose consciences are seared" because they have corrupted their conscience and have reached a condition in which they lack both a desire for virtue and a hatred of sin. When the person sins, the corrupted conscience no longer pricks the person, no longer makes the person suffer guilt (see also Titus 1:15). Thus, it is necessary for a Christian to serve God "with a clear conscience" (2 Tim. 1:3; cf. 1 Tim. 1:19) and to "hold the mystery of the faith with a clear conscience" (1 Tim. 3:9). In light of 1 Peter 3:21, Pierce adds that the path to "a clear conscience" runs through faith and baptism, by which people are united to the healing power of Christ's cross and resurrection. He also examines Hebrews 9:9, which argues that the Old Testament's "gifts and sacrifices . . . cannot perfect the conscience of the worshiper." Through Christ, worshipers "no longer have any consciousness [or conscience: *syneidēsin*] of sin" (Heb. 10:2). The author of Hebrews urges that now that "we have a great priest [Christ] over the house of God, let us draw near with a true heart in full assurance of faith, with our hearts sprinkled clean from an evil conscience and our bodies washed with pure water" (Heb. 10:21–22). For the author of Hebrews, Pierce concludes, "the Christian life moves steadily away from the pain of conscience."[40]

In Pierce's view, the New Testament authors did not significantly alter the popular Hellenistic understanding of *syneidēsis*, although they did place the concept in the context of the Creator God and of Christ the Redeemer. In the New Testament, conscience judges past actions (which may be ongoing) on the basis of whether they have violated the norms befitting to our created human nature; conscience causes interior pain and guilt when it discerns a violation; conscience can be fallible and can be corrupted or obscured by habitual sin; conscience is strengthened and awakened by faith; conscience is corrupted by apostasy from Christian faith; conscience must be obeyed when one has tested it to see whether it is in accord with other sources of moral knowledge; and conscience can be clear through

Christ's power. The expectation is that the Spirit's outpouring will enable the Christian to live without violating conscience, although later Christians had "to revise this expectation as still too optimistic."[41]

When Pierce reflects upon the contemporary relevance of the New Testament's doctrine of conscience, he critiques Rashdall's claim that "the conscience ought to prevail against the *ipse dixit* of any authority, however justly venerated (including Christ)."[42] Pierce notes that, unfortunately, "modern English usage regards conscience as a guide to future action independent of and superior to any other such guide, and to the counsel or command of any authority whatever."[43] This modern notion of conscience, advocated by Rashdall and many others, has no grounds in the New Testament. For one thing, conscience in the New Testament has to do with judging past action; conscience is not presented as a guide to, or a justification for, a future action. For another thing, conscience in the New Testament is fallible and requires to be purified and informed by other authorities. Pierce goes so far as to hold that in modern England, conscience has become an idol, since the autonomy of God-given conscience is often taken as the basis for claiming that one has no "need of Bible, Church, Ministry, Creeds, Sacraments, worship or devotion."[44] In this context, Pierce warns against exaggerating the place of conscience in Paul's moral teaching, as though conscience were "the most important of moral terms, the crowning triumph of ethical nomenclature."[45]

Pierce is especially concerned with what happens when Christians conceive of conscience as an infallible guide and at the same time understand conscience to be about determining *future* action. This turns the New Testament's understanding of conscience on its head by supposing that to justify our future actions all we need to do is consult our conscience. Pierce urges a return to the New Testament's more limited view of conscience. He also draws attention to the task of *proairesis*, which he translates as "choice." He explains that in our moral decision-making, we require not only conscience but also faith, love, hope, joy, persistence, conversion of heart, cultivation of good habits, instruction in divine revelation, imitation of Christ, spiritual direction, and more.

Yves Congar, OP

Undertaking exegetical work on the Pauline letters, the Catholic theologian Yves Congar, OP, provides a second angle of biblical critique of conscience-centered morality. In his 1958 essay "St. Paul's Casuistry," he focuses not on conscience but on what may be called cases of conscience. His purpose is to exposit Paul accurately while undermining preconciliar Catholic casuistry.

He begins by opining about the relative value of casuistry: "That casuistry of some kind is necessary no one, surely, will deny."[46] Casuistry's defenders argue that both Jesus and Paul employed casuistic moral reasoning. Congar agrees, but he holds that "Paul's casuistry" never gives evidence of "a juridical or legalistic outlook."[47] Taking preconciliar Catholic anti-Judaism for granted, he tars the moral manuals of his day with the supposed taint of Judaism. He states that "all law is carnal and Jewish, whenever it is taken as law, and not as the response of *agape* to the demands in us of the *agape* of God."[48] As a response of *agape*, however, both Jesus and Paul retain some juridical aspects of Jewish casuistry. Such aspects are found in the church's canon law as well, but "pure juridicalism" does not properly belong to the church.[49] Unfortunately, Catholic moral theology has fallen into a "juridical spirit" due to abandoning "an ethic of the Good and the Call to perfection."[50] On this view, the moral manuals are guilty of displaying an ethic of "mere legal obligation, a wholly juridical casuistry of the permitted and the forbidden" in which liberty and law are at odds and in which the legal minimum takes center stage.[51]

In opposition to this "juridical spirit," Congar calls for theocentric charity—the imitation of God and the imitation of Christ—for the purpose of divinization or sharing in the divine beatitude, in accord with the Spirit's "renewal of our minds."[52] Congar indicates a degree of appreciation for situation ethics (or existentialist ethics), though not in its subjectivist enthronement of the individual's sovereign conscience above universal norms.[53] He deems that the true "situation ethics" will be found in a moral life governed by charity and prudence in accord with "the specificity of the practical order."[54]

According to Congar, what are the moral cases or "cases of conscience" that Paul confronts? Congar summarizes them succinctly. In the Thessalonian correspondence, Paul reflects on the obligation to work and on his own commitment to working to support himself. In the Corinthian correspondence, Paul discusses a long list of difficult cases: the excommunication of the incestuous man and the way in which the Christian community should treat him, recourse to non-Christian judges, marriage between a Christian and a non-Christian, whether an enslaved person should accept his or her enslavement, whether an unmarried person should get married, whether food sacrificed to idols should be eaten, how a woman should wear her hair, whether a woman should wear a veil in public worship, how the eucharistic liturgy should be celebrated, what should be expected from those who speak in tongues during worship, what the expectations for almsgiving should be, and whether Christians should associate with non-Christians. It is easy to see that these cases are not easily resolvable by the application of universal norms; this is why they are difficult cases of conscience and why Paul is asked to speak to them.

In Galatians, Paul addresses the case of whether (Christian) Jews should eat with (Christian) gentiles. In Romans, Paul addresses the question of whether meat sacrificed to idols can be eaten, and also the question of whether particular days should be observed. In Philemon, Colossians, and Ephesians, Paul addresses slavery, as well as (in the latter two letters) the relationship between husband and wife. In 1 Timothy, Paul discusses the excommunication of Hymenaeus and Alexander; the clothing, jewelry, and behavior of women; the goodness of marriage and of foods; the deportment of widows and the community's responsibility toward them; and the obedience of slaves to their masters. In Titus, Paul discusses the proper attributes of a bishop, the proper deportment of men and women, and the obedience of slaves.

For Congar, many of Paul's casuistic determinations applied only to the specific circumstances of his day and require to be sifted and evaluated within the broader context of his moral teaching. While Paul's casuistic determinations rely upon moral principles that are binding and enduring in their authority, Paul's casuistic determinations are often timebound. Casuistic determinations regarding particular acts in particular circumstances should not be thought to apply in all circumstances, as though everything that Paul says casuistically is a moral dictate for all time.[55]

Congar focuses on three issues: whether a preacher is bound to support himself, whether food used in idol worship can be eaten, and "the observances concerning foods and days."[56] His goal is to perceive, behind Paul's casuistic judgments, the authoritative moral principles or criteria upon which Paul depends. As Congar observes, it is these principles, rather than the specific casuistic determinations, that are "of permanent validity for Christian pastoral work."[57]

Congar begins with the question of whether Paul, as a preacher of the gospel, should have supported himself through manual work. As Congar notes, Paul was frequently willing to accept gifts from his congregations to cover part or all of his material upkeep. Yet, Paul also often worked with his hands to support himself. He recalls this fact in 1 Thessalonians 2:9:

"For you remember our labor and toil, brethren; we worked night and day, that we might not burden any of you, while we preached to you the gospel of God." Paul considers this fact important enough to repeat in his second letter to the Thessalonians, as part of his warning that able-bodied members of the Christian community should not be permitted to be idle or to rely upon the community's alms.[58] Paul urges all believers to imitate him in working "night and day" and in refusing to "eat any one's bread without paying," even though he had a "right" not to work since he was preaching the gospel to the community (2 Thess. 3:8–9).

Paul explains the principle at stake more fully in his Corinthian correspondence, but here he does so with a tone of complaint, apparently because his apostolic credibility has been challenged. He asks rhetorically, "Do we not have the right to our food and drink? . . . Or is it only Barnabas and I who have no right to refrain from working for a living? Who serves as a soldier at his own expense? Who plants a vineyard without eating any of its fruit? Who tends a flock without getting some of the milk?" (1 Cor. 9:4, 6–7). He goes on to explain that among the Corinthians he chose not to exercise his right but instead did manual work to support himself, in order to show the Corinthians that he was not preaching the gospel for material gain. He insists strongly—invoking a command of Christ—that preachers of the gospel should be supported by the community: "the Lord commanded that those who proclaim the gospel should get their living by the gospel" (1 Cor. 9:14). At the same time, he defends the truth of his apostolic commission by emphasizing that he proclaimed "the gospel free of charge" (1 Cor. 9:18).

The Acts of the Apostles describes Paul's tentmaking, which he undertook in Corinth with Aquila and Priscilla (Acts 18:3). Paul underscores that his preaching has been free from a desire for profit: "I coveted no one's silver or gold or apparel. You yourselves know that these hands ministered to my necessities" (Acts 20:33–34). Yet, he praises the Philippian congregation for repeatedly sending him gifts in support of his ministry, when otherwise his ministry would have been imperiled (see Phil. 4:15–18). He also admits to the Corinthians that part of the cost of his preaching to them had been borne by other churches: "I robbed other churches by accepting support from them in order to serve you. And when I was with you and was in want, I did not burden any one, for my needs were supplied by the brethren who came from Macedonia" (2 Cor. 11:8–9).

The fact that Paul takes different approaches to this issue shows, in Congar's view, that Paul is engaged in casuistry, aiming to bring Christian principles to bear on particular acts in particular circumstances. What were the principles that in certain cases led Paul to work with his hands in addition to his work of preaching? Certainly one of the principles was the great dignity of the gospel, which would be impugned if preaching the gospel were merely about money. Paul could not seem to be greedy or a mere burden upon the community. His preaching is commanded by the Lord, and he "seeks a gain only for his Lord."[59] As a second principle, Congar names Paul's desire to be a model of life in Christ. He did not only preach the gospel intellectually; he also wanted to embody it for his communities. The principle is this: "The shepherd must be a pattern to his flock."[60] Given that some converts were shiftless and that other converts (believing that the end was imminent) felt no need to do any work, Paul had to set an example—and he also had to insist, in his preaching, that able-bodied people who do not work are failing the community. In obeying God's commission, Paul understood himself to be imitating the pattern of Christ's self-sacrificial service in love for all.

The third principle behind Paul's choice to support himself by his manual work was his commitment to "Christian *agape*," marked by giving of oneself.[61] Paul sought to make manifest the free character of God's grace. God freely loves us, not seeking gain for himself. Insofar as possible, Paul wants to be a giver of this sort to his congregations. By working with his hands, Paul is able to give to others. Paul seeks "a sovereign liberty for the service of the gospel and the kingdom, indifferent to the alternations of comfort and want."[62]

The enduring moral principles behind Paul's casuistic judgment about his manual work, therefore, are at least three: care for the gospel's divine dignity, imitation of Christ's service, and manifestation of the free gift of grace. In all times and places, these principles should undergird Christian pastoral and moral judgments, even though the church must pay its ministers a salary.

What about Paul's judgments regarding food sacrificed to idols? Since he does not believe in the reality of idols, he is willing to eat such food, but not if the eating of such food might draw newly converted Christians back to their old idolatrous patterns of life. Congar describes the situation in Corinth as one of poorly formed conscience, in which the Corinthian Christians freely associated with their old pagan friends (including by joining with them to eat food sacrificed to idols within temple precincts) and were prone to moral laxity, a division between the rich and the poor, and pride in glossolalia.

Focusing on the issue of foods sacrificed to idols, Congar observes that Paul lays down three principles. First, the idols do not exist and therefore, in reality, food cannot be offered to them; second, Christians are free to eat whatever is available in the market, since all food is from God; and third, Christians are not free to participate in pagan religious acts, since such acts are idolatrous. The Corinthians understood themselves to be following all three of these principles. Thus, they assumed their behavior to be good.

Congar argues that their mistake consisted in thinking "that wisdom and science were supreme values."[63] Put simply, they forgot about love. They forgot that their freedom must take account of the perspective of the less knowledgeable neighbor. Life in Christ is not about freedom to do whatever one has the moral right to do but rather is about using freedom to serve the needs of others in love. Freedom, then, is not an absolute—even when it has to do with things that are morally permissible. The absolute for Christians is charity.

Christian casuistry, therefore, should keep the full situation in view when deciding upon whether to do a permissible thing. Charity must be the guide for the casuistic judgment. For example, when a Christian is eating with a recently converted Christian, it may be necessary not to eat the meat, lest one's partner at table "be tempted to think one was eating offered meat precisely as such."[64] This could scandalize a person who does not know what better-informed persons know. Paul is eager to avoid scandalizing anyone, because he wishes to proclaim the gospel effectively to everyone.

Congar holds that this eagerness to avoid scandalizing applies to Paul's decision to have Timothy circumcised (Acts 16:3) and to other similar decisions with regard to Torah observance on the part of Christians. He notes that here Paul's casuistry differed from James's. James requires that gentile believers not eat strangled meat or meat with the blood in it (Acts 15:20); in other words, he advises that gentile believers follow the Torah's food laws on these points. In James's view, this is the minimum that should be required of gentile followers of Christ. Congar is critical of James, whom he associates with modern casuists who seek to identify the legal minimum. He argues that Paul, in teaching about food offered to idols, aims not to find a legal minimum but to follow "the maximum of the demands of charity."[65] I doubt this is fair to James, but it is certainly accurate with respect to Paul. For Congar, the point is that casuistry—dealing with difficult cases of conscience—needs to be guided not by a focus on one's minimum obligation, but by a focus on charity in imitation of Christ.

Lastly, Congar treats "observances concerning foods and days." In regard to this subject, Paul builds his casuistic case on four principles. First, Christian faith must instruct and guide practical judgment. In faith, we believe that all food comes from God and therefore no food is unclean per se. Second, however, if our judgment of conscience erroneously deemed that a particular food is unclean, we would sin by eating that food. An "erroneous or doubtful" conscience still binds. Third, while faith must inform practical judgment, the action must be guided by charity. Since this is so, we cannot suppose that our conscience is adequate to judge others' actions in difficult cases. Fourth, charity requires not only that we refrain from judging, but also that we avoid causing scandal by doing something that others, in erroneous conscience, consider to be forbidden. Our freedom should not be used in a way that ignores the perspective of others or harms the unity of the Christian community. In charity, therefore, "we should refrain from obstinately following our personal point of view, even when it is lawful."[66] In cases of conscience, we should follow Christ, who did not seek his own will but sought to give his life in service to others.

Congar remarks in conclusion, "Casuistry of the gospel kind does not, for all that, despise the letter: the juridical laws form part of the given facts of the action, but they do not exhaust them."[67] At the center of every good act of casuistry is charity, since God is love. We are called to act in such a manner as to be drawn into the divine life of love revealed by Christ. Ultimately, for Paul, casuistry about cases of conscience "is scarcely casuistry at all," in the sense that it is determined by faith and charity rather than by the legal minimum, and therefore "is 'divinising', not moralising."[68]

Congar's approach serves both to affirm casuistry and to critique the preconciliar conscience-centered understanding of it. His reading of Paul should be kept in view when I discuss the positions of Labourdette and Pinckaers in chapter 3.

Johannes Stelzenberger

A third biblical critique of conscience-centered morality comes from the German Catholic moralist Johannes Stelzenberger, whose approach bears the imprint of Christian existentialism. Stelzenberger published books treating the place of conscience not only in the New Testament but also in Origen and Augustine.[69] The latter studies demonstrated that the early church conceived of the moral life in a manner that involved conscience but certainly did not give the central place to conscience.

In his 1961 *Syneidesis im Neuen Testament*, Stelzenberger begins with a survey of German-language scholarship on this topic, and he also examines nonbiblical antecedent uses of the term. He devotes the main section of his book to an analysis of the various biblical instances of *syneidēsis*. As he observes, German scholars can be misled by the wide range of meanings that pertain to the German word for "conscience" (*Gewissen*). For this reason, he seeks to identify with clarity the meanings that the New Testament allots to *syneidēsis*, as background for understanding how conscience should function in Catholic moral theology today.

Although *syneidēsis* is a concept that was in circulation in the Hellenistic world of Paul's day and that was used by Stoic philosophers and by Jewish thinkers such as Philo, Stelzenberger considers that *syneidēsis* "in the New Testament is a *novum*. . . . Interpreting it in light of the Greek does not bring out what is proper to it. Even the Old Testament must be excluded as a source" (94). In defending this distinctive position, Stelzenberger argues that there are a wide diversity of meanings of *syneidēsis* in the New Testament.

With regard to Acts 23:1—where Paul states that he has "lived before God in all good conscience up to this day"—Stelzenberger notes that commentators generally assume that Paul means that he has obeyed God's moral law and is righteous. Disagreeing with this interpretation, he proposes that Paul instead intends to indicate his fidelity to God's commission. Paul is describing his consciousness that he has obeyed God's call or, in other words, has lived "in perfect solidarity with God" (50). Stelzenberger offers a similar reading of Acts 23:15, "I always take pains to have a clear conscience toward God and toward men." He thinks this statement pertains to Paul's desire to have a pure "consciousness" or "attitude" in his religious-moral activities.

Syneidēsis functions along the same lines in Romans 9:1, "I am speaking the truth in Christ, I am not lying; my conscience bears me witness in the Holy Spirit"; and 2 Corinthians 1:12, "For our boast is this, the testimony of our conscience that we behaved in the world, and still more toward you, with holiness and godly sincerity, not by earthly wisdom but by the grace of God." In these passages, Paul is describing his awareness or consciousness of his actions and experiences. He invokes his consciousness as true and trustworthy because the Holy Spirit has been at work in him, with the result that "he knows himself to be fully in harmony with God's directives," not due to his own power but due to God's grace (54).

Another meaning of *syneidēsis* appears in Romans 13:5, "Therefore one must be subject, not only to avoid God's wrath but also for the sake of conscience." Stelzenberger holds that the purpose of Paul's reference to *syneidēsis* is to make clear that believers should be subject to the governing authorities not solely out of fear but also out of an interior sense of the obligations and values intrinsic to believers' relationship with God. The meaning of *syneidēsis* in this case is the interior relational bond to God, which is the ground of Christian obedience. Similarly, treating 1 Peter 2:19—"For one is approved if, mindful of God [*dia syneidēsin theou*], he endures pain while suffering unjustly"—Stelzenberger rules out translating *syneidēsis* here as "conscience," since this verse has in view the recognition of one's relationship to God and the inherent obligations that arise therefrom.

In various other New Testament instances, *syneidēsis* has a meaning that accords with the Old Testament use of "heart" to mean the deep interior of the person. These instances occur in letters that are not generally considered Pauline, especially Hebrews and 2 Timothy. In Stelzenberger's view, *syneidēsis* does not mean "conscience" in these instances but rather involves one's religious-moral standing, "one's interior, the bearer of worship and religious adoration" (68). What is in view is "the quality of the heart that is bound to God" (68).

What is Stelzenberger's interpretation of the passages in 1 Corinthians 8 and 10 (and 2 Corinthians 4–5) that discuss conscience? He finds that *syneidēsis* is here being used "in the sense of the believer's faculty of judgment in matters related to God" (69). But he again denies that Paul has in view what we today mean by "conscience." He remarks, "In 1 Cor 8:7–12, a totally false point of departure is chosen, when one works with the function of moral conscience. The fundamental notion is the *gnosis* and the religious-moral ability to judge that is given with it. *Syneidesis* is the faculty of judgment based on insight concerning the relationship between God and man" (70). The Corinthians who are tempted toward idolatry (and who are endangered when Christians willingly eat food sacrificed to idols) are deficient not in "conscience" as we understand it but rather in their religious-moral knowledge about idols and sacrificial food. Similarly, Stelzenberger proclaims, "*Synedeisis* in 1 Cor 10:25 and 27 is the religious-moral perception of values. There is no discussion at all of 'conscience' [*Gewissen*]" (73).

Romans 2:15 is another central text often quoted in traditional Christian analyses of conscience. In discussing this passage, Stelzenberger gives insight into his own existential understanding of "conscience," separated from religious-moral knowledge. He remarks, "Conscience in the actual and strict sense of the word only occurs in crises in activity. The human being stands before a personal decision. . . . [Conscience] is stirred by our sense of responsibility before the intrinsic values of life. It revolts when we are in danger of acting against our sense of values or when we have done something that contradicts our personal scale of values" (78–79). For Stelzenberger, then, conscience applies our personal sense of values to a particular action that we are poised to do. Stelzenberger goes on to clarify in his discussion of Romans 2 that our "sense of values" reflects real "trans-individual norms," and conscience urges us to act in accordance with these norms (80). He concludes that in Romans 2 we find a suitable grounding of both antecedent and consequent conscience.

A number of New Testament passages refer to a good conscience, including four verses in 1 and 2 Timothy. Likewise, three passages named by Stelzenberger have to do with a bad conscience, including 1 Corinthians 8:7, which he considers to be an exception to his general rule that 1 Corinthians 8 and 10 are not about conscience as we understand it. If one's sense of values includes the rejection of eating food offered in ritual sacrifice to idols, then if one eats such food anyway, one is acting against conscience (91). When one acts in such a way, one experiences the pain of "bad" conscience: "a strong feeling of disappointment and disapproval arises in the examination of conscience, which is experienced as acute suffering. The conscience blames and accuses" (94).

Stelzenberger draws in part upon the first edition of the Catholic biblical scholar Rudolf Schnackenburg's *The Moral Teaching of the New Testament*, which has a discussion of Paul's use of this concept in "Conscience and Its Formation as a Concern of St. Paul."[70] Schnackenburg recognizes that Catholics are especially interested in what Paul says about conscience because of the importance that conscience has come to have in the Catholic moral life. Not surprisingly, however, Schnackenburg emphasizes that "the concept of *syneidēsis* in Paul is . . . not yet entirely identical with what we call 'conscience.'"[71] Schnackenburg influences Stelzenberger's presentation by singling out Romans 2 and 1 Corinthians 8:7 as teaching that "everyone possesses a faculty of making moral judgements," so that Christians, like other people, make a "judgement of conscience."[72] Yet, for Schnackenburg, unlike Stelzenberger, 1 Corinthians 8 and 10, along with various other Pauline passages, truly have to do with the formation of "conscience" (as we understand it) insofar as they insist upon the need to seek "true moral values."[73]

Philippe Delhaye

The Belgian Catholic moral theologian Philippe Delhaye examines con-science in the Bible from an exegetical perspective shaped by his commit-ment to the moral manualist tradition. Although his viewpoint is quite different from those of Tyrrell, Rashdall, and Bultmann, he joins them in affirming the biblical centrality of conscience. Delhaye explains his 1964 monograph on conscience by observing that since moral theology treats of the encounter of God and man, it is of paramount importance to study the "privileged encounter between God and men which is to be found in the moral conscience."[74] For Delhaye, conscience is "God's voice" and "God's abode in us" (19). He also describes conscience as "the reflection of divine wisdom" (20). Against the increasing tendency to posit an opposition be-tween conscience and law, he notes that conscience follows "the laws of the spirit" (20). Christian conscience has the task not of rejecting the law but of "interiorizing the law" (21).[75]

At the outset of his book, Delhaye identifies the diverse schools of Catholic conscience-centered moral theology, among which he names seven: "absolute tutiorism, mitigated tutiorism, probabiliorism, equiprob-abilism, probabilism, compensationism, laxism" (21).[76] He also notes that the moral manuals typically distinguish between "actual" and "habitual" conscience. Among the medievals, habitual conscience was called "syn-deresis," that is, "the habit of the first principles of the practical reason" (27)—although Bonaventure instead joins synderesis to the will. In Del-haye's view, habitual conscience can be "right," "lax," or "scrupulous" (27). Actual conscience includes "*antecedent* conscience" (a judgment prior to the act) or "*consequent* conscience" (a judgment after the act) (27). Actual conscience can be true, false, lax, scrupulous, perplexed, certain, doubtful, probable, or right. It judges everything, both "what we intend to do as well as what we have done with all particulars and characteristics" (29). Although conscience is in a certain sense impartial, it also registers the intentions of the person, and therefore it is deeply personal in its judgments. Delhaye appreciatively cites René Le Senne's *Traité de morale générale*, in which Le Senne holds that there is a "plenary conscience," participated in by a "psychological conscience" (self-knowledge) and an "artistic conscience."[77] For Le Senne, along existentialist lines, conscience becomes "religious" and "moral" when it moves beyond pure knowledge and experiences conversion from self-centeredness to self-giving love. Advocating an expansive view of conscience, Le Senne states that "the 'ego' is the universality of the conscience in connection with all consciences" (Delhaye, 32).

Delhaye argues that progress may be made in understanding conscience by investigating what Scripture says on the topic. He takes inspiration from various exegetical articles, especially Ceslas Spicq, OP's "La conscience dans le Nouveau Testament."[78] In chapters 1 and 2 of the first part of his book, therefore, Delhaye reflects on the New Testament depictions of conscience. He focuses on the Pauline epistles and the sermons of Paul recorded in Acts, and he finds twenty-two references to *syneidēsis*. He divides his discussion into a section on "habitual conscience" and a section on "actual conscience."

According to Delhaye, "St. Paul often speaks of the conscience as the power to direct one's moral life" (37). As an example, he cites Romans 2:14–15, "When Gentiles who have not the law do by nature what the law requires, they are a law to themselves. . . . They show that what the law requires is written on their hearts, while their conscience also bears witness and their conflicting thoughts accuse or perhaps excuse them." Romans 2:14–15 shows that all persons "have within themselves a moral faculty"—conscience—"that indicates to them what good acts they must do" (37). For Delhaye, conscience also gives us the ability "to judge others' acts in relation to the 'good'" (37). In his view, "conscience" contains within it the natural law, and therefore it is able to render "a moral judgment" and to compare "behavior with the indications of the moral imperative" (38).

In support of conscience's wide-ranging powers, Delhaye also cites Romans 9:1 ("I am not lying; my conscience bears me witness in the Holy Spirit") and 2 Corinthians 1:12 ("For our boast is this, the testimony of our conscience that we have behaved in the world, and still more toward you, with holiness and godly sincerity, not by earthly wisdom but by the grace of God"). Here Delhaye finds evidence that the conscience is not merely a human word; it is a divine word, "God's witness in him [Paul]" (38). This divine word can be natural, in a fallen person; or it can be guided supernaturally by the Holy Spirit, in a Christian. Its primary purpose is to judge our past action, but, as noted, Delhaye thinks it can also judge other people's actions. He cites 1 Corinthians 8 and 10, where Paul describes the case of a person with a "weak" and erroneous conscience, who would be scandalized if a fellow believer ate food that had been offered up in sacrifice to a false god. In conscience, a "weak" believer would judge the action of a fellow believer who ate such food.

Delhaye cites 2 Corinthians 5:11 as a further example of how conscience can judge others. Paul states that "what we [Paul] are is known to God, and I hope it is also known to your conscience." Delhaye assumes that Paul means "moral conscience" here rather than simply meaning "consciousness." The Corinthians' consciences are "their inmost hearts" in which they are able to reflect upon Paul's actions and to pass "a serene and objective judgment" (40). Delhaye also draws upon 2 Corinthians 4:2, where Paul says, "we refuse to practice cunning or to tamper with God's word, but by the open statement of the truth we would commend ourselves to every man's conscience in the sight of God." If "conscience" is the correct translation here, Paul is suggesting that a person's conscience not only judges the person's own actions but also judges other persons' actions. In Delhaye's view, Paul thereby "acknowledge[s] not only the existence of universal norms of good but also the existence of the subjective capacity, that exists in every man, of discerning in depth whether human behavior conforms with the moral law or not" (40).

Delhaye notes that a good or clear conscience is frequently described in Scripture. He cites 2 Timothy 1:3, 1 Timothy 1:19 and 3:9, Acts 23:1 and 24:16, and Hebrews 13:18. To have a clear conscience means to "persevere in the good," and having a clear conscience is "allied to faith," since "the life of faith requires the purity of moral existence" and also since faith strengthens one's conscience (41). With regard to faith's flourishing in good works, Delhaye gives a crucial role to conscience: "By his conscience, man is aware of God's will and applies it to his moral life" (41).

In some of the same letters, a bad or corrupted or faithless conscience also appears. Delhaye cites 1 Timothy 4:2, Titus 1:15–16, and Hebrews 9:9, 14 and 10:2, 22 in order to show that in people who have corrupted themselves by evildoing, "their conscience, the organ of moral life, becomes incapable of performing a good action" (41). He identifies conscience as the fundamental "organ of moral life," and he suggests that this claim is supported especially by Titus 1:15: "To the pure all things are pure, but to the corrupt and unbelieving nothing is pure; their very minds and consciences are corrupted." For Delhaye, again, the role of conscience is more than bearing witness regarding past acts. Conscience must "choose what is good" and "impose its judgment" (41), and thus has a crucial role in future actions. Delhaye argues that in Hebrews 10:22 ("let us draw near with a true heart in full assurance of faith with our hearts sprinkled clean from an evil conscience and our bodies washed with pure water") we find conscience identified with the person's whole moral organism in the sight of God: "The identification of the conscience and the moral personality is here complete" (41).

In 1 Corinthians 8, Delhaye finds a conscience that is neither clear nor corrupted but simply weak. Persons with a "weak" conscience are, as Delhaye says, erroneous or "weak in their judgment . . . because they consider an objectively indifferent action to be bad" (42). He infers that one aspect of their weakness is that they are easily led astray by others. Because they have a "weak" conscience, they are open to doing things that will corrupt their conscience. Paul states that if they see a fellow Christian eating food at an "idol's temple," then they too may eat the food, and they will eat it "as really offered to an idol" (1 Cor. 8:7, 10). Once they have done this, they will be poised to return to their idolatry. Their "weak" conscience will have been corrupted and their moral life will be "destroyed" (1 Cor. 8:11). Delhaye draws the conclusion that the conscience is "not only the witness and interior judge, or the impersonal expression of duty," but is also—most fundamentally and importantly—the very "center of the soul where choices are worked out and responsibilities taken on" (42). This gives to conscience a large role indeed.

Delhaye also treats Romans 14:22, which in Delhaye's Vulgate version reads "consider the man fortunate who can make his decision without going against his conscience."[79] The point is that one must follow one's conscience, rather than disobeying it. Citing Romans 13:5, which teaches that one must obey the ministers of God "for the sake of conscience," Delhaye explains that "we must be subject to legitimate authority because that is God's will. And this will of God is manifested to us through the conscience, and grounded in the conscience" (42). Paul makes clear that acting against a misinformed or erroneous conscience has spiritually harmful effects. Delhaye underscores "the obligatory force of the judgment of the personal conscience" (44).

Delhaye gives careful attention to "concrete cases of conscience and the principles which must guide the Christian in case of doubt" (44). Citing 1 Corinthians 8:1, he differentiates between knowledge and love in conscience's judgment of whether an act is licit. Conscience may know that an action is licit in itself (i.e., in the abstract), but it may also be the case that this action does not build up charity and therefore should not be done.

Inquiring into the originality of Paul's teaching on conscience, Delhaye notes that Paul employed the Greek term for "conscience" rather than Old

Testament phrases such as the "heart." This allowed Paul to show more clearly how it is that the *interiorized* law guides and judges the action and even "pronounces on the actions of others as an objective norm" (49). The conscience can be said to be the "moral person" because, if the conscience is bad, then the person is morally bad. Delhaye concludes that the idea of conscience "was valuable in the Judeo-Christian sense and also had an appeal to the pagans because they were spoken to 'in their own language'" (50).

The second chapter of Delhaye's first part is titled "Biblical Themes Analogous to Conscience: Heart, Wisdom, Prudence." The significance of the "heart" for the moral life can be seen in Scripture's insistence that God probes the heart and that the heart is the locus of moral decision-making where God's word is heard (or rejected) and where the Holy Spirit converts the person. Delhaye shows that the New Testament, including Paul's writings, still contains frequent references to the heart. To the degree that "conscience" serves to replace the "heart," it is no wonder that Delhaye gives conscience such a significant place in his moral theology. In the Old Testament and in many New Testament texts, the heart is the center of moral interiority and the source of moral action.

The brief remarks that Delhaye makes about prudence are also important. Delhaye describes prudence as "wisdom-prudence." Among other proverbs, he cites Proverbs 10:5, "A son who gathers in summer is prudent." He cites various biblical texts that mention "insight" or discernment, though not specifically "prudence." In addition, he describes virtues that flow from prudence, and he sets forth the *infused* virtue of prudence. His discussion draws upon Wisdom 7–9 and various New Testament texts, such as Luke 16:8, "The master commended the dishonest steward for his prudence." In general, he relies upon texts that do not mention prudence but that can be seen to describe it, as for example the supernatural prudence shown in Jesus's command to the rich young ruler: "Sell all that you have and distribute to the poor . . . and come, follow me" (Luke 18:22). Delhaye emphasizes that for Paul, one must exercise a constant virtuous discernment regarding what is pleasing to God (see Rom. 12:2; Phil. 1:9–11; 1 Thess. 5:21). Such discernment is rooted both in prayer and in the practice of the virtue of prudence. Here the Letter of James also plays a role, by showing the connection of prudence with the moral virtues: "the wisdom from above is first pure, then peaceable, gentle, open to reason, full of mercy and good fruits, without uncertainty or insincerity" (James 3:17).

Richard B. Hays

Whereas on Delhaye's reading the morality of the New Testament is in many ways centered upon conscience, for the Reformed New Testament scholar Richard B. Hays, there is no need even to mention conscience in a book on New Testament ethics—although he does take up a number of what might be called cases of conscience. Hays's approach will bring my biblical section to an end, having surveyed four exegetical critiques of conscience-centered morality and four defenses of it.

In his 1996 book *The Moral Vision of the New Testament*, Hays argues that there are "three recurrent, interlocking theological motifs that provide the framework for Paul's ethical teaching: eschatology, the cross, and the new community in Christ."[80] By "eschatology," Hays means the inauguration of the kingdom of God, the beginning of the new creation. The new creation will bring to an end creation's bondage to sin, injustice, and death. Jesus Christ has inaugurated the new creation by his cross and resurrection. The messianic community that he gathered around himself lives by the Holy Spirit that he has poured out, and in this way it represents the beginning of Israel's eschatological restoration. Even so, in the present time prior to the coming of Christ in glory, "the power of the old age persists: mundane obligations (e.g., marriage, obedience to ruling authorities) remain in force, and sin and suffering continue to best the church" (21). But to live in Christ means to live already in the new creation, because Christ's redemptive power is present and active in the lives of his people through his Spirit.

From this perspective, the task of the church is to serve God in love and to be configured in every way to the love of Christ, in "relationships of loving mutual edification" (23). Indeed, in Christ, the church must "*become the righteousness of God*," because "where the church embodies in its life together the world-reconciling love of Jesus Christ, the new creation is manifest" (24). Primarily, then, the church must follow Jesus to the cross, as Christians give their lives for the sake of others. The Christian life therefore involves suffering, since real service to others and real configuration to Christ inevitably involves suffering. Hays maintains, "For Paul, Jesus' death on the cross is an act of loving, self-sacrificial obedience that becomes paradigmatic for the obedience of all who are in Christ" (27).[81]

Although Christians are unlikely to be crucified, the cross functions metaphorically as the pattern for the self-sacrificial love to which all Christians and all humans are called. We must imitate Christ's obedient humility and his self-emptying love. Configuration to the cross is not op-tional for followers of Christ. It is not something that we do for ourselves but something that the Holy Spirit does in us, if we cooperate with the Spirit's work. A mark of self-sacrificial love is found in the church's unity. For Paul, Christian unity is fundamental, given that the church is called to be in fellowship with Christ. The outpouring of the Spirit has the goal of building up the unity of the messianic community. Hays comments, "Love binds the body of Christ together in mutual suffering and rejoicing; love seeks the upbuilding of the whole community rather than private advantage" (35).

But if we believers are "led by the Spirit" and "live by the Spirit" (Gal. 5:18, 25), then how is it that moral norms such as the Decalogue apply to us? Hays notes that Paul is aware "that his gospel could be heard as license for antinomianism," and therefore Paul commands: "do not use your freedom as an opportunity for the flesh" (Gal. 5:13). There are actions that involve using our bodies in ways contrary to Christ's charity, in ways that pertain to the flesh rather than to the Spirit. Believers are not liberated from God's law by the Spirit; rather, believers "have been set free from sin and have become slaves of God" (Rom. 6:22).

Repeatedly, Hays observes that the Christian moral life is defined by entering "the sphere of the Spirit's power," where believers "find themselves changed and empowered for obedience" (45). But he recognizes that Paul does not simply entrust believers to the Spirit's unmediated guidance. In Paul's vision of the Christian moral life, there are authoritative "instruments and mediating structures through which the Spirit works: Scripture, Paul's own teaching, the emissaries that Paul sends back to his churches (see, for example, Phil. 2:19–30), the community's worship" (45). Notably, Hays does not include human nature on this list. He observes, "For Paul, the moral life can never be a matter of reason controlling the passions (as in Platonist philosophical traditions) or of any exercise of unaided human will or ca-pacity" (45). This is because humans are saved not by their own powers but by the redemptive work of Christ and the outpouring of his Spirit. Hays states, "Obedience [to God's will or law] is possible at all only because God has broken the power of sin and begun the work of conforming believers to the image of Jesus Christ" (45).

There is no human moral power whose exercise, outside the Spirit's transformative work, can guide us along the saving path of life in Christ. In this regard Hays cites Romans 8:8, "those who are in the flesh cannot please God." Or as Hays puts it shortly afterward, the Christian moral life must be "christomorphic" through imitation of Christ's self-sacrificial love; and this is possible for no created faculty outside of "Spirit-empowered, Spirit-discerned conformity to Christ" (46).

The strength of Hays's analysis is that he puts his finger on the elements that are central to Paul's moral vision, including Christ's cross, the upbuilding of the church by self-sacrificial life in imitation of Christ, the outpouring of the Holy Spirit, and so forth. By ignoring the place of conscience in Paul's moral vision, he misses an opportunity to reflect upon how Paul thinks moral reflection and moral action work in the human person.[82] But he also shows where moral theologians should lay the emphasis—and the answer is not conscience.

With regard to the ethical ideal, Tyrrell does not envision any significant disjunction between church, Christ, and conscience, which he names as the three great authorities—so long as "church" and "Christ" are understood to be the sum total of collective conscience and the most perfect expression of conscience, respectively. Conceiving of Christ as the incarnation of collective conscience, Tyrrell considers that the key "vehicle" of divine revelation is "the gradual evolution of [God's] Mind and Will in the collective spirit of mankind."[83] This divine, evolving "collective spirit" is our collective conscience. For Tyrrell, the church's authority, properly understood, is strictly coterminous with and limited by "the imperativeness of the collective conscience."[84] Rashdall concurs with this position, holding that if contemporary collective conscience were to disagree with certain moral teachings found in the New Testament, then it is always the latter that would need to give way. By contrast, Pierce seeks to limit conscience's role in ethics, on New Testament grounds. He denies that conscience has anything to do with judging future actions, let alone with directing them, even though Paul presumes that the Spirit will preserve Christians from acting in ways opposed to a clear conscience.

Bultmann argues for an existentially resonant understanding of conscience as the locus of the self-constitution of the "real" self—or of the failure to attain the real self. Conscience constitutes the real self by receiving and obeying the transcendent judgment and commandment of God. Conscience must be obeyed because it communicates God's word and allows for the interior constituting of the authentic self. Like Tyrrell's perspective, this expansive view of conscience sheds light on later postconciliar conscience-centered ethics.

Congar, Stelzenberger, and Delhaye respond in the late 1950s and early 1960s to the Catholic emphasis on conscience as the center of the Christian moral life. In exploring Paul's casuistry, Congar's purpose is to overthrow conscience-based morality and to replace it with a morality centered upon charity and prudence, which provide the basis for Christian casuistry. Stelzenberger, from a Christian existentialist perspective, examines all the New Testament's references to *syneidēsis*. In Stelzenberger's view, the connections between the New Testament's *syneidēsis* and traditional understandings of "conscience" have been greatly exaggerated. Instead, he emphasizes conscience's role in personal decision during moments of crisis. Delhaye, who also examines the New Testament's uses of *syneidēsis*, goes further in associating conscience with the very core of Christian moral identity and agency. Writing in the midst of the Second Vatican Council, he defends conscience-centered morality.

By contrast, Richard Hays does not mention conscience in his lengthy book *The Moral Vision of the New Testament*, given that many other themes—including cross, community, and new creation—are more central to the New Testament's understanding of the Christian moral life. Lest it seems that only Protestants held such a viewpoint in the twentieth century, I should note that the Catholic biblical scholar Frank Matera, in his *New Testament Ethics: The Legacies of Jesus and Paul* (published in the same year as Hays's book), likewise barely mentions conscience, although he does mention it very briefly in passing.[85] No doubt the reason why Matera does not discuss conscience is that he, too, has so much else to discuss. He makes clear that to understand Paul's approach to ethics requires appreciating what it means to be an elect people, to be a sanctified community, to walk by the Spirit, to imitate Christ, to live by the obedience of faith, and to be a new creation. Emphasis on conscience or on any human power would miss the point of Paul's moral vision; and Jesus never talks about conscience.

In my view, the New Testament references to conscience support a role for conscience, but a limited one. For Paul, faith, hope, and cruciform love have primacy. They are spelled out in a virtuous life, in imitation of Christ and under the Spirit's transformative direction of believers as adopted children of God and members of Christ's body. There is a connection in Paul between being purified by Christ's cross and illuminated by his Spirit in faith, hope, and charity, on the one hand, and having a clear conscience and perceiving holiness and truth, on the other hand. But the dictates of conscience must be informed and guided by other authorities such as Christ himself and the church as the "pillar and bulwark of the truth" (1 Tim. 3:15).[86] Paul warns sharply against a number of sins that members of his congregations are committing, and he has no room for the notion that the members of his congregations could legitimately continue doing these sinful actions if it seemed good to them in conscience.

Thus, conscience is not the center of Christian moral life according to the New Testament, nor is conscience (individual or collective) the main way in which Christians know what is right to do, let alone determinative of what it means to be the church. At the same time, the interior judgment of conscience has an important role for both Christians and non-Christians in differentiating good and evil actions. Paul does not propose a "universal ethic" outside of Christ and the Spirit, but neither does he fail to recognize the universal elements (due to our created human nature) of human morality. As the New Testament scholar Brendan Byrne, SJ, says about conscience, "Conscience is that element of self-awareness that submits one's thoughts and actions to constant evaluation in view of a responsibility that presses in on one from without, independently of one's own being and for which one will ultimately be called to account on the day of judgment."[87] This seems a fair enough summary of the New Testament's view of the place and function of conscience in the moral life. It should provide a standard for assessing the approaches to morality found in the next three chapters.

Chapter 2

Conscience and the Moral Manuals

T hough he has sometimes been accused of being a "manualist,"[1] one
could hardly find a more trenchant critic of the post-Tridentine
moral manuals than Réginald Garrigou-Lagrange, OP. He remarks
in an essay published in 1925: "A great difference separates his [Aquinas's]
idea of moral theology from that which can be found in a number of works
written on this subject from the seventeenth century onward."[2] Among
other concerns, Garrigou-Lagrange challenges the sharp distinction between moral and dogmatic theology on the grounds that theology is a unified science, having God as its formal object.[3] He also warns that moral
theology, properly speaking, "*cannot be reduced to casuistry*, which presupposes (but does not treat) the fundamental questions concerning the
last end, the nature of human acts, the foundation of morality, the nature
of law, the nature of the virtues and the Gifts of the Holy Spirit, the various states of life, and so forth. Casuistry is only the inferior application of
moral theology."[4] Even more clearly, Garrigou-Lagrange calls upon Catholic
theologians to restore to moral reflection the centrality of God's grace and
the graced life of virtue, including faith, hope, charity, and supernatural
prudence. He complains, "numerous modern theologians, more or less
reducing moral theology to casuistry, remove the treatises on grace and
the infused virtues."[5]

Garrigou-Lagrange is deeply critical of the moral manuals' approach
to conscience. He advises that in order to understand what has been lost
in the moral manuals, we should compare Aquinas's treatise on prudence
with the moral manuals' treatment of conscience. Generally speaking, the
moral manuals "not only ask whether conscience is the proximate rule of
human acts and if it must always be right and certain, but furthermore
pose numerous questions about how one is to form a right and certain
conscience and about how one is to correct an erroneous conscience."[6] In

other words, the moral manuals move almost immediately into "special" or "particular" moral questions rather than reflecting adequately upon "general" moral theory—or even upon the various virtues. The moral manuals expansively discourse upon conscience very early, prior to the discussion of other topics: "they ask questions about the species and gravity of sin entailed by every action against conscience, about cases of doubtful and probable conscience, about a lax or a scrupulous conscience, and so on."[7] When they turn to "special" morality, furthermore, they devote hardly any attention to prudence.

For Garrigou-Lagrange, the neglect of prudence in most moral manuals is scandalous. He proposes that the key to all the more troublesome questions about conscience (such as those in the probabilist controversies) is to perceive the real nature of prudence. He explains, "the truth of the practical intellect (i.e., prudence) consists in *conformity with rectified appetite*, meaning conformity with the *sensitive appetite* rectified by the virtues of temperance and courage, as well as (and especially) conformity with the *rational appetite* rectified by the virtue of justice and the other virtues of the will."[8] Much moral casuistry would be unnecessary were it perceived that when a person possesses rectified appetite, such a person can move forward confidently in prudential judgment. Indeed, Garrigou-Lagrange concludes that a virtuous person, especially when aided by counsel, "can generally succeed at forming a right and certain conscience without recourse to a meticulous comparison of probabilities for and against an action."[9]

To Garrigou-Lagrange's critique, Servais Pinckaers, OP, adds further details. Specifically, he addresses the approach taken by Dominic Prümmer, OP, one of Pinckaers's predecessors in moral theology at the University of Fribourg, where Prümmer taught from 1908 to 1930. Pinckaers deems that Prümmer's moral manual fails to measure up to Aquinas. He explains, "Father Prümmer, in an effort to return to St. Thomas, had undertaken a renewed presentation of this classic morality, centering it on the virtues rather than the commandments. But the virtues never furnished him with anything more than a different framework; the material itself was still limited to obligations and sins."[10]

Pinckaers is much more positive about Santiago Ramirez, OP, who taught moral theology at Fribourg from 1923 to 1945. Regarding Ramirez, Pinckaers offers high praise: "Father Ramirez pondered deeply and speculatively on a vast amount of material including, besides the works of St. Thomas, ancient and modern philosophers, Scripture, the Fathers, Church documents, theologians, mystics, and literature concerning them."[11] Likewise, Pinckaers praises the work of Thomas Deman, OP, who taught at Fribourg from 1945 to 1954 and was a critic of casuistic moral theology.[12] By contrast to Prümmer, neither Ramirez nor Deman wrote a moral manual. Pinckaers also credits Ramirez and Deman for refusing to separate moral and ascetic-mystical (spiritual) theology.

Pinckaers goes on to describe the standard approach taken by the moral manuals. He observes that "the table of contents in the manuals proposed only four pillars for fundamental moral theology: firstly the law, that is, natural law, identified with the Decalogue, which, since the commandments replaced the virtues, served to organize special moral theology; and then conscience, human acts, and sins."[13] While each of these topics is important in itself, these four elements—natural law, conscience, human action, and sins—do not suffice for Catholic moral theology, which must attend preeminently to the grace of the Holy Spirit and to the inaugurated kingdom with its foretaste and promise of beatitude. In the moral manuals, Pinckaers remarks, obligation or duty becomes the main focus, the virtues receive at best brief consideration, and the purpose of studying moral theology is largely to learn how to make external determinations regarding "cases of conscience."[14]

From early in his career, Pinckaers traced the problems in the moral manuals to a faulty understanding of freedom. He argues that the moral manuals present human freedom as an indifferent power for choosing, a neutral dynamism. However, as Pinckaers remarks, freedom fully exists only when it engages "the intellect and will according to their natural inclinations to the true and the good."[15] This is a "freedom for excellence" rather than a "freedom of indifference."[16]

Tom Angier has criticized Pinckaers for neglecting the Jewish and Old Testament roots of Christian ethics and for being too negative toward commandments and obligations.[17] I agree that Pinckaers should have devoted more attention to the Old Testament and the Mosaic law.[18] But in *The Sources of Christian Ethics*, Pinckaers writes at length and positively about the Decalogue, natural law, and natural inclinations.[19] Pinckaers's critique of obligation and commandment-based ethics is not based on neglect of or negativity toward the Jewish/Old Testament roots of Christian ethics. A morality of obligation—in the Kantian sense, which is what concerns Pinckaers—will not be able to appreciate either why Christians obey the commandments or what place the divine commandments have in Christian life.

For Pinckaers, as for Aristotle and Aquinas, the virtues are "coordinate with other notions: notions such as nature, law, function and fulfillment."[20] To say that Catholic moral theology should be virtue based is not to deny or denigrate these crucial coordinates, without which "virtue" could not be understood. Rather it is to make a point with regard to the moral manuals as well as certain forms of post-Kantian modern ethics.[21] Pinckaers is well aware that, for Aquinas, God moves the human person to himself by means of law and grace. The issue has to do with recognizing the proper place of the concept of "law" in the Thomist moral lexicon,[22] as well as with reclaiming the structure of the *secunda pars* of the *Summa theologiae*, and above all with appreciating the elevation to supernatural beatitude accomplished by the new law of the grace of the Holy Spirit through the theological virtues, the infused moral virtues, and the gifts of the Holy Spirit.[23]

In *The Sources of Christian Ethics*, Pinckaers asks whether Catholic moral theology underwent a definitive rupture in the period after Aquinas. Put simply, has the moral teaching of the Catholic Church been fundamentally compromised by the casuistic moral theology of the period 1600–1965? He answers that the bond with the sources of Catholic moral doctrine was never broken, but there was "a shrinkage" and "a slight distortion."[24] Despite his disagreements with St. Alphonsus, he affirms that Alphonsus's stature as a Doctor of the Church and as the patron of moral theologians "merits our respect and esteem for his achievements."[25] He also praises the spiritual writings of Alphonsus. Alphonsus is not to blame, since the moral manuals mirror the centrality of obligation in Kantian ethics and also react to Protestant criticisms of law.[26] This cultural context explains why Catholic moral theology, including Alphonsus's, went in the direction it did.

Pinckaers thinks that Catholic moral theologians today are tempted to become neo-manualists, but now committed to conscience *over against* law. In response, he urges returning to the Sermon on the Mount, Augustine, and Aquinas and building from there. In so doing, however, moralists should take advantage of historical studies both of Scripture and of the development of theology, so as to understand the sources of Catholic moral theology more deeply and thereby be able to renew it more richly.[27]

In a recent article titled "Reappraising the Manual Tradition," Brian Besong challenges the accuracy of Pinckaers's perspective.[28] Besong has in view Pinckaers's argument that the moral manuals relied upon an account of freedom derived from Ockham. As will become clear, I agree with Besong that the manuals' view of freedom was often much richer than this, at least if the moral manuals I survey in what follows are representative. I also partly agree with Besong's point that the moral manuals' "strong, practical emphasis on duty in no way implies a derogation of the virtues; in contrast, such an emphasis strongly complements the virtues, albeit with a focus on their more practical side, rather than the metaphysics of perfecting powers."[29] In a certain way, too, the manuals' casuistry can be said to have offered a training in the paths of prudent decision-making. But I think that the moral manuals' conscience-centered morality was not adequate to articulating the Christian moral life and did indeed minimize the virtues and the gifts of the Holy Spirit, just as Garrigou-Lagrange and Pinckaers say.[30]

In this chapter, I examine five representative twentieth-century moral manuals. I explore how each manual orders its topics and, in a more focused way, I survey the content of its discussion of conscience. I have selected manuals published in the early to mid-twentieth century in the United States, Ireland, and Europe. Two are by Jesuits, two by diocesan priests, and one by a Dominican at Fribourg. Three are by philosophers and two by theologians. I will begin by giving lengthy attention to an American philosophical moral manual that appeared in the 1950s and that sought to be fully Thomistic in outlook.

Austin Fagothey, SJ

The first edition of Austin Fagothey's *Right and Reason: Ethics in Theory and Practice* was published in 1953, and the second and final edition—from which I will quote—in 1959. Fagothey taught philosophy at the University of Santa Clara, a Jesuit institution in California. The text is one of moral philosophy, not moral theology, but of course the two were very closely related in his day.

Fagothey opens his book with a striking sentence: "The point of view adopted in this book is that of the Aristotelian-Thomistic synthesis, the living tradition of the *perennial philosophy*, that applies the wisdom of the ancients, tried and proved in the crucible of historical experience, to the discoveries and problems of modern life."[31] At the same time, Fagothey notes that Aquinas's synthesis can be augmented in light of more recent developments; and thus part of his task will be to bring Aquinas into critical conversation with existentialism, logical positivism, and relativism.

After an introduction titled "Ethics as a Study," he proceeds with chapters in the following order: "The Good," "Happiness," "Pursuit of Happiness," "The

Human Act," "Voluntariness," "Morality," "The Norm of Morality," "Sources of Morality," "Law," "Natural Law," "Obligation and Sanction," "Conscience," "Virtue," "Rights and Duties," "Worship," "Life," "Health and Safety," "Truthfulness," "Justice and Contracts," "Charity," "Society," "The Family," "The State," "Government," "Civil Law," "Education," "Property," "Titles to Property," "Work and Wages," "Communism and Socialism," "Social Order," "International Relations," "War," and "Peace." It will be clear that beginning with the chapter entitled "Worship," the book turns to specific moral actions, institutions, or problems. The chapter on worship makes this explicit by describing itself as the beginning of the book's movement to applied ethics.

Fagothey is aware of his difference from Thomas Aquinas in this regard. As Fagothey says with regard to the kinds of actions that he will study in the second half of his book (the section on applied ethics), "Older writers, such as St. Thomas, built their whole treatment of applied ethics around the classification of the virtues and opposed vices. Modern writers prefer to make a specific investigation of the rights conferred and the duties imposed by the natural law, and we shall follow this method" (263). He justifies his approach by pointing to the contemporary spread of moral relativism. By grounding himself in natural law, he aims to insist upon binding moral norms against relativistic approaches to ethics.

He also defends his overall approach in his discussion (in the chapter preceding "Worship") of rights and duties. Humans have duties toward God and rights and duties vis-à-vis each other, as well as "rights against our fellow man concerning ourselves and duties to God concerning ourselves," such as not to commit suicide (263). Our central duty is toward God. It is our duty toward God that grounds the duty of living a moral life. The central duty that we have toward God is the duty of worship. We owe God love as our ultimate end, we owe God reverence because of God's greatness, and we owe God service because God is our Creator on whom our existence depends absolutely. The debt that we owe God as our ultimate end is listed third by Fagothey because it has to do with God as final cause.

He defines worship in terms of adoration, prayer, and sacrifice. His main opponent here is Immanuel Kant and specifically his *Religion within the Limits of Reason Alone*. For Kant, religion is simply the work of living a moral life by obeying, for its own sake rather than for personal gain, the categorical imperative to do unto others as you would they do unto you. Kant's religion does not really involve anything vis-à-vis God. Fagothey also addresses the position of Friedrich Schleiermacher, who supposes that religion is simply the consciousness that we have of our absolute dependence, without being able to say more about the mystery upon which our lives depend. In answer to such positions, Fagothey argues that the natural law requires the worship of God because God can be known by human reason as the source of our being whose infinite excellence must be acknowledged. This rational acknowledgment of God's excellence is what is primarily meant by "worship."

Why then should worship include sacrifice, and why does it need to take place publicly in a church? It must include exterior sacrifice or offering in order to express bodily the interior self-offering that we give to God. As body-soul creatures, we cannot worship rightly if our bodies have no part in it. Moreover, since we are social creatures, our worship must be communal and public; even nation-states, therefore, owe worship to the true God. *Pace* Kant, worship requires more than intrahuman morality; *pace* Schleiermacher, religion consists in more than religious consciousness, since religion "is directed to a personal being" rather than simply consisting in our interior awareness of the sublime and mysterious character of our existence (271).

Fagothey's opening chapter on philosophical ethics is structured as a response to Kant. He begins by asking what the good life is, and he notes that not every action is good. Throughout the ages, people have deemed some acts praiseworthy and other acts blameworthy. He notes that in human legal systems "we punish people and even put them to death for doing what we think they ought not to do, or for not doing what we think they ought to do" (21). His point is that the human being, in society, is a creature for whom the difference between right and wrong action is profoundly important. He continues this introductory chapter by reflecting upon the foundations of "ethics." How is it that there is a "right" and "wrong" action? Can we really be held accountable to these standards, and does living in obedience to them actually benefit us? After all, the wicked flout these standards by doing many actions deemed "wrong," but they seem to enjoy a good deal of pleasure and power, and they often oppress and even put to death those who are attempting to live by the standards of right and wrong. Moreover, the latter often gain little tangible benefit in this life from adhering to right and wrong. Could it be that human beings who live by self-interest, rather than by morality, are the ones who are acting more wisely?

Metaphysically, Fagothey proposes that three affirmations are necessary for ethics to make sense, in light of the above questions. First of all, determinism cannot be true. Despite the increasing popularity of determinist viewpoints in the modern age, humans have freedom in their actions; otherwise, the insistence that people should live in accord with ethical standards would make no sense. Second, humans—as rational creatures—have a spiritual (and thus immortal) soul. Philosophically speaking, if there were no immortal soul, then human reason (without the benefit of revelation) would be justified in concluding that, in particular circumstances at least, it is more beneficial for one's own flourishing to live by self-interest than by ethical standards. Third and finally, God exists. If God did not exist, then the Good—the standard that measures in a transcendent manner all finite goodness—would not exist. Nor would there be any beatitude for humans, any life after this life in which justice is done for the righteous who have suffered for refusing to do evil.

Fagothey grants, "It is probably due to the influence of Immanuel Kant that these three truths have been singled out as having special reference to ethics" (27). Kant defends each of them, but on ethical rather than metaphysical grounds. Kant argues for human freedom as a datum of experience, and then he postulates, as a matter of practical reason, the immortality of the soul and the existence of God. Fagothey urges that the opposite path must be taken: metaphysics must ground ethics. But he considers that ethics cannot get underway without first defending the realities that modern skepticism, ever since Michel de Montaigne and David Hume, has been attacking: human freedom, the immortality of the soul, and God's existence. As he puts the matter, "Ethics begins with a definite view of the universe and of man drawn from experience and refined by metaphysics (our three presuppositions being particularly important), from which certain moral principles follow as logically demanded" (28).

After this opening chapter, Fagothey—partly shaped by his context in the 1950s, by which time the Thomistic criticisms of the moral manuals were widespread—offers chapters on the Good and on Happiness. He observes that "ethics originated in speculation on the good life" among the Greeks (29). Thus, the Good must be given its place; but in understanding the contents of the good life, ethics focuses upon human actions and specifically the difference between right and wrong acts. Fagothey therefore defines philosophical ethics as "the practical normative science of the rightness and wrongness of human conduct as known by natural reason" (29; italics removed).

At the same time, Fagothey has a teleological understanding of philosophical ethics. He begins with the Good because, as he notes, "If man distinguishes a good life from a bad, a right way of living from a wrong, a doing of what he ought as opposed to what he ought not, he can do so only because the good, the right, and the ought lead to some worthy goal that the opposite modes of conduct make unattainable" (31). For Fagothey, everything depends upon asking the question of what "will bring him [the human person] to the fulfillment of the highest good possible for him, to the accomplishment of the purpose for which he exists" (31). After all, humans act for ends, and these ends are goods. In describing this principle, Fagothey presents human freedom as indeterminate: "before it acts, a being with potentiality for acting is in an indeterminate condition, and can either act or not act, act in this way or in that way. No action will ever take place unless something removes this indetermination, stirs the being to act, and points its action in a certain direction" (33). Fagothey could have been clearer that the will's natural inclination toward the good means that our indetermination is always grounded in a deeper inclination toward the good, but his point remains accurate regarding the motivating factor in human action.

Fagothey grounds all ethics in the fact that humans have one ultimate end or highest good, encompassing all other ends. He notes that, for ethical relativists, the idea of one ultimate end seems restrictive and confining; how could one end satisfy the wide diversity of our human desires and truly satiate our desire? Besides, says the ethical relativist, any "total and ultimate meaning" that life might possess is in fact "undiscoverable by us now and unnecessary for relatively successful living" (36). In response, Fagothey notes that the ultimate end is not and cannot be a means to something further. Quoting Aquinas (*Summa theologiae* I-II, q. 1, a. 4), he shows that if there were no ultimate end, no rational action could ever get started, since there would finally be no reason for the will to move—given that the will could not hope to be satisfied. People may act for an end that they mistakenly identify as ultimate, but rational action always has in view an ultimate end. In fact, there is only one end that can truly be ultimate in the sense of providing the happiness that we seek. Actions that are morally good conduce to this ultimate end of human flourishing; actions that are wicked lead away from true human flourishing. As Fagothey says, "human conduct derives its moral goodness from the last end" (41).

In his next chapter, "Happiness," Fagothey remarks that this ultimate end must, when possessed, make us truly happy, so that we are not striving for a still further good that we imagine will make us happy. God, in himself, is infinitely happy; and the happiness that humans possess in God, while not infinite, is utterly full and complete. Every human desires rationally to be happy. Even despair is rooted in a radical, but seemingly unfulfillable, yearning for happiness. Such happiness is found only in union with God as our good and end. To strive for this end does not mean that we have to be conscious of it, since everyone acts at least implicitly for happiness. Here Fagothey contests the materialism of Bertrand Russell, who despaired of any ultimate meaning or purpose in human life. Fagothey agrees with Plato and Aristotle in their estimation of the goal of human life, and he finds their viewpoint beautifully developed and articulated by Aquinas.[32] Humans will not rest until they find happiness; this desire continually presses upon us and cannot be negated or resisted, although we can incorrectly identify the ultimate end. God has made us with a natural desire for happiness, for union with himself as the infinite Good. If this desire were not possible to fulfill, then God would have created us for a condition of perpetual frustration, which the wise and good Creator would not have done.

Fagothey's next chapter discusses the pursuit of happiness, first with respect to four mistaken paths: hedonism, utilitarianism, Stoicism, and evolutionism. The first two involve a commitment to maximizing pleasure for the individual and for the group. Against Epicurean hedonism, the Stoics taught that virtue is happiness itself and, in addition, that virtue means attunement to the world soul, which is "God." The evolutionist view is that happiness consists in the eventual historical perfecting of the human being, so that the historical process ("progress") is what really counts. Fagothey also mentions a type of evolutionism that is indebted to Kant and that identifies self-realization (as a member of the whole of humanity) as happiness. He shows that none of these actually satisfy our desire for happiness. For example, he observes: "The Stoic might stand firm while the world topples about him, but he could hardly be happy about it. Virtue is an indispensable means to happiness, but it is not that happiness itself" (72). God alone is required for our happiness, and God alone is sufficient for our happiness.[33] This is because God is the infinite Good whose infinitely delightful riches we can never exhaust. He explains that even our bodily desires are satisfied by God, both because the body is ordered primarily to the good of the soul and because God in his omnipotence is able to draw our bodies into beatitude (as he will do in the resurrection of the dead at the end of time).

At this stage, Fagothey—like Aquinas himself in the *prima-secundae*— turns to human acts, which Fagothey conceives of as the means by which humans attain to the ultimate end or happiness. Why is it, he asks, that God does not simply create humans in the state of beatitude? Why make humans work for it by action? Fagothey answers that this path pertains to the dignity of the human beings as created with intellect and will, which are intended to operate toward their end. He defines a "human act" as a conscious, free act, by contrast to an "act of man," in which the element of conscious freedom is absent. He explains that action is rooted in the apprehension of an attractive good: "For a man to act he must first be attracted by some good. When the intellect knows something as good, there arises in the will a liking for it" (89). This element of attraction to the good and natural inclination (of both the intellect and the will) is important. In developing his analysis, Fagothey follows Aquinas quite closely: "If the intellect further sees it [the thing known] as a possible good that may be striven for and obtained, this moves the will to an act of spontaneous *intention* or tending toward the good, a stretching forth to gain the object without yet considering the means necessary to it" (89).

Fagothey addresses the voluntariness of an action and the freedom of the will. He defines a voluntary action as "one which proceeds from the will with a knowledge of the end" (94; italics removed). He defines freedom or free will as essentially a freedom to choose, so that one is responsible morally for one's choices: "Freedom (in the sense of free will, as we take it here) is the ability, when all requisites for acting are present, of either acting or not acting, of doing this or doing that. . . . A free act supposes two or more eligible alternatives, at least the alternatives of acting or not acting" (94). Yet, Fagothey is aware of a case of a voluntary action that does not involve "freedom" in this sense and still would be fully voluntary. Namely, the manifestation of the perfect Good (God himself) would *impel* our will to accept it and yet our will would act *voluntarily*. Moreover, he points out that our desire for happiness is not something that we choose—since we cannot help but desire happiness—but it is still something we voluntarily embrace. His focus, however, is on distinguishing free human acts for which we are morally responsible from other kinds of human acts.

Fagothey next asks whether moral positivism is true, or whether (as he holds) there are acts that "are right or wrong of their very nature" (114). He critiques Thomas Hobbes, Jean-Jacques Rousseau, Auguste Comte, Herbert Spencer, and others. In this discussion, he also pauses to criticize John Duns Scotus and William of Ockham for their misunderstanding of the human will. For Scotus, adultery and murder (though naturally bad for human beings) "would not be wrong if God did not forbid them"; and William of Ockham "makes the goodness or badness of acts depend solely on the divine will. In one passage he says that God could even command His creatures to hate Him, and this hatred would then become meritorious" (122). Like Pinckaers, Fagothey condemns such a view of human freedom. It is emphatically not the case that "all acts are indifferent in themselves and become good or bad only because commanded or forbidden by God" (122).[34]

Fagothey goes on to distinguish carefully between what he calls "freedom of choice" and "freedom of independence," noting that the latter is impossible with regard to the natural law. Even more tellingly, he then adds: "The freedom we have been considering is *freedom from*. More important is *freedom for*. The only reason why it is good for a person to be free *from* various restrictions and hindrances is that he may be free *for* the kind of life he is meant to live, for the attainment of his end. Freedom *from* is merely negative; freedom *for* is its positive complement" (166).[35] He specifies the meaning of "law" under the rubric of "freedom *for*," insisting that even though "law curtails freedom *from*, . . . it enhances freedom *for*, because it enables a man to live the kind of life he has been created for. . . . Law tends to make men good, directing them to their last end and pointing out to them the means necessary to this end" (166). Pinckaers would fully agree.

Let me skip over Fagothey's account of eternal law and natural law; he presents the viewpoint of Aquinas on these matters. In the chapter that follows, titled "Obligation and Sanction," far from centering everything on duty or obligation, Fagothey firmly opposes this Kantian perspective. As he notes, "Kant's ethics is a stern *deontologism*, the theory that man's last end is the fulfillment of duty" (191). He treats at length Kant's *Foundations of the Metaphysics of Morals*. While granting that Kant's approach is significantly better than mere materialism or hedonism, he observes that "to rest all morality on the motive of *duty* is unnatural and inhuman" (195). He warns against "overplaying the role of duty" and "cold obligation" (195). It should be evident, he argues, that duty is a valuable thing. But much more valuable and central in the moral life is love. He remarks in this vein that "love and generosity are always esteemed as higher motives than mere duty and give the act a greater moral worth. We fall back on duty only when other motives fail" (195).[36]

Moreover, Fagothey roots obligation in the fact that we are ordered to the ultimate end that is God himself. Obligation, then, has to do with our ordering to beatitude and is inseparable from the fact that God created us to flourish. It is not a stern legalism but a life-giving reality. He states, "Moral necessity, which binds a free will without destroying its freedom, must come from the final cause, for only an end or good known by the intellect can move the will, either to arouse or to restrain it" (198).[37]

We now arrive at Fagothey's treatment of conscience. Does this treatment suffer in the ways that we would anticipate from Garrigou-Lagrange's and Pinckaers's critiques of the moral manuals, namely, by neglecting the context of the virtue of prudence (as well as neglecting the gift of wisdom, the importance of faith and prayer, and the healing and sanctifying power of grace)?

Fagothey presents conscience as the "connecting link between the law and the individual act," or the way in which a person is able to "apply the law to the concrete situations in which he finds himself" (207). He adds that conscience is "the subjective basis of morality" (207). Against exaggerated views of conscience, he notes that it is "not a special faculty distinct from the intellect," as though it were a particularly acute moral instinct or a supernatural intrusion of the divine voice (208). Instead, like Garrigou-Lagrange, he argues that conscience consists in "a function of the practical intellect," or "the practical judgment of reason upon an individual act as good and to be performed, or as evil and to be avoided" (208–9). He goes on to explain that *synderesis* is "the habit of general moral principles," such as "Do good and avoid evil" and "Do unto others as you would be done by"— the first principles of practical reasoning, which are either self-evident or immediate conclusions from self-evident principles (209). These immediate conclusions include, if I understand Fagothey correctly, the precepts of the Decalogue. On this view, conscience is simply a judgment of practical reason, in which the major premise is a principle that comes from synderesis and the minor premise brings in the particularity of the act to be done or not done here and now.

In its judgments, conscience reflects upon both future actions and past ones. Fagothey considers that conscience is at its most important when reflecting upon possible future actions. In this situation, conscience, as practical judgment, functions in four ways: commanding, forbidding, persuading, or permitting. Given that conscience involves a process of practical reasoning, it "can err, either by adopting false premises or by drawing an illogical conclusion," due in some way to ignorance (210). The question then becomes whether the ignorance involved is vincible (in which case the person is culpable for the erroneous conscience) or invincible (in which case the person is not culpable). Conscience can "also be certain or doubtful," depending upon the strength and firmness of the practical judgment (211). There are various kinds of doubtful conscience, which Fagothey also terms "probable conscience." As he says, "There are varying degrees of probability, running all the way from slight suspicion to the fringes of certitude" (211).

Not only are there varying degrees of probability in the practical judgment that is conscience, but also there are differing tendencies or states of conscience. Fagothey lists some of them. A person's conscience can be lax or strict; it can be "perplexed" in the sense of unable to make a determination; it can be painfully scrupulous, constantly rehashing past decisions from new and troubling angles. He warns against scrupulosity as a "form of spiritual self-torture, mounting to neurotic anxiety" (211).

Given the possibility that conscience may err in its practical reasoning, should we obey conscience? Fagothey holds that we must obey a certain conscience. This leads to various questions, however. For example, "What degree of certitude is required?" (212). Do we need absolute certitude about the correctness of the practical judgment that is conscience's rational dictate? In his view, rather than requiring absolute certitude, we require only "prudential certitude." But how do we know when our certitude is "prudential"? Fagothey does not appeal to the virtue of prudence, though he does not reject it either. His understanding of "prudential" appears to be simply what a reasonable person would consider sufficiently well grounded and likely to be correct. He states that prudential certitude—unlike mathematical certitude or the certitude of physical events—simply "excludes all *prudent* fear that the opposite may be true," even while not excluding "imprudent fears based on bare possibilities" (212). He appeals to what a reasonable person would think, much as is done in courts of law. When conscience has the necessary prudential certitude, its "reasons are strong enough to satisfy a normally prudent man in an important manner, so that he feels safe in practice though there is a theoretical chance of his being wrong. He has taken every reasonable precaution, but cannot guarantee against rare contingencies and freaks of nature" (212).

In Fagothey's presentation, common sense can help us to recognize a properly certain conscience. He compares a prudentially certain conscience to other reasonable determinations that prudent people make. He states, for example, that "a prudent man, having investigated the case, can say that he is *certain* that this business venture is safe, that this criminal is guilty, that this employee is honest" (213). In my view, Fagothey should here have engaged at length the virtue of prudence.

Fagothey affirms that an erroneous conscience must be followed. But he adds an important clarification: it must only be followed if it is invincibly erroneous. This is so because "vincibly" erroneous means, by definition, that the person knows that he or she does not yet have prudential certitude about the matter. When one is in a state of invincible ignorance, one has certitude; one does not know that one lacks the needed knowledge. By contrast, when one is in a state of vincible ignorance, one knows that one lacks the needed knowledge, but one has not yet tried to remedy one's ignorance. A vincibly erroneous conscience, therefore, must not be followed, since one is morally required first to seek to overcome the ignorance that is impeding one's practical judgment. In giving examples of a vincibly erroneous conscience, Fagothey observes: "A man may merely have a probable opinion which he neglects to verify, though able to do so. Or he may once have judged certainly yet erroneously, and now begins to doubt whether his judgment was correct or not. As long as he did not realize his error, his conscience was invincibly erroneous" (213).

When one follows the practical judgment of an invincibly erroneous conscience—as one must do—one thereby commits a sin objectively speaking, but subjectively speaking one is not culpable because one has done the right thing by following a certain judgment of conscience. An invincible error has been made by the intellect, but the will is not wrong. Fagothey comments, "If a man is firmly convinced that his action is right, he is obeying the moral law as far as he can" (214). The main point, however, is that one cannot act upon the basis of a conscience that is in doubt. If one is unsure whether the action one is about to commit may be wrong, and if one does it anyway (absent any requirement to act), then one has sinned. This is because one has refused to "take the means to avoid this probable violation" and, in fact, one is "prepared to perform the act whether it violates the law or not" (214).

Actions, however, often involve many angles. Regarding future actions, indecision about what to do can paralyze a person; and, regarding past actions, fear that one has not done what one should have done is sometimes hard to avoid. In this light, Fagothey points to the solution: namely, one must form one's conscience. If one is in any significant doubt, if one lacks certitude about a course of moral action, one "must use all the means that normally prudent people are accustomed to use" in order to "investigate the facts in the problem and make certain of them, if possible" (215). But what if, in the end, a person still remains unsure about the facts? Often a person cannot simply *do nothing*, because the matter may be one in which the person will be culpable if he or she does nothing. Still, the person's conscience remains in a state of doubt. Is there a path forward?

Fagothey answers in the affirmative. If one has sought assiduously to learn the relevant information but has not been able to arrive at certitude, one must strive to identify "the kind of conduct that is *certainly* lawful for a *doubting* person" (216). According to Fagothey, this is the fundamental work of the formation of conscience. In forming conscience, a person must observe two principles above all: "(1) The morally safer course is to be chosen. (2) A doubtful law does not bind" (216).

Much work, then, will need to be done in order to be certain that one has identified the morally safer course. No doubt there are relatively easy cases. For example, "If a man is certainly not obliged to act but doubts whether or not he is allowed to act, the morally safer course is to omit the act; thus if I doubt whether this money is justly mine, I can simply refuse it" (216). It is relatively easy to turn down money that one doubts is really owed. Likewise, if a doctor knows that one medicine is safer than the other, and if the patient truly needs medicine, then the doctor must give the medicine and must choose the safer or better medicine. These cases seem clear enough, but others will be much more difficult.

For Fagothey, a pressing problem is what to do when one is not sure whether one is bound by an obligation. He explains: "Out of a desire to do the better [morally safer] thing we often follow it without question, but, if we were obliged to follow it in *all* cases of doubt, life would become intolerably difficult. To be safe morally, we should have to yield every doubtful claim to others who have no better right, and thus become victims of every sharper and swindler" (217). Fagothey proposes that the solution consists in reminding oneself that one is not bound by a doubtful law. Either the law that seems to obligate may not actually exist as a true law, or the law may not apply to our particular situation. His conclusion is that "a man is presumed free until it becomes certain that he is restrained, and therefore a doubtfully existing restraint or law loses its binding force" (218).

Fagothey goes deeply into questions regarding the tension between law and liberty, and the necessity of seeking the moral (legal) minimum. For example, he asks: "How doubtful does the law have to be to lose its binding force? Must the existence or application of the law be more doubtful than its nonexistence or nonapplication, or equally so, or will any doubt suffice to exempt one from the obligation?" (219). Fagothey notes the various schools or approaches to such questions: tutiorism, probabiliorism, equiprobabilism, probabilism, and laxism. The first of these, tutiorism, is too strict according to Fagothey. It requires that a person, in the face of a doubtful law (or doubtful obligation), be *certain* or *nearly certain* regarding "the nonexistence of a law imposing such obligation, or the non-applicability of the law" in the specific case (219). Laxism, too, is not a real option, because in this case the nonexistence or inapplicability of the doubtful law can be merely "barely possible" in order to justify ignoring it in conscience (219). So the real options are probabiliorism, equiprobabilism, and probabilism.

Like almost all Jesuit manualists, Fagothey favors probabilism. This is the most "lax" option other than laxism, but it is not laxist. According to probabilism, we are not bound by a doubtful law (or obligation) in a specific case if it is "a law against whose existence or application there stands a solidly probable argument" (219). Fagothey thinks that this should suffice to assuage conscience. He argues against equiprobabilism (Alphonsus's position) and probabiliorism (generally the Dominican viewpoint) as "too severe" (219). Forming conscience here is a matter of adjudicating relationships to laws and obligations. He emphasizes, "Obligation does not exist unless it is certain, for the law imposing such an obligation would not be sufficiently promulgated" (220).

According to probabilism, even if there are many probable arguments, including quite solid and weighty ones, in favor of the existence or applicability of a law, the existence of even one probable argument *against* the existence or applicability of a law suffices to ensure that one is not bound in conscience by that law in the case of conscience. Again, freedom from the law has priority; it is the obligation that must be shown with certitude.

Fagothey understands that legalism (as distinct from law) should be avoided if possible, and he tries to do so. But he is constrained by the framework of his discussion of cases of conscience. Thus, against legalism (and against equiprobabilism), he reasons quite plausibly that "the weighing of probabilities on each side to determine whether they are equal, or greater on one side than the other, would be an unreasonable burden. The average man has neither time nor knowledge nor ability for such a comparison. The learned after years of study are often unable to fix the exact amount of probability on each side of the case" (220). Certainly this is true, but it is little consolation to think that Christian life comes down to trying to find one "probable argument" for the nonexistence or inapplicability of a law. This gives the impression that the Christian moral life is fundamentally about laws and loopholes. Fagothey is aware that equiprobabilism does not require an exact counting up of probabilities on each side; rather, it only asks for a general sense of which side is more probable. But as Fagothey says, "Even the roughest estimate of the weight of probability may often be very difficult, too much so for practical use" (220).

Fagothey raises an objection to his own position. Namely, if probabilism requires finding at least one truly probable argument for doubting the existence or applicability of a law to one's specific case of conscience, this requirement may be found to be just as difficult as is the equiprobabilist task of identifying the comparative weight of the probable arguments in favor and the probable arguments against. After all, how do we know when a view counts as *solidly* probable? Fagothey responds that, actually, it is not hard to determine whether a view is solidly probable. He states, "To determine that an opinion is solidly probable, it is sufficient to have a few or even one good weighty argument in its favor, although the arguments against it may be stronger" (221). The argument of one weighty authority in favor of a particular casuistic solution will suffice.

Fagothey raises one further query before he concludes his discussion. He asks, "Must one be consistent in the use of probabilism? . . . May a person in one case follow the opinion that the law binds, and then in another but exactly similar case follow the opinion that the law does not bind?" (221). In other words, if one finds a probable argument in favor of the nonexistence or inapplicability of a law, does one have to adhere to this probable argument in every similar case? Fagothey grants that one does not have to do so. A probabilist does not have to incline in the same way in each case of conscience. When a new case arises, the favorable probable argument that resolved the earlier case need not now be deemed conclusive. The point simply is that it *can* be conclusive. Fagothey argues that it is enough if the probabilist does not try to have it both ways in the very same case. In dealing with the question of whether a person's last will and testament is legally binding, for example, a probabilist lawyer cannot rightly hold both that the will is valid (meaning that his client can accept the inheritance) and that the will is invalid (meaning that his client would not have to pay to others the individual legacies contained in the will).

Fagothey knows the critique of this conscience-centered moral system well enough to remark, "This whole matter of forming one's conscience may seem to involve a great deal of subtlety and casuistry" (221). It does seem so. But Fagothey supposes that critics are motivated by "an emotional rebellion against these refinements, as contrary to straightforward simplicity and sincerity" (221). The fact of "refinements," though, is not the problem. The problem is the conscience-centered framework in which the moral life is reduced to a struggle between law and liberty and to the identification of the legal minimum. Without recognizing this as a problem, Fagothey urges that "in ethics we are studying not only what is the better, nobler, and more heroic thing to do, but also exactly what a man is strictly obliged to do" (221). For Fagothey, the approach taken by the moral manuals flows from generosity toward one's neighbor: "In our personal lives we may be willing to waive our strict rights and to go beyond the call of duty, but we have no business imposing on others an obligation to do so. . . . We are not allowed to accuse another man of wrongdoing if he has not done wrong" (222).

Before moving on from Fagothey's manual, let me note that after the above chapter on conscience, he turns to a chapter titled "Virtue." The chapter on conscience is sixteen pages, whereas the chapter on virtue— including sections on habitus, virtue, the intellectual virtues, the moral virtues, and all four cardinal virtues—is thirteen pages. Even if this were not disproportionately short, the chapter is placed too late. By this time in Fagothey's book, individual acts viewed in light of obligation, cases of conscience, and law (as the opposite of freedom) already have impressed their form upon the moral project. This is so even though Fagothey affirms, for example, that "the importance of prudence in the ethical life cannot be overestimated. Whenever a general rule of conduct, such as ethics devises, must be applied to a concrete case, prudence is called for" (232).

Let me now more briefly examine four other representative moral manuals. I hope to provide the reader with a sense of the distinctive qualities of these four manuals, while also exhibiting the place of conscience in their approaches to the moral life.

Thomas J. Higgins, SJ

In 1949, another American Jesuit, Thomas J. Higgins, published a moral manual on philosophical ethics: *Man as Man: The Science and Art of Ethics.* This work has more of the feeling of a scholastic manual, as he identifies his main points as "THESIS I" or "THESIS II" and intersperses regular sections titled "PROOF." He begins with the ultimate end and demonstrates that this (natural) end must be union with God by knowing and loving. He includes some elements not found in Fagothey's manual, such as a more detailed presentation of human life as a "probation" in which the miseries of life test us and lead us to realize that not creatures but God alone can be our true end.[38] He condenses the discussion of the ultimate end (happiness) to one chapter rather than the three given to the topic by Fagothey.

Higgins's overall path, however, is basically the same. He moves from the ultimate end to human acts and morality, focusing on good and evil and criticizing modern ethicists such as John Stuart Mill, David Hume, Herbert Spencer, Immanuel Kant, and others. Like Fagothey, but in a much more compressed way, he criticizes William of Ockham. He devotes a chapter to duty and law, followed by chapters on sanction and merit and the properties of natural law. Throughout, he guides readers to discussions found in moral manuals published in the period 1900–1930; for example, he references works by Michael Cronin, Victor Cathrein, SJ, Joseph Donat, SJ, Theodore Meyer, SJ, Thomas Slater, SJ, and Marcel Nivard, SJ.

After the chapter on natural law, he devotes a chapter to conscience. This chapter is thirteen pages, and it is followed by a chapter on virtue and vice that is twenty-four pages. Somewhat more briefly than Fagothey, he defends conscience-centered morality and probabilism. He also leads the reader through the other options (from rigorism to laxism). In his view, "Probabilism offers a sure and ready solution to the anxieties of conscience. Provided my reason is worthy of an honest man, I can readily reach a certain dictate of conscience."[39] He appeals to someone possessed of basic common sense, "an honest man," as sufficient for being able to reach sufficient certitude in cases of conscience.

Higgins grants that abuse of probabilism is possible, and he warns in this regard, "If a person imagines probabilism to be a license to pare one's obligations down to the barest minimum and converts it into a clever scheme whereby a certain conscience can be rendered probable and obligation avoided, he is not a probabilist but a laxist."[40] But he thinks that probabilism generally works quite well. Its purpose is simple: to lay bare the legal minimum, the place where law and liberty intersect. He states, "The function of probabilism is to cut the knot of doubt and rigidly expose the extent of one's obligation."[41] In his chapter on virtue and vice, he gives only two short paragraphs to prudence, without noting a relationship to the judgment of conscience.

Michael Cronin

In his manual *The Science of Ethics*, published in 1909, the Irish Catholic philosopher Michael Cronin devotes his lengthy first volume to general ethics. He announces in his preface that his goal is "to present to Students of Ethical Science a full and connected account of the ethical system of Aristotle and St. Thomas Aquinas. To this system the author gives his fullest assent and adherence."[42] He organizes his chapters somewhat differently from the two Jesuit manuals I examine above, but the overall pattern is the same. After an introductory chapter on ethics, he explores human acts insofar as they are voluntary. The third chapter takes up the ultimate end, demonstrating that it is God. He then treats good and evil in chapter 4, remarking that "the 'good' is the object of appetite" and thereby ruling out a perfectly neutral will (88). He defines a good moral act as one that is governed by reason and conduces to the attainment of the ultimate end (95).

Chapter 5 is devoted to moral "criteria," emphasizing the natural use of our faculties as a criterion for a good act and pointing out that "actions that oppose our natural appetites and their objects are bad" (128). In this chapter, he also criticizes utilitarianism and reflects upon the relationship between virtue ("the *moral* good"), the good as a whole, happiness, and moral feelings (145). The range of his dialogue partners is impressive, from Claude Levy-Bruhl to Georg Simmel and many others.

Chapters 6 and 7 take up freedom and morality, and chapter 8 is on duty. These chapters are followed by chapter-length engagements with Stoicism, hedonism, utilitarianism, and evolutionism (biological and Hegelian, in separate chapters). In discussing freedom, he addresses the will's "antecedent indeterminateness" and ability of self-determination (169). He explains: "Freedom, therefore, or the causation of our own act, supposes antecedent indeterminateness of the will, which excludes, first, previous determination by object, secondly, previous determination by the very nature of the will or by any quality or disposition of nature not controlled by the will" (173). He carefully distances his position from the notion that freedom must be autonomous from natural ends, and he insists that "motives or ends are the final causes of the free acts of the will," so that freedom is not a "purely negative" concept (174).[43]

In chapter 14, he treats conscience as "the moral faculty," rooted in reason. This chapter begins on page 448, and so much ground has already been covered. But the contents of the earlier chapters suffice to show that Cronin's approach remains within the basic framework of ethics that we found in the Jesuit authors discussed above.

What "ordinary life" indicates to us, says Cronin, is that the moral life consists in the constant "reasoned application of one or many general laws to an individual case," as we move from case to case each day (449). Conscience is nothing other than the faculty of human reason at work in identifying and applying the law to particular moral cases, to actions that we may do or have done. Cronin explains that the "practical intellect of which Conscience is a function is the ordinary practical intellect—the very same intellect which tells a man what to do or to avoid in ordinary extra-moral questions of the business of life—how, for instance, he ought to invest his money, or carry on a business, or preserve his health" (450).

Does this notion of conscience downplay its authority or "sacredness"? Cronin thinks not. The authority of conscience is rooted simply in the fact that the practical reason has the ability to arrive at certitude (if not infallibility). Cronin states, "Reason in the sphere of morals is as reliable as in any other sphere, and can lead the mind to certitude in simple as well as in complex cases, unless, indeed, the case be exceedingly complex, in which case the fault lies not with Reason, but either with the way in which the materials of our moral judgments are presented to us, or with the will" (449). The point is that practical reason can arrive at certitude on moral matters, and when it addresses itself to such matters, this is the act of conscience.

Cronin argues that ethicists are mistaken if they suppose that conscience has a "sacredness" over and above the practical reason. The "sacredness" of conscience attaches to it not because it is a special faculty but because of the work that it accomplishes in reasoning about moral questions regarding "'the good' and duty" (450). Thus Cronin denies that conscience is "a perceptive sense, a feeling or sentiment, a spiritual power, or even a Divine power transcending, yet dwelling in, human nature" (451). Strictly speaking, conscience is simply the "act of the Practical Reason whereby a man recognises that certain things are good and to be done, others evil and to be avoided" (451).[44]

Cronin recognizes his view to be at odds with that of Joseph Butler, who influenced John Henry Newman. He states, "Butler is not always quite consistent on the question of the function of Conscience, for he tells us also that the three functions of Conscience are *judgment*, direction, and superintendence—and judgment is certainly a function of intellect" (455).[45] Correctly, Butler thinks of conscience as "a *deliberating* faculty," a function that pertains to the practical intellect (455). Butler, however, differs from Cronin in considering conscience to be the voice of God. Conscience passes judgment upon our deeds; it accuses or excuses us, and it commands us regarding future actions. Conscience does all this "coldly and impartially," without being influenced by our desires or inclinations, and in a manner that shows its independence and supremacy (472). Conscience manifests itself to us interiorly as a powerful authority, perfectly holy and supreme, that we cannot evade or relativize. As Cronin says, Butler concludes that conscience "is not a creature, for no creature could exact from us such absolute homage, such unconditional reverence, nor create in us the confusion which this Invisible Power creates. Putting together all the attributes that are exhibited in its least word . . . we can only say that it bears all the marks of the Supreme Being" (473).

Cronin sums up Butler's position eloquently: conscience "is the voice of the Creator Himself, and when I [i.e., any person listening to his or her conscience] hear it I am listening to God Himself, am in His presence, just as I am present to any friend that I hear and do not see" (473). For Butler, conscience stands as an interior proof of God's existence.

Cronin is aware that in disagreeing with Butler, he is also disagreeing with Newman. He pays particular attention to Newman's distinctive way of arguing that conscience offers a proof of God's existence. In Cronin's view, "It is because we know *aliunde* [i.e., from elsewhere] the existence of God, and know also *aliunde* that the intuitions of Conscience *represent* the Divine will that therefore we conclude that the objective moral relations revealed by Conscience are commands of God" (476). For Cronin, in other words, if we did not know on other grounds (whether by revelation or by reason) that God exists, we would not receive the dictates of conscience as evidence of God's existence. Instead, we would receive them as flowing from practical reason. Cronin points out that when our conscience arrives at a mistaken judgment (something that can happen relatively frequently), our experience of conscience is the same as when conscience arrives at a true judgment. This would not be the case if conscience were the voice of God rather than a judgment of practical reason.

Cronin grants that conscience is the voice of God in the sense that a conscience that perfectly reflected "objective truth" about the moral law would be "an exact replica of God's mind on Morality" (474). But this is merely to say that when practical reason gets things right, it really does reflect God's wisdom about what is good and bad for humans. To this observation, Cronin adds that if one views conscience as the "voice of God" rather than as the judgment of practical reason, one will have difficulty distinguishing what is forbidden because it is intrinsically evil from what is forbidden simply because of God's will. In sum, if one does not recognize the role of practical reason, one will fall into a divine command theory of morality. Besides, if conscience were the voice of God, in complex situations God's voice would resound strongly and we would never experience moral perplexity or doubt.

Cronin ranges widely and offers many significant insights regarding conscience in his thirty-page chapter on the subject. He concludes the chapter with a dense two-page discussion of probabilism, which he firmly upholds. While probabilism is not the center of his discussion of conscience, it provides the culminating note of the chapter. In his view as a philosopher, the moral life consists in acting with attention to the lawfulness of one's action. The key question for the moral agent, then, is how a potential action relates to natural law. For a law to be operative, it must be clearly and fully promulgated. It follows that, in moral decision-making, we should remember that "it is *certain* that no law can bind in conscience in such a way that to violate it is a sin, unless the law be fully and certainly promulgated to our reason; but a law which is only probable, or which only probably forbids a certain course of conduct, is not fully promulgated to us, and hence it is *certainly* lawful for us to ignore such a law" (479). Cronin deems that even if it may be more probable that an action is not lawful, it is the case that when we have a "prudent and well-grounded" reason for thinking that the action is lawful, we are justified in undertaking the action (479). It will not be a sin, at least not subjectively.

Before moving on, let me note that after his chapter on conscience, Cronin offers a chapter on commonsense moral intuitionism (the notion that morality is self-evident) and then a chapter on synderesis. The chapter on synderesis deserves brief comment here. Cronin states, "Synderesis is the name given to the group of primary moral principles which belong naturally to the human mind," in the sense that "without reasoning the mind comes quickly and easily to acquire them, and cannot help doing so" (509). Some of these principles are intuitions and others are such easy inferences that they "are generally regarded as self-evident truths" (509). Among the primary self-evident principles natural to the human mind and included in synderesis, Cronin lists "the goodness of honesty, and bravery, and kindness, and filial pity, and the care for offspring, and marriage, and . . . the evil of indiscriminate murder" (509). Of course, the fact that these principles are self-evident does not mean that people cannot act otherwise.

Cronin goes on to address the question of whether conscience can be corrupted. He answers in the affirmative, due to the weakening and darkening of the practical reason, as for instance by the regular "misuse of conscience" against our "better judgment" and through the distortive impact of fallen desires (520). Yet, he holds that conscience cannot be completely expunged in people of sound mind; for example, "no developed mind could ever believe that wanton murder was the good thing and to be done, and its opposite the bad thing and to be avoided" (521).[46] Even murderers do not think it good to be murdered, nor do they think (if they are sane) that they are doing a good thing toward those whom they wantonly murder.

Let me note, too, that Cronin's eighteenth chapter takes up habits and virtues, prior to his nineteenth chapter, which treats law (the twentieth and final chapter of the book treats rights). His account of prudence is helpful. He warns against the tendency of modern philosophers to imagine that prudence is the same as a mere sense for self-interest. He also remarks that "he only is prudent in the full sense who seeks the means that will lead him to his final end" (567).

Overall, Cronin's approach fits with the concerns expressed by Garrigou-Lagrange and Pinckaers, but his equation of conscience with practical reason at least opens the door to more reflection upon prudence. His account of freedom emphasizes natural ends and thus differs from Ockham's. Like all the moral manualists, he remains a firm defender of moral probabilism. For those who know only the stereotype of the moral manuals, his lively style and impressive range of insight will be appreciated.

Antony Koch

The first volume of Antony Koch's five-volume *A Handbook of Moral Theology* appeared in an adapted and edited English version in 1918.[47] This volume, which runs to 293 pages, contains the following chapters: an introductory overview of moral theology, a chapter on the subject of morality (focusing on free will), a chapter on law as morality's objective norm, a chapter on conscience as morality's subjective norm, a chapter on duty, and a chapter on human acts and habits.

This moral manual conforms closely in certain ways to what was critiqued by Garrigou-Lagrange and Pinckaers, but in other ways it is much better than critics would anticipate. In the introductory chapter, Koch distinguishes moral theology sharply from dogmatic theology, on the grounds that "whereas the latter deals with God, His essence, attributes, outward operation, etc., and shows Him to be the sovereign good and source of all created goodness, the former is entirely concerned with directing man to his eternal goal" (5). He then distinguishes Catholic moral theology from Protestant ethics, taking Luther's conception of freedom and original sin as normative for the Protestant tradition. According to Koch, Protestant ethicists charge Catholic moral theology with "a false empiricism, which wrongly distinguishes between mortal and venial sin and between perfect and imperfect contrition, thereby catering to human frailty and derogating from the spirit of the Gospel" (8–9). Protestants mount other criticisms, from linking the Catholic view of the sacraments to magic to holding that Catholic morality, "like that of the ancient Pharisees, exaggerates external acts at the expense of character and thus breeds servility and hypocrisy" (9). Koch sets out to refute such charges.

In his introductory chapter, Koch identifies the ultimate end of human life as "eternal happiness in Heaven (*beatitudo*)" (17). This leads him into a discussion of eudaimonism and merit, in critical conversation with Kant, the Stoics, and Catholic quietists. In the same context, Koch identifies three methods of moral theology. The first he calls "scholastic" or "speculative"; this method bases itself upon the teachings of Scripture and tradition in the light of reason, without ceasing to attempt to serve the needs of confessors. The second method is casuistry, which focuses on resolving specific cases of conscience. Koch considers this method to be "a legitimate, nay an indispensable instrument for testing the morality of human acts"; but he cautions that casuistry "embraces only a narrow sector of life, and appraises human conduct mainly from the external, juridical, and legal point of view, and hence easily leads either to excessive rigorism or undue laxity" (38–39). The third method is focused on the way of perfection and is called "ascetic" insofar as it describes the mystical path open to all Catholics. Koch urges that all three methods "should be employed together," just as was done by medieval masters such as Aquinas (39). His own first volume is offered as a scholastic or speculative exercise; and indeed his five-volume work, while certainly a moral manual of the kind we today associate with the era of casuistry, does not take up specific complex cases in the way that a casuistic manual would.

Later in his introductory chapter, Koch offers a short history of moral theology, with special attention to the Fathers and to Aquinas as well as to the roots of casuistry in the numerous penitential handbooks produced from the twelfth through the early sixteenth centuries (for example, Raymond of Peñafort's *Summa de casibus poenitentiae*). As he observes, "From the close of the sixteenth century Moral Theology began to be treated as a separate discipline" (57). He credits Alphonsus de Liguori, in the late eighteenth century, with purifying the excesses of casuistry. Unfortunately, he says, during the same period in which Alphonsus was active, "Moral Theology was detached from its supernatural basis and almost completely identified with moral philosophy" (67). Yet, according to Koch, the nineteenth century saw a strong renewal of moral theology, both speculative and casuistic.

The central subject of Koch's first chapter is free will. Citing 2 Corinthians 3:17, Ephesians 4:13, and Romans 8:21, Koch grounds his interest in freedom biblically: the human being "is called to attain 'moral liberty,' to develop into 'a perfect man unto the measure of the age of the fulness of Christ', and thereby to reach that blessed freedom which is 'the glory of the children of God'" (81).[48] He notes that our freedom is not intended to be unlimited in this life. Bodily needs and our external environment ensure that our freedom is limited. In his treatment of free will, he defines it in terms of "self-determination, and the power of choosing between different actions" (108). This may sound like "freedom of indifference," but he goes on to say that "moral indifference is not a prerogative but rather a defect of the will," and he urges that true freedom is graced freedom, "the freedom of the children of God" (see 1 Cor. 15:28; 2 Cor. 3:17; Gal. 5:13; John 8:31–36) (110). In fact, the highest point of freedom is to will to do the good and not even to be able to sin.

The second chapter treats law, understood as "the will of God as manifested through nature and Revelation" (119). In accord with Romans 2:14–15, God's law includes natural law. Koch thinks that Deuteronomy 30:1–14 has to do with natural law, which is what was revealed to the Israelites. Against voluntarism, he notes that "though God is the Author of all law, His will is not arbitrary, but based on His wisdom" (133). Humans can participate in this wisdom for our flourishing by the light of our reason (natural law) as well as by divine revelation. He examines both the Noachide laws and the various precepts of the Decalogue and the Mosaic law, which he praises as good (Rom. 3:31; Rom. 7:12). He praises even more the "moral law of the New Testament," which he deems to be "the purest and most perfect expression of the divine will" (141). It is a "law of love" whose "motive, content, and fulfilment is charity"; thus it is "a law of grace and liberty" (142). While continuing to value the Old Testament's law, he quotes much from Paul and other New Testament texts, and he gives a special place to the principles "contained in the Sermon on the Mount, the description of the Last Judgment, and the parables of the Gospel" (147). Against Protestant scholars, he holds that the New Testament retains a "legal" character, not only because Christ taught moral principles and did not abrogate the Decalogue but also because law and liberty should not be set in opposition (see Gal. 5:13; 1 Pet. 2:16), given the fact that love fulfills rather than negates the law (Rom. 13:10).

The third chapter treats conscience. Koch argues that conscience is a biblical reality, attested in the Old Testament by the term "heart" and in the New Testament repeatedly by the term *syneidēsis* (though not by Jesus). In a certain sense, conscience can be understood as "the voice of God," given that it manifests the divine law. Even so, it should be clear that conscience is a human judgment, since otherwise it would be unable to err (186). Indebted to the medievals, Koch speaks of antecedent and consequent conscience. Indebted to the mystics, he suggests that conscience is more than "a dictate of practical reason" and instead may be conceived of (in a manner that escapes definition) as "a spark of eternal life (*scintilla animae*), which God Himself has put there to preserve the soul from destruction" (191).

Notably, along lines carried forward by some postconciliar theologians (such as Bernard Häring), Koch proposes that conscience "engages all the faculties of the soul, and consequently is not a separate and distinct faculty, but something which lies beneath all faculties, at the very basis of the soul" (192). Conscience is not only "moral" but also "religious." Conscience may err in concrete application but, in itself (in "its innermost essence"), conscience "is never mistaken" (192). As something that is like a faculty, but that is deeper than and ties together all faculties, conscience is the core of a person's "ethical personality" (192). No wonder conscience has an exalted place in the moral life. It is the deepest and most central core of interiority where the human person responds to the God who has revealed his law of love in Christ.

Koch proposes three ingredients for a healthy conscience: it "must be right, certain, and watchful" (194). He explains the meaning of these three terms briefly, and he describes the practices needed for ridding oneself of doubts, attaining to certainty of conscience, and being watchful. We need to be conscientious in observing the commandments, and we need to undertake "regular daily examinations" (197). We need to avoid allowing our conscience to corrupt into sleepiness or laxity. Yet, we also need to avoid scrupulosity. Koch notes that penitents can sometimes hypocritically pretend to possess scrupulosity in order to conceal their sins.

In chapter 4, Koch takes up the topic of duty. At the outset of this discussion, he strongly emphasizes charity, which is the key to all obligation given that the goal of all human life is perfect love of God and neighbor. Koch devotes significant attention to how to choose between competing duties and to avoid a perplexed conscience. For example, he lays down the rule that "the duties of one's vocation or office take precedence over purely personal and family duties, but only in so far as their non-observance would jeopardize the common good" (214). He adheres to Alphonsus's equiprobabilism, which he suggests develops probabilism in a positive way by overcoming "the logical and moral objection that probabilism permits men to follow a less probable opinion . . . even though its opposite is perceived to be more probable" (227). Having already rejected laxism, he is most concerned to criticize the rigorists who attack probabilism. Even if equiprob-abilism is better than simple probabilism, the latter is much better than rigorism. He devotes a section to the status of the obligations involved in the Evangelical Counsels, insisting that "the Church has one standard of morals for all" while also insisting (in light of Matt. 19:11–12 and 1 Cor. 7) that the Evangelical Counsels "are means of fulfilling the precept of charity more perfectly" (244).

The fifth and final chapter of the first volume discusses human acts, with an initial focus upon culpability. Koch states, "A man is responsible for an act (be it of commission or omission) in exact proportion to the degree of liberty which he enjoys" (257). In this chapter, he briefly discusses habits, the moral virtues (acquired and infused), and the theological virtues. He also discusses the gifts of the Holy Spirit, ranking them below the theo-logical virtues and above the infused moral virtues; and he sets forth the beatitudes (enumerated in the Sermon on the Mount) and the fruits of the Holy Spirit mentioned by Paul in Galatians 5:17.

There is much in Koch's moral manual, therefore, that Garrigou-Lagrange's and Pinckaers's discussions would lead us to expect *not* to find. Even given the necessary brevity of Koch's work as adapted and edited by Preuss, there is ample consideration of Scripture, the new law of grace, the gifts of the Holy Spirit, and so on. On the other hand, Koch advocates an especially expansive view of conscience, and he gives little real role to prudence.

Dominic M. Prümmer, OP

As a final example of the twentieth-century moral manuals, I have chosen Dominic Prümmer's one-volume *Handbook of Moral Theology*, a concise summary of his multivolume manual of moral theology. Prümmer was a Thomist, but because of his influential moral manual, I survey his perspec-tive here rather than in the next chapter. As noted above, Prümmer was a predecessor of Pinckaers at Fribourg. After the publication of Prümmer's one-volume summary, it went through multiple editions after his death in 1931. The one translated into English and published in 1957 was the fifth edition, whose publication was overseen by Englebert M. Münch, OP.

After a very brief introduction regarding the nature and methods of moral theology, Prümmer offers numerous "Treatises," comprised in scho-lastic style of short chapters and articles. The first part of the volume treats subjects that we normally associate with moral theology today. The volume's second part is a treatise on the seven sacraments, along with the status of indulgences and of ecclesiastical punishments such as excommunication. The lengthy attention to the sacraments is appropriate given the fact that it is hardly possible to live out the moral teachings of Christ without the aid of the sacraments.

The thirteen treatises that comprise the first part of Prümmer's one-volume manual are arranged in the following order: "The Ultimate End of Man," "Human Acts," "Law," "Conscience," "Sin in General," "Virtue in General," "Theological Faith and Contrary Vices," "Theological Hope and Contrary Vices," "Theological Charity and Contrary Vices," "The Virtue of Prudence and Contrary Vices," "The Virtue of Justice and Contrary Vices," "The Virtue of Fortitude and Contrary Vices," and "The Virtue of Temperance and Contrary Vices." It is clear that what Prümmer has done is to attempt to join together the *prima-secundae pars* and the *secunda-secundae pars*, keeping intact as much of Aquinas's structure as possible—including its starting point, beatitude ("the ultimate end"). His placement of the sections titled "Law" and "Conscience" prior to "Sin in General" and "Virtue in General" departs from Aquinas's ordering, and of course Aquinas's discussion of conscience is limited in the *Summa theologiae* to two articles contained within the treatise on human acts. In addition, the questions on grace at the end of the *prima-secundae* of the *Summa theologiae* are absent. Otherwise, by and large, Prümmer's table of contents in the first part of his book strives to mirror the *Summa theologiae*.

Whereas Aquinas's discussion of the ultimate end (beatitude) is quite lengthy, Prümmer's discussion of this topic occupies only three short pages, short even given the condensed nature of his one-volume manual.[49] In scholastic format, he first defines his terms, and then offers three "Propositions" about the ultimate end, each of which he proves in a formal manner. For example, his third proposition states: "The ultimate end of man (viz. perfect happiness) cannot be attained without supernatural grace which is given in sufficient degree to every man through the redemption of Christ."[50]

By comparison, his treatise on human acts is much more extensive, around twenty pages. Much of his attention focuses upon whether we have sufficient knowledge to be responsible for our actions. He treats vincible and invincible ignorance. He explains that even vincible ignorance lessens culpability, assuming that one is not merely pretending to be ignorant. Other obstacles to full responsibility for an action include coercion, fear, and passion. He identifies sins committed due to a burst of passion—anger, lust, and so on—as "sins of human frailty" (18; italics removed). Throughout this discussion, he keeps an eye on the confessional, as, for instance, when priests have to deal with penitents confessing (unnecessarily, and therefore without the need of absolution) "voluntary omissions of a good act" such as daily Mass (25).

In treating law, Prümmer discusses eternal law and natural law, as well as the Mosaic law. He mentions the law of the New Testament only very briefly in what is already a highly compressed discussion of law. He focuses on the specific laws commanded in the New Testament, rather than examining the grace of the Holy Spirit as itself the new law. As he says, given the human vocation to a supernatural ultimate end, "it is impossible to attain to supernatural happiness without observing supernatural laws made known by God," and these laws have to do primarily with morals, the reception of the sacraments, and the eucharistic sacrifice (31).

Comparatively speaking, he gives more attention to human law, including ecclesiastical law. He is concerned with such questions as whether ecclesiastical laws bind non-Catholics, as, for example, the law that a marriage must take place in the presence of the couple's parish priest. He asks also whether some laws can be "purely penal" by requiring the obedience of citizens under pain of punishment without thereby obligating consciences under pain of sin (40). He examines how laws are fulfilled: for example, it is possible (given due circumstances) for a priest to fulfill in the morning the binding law that he recite the daily Office's evening prayer. With particular attention to ecclesiastical laws, he inquires into who has the authority to grant dispensations from the observance of established law. Not surprisingly, this section is relatively lengthy. With regard to civil law, he again goes into detail, as, for example, in his argument that paying taxes is a binding obligation in conscience so long as the taxation is not unjust.

Prümmer's treatise on law is thirty-one pages; by contrast, the treatise on conscience that follows is only eight pages. It should already be clear that even where the topic is linked with the *secunda pars* of the *Summa*, the content differs significantly. The structural place of conscience in Prümmer's manual should caution us against equating Aquinas's position with Prümmer's. There is also a notable difference in content.

Like Aquinas, Prümmer holds that conscience is "the judgement or dictate of the practical intellect deciding from general principles the goodness or evil of some act which is to be done here and now or has been done in the past" (58). Like Aquinas, too, Prümmer begins with synderesis and connects conscience with prudence. But, in accord with other moral manuals, Prümmer devotes more space to different kinds of erroneous conscience: lax, scrupulous, perplexed, hardened, and Pharisaic. He distinguishes between a vincibly erroneous conscience and a certain conscience—the latter is inclusive of invincibly erroneous conscience. He notes that in cases of conscience, we should not suppose that we will always be able to reach certitude of conscience. In ordinary circumstances, we can follow a probable opinion, so long as we believe that it has a strong probability. Yet, in following the probable opinion, we must not be in a state of "positive" doubt, namely, a condition where our fear of error "is based on grave reasons" and thus we risk committing a sin for which we would be culpable (63). As an example, he gives the case of a judge who follows a less probable opinion when making a decision, not about his own life but about someone else's; in such a case, no judge can rightly act upon a less probable opinion in the face of a more probable one.

In light of Pope Alexander VIII's censuring of Jansenist tutiorism in 1690, Prümmer reviews the various schools of thought—tutiorism, moderate tutiorism, probabiliorism, equiprobabilism, pure probabilism, laxism, and compensationism—and concludes: "Apart from Rigorism and Laxism each of the above systems is tolerated by the Church, and in consequence the confessor is not entitled to force his own system on the penitent or to demand something from his penitent to which the latter is not obliged according to the principles of one or other of the systems" (66). In general, he favors the positions of equiprobabilism and probabiliorism because it seems best to do what one can to follow the more probable opinion rather than to risk sin. But he accepts that his judgment here cannot be imposed upon penitents, even if "the confessor may prudently advise the safer and more probable opinion" (66).

He adds that probability itself needs to be defined. Intrinsic probability arises from the nature of the situation; extrinsic probability arises from the number of eminent authors who support one or the other position regarding the specific case of conscience. He ends his discussion of conscience by reflecting upon the formation of conscience. Such formation, he says, begins with a good childhood education and requires sincere examination of conscience, as well as prayer, seeking the help of divine grace to heal the passions, and "sacramental confession and obedience to one's spiritual director" (67).

In his appreciative study of the moral manuals, Brian Besong urges "contemporary moral theologians and philosophers to return to these rich sources of insight."[51] Having examined five moral manuals, I agree with him that there are many valuable insights in these texts. Nevertheless, it remains true that the moral manuals characteristically perceive conscience to be "an intermediate faculty placed between law and freedom" that functions as a "judge."[52] As Pinckaers says, given that "the law was fixed and general, conscience had to act as an interpreter of the law, so as to determine with precision the line between the allowable and the prohibited."[53] The manualists sought to help conscience by informing it about the law and assisting in the practical application of the law. As a result, the manuals focus on the various states of conscience and on whether, in a particular case, there is a law that should be allowed to restrict liberty.

Of course, the Christian moral life regularly involves cases of conscience. It is therefore understandable that Catholic theologians have advocated conscience-centered morality, as does James Keenan when he emphasizes that he consistently tries "to teach my students that they need to form and follow their consciences."[54] We need not deny the value of the manuals' discussions of conscience, vincible and invincible ignorance, synderesis, and so on. Kevin Flannery, SJ, has shown that an appreciation for conscience and invincible ignorance stands behind the important developments found in Vatican II's Decree on Ecumenism, *Unitatis Redintegratio*. Flannery comments, "The church is thereby respecting the bond of conscience of people who grow up in such [non-Catholic] traditions and exonerating at least some of them on the grounds that their ignorance of the full truth is not due to choice or to negligence."[55] Just as we pay close attention to conscience, so also should we reflect carefully upon the contents of natural and divine law, as Flannery shows at the outset of his book.[56]

We can gain a great deal of insight from the twentieth-century moral manuals. Contrary to caricatures, they often begin with beatitude and demonstrate a rich understanding of human freedom. The manualists also recognize that there is much more to Catholic moral theology than obligation and law. Their engagement with modern philosophers is often profound.

But even while we appreciatively turn again to the manuals in certain regards, we should not pattern Catholic moral theology upon them. They place conscience, along with the tension between law and liberty, at the very center of the moral life. In so doing, they distort the shape of Christian ethics.

The better path consists in apprehending the Decalogue and the moral precepts taught in the New Testament within a virtue-centered framework, constituted by communion with Christ and the grace of the Holy Spirit. Conscience has its proper role within this framework. Receiving the principles of God's moral law through synderesis, conscience makes judgments about the goodness or badness of our actions. Conscience does so within the context of faith, hope, charity, and the infused virtue of prudence. Love stands at the center, as befits the fact that "God is love" (1 John 4:8). As the form of all the virtues, love oversees the virtuous organism that guides us to our ultimate end, along paths sketched in Christ's Sermon on the Mount.

Chapter 3

Conscience and the Thomists

In recent Thomistic studies of the Christian moral life, conscience has not played a central role, but neither has it been ignored. To give a notable example, in his chapter on the dignity of the human person in *Saint Thomas Aquinas: Spiritual Master*, originally published in 1996, Jean-Pierre Torrell, OP, devotes a section to conscience.[1] He distinguishes two ways of relating to God in personal dignity: through conscience and through God's personal call to communion. He notes that our contemporary understanding of conscience is distorted, so that many people conceive of conscience as a sphere of autonomy where one is answerable only to one's own intuitive sense of right and wrong. For Aquinas, by contrast, conscience has dignity because it is a realm of dependence upon God, through which God's law resounds.

Torrell goes on to explain how the habitus of synderesis contains the first principles of practical reason[2] and how the judgment of conscience unites principles known by synderesis to moral wisdom gained by reflection and by divine revelation, in order to make a judgment about the moral status of a particular human act. The judgment of conscience is binding; and yet conscience must constantly seek truth and be docile to revealed Truth. True conscience has real dignity, but the greatest dignity is that God speaks to us not simply in conscience but as a friend, within the ecclesial communion to which we are called in Christ.

Similarly, Leo Elders, SVD's philosophical work *The Ethics of Thomas Aquinas*, originally published in Dutch in 2001, carefully follows the order of Aquinas's *Summa theologiae*. Elders's fourteen chapters, beginning with the ultimate end (happiness) and ending with natural love and friendship, do not include a chapter on conscience. Yet, Elders examines the key discussions of conscience in Aquinas's corpus, including *In II Sent.*, distinction 24, question 2; *De veritate*, question 17; and *Summa theolo-*

giae I, question 79 and I-II, question 19, article 5. Elders explains that for Aquinas, "Conscience is a norm, which depends on a higher norm (it is a *norma normata*), which derives its principles from the order of things. . . . Conscience is judgment of the mind and witnesses to the order present in creation."[3]

Many contemporary Thomists, however, steer clear of conscience. For example, Denys Turner's introductory 2013 *Thomas Aquinas: A Portrait* takes up many moral topics but does not mention conscience. Understandably, Turner focuses instead on the quest for happiness, friendship with God, the grace of the Holy Spirit, the three theological virtues (faith, hope, and love), prudence, and natural inclinations and natural law.[4] Likewise, Bernard McGinn's 2014 *Thomas Aquinas's "Summa theologiae": A Biography* briefly treats human acts, the ultimate end (beatitude), grace, the life of charity, and other moral topics, but does not refer to conscience.[5] A more specialized study, Daniel McInerny's 2006 Thomistic analysis of practical reasoning and moral conflict, alludes to conscience only very briefly, in the context of the problem of an erroneous conscience.[6] John Rziha's 2009 study of our cognitive participation in God's eternal law treats the practical intellect, synderesis, natural law, and prudence, but leaves out conscience.[7] The same trend holds for Thomas Hibbs's 2001 *Virtue's Splendor: Wisdom, Prudence, and the Human Good*.[8]

Contemporary Thomists who discuss conscience emphasize the connection of conscience to prudence and to the entirety of the Christian life. Romanus Cessario, OP, in his *Introduction to Moral Theology*, notes that the judgment (or "decision") of prudence is "traditionally identified with the act of conscience."[9] As we will see in this chapter, the precise relationship of the judgment of conscience to the judgment of prudence was debated among Thomists in the twentieth century, though by the latter part of the century they inclined toward distinguishing the judgment of conscience from the judgment of prudence. Thomists today are agreed that, as Cessario goes on to say, "casuistry's emphasis on the role of conscience relegated prudence to a subordinate place in accounts of the moral life."[10]

Some Thomists in the early twentieth century attempted to square the moral manuals' tradition of conscience-centered ethics with Aquinas's understanding of ethics. Their efforts should not be despised. As part of prudence and the graced life of charity, we need to form our conscience and obey its judgments about particular acts. Nevertheless, by the mid-twentieth century, and in some cases earlier (as we saw in Garrigou-Lagrange), Thomists were challenging the regnant post-Tridentine moral theology and were seeking to replace it with an approach that was more firmly grounded in Aquinas's moral theology.

In what follows, I survey five significant twentieth-century Thomistic authors—four of them Dominicans—on the topic of conscience. Benoît-Henri Merkelbach, OP, seeks to advance a Thomist position on conscience, reintegrating it with prudence, while retaining the Dominican probabiliorist tradition. Michel Labourdette, OP, carefully distinguishes between prudence and conscience and shows the centrality of prudence. He offers a powerful rationale for rejecting the manualist tradition and adopting a fully Thomistic approach. Eric D'Arcy engages the issue of the treatment of non-Christians and non-Catholics. He explores Aquinas's account of conscience with the purpose of showing that Aquinas's position should mean that no state should force a person to act against conscience in religious matters. D'Arcy's reflections are important, lest Thomistic discussions of conscience be rejected on religious freedom grounds.

Lastly, I survey the contributions of Reginald G. Doherty, OP, and Servais Pinckaers, OP. Doherty analyzes the relationship between the judgment of conscience and the judgment of prudence according to Aquinas. He offers a nuanced perspective that recognizes the formal distinction between the two while allowing for the integration of the judgment of conscience into the act of virtuous prudence. For his part, Pinckaers begins with an investigation of the scriptural testimony. Like Labourdette, he emphasizes that the full scope of Christian morality is neglected in the moral manuals, and he highlights the role of prudence. Pinckaers carries forward Labourdette's project but in a manner shaped also by the mid-twentieth-century biblical movement, which encouraged returning to Scripture as a path for overcoming the limitations of the moral manuals.[11]

Benoît-Henri Merkelbach, OP

Between 1931 and 1940, Benoît-Henri Merkelbach (who died in 1942) published his masterwork, the three-volume *Summa Theologiae Moralis*.[12] I will here explore his reflections on conscience and prudence. Merkelbach splits the treatise on conscience into two parts, one belonging to "general" moral theology and the other relegated to "special" moral theology, specifically to the treatise on prudence.

For Merkelbach, "there are two rules of human acts: the remote, objective, and intrinsic rule, which is the *law*, and the proximate, subjective, and intrinsic rule, which is *conscience*."[13] After treating human acts, therefore, Merkelbach treats conscience. As he says, "just as the archer must know the rules by means of which he must rightly aim at his target, so too man must know the rules by means of which his acts are made orderable to the ultimate end" (155). Conscience is not all that we need for this task; we also need the whole organism of the virtues. But if conscience were lacking, we would not be able to make judgments about right and wrong in particular actions, and so we would not get very far in ordering our particular actions toward our ultimate end.

According to Merkelbach, the act of virtuous prudence is an act of practical judgment, and thus this act is "right and well-formed conscience" (155). In the state of grace, conscience can be said to be the "rule of supernatural acts," making judgments about what is right or wrong to do in a particular circumstance (155). Conscience can have to do either with testifying ("psychological" conscience: Rom. 9:1) or with judging the morality of acts ("moral" conscience, whether consequent or antecedent). Merkelbach cites various biblical instances of consequent conscience, which accuses or excuses a past action: Romans 2:15, Hebrews 9:14, and 2 Corinthians 1:12, among others. Regarding antecedent conscience, which induces or hinders a possible future action, he cites Romans 13:5. He considers the heart of the treatise on conscience to be antecedent conscience, through which, prior to performing an action, the human person is able to make a judgment about its moral quality. Antecedent judgment is "moral conscience in the strict sense because it alone is the rule of human acts" (156).

In addition to these senses of "conscience"—psychological and moral (consequent and antecedent)—there are also two improper senses of "conscience" identified by Merkelbach. First, conscience can be seen as a repository of judgments. This sense of "conscience" is found in 1 Timothy 1:5, where we are said to have a "good conscience" if we have been living in purity. Merkelbach deems this to be a technically "improper" sense of conscience because, properly speaking, conscience is an act, a judgment rather than a repository of judgments. Second, "conscience" can be improperly conceived of as a habitus by which we are able easily and promptly to make a correct judgment about the goodness or wickedness of a particular action.

Not all judgments about actions count as conscience. Merkelbach describes what he terms "a *speculatively-practical* judgment (i.e., a speculative judgment concerning do-able things)" (157).[14] A speculatively practical judgment is not conscience because, although it reflects upon the morality of acts in general, it does not have to do with judging the actual action that may be or has been undertaken by a specific person here and now. In a speculatively practical judgment, one may simply be assenting to the truth of the universal principles known by synderesis. Speculatively practical judgments also include assent to universal conclusions immediately derived from the universal first principles. An example of such a conclusion is "One should not steal." The habitus of moral knowledge (*scientia*) enables a person to draw such universal speculatively practical conclusions with accuracy.

What kind of judgment, then, is conscience? Merkelbach terms it "practically-practical." It has to do with a particular action, "concretely posited here and now by an acting subject" (157). In the practically practical judgment that is conscience, a person applies his or her moral knowledge (the habitus of moral *scientia*) and the universal principles known by the habitus of synderesis to a particular action under consideration. Thus, Merkelbach defines conscience as follows: "A *dictamen* or judgment of the practical intellect affirming that a particular act is permitted and therefore must be done (or, can be done) or must be set aside by us" (158). Conscience is not formally good or bad but rather "is called good or evil *regulatively* and from its effect inasmuch as it directs good or evil works" (158).

As practically practical, conscience belongs within prudence (or, when it is wrong, within imprudence) because prudence inclines the person toward right judgment (that is, right conscience). Without the virtue of prudence, one is unlikely to make a correct judgment about the goodness or badness of a particular act, or at least one is unlikely to follow one's correct judgment. Merkelbach considers that conscience involves only one's own actions, never someone else's. With regard to this latter point, he cites Romans 14:4 and 1 Corinthians 4:4–5. Conscience is simply the conclusion of practical reasoning in a specific case, with the major premise coming from the universal principles of synderesis and the minor premise from one's moral knowledge.

Two issues arise at this stage: Can conscience err, and why is conscience binding? It is clear that practical reasoning can err, and therefore conscience can err. It can do so by wrongly applying true principles, or it can do so by adopting a false principle drawn from erroneous moral *scientia*. Synderesis, of course, cannot err: its universal principles express God's eternal law. But synderesis operates at the level of the first principles of practical reasoning, not at the level of the derived precepts of acquired moral knowledge. Since the latter precepts are the minor premise of practical reason's syllogism in coming to a judgment in a particular case, the judgment of practical reason (i.e., the judgment of conscience) can be based on erroneous moral knowledge.

If it is so easy for conscience to err, then it seems that conscience should not be binding. But Merkelbach insists that conscience is binding, on the ground that conscience applies a universal principle drawn from synderesis to the particular case—and the universal principle expresses God's law. He quotes both Bonaventure and Aquinas to the effect that because conscience communicates divine law, conscience must be obeyed, even if it is in error. For us to be bound by conscience, the judgment of conscience (whether right or erroneous) must have certitude. If our judgment contains doubt or ambiguity, conscience does not bind. To be *absolutely* binding, our conscience must be in accord with right reason. If we are in a state of invincible ignorance, our conscience is internally binding, but we do not have a right to obey it (since it is out of joint with objective reality) and certainly we have no absolute right to act upon it externally. In Merkelbach's view, then, the state can legitimately impede external obedience to erroneous conscience. Merkelbach gives the example of suppressing heretical worship or suppressing the worship of non-Christians.

The possibility of vincible ignorance complicates matters further. A vincibly ignorant conscience exists when, if we bothered to instruct ourselves, we could easily rectify the error in our moral knowledge. Even if the vincibly ignorant person cannot set aside the dictate of his or her (erroneous) conscience, a person sins in acting in accord with a vincibly ignorant conscience. A vincibly erroneous conscience does not bind.

It is possible for practical reason to make a judgment about the moral goodness or wickedness of a particular action without being *certain* of that judgment. One's conscience (or practical judgment) may be doubtful or "opining." To be certain about the moral safety of our action, we need certitude in conscience. If we go ahead and act without such certitude, when it is possible *not* to act, then we have sinned. If we *must* act one way or the other, then it is incumbent upon us to choose the safer path. There are exceptions, as, for example, when we are under obedience to a superior who legitimately possesses the right of command. Merkelbach notes in this regard, "the right order of the common good forbids the subordinate to refuse his obedience unless it is completely certain that the superior is abusing his power" (168). He remarks that the safer path is to be judged not only on the basis of moral security, but also on the basis of whether a particular path enables one to avoid an evil or obtain a great good. He appeals here to prudence: "Prudence, taking all of the circumstances into consideration, points out how one is to proceed in various cases and doubtful situations" (169).

Is conscience present in the same way in all people, whether or not they are in a state of grace? Merkelbach thinks the answer is no. After all, in the supernatural order, practical reason does not simply make a judgment about whether a particular act is good or evil per se but also makes a judgment about whether the act leads to our ultimate (supernatural) flourishing. An act is "good" if it conduces to our supernatural end; its goodness cannot be judged solely on the natural level. Merkelbach states that there "must be a supernatural conscience which decides upon the supernatural quality and worth (or, the supernatural morality) of our acts" (169).

Supernatural conscience thus differs from natural conscience.[15] Does it displace natural conscience or simply augment natural conscience? Natural conscience conforms our acts to right reason and the natural law; supernatural conscience conforms our acts to supernatural charity and to the flourishing that is eternal life, rooted in the divine law (that is to say, the new law of Christ and the Holy Spirit). It might seem that this means that Christians have two consciences. Merkelbach, however, insists that the Christian has one conscience, a supernatural one, which includes within itself natural conscience. Put otherwise, in a Christian, natural conscience is supernaturalized, not in such a way as to negate natural reason and its ends but in such a way as to include them while also going beyond them. It is not therefore a matter of rejecting natural law or rejecting the measure of right reason. Rather, the Christian's task, aided by supernatural conscience, is "to do good and *cultivate virtue according to the measure of reason* but also to do so *according to the more excellent measure of the divine law,* as ordered to the more excellent divine life in accord with the exemplar of Christ Jesus" (170).

Merkelbach's principle here is consistently that "grace perfects and does not destroy nature" (170). As noted above, natural conscience relies upon synderesis as the major premise of its judgment. Synderesis bespeaks the eternal law, and supernatural conscience does not reject the eternal law. But the first practical principles that govern supernatural conscience do not come from synderesis; rather, they come from the "first practical principles of faith," such as "we must seek the happiness of the beatific vision" (171). Faith does not negate the principles given by synderesis, but faith's content informs, elevates, and subordinates synderesis. The gifts of the Holy Spirit—specifically understanding, knowledge, and wisdom—shape faith's content. Moral knowledge now includes all that follows from infused prudence and the other infused virtues, as well as from the Spirit's gift of counsel. Merkelbach adds, presumably with non-Christians and non-Catholics in view, that an invincibly erroneous conscience cannot suffice as "the rule of supernatural acts" (172).[16]

In his treatise on prudence, Merkelbach has supernatural prudence in view from the outset, although he also describes natural prudence. He notes that prudence is absolutely necessary for moral goodness, because just as the moral virtues rectify the appetite and therefore order a person to the due end, prudence judges the proper means and commands the means. Prudence is requisite for "the discovery, formation, and execution of the judgment of right conscience" (175). Prudence is the virtue of practical reason, and therefore has to do with particular things to be done, in relation to the ultimate end of human life. To accomplish its work, prudence requires (among other things) remembering past actions, understanding present matters rightly, and shrewdly identifying means of action. Prudence "directs the moral virtues, over which it rules as moderator"; and prudence "serves the theological virtues, though it directs them as regards the exercise of their acts inasmuch as it discerns when they ought to be exercised" (181). For prudence to serve the supernatural end, not only prudence but also the Spirit's gift of counsel is needed, since we are "in need of being moved by God Himself for the sake of a supernatural inquiry of reason concerning the means ordered to the supernatural end" (192).

In the discussion of conscience that he attaches to his treatise on prudence, Merkelbach distinguishes "certain" conscience from the varieties of doubtful conscience and from "opining" or probable conscience, and he also addresses lax and scrupulous conscience. He emphasizes the need for constant diligence in forming conscience. He describes a helpful process for discerning a vincibly erroneous conscience: for example, we should be concerned about the condition of our conscience when we see "good people acting differently" than we are, or when we suspect that our action may be wicked but nevertheless judge it to be permissible (212). He cautions that people need to focus on present things to be done, rather than constantly reconsidering past actions. In advising scrupulous penitents, confessors should keep in mind that the judgment of antecedent conscience is what matters; a later judgment of consequent conscience does not mean that our action was done in sin (213).

In addition, Merkelbach details the natural and supernatural means of forming conscience. Much depends upon teachers and catechists being able to "carefully and gradually teach . . . students to be able to discriminate between good and evil," in a manner that enables young people to do "the good out of conviction of its goodness and not only out of a desire for reward or in order to receive praise, or to avoid punishment" (215). Among the supernatural means of forming conscience he names frequent prayer, battling against disordered passions, frequent recourse to the sacrament of penance, and receiving spiritual direction.

Briefly, he explores certitude, doubt, and degrees of probability in relation to conscience. He notes that "if conscience is sufficiently certain, it can be a prudent rule of acting"; but otherwise "one must make further inquiries about the course of action to be taken," assuming there is time to do so (223). He then spends a few pages summarizing the differences between rigorism, equiprobabilism, probabiliorism, probabilism, and laxism. Like Alphonsus, he thinks that "certitude broadly speaking" suffices for prudent moral action (226).

In an essay originally published in 1923, Merkelbach asks what place the discussion of conscience should have in moral theology. He urges that "the study of prudence and conscience must unhesitatingly be pursued simultaneously."[17] In this regard, he complains about the lack of attention presently paid to the virtue of prudence: "It is dumbfounding that the most perfect, most essential, and most fundamental of the moral virtues occupies such a diminished position in moral science today—a quite bizarre state of affairs indeed, given that no good act can fail to be simultaneously prudent."[18] As he notes, many manuals either ignore the virtue of prudence or devote only a very few pages to it. It is for this reason that, as we have seen, he first discusses conscience in his "general" moral theology and then adds further comments about conscience in connection with his treatise on prudence in his "special" moral theology.

Michel Labourdette, OP

Michel Labourdette, OP, editor of the *Revue Thomiste* in the years before and after the Council and the greatest Thomist moral theologian of his generation, next deserves our attention. His work on conscience is of interest in part because, unlike Merkelbach, he utterly rejects the structural principles of post-Tridentine moral theory. He calls for a return to a fully Thomist approach to morals. In his *"Grand cours" de théologie morale*, unpublished during his lifetime but now published in a multivolume set, he guides students through the *secunda pars* of the *Summa theologiae*. He treats conscience where Aquinas treats it, namely, I-II, question 19, in the section of the *secunda pars* where Aquinas is discussing human acts.

In question 19, Aquinas first shows that the goodness of the will depends on its object, as proposed to the will by right reason measured by the eternal law. Articles 5 and 6 of question 19 address conscience. In question 19, article 5, Aquinas refers back to I, question 79, article 13, where—reflecting upon the intellectual powers of the human being—he explained that "conscience is not a power, but an act." Conscience is the application of moral knowledge (rooted in synderesis) to a particular action, either before or after the action.

Labourdette devotes forty-two pages to articles 5 and 6, discussing "the problem of conscience."[19] He finds himself needing to move well beyond Aquinas's short texts in the *secunda pars*, and he draws especially upon Aquinas's extensive Disputed Question on Conscience, question 17 of *De veritate*. The Disputed Question on Conscience contains five articles, each of which Labourdette sets forth in some detail. These articles address the following topics: "Is conscience a power, a habit, or an act?" (a. 1); "Can conscience be mistaken?" (a. 2); "Does conscience bind?" (a. 3); "Does a false conscience bind?" (a. 4); and "Does conscience in indifferent matters bind more than the command of a superior, or less?" (a. 5).[20]

Regarding the first article of question 17—whether conscience is a power, habit, or act—Labourdette notes that Aquinas distinguishes between "psychological conscience" (which is a judgment of existence, of truth) and "moral conscience." The key reality, for Aquinas as for Labourdette, is moral conscience, which is an act of practical reason. Moral conscience draws upon a variety of sources in seeking to judge the moral status of a particular act: "synderesis, moral science, convictions and opinions, experience, memory, etc." (206). Christian moral conscience also draws upon "faith and all that is attached to it" (206).

Conscience is not the practical intellect's final step with regard to a concrete action. The virtue of prudence involves conscience's judgment, but prudence itself rectifies "the judgment of election," that is, free *choice* about what to do. Labourdette considers that this point explains why Aquinas "does not mention prudence among the habits which the judgment of conscience applies to the particular case" (207). Even when conscience makes the correct moral judgment, therefore, prudence can err in the judgment of election. This distinction between conscience's judgment and prudence's judgment of election is crucial in distinguishing the work of the practical intellect in conscience and the broader work of the practical intellect in prudence.

Labourdette notes that in thinkers after Aquinas, "the more the idea of conscience is foregrounded, the more the idea of prudence is effaced" (207). Indeed, in the moral manuals, conscience took over the work of prudence. Labourdette comments, "Nearly all that St. Thomas says about prudence and about its properly practical truth has been ascribed to the judgment of conscience" (208). He notes that many Thomists since Charles Billuart, including Merkelbach, have understood conscience to be simply the judgment of prudence, whereas in fact the defining judgment of prudence is the judgment of election (208). Aquinas insists that conscience does not apply the knowledge gained by prudence to a particular action. Prudence has its own quite different work to do (namely, choice), and conscience is not a prudential judgment.

Turning to the second article of question 17, Labourdette asks whether conscience can be mistaken. Conscience is not simply a passive receptor, let alone some form of innate knowledge. Rather, conscience involves the practical intellect's activity. The judgment of conscience is the fruit of active reasoning. Synderesis, which informs conscience, comes from spontaneous knowing and does not require work on the part of the mind. Labourdette cautions against conflating conscience with synderesis. If conscience were simply a set of divinely given moral dictates that arise spontaneously in the human mind, then conscience could never be wrong and would always carry maximal certitude. Indeed, this is how conscience is understood in some quarters today.

What can cause an act of conscience to be erroneous? Either one misapplies true moral principles or one relies upon false moral ideas due to negligence in inquiry, cultural biases, or the influence of the will and affectivity upon one's exercise of reason. When one's mind is turned away from the truth by one's will, one is culpable for an erroneous conscience. The point Labourdette highlights, however, is that "the conscience is an object of cultivation" (209). The ability of conscience to arrive at truth depends upon the cultivation and exercise of multiple habitus. We are responsible, therefore, for carefully forming our conscience. Conscience must be maintained in an attitude of "fidelity to the light" or else it will become biased and corrupt (209).

As Labourdette remarks, modern moralists tend to emphasize the importance of following one's conscience. Aquinas affirmed this importance, but conscience is not about being "authentic" or "sincere" vis-à-vis oneself. Rather, it is about orienting one's life according to natural law and, thus, eternal law. It is not so easy to be entirely innocent when one errs in conscience against the natural law; and even when one is not culpable, it is a serious matter rather than a noble instance of conscience's autonomous authority.

If conscience can err and relatively often does err, then the question (taken up in article 3 of question 17) is why conscience obligates us to obey it. Clearly, this obligation is not absolute, but rather is a conditional necessity of the kind that presumes freedom. In the moral life, the purpose is to attain to the ultimate end, God himself. This requires obeying the eternal law as participated in by the natural law; and it requires obeying the commands of divine revelation and of one's legitimate superiors. Conscience, then, differs from obligation. Conscience awakens us to an obligation, rather than itself being reducible to obligation. The obligations to which conscience awakens us do not derive from conscience. They derive instead from God's eternal law. It follows that conscience really is, in a certain way, "the Voice of God in us" (211).

Although the human person is obligated to follow conscience due to its mediation of God's law, however, its authority must not be exaggerated. Labourdette comments that conscience is not another Sinai; it is not an immediate revelation of God's commandments. Logically, then, it may seem that a true conscience is binding but an erroneous conscience does not obligate us. This is the topic of *De veritate* question 17, article 4; and Aquinas also treats this particular problem at length in question 19, articles 5 and 6 of the *secunda pars*. Aquinas holds that in every case, "one cannot transgress what the conscience presents as an obligation, without transgressing the divine law" (213).

If so, however, do we end up in a situation of perplexed conscience, where one is damned if one does and equally damned if one doesn't (because both obeying *and* disobeying one's erroneous conscience, unless the error is utterly invincible, are sins)? The fifth article of *De veritate* asks whether conscience binds more or less than does the command of a superior. This seems to be a classic situation of perplexity, since disobeying one's conscience is wrong and disobeying the legitimate command of a superior is wrong. But there is no need to fall into perplexity. As Aquinas states in his *respondeo* in article 5: "A correct conscience binds absolutely and perfectly against the command of a superior. . . . But a false conscience binds against the command of a superior even in indifferent matters with some qualification and imperfectly."[21] The qualification is that "one can and should change such a conscience" by forming it better and freeing it from error.[22]

In the *secunda pars*, Aquinas takes up this same issue against the Franciscan viewpoint that an erroneous conscience obligates only with regard to indifferent matters. The Franciscans reason that conscience cannot substitute for God's law or for the "objective order founded upon God" (215). In Aquinas's view (and Labourdette's), they thereby misunderstand conscience's intermediary role. We cannot receive the dictate of God's law vis-à-vis particular acts except through conscience. Therefore, to reject the dictate of conscience is not a good act. Admittedly, following erroneous conscience is not, as such, a good act either, given that erroneous conscience is opposed to God's law.[23] The solution is to form our conscience.

Labourdette observes that at the center of Aquinas's understanding of conscience is the Good, knowable by reason and constitutively the object and end of the will. As the Good, God is our ultimate end, "calling us to partake in his own beatitude" (217). Humans have responsibility in the relationship with God, rather than being merely passive. In human action, this responsibility or cooperation takes shape not least through conscience: "To each of a person's acts, the eternal Law is applied by the person's own reason in a regulative judgment that is called *conscience*" (218). Conscience communicates obligation—not an extrinsic or arbitrary obligation, but an obligation vis-à-vis attaining to human flourishing and to the ultimate end of beatitude. Love, therefore, is at the core of such "obligation," because obeying "obligation" means fulfilling the will through, ultimately, the attainment of the Good.

However, this makes failures of conscience even more devastating. A bad act is always against God's law and therefore against our movement toward the Good, even if we are not culpable of sin. Modern Catholic moralists, Labourdette notes, generally hold that "following an invincibly erroneous conscience can be good" (220). Aquinas, however, denies this. To deviate from the eternal law is not a good path for human flourishing.

The above remarks have to do with conscience that (even if erroneous) possesses subjective certitude. What happens when the judgment of conscience contains doubt? In such a case, one will want to suspend judgment and do nothing. But what if the action has a certain urgency to it: one must either act or do nothing? Aquinas, like the other medievals, holds that one must choose the surer course. Labourdette remarks that historians today term this stance "medieval tutiorism," thus suggesting that the probabilist debates go back behind the sixteenth century to the Middle Ages.

As Labourdette observes, however, the word "tutiorism" has connotations that were not part of medieval theology. After all, "tutiorism" in context means absolute rigorism, which was not the position of Aquinas. For Aquinas, a "probable" conscience—in which the judgment of conscience arrives at the opinion that a particular course of action is probably true—"is, when certitude is lacking, a just and sufficient rule of action" (220).

Moreover, as Labourdette emphasizes, "in the moral theology of St. Thomas, conscience is not all!" (220). The crucial point is that the final practical judgment belongs to prudence. Prudence gives "a just rational measure to an act that it conforms to rectified appetite" (223). In this sense, prudence (with its connection to the will and affectivity), not conscience (with its focus on moral knowledge and the eternal law), establishes the "truth of the action" and completes practical reason's judgment of what constitutes a good action (222).

It follows that conscience-centered moral theology, or what Labourdette terms the "morality of conscience" or probabilism, is opposed to Aquinas's moral theology. When probabilism came on the scene as a moral theory in the sixteenth century, various reactions expanded its domain: laxism, tutiorism, probabiliorism, and equiprobabilism. These alternatives differ from each other but share core principles regarding the foundations of moral theory. Although post-Tridentine Dominicans thought they were remaining faithful to Aquinas's moral theory in advocating probabiliorism, they were not. The problem was simply that conscience-centered morality cannot do the work done by the prudence-centered (along with the other virtues and gifts of the Holy Spirit) morality of Aquinas.

Labourdette describes this problem in detail. Little by little, under the influence of nominalist and voluntarist thought, obligation came to take the central place in moral matters, displacing the Good and the ultimate end (toward which the will is drawn). In answer to the question of "why do this rather than that?" a morality of obligation states: "because it is commanded" (224). Rather than understanding the commandment as good because it expresses the exigency of a nature in tending toward its good (its flourishing), the commandment is increasingly understood in voluntarist terms "as a precept that is imposed as a positive given" (224). Obligation here responds to commandment and law conceived not in terms of flourishing and happiness but in terms of God's will. Obligation addresses our free will—but now conceived in terms of a "freedom" separated from a "primal orientation toward the Good as such" (225). No longer teleologically defined, freedom is simply autonomy, our "natural right to do all that is not forbidden" (225). Obligation puts a check or limit upon the will's freedom; the will must accept God's authority and obey God's command. In this perspective, conscience is central because it communicates the divine command that the will must obey. Since the most important question of morality here consists in discerning what we are obligated to do—the boundary lines that limit our freedom—conscience plays the most central role. Labourdette quotes Alphonsus to the effect that conscience is the "tribunal" that decides between liberty and law.

In the contest between liberty and law, Labourdette comments, moral theologians of different temperaments leaned toward one side or the other. Some favored more restrictive law; some favored a great deal of liberty. But for almost all of these theologians, liberty stood as the primary reality. In order to curtail human freedom, there needed to be a clear commandment. Conscience became preeminent because conscience was normally how the commandment was communicated in the case of particular actions. Conscience could be true or erroneous; conscience could have certitude, probability, or doubt.

Even these traditional terms underwent a change in the new moral theory. Obeying certain erroneous conscience became a "good" act since "goodness" was now measured simply by adherence to obligation and commandment. Likewise, probability and truth came to be separated. For Aquinas, something was "probable" and worth adhering to because of the light of truth. In the new moral theory, by contrast, "probable" meant an intermediate position between true and false. Instead of saying "probably true," one said simply "probable." Probability came increasingly to depend upon the number of authorities that favored a particular position, or the number of arguments in its favor. "Opinion" too came to have an impersonal sense, as a "probable assertion" (228). Opinion no longer was the mind inclining toward truth, though without being absolutely certain. Probability became something extrinsic to the mind, rather than being the mind's inclination toward something as true.

Thus, in conscience-centered moral theory, it was perfectly possible to hold in an equal way two contrary opinions or probabilities. Clearly, such an outcome exhibits a sharp difference from the meaning of "opinion" and "probable" for Aquinas. Since having an opinion no longer meant inclining toward something as true (though without demonstration or certitude), one might incline equally toward opposite opinions. In cases of conscience, the person would identify various expert opinions favoring liberty and various expert opinions favoring law, and then try to figure out which viewpoint was more likely, often on the basis of the weight of authorities on one side or the other. Moral casuists listed the authorities on each side and weighted the alternatives accordingly. The question was also whether to put weight on the side of liberty or instead to favor law.

In this new moral system, there was the possibility that *neither* side contained a probability sufficient to enable a solid judgment of conscience. As noted above, for Aquinas, one should strictly avoid what one fears to be a sin. In the new moral theory, however, both sides might give warrant for fearing a sin. Francisco Suárez developed the solution that although one can never act with a practical doubt about the goodness of one's action, one can form one's conscience by referring one's doubt to the speculative level—for example, by applying the principle that *a doubtful law does not obligate.* One can thereby act with a "practical certitude" that one does "good," so long as one is acting "in good faith" (229).

Labourdette discusses the various perspectives that arose within the new conscience-centered morality. The first was probabilism itself. Developed by the Dominican Bartolomé de Medina in the late sixteenth century, probabilism proposes that it is acceptable for conscience to follow any opinion that is judged probable—even if there may be a *more* probable opinion. When exaggerated, probabilism became laxism, which held, for example, that "the precept of love of neighbor only requires exterior acts, not internal acts of love" (232). On the other extreme was tutiorism, which strongly favored law over liberty, so that the *least* probability would suffice for strict obligation, whereas absolute certitude would be necessary for liberty. Labourdette points out: "For modern tutiorism, the supreme category is security, just as for laxism it is liberty. For St. Thomas . . . the supreme category is *truth*" (235).

Labourdette then reviews probabiliorism, the standard position of Dominican theologians since the seventeenth century. While he thinks this position is a reasonable one given the constraints of the conscience-centered moral system, it certainly is not Thomistic morality. He also examines Alphonsus's equiprobabilism. Alphonsus sought to pay due respect both to liberty and to law, keeping the two poles in strict balance rather than favoring one or the other. Labourdette credits Alphonsus with assisting the church in arriving at a body of received moral opinions that avoided the extremes of rigorism and laxism. In Labourdette's view, these moral opinions merit respect, even while the actual moral system merits critique. One cannot follow both the moral system of Alphonsus and the moral system of Aquinas; and it is the latter that provides better grounds for Catholic morality.

Labourdette also questions the value of a separate moral theology as developed since the sixteenth century. For Aquinas, moral theology is one part of an integrated theology, whose heart is knowledge of God. Moral theology is thereby "organized around God as the supreme Ultimate End, because he is the sovereign Good, calling the rational creature to share in his own divine beatitude" (239–40). Moral theology (as part of an integrated theology) is about the return to God through the dynamisms of nature and grace, given the historical conditions of the fall and of redemption in Christ, and within the communion of his mystical body. The topics treated in moral theology should include sin, precepts, counsels, ascesis, mysticism, and much more—all in light of progress in virtue and holiness, and thus in light of free human actions conforming to the truth of reality, determined by the eternal law, and fulfilling human nature and the human vocation to beatitude.

In Aquinas's approach to the moral life, Labourdette notes, "conscience has a significant but subordinate role" (240). Conscience is simply the application of moral knowledge to a particular action; and in this way true conscience communicates God's eternal law—keeping in mind that God's law is not an arbitrary command but is his wise order for human flourishing, for our fulfillment and beatitude. Since conscience can err, however, we have to be diligent in seeking moral truth and in forming conscience. Even more important is not to conflate conscience with prudence. Labourdette comments that when, through conscience, "one knows the moral truth, in a particular case, it still remains to do it, to conform one's acts to the truth one knows, to guide one's acts by the truth as their rule. . . . This is all the role of prudence" (241). It is prudence that achieves "*practical truth*" in action, in accord with knowledge and affectivity, by freely choosing the means of action in the judgment of election or choice (241). It is prudence that makes a person not only to *know* what is morally good but truly to *be* morally good, through "the accord of the concrete action to the virtuous ends" (241).

By contrast, the post-Tridentine conscience-centered morality is a complete change from the Thomistic understanding of morality. The "morality of conscience" is both subjectivist (in the sense of losing a strong sense of the eternal law, the teleological ordering of all things to the Good) and impersonal (in the sense of entrapping the person within the opinions of various authorities). Here, conscience "becomes the arbitrary sovereign" (241). An act is deemed "good" simply on the basis of whether it has been done through a good-faith exercise of conscience. The notion of probability is separated from the person's holding a *truth* as probable. The whole moral system becomes an "impersonal mechanism" (242). Prudence is reduced simply to the act of conscience, to conscience's prudently judging between the various probable opinions. Commandment and obedience become the heart of the matter, in a casuist manner separated from actual human subjectivity and affectivity. The result is "an algebraic mechanism, a pseudo-universal schematization of singular cases," opposed in every way to the Thomistic emphasis on personal decision and responsibility through prudence, whose decision is always new and directed to the uniqueness of each particular action (243).

Once more, Labourdette criticizes the separation of moral, ascetic, and mystical theology, as though the theology of the return to God—of human acts—could be separated from the whole of theology along the lines required by the "morality of conscience." He notes that even probabilists admit that if the Christian moral life consisted solely in what is required according to the principles of probabilism, it would not rise to the dignity of a *Christian* life.

Labourdette ends by observing that there has emerged at the time of his writing (in the 1950s) a strong reaction against impersonal objectivism in morality. But this reaction goes to the opposite extreme, by adopting a subjectivist view of moral action. Absent any universal moral laws or rules, the "creative activity of conscience" reigns anew, now as the "sovereign will" (245). Labourdette notes that Pope Pius XII has spoken out against this situation ethics (which I will examine in chapter 4), notably in two radio addresses in 1952. Importantly, in these addresses, Pius XII directed attention to Aquinas's treatise on prudence as the path for uniting the objective and subjective—intellectual and affective—dimensions of moral action.[24]

Eric D'Arcy

Labourdette is clearly a giant of twentieth-century moral theology. But he leaves room for further reflection in two areas that respectively occupy the next two figures to be surveyed: the relationship of conscience to religious freedom, and the relationship of the judgment of conscience to the judgment of prudence.

In 1961 the philosopher Eric D'Arcy published his doctoral dissertation, written at Melbourne University and the University of Oxford and guided by Peter Geach, Elizabeth Anscombe, and other notable Catholic scholars, under the title *Conscience and Its Right to Freedom*.[25] D'Arcy later became Archbishop of Hobart (Australia) and contributed much to the life of the church.

In *Conscience and Its Right to Freedom*, D'Arcy begins by observing that, for Aquinas, conscience is not a distinct faculty or a divine voice resounding in the soul. Turning to the sources behind Aquinas's position, he distinguishes between judicial conscience (judging past actions) and legislative conscience (dictating what action we should do). D'Arcy argues that in the pagan world, conscience or *syneidēsis* was about past actions, whereas St. Paul thinks that conscience can also judge future actions and that conscience can err. D'Arcy also discusses the scribal error in copying Jerome's commentary on Ezekiel that produced the word "synderesis." Jerome's original word seems to have been *syneidēsis*.

In the early thirteenth century, Stephen Langton held that synderesis has to do with the universal principles of practical reason, not with concrete cases per se. Around 1230, Philip the Chancellor identified synderesis as being like a habitus (a *potentia habitualis*), and he also argued that synderesis provides the universal principles that conscience then applies to a particular case. For Philip, synderesis pertains to the will and assists the will in moving toward the morally good. The thirteenth-century Franciscan theologians followed this line of reasoning, locating synderesis in the will and conscience in the intellect. For Bonaventure, synderesis is a habit-like power in the will and conscience is a habitus of the practical reason.

Aquinas holds that synderesis is an innate habitus containing the first principles of practical reason—innate in the sense that once the terms are learned through experience, "the truth of the principles is seen without discursive reasoning."[26] D'Arcy examines Aquinas's remarks on synderesis in his *Commentary on the Sentences*, showing that Aquinas's viewpoint develops between this first work and his *Summa theologiae*. Namely, in his earliest work, Aquinas is not quite sure that synderesis is a habitus. He is certain, however, that synderesis cannot err (unlike conscience) and that conscience, drawing upon the universal principles given by synderesis and also upon other moral knowledge, judges the goodness or badness of particular actions.

Question 17 of the *De veritate* presents Aquinas's mature position on conscience, from which he does not deviate in later writings. Conscience is an act of the practical reason that involves "the application of general moral principles to a particular case" (43). It can err because it formulates a practical syllogism: the universal premise (drawn from synderesis) is always true, but the minor premise may be in error or the person may reason mistakenly.

In the *Summa theologiae*, Aquinas sets forth the nature of synderesis and conscience in question 79 of the *prima pars*, and he discusses the binding character (and potential errors) of conscience in question 19 of the *secunda pars*. Aquinas insists that synderesis is not a distinct faculty within the human intellect; rather, synderesis is a habitus that enables practical reason to know its first principles. While carefully distinguishing conscience and synderesis, Aquinas accepts that "common usage often identifies a faculty or a habit with its act," and in this sense some people speak of the interior voice of conscience when they actually have in view "synderesis, the habitual grasp of the fundamental moral principles" (47). D'Arcy suggests that the universal first principles known by synderesis are broad claims such as "Sexual conduct must be ordered by some rules" or "Killing a man is different from killing a rabbit" (65).[27]

Having established the nature and work of synderesis and conscience according to Aquinas, D'Arcy turns to the issue of religious freedom and the authority of conscience, which is the central concern of his book. He begins by summarizing the argument he wishes to make: there is an absolute duty to obey one's conscience in order to attain to the ultimate end of happiness, and so the state should assist the person in obeying conscience and should never compel a person to worship in a manner that violates his or her conscience.

For Alexander of Hales, however, an erroneous conscience does not bind and may therefore be overruled by our superiors. Similarly, John of la Rochelle argues that if there is a promulgated law (natural or divine), then conscience must be disobeyed in order to obey this law. Bonaventure argues that one is always sinfully culpable for obeying an erroneous conscience rather than God's law.

Albert the Great made a breakthrough by reflecting not only upon the objective situation (violating God's law) but also upon the subjective situation. In his view, conscience is binding whenever we believe, either with probability or with certitude, that God's law requires a certain action.

For Aquinas, no action done in erroneous conscience is "good," but "any act done against conscience is morally evil" (88). In his *Commentary on the Sentences*, admittedly, Aquinas states: "In any person at all, ignorance is always culpable if it concerns sound morals or the truth of the Faith."[28] The result is that all persons who are not Catholic—assuming that they could have heard the gospel proclaimed—are in a state of mortal sin, bound for damnation unless they convert. As D'Arcy points out, this viewpoint assumes that "the religious truth [has] been so proposed that it produced a conviction of authenticity, and was then rejected in bad faith" (94).

Aquinas takes up the same topic in *De veritate* and the *Summa theologiae*. In *De veritate*, he argues once more that an erroneous conscience is binding; we cannot act against it without sinning. He also argues that "ignorance of the law" is always culpable, given that a law (by definition) is something that has been effectively promulgated. With regard to the divine law in Christ, he grants that "unbelief is no sin in lands where the Gospel has not been preached," but he supposes unbelief to be a mortal sin wherever the gospel has been preached (103). In *Summa theologiae* I-II, question 19, however, Aquinas underscores that an erroneous conscience binds absolutely, so that disobeying it (even for the sake of converting to Christianity) would be a sin.

For D'Arcy, it is unclear why the act of following an erroneous conscience cannot be considered a good act, since it is not a sin. D'Arcy points out that modern moralists agree with him. Alphonsus de Liguori deemed an act done in accordance with conscience (even erroneous conscience) to be formally good. If done in good faith, it is, formally speaking, a good act.[29] Almost all moralists since Alphonsus's day have accepted his position.

D'Arcy grants that actions against natural and divine law are certainly not "objectively good"; this would be to condone moral relativism (128). In this sense, it does not matter whether we violate natural or divine law "in good faith," since such a violation cannot conduce to our flourishing (our happiness) and therefore cannot be objectively good. Subjectively, however, "no man is under formal responsibility to obey a law except in so far as he knows it" (128). Since it is possible not to know a law without culpability—and D'Arcy grants this in more cases than does Aquinas—an action against divine law (e.g., against the new law promulgated by Christ), when undertaken in good faith, is subjectively good even if not objectively good.

D'Arcy recognizes that, given the scope of erroneous conscience, calling an act "good" that is committed in erroneous conscience (even if non-culpable erroneous conscience) may lead to some disturbing conclusions. For example, in the social world of the Nazi leaders, Heinrich Himmler thought himself to be acting in good faith in directing the slaughter of Jews. D'Arcy responds that in such a case, Aquinas's point that a person can be culpable for an error of conscience is correct.[30] As a more appropriate example, then, D'Arcy notes that some nineteenth-century Catholic moralists thought that abortion was acceptable in cases in which otherwise *both* mother and child would die. In D'Arcy's view, these moralists were wrong about the natural law; yet they were not *culpable* for their error, given the complexity of detailed natural law decision-making. Whereas Aquinas thinks that error in matters relating to God's law is always culpable, D'Arcy thinks that more room needs to be given for invincible ignorance.

Modern Catholic moralists, D'Arcy says, benefit from anthropological studies that show in detail how cultures have differed in terms of moral values. Modern moralists also benefit from a greater awareness that in most societies people simply do not question their principles. In many societies, adultery (at least on the part of the man), polygamy, and contraception have often been encouraged, so that people in many societies do not even think twice about them. It would be a serious mistake to accuse *all* these people of being in a damnable state of culpable ignorance. The fact is, "without divine revelation it is morally (though not absolutely) impossible for most men, given the present condition of the human race, to arrive at such knowledge with certainty, accuracy, and 'no admixture of error'" (139). This is why God revealed the basic precepts of the natural law at Sinai. Culturally grounded ignorance is even more likely in matters that require supernatural revelation. Generally speaking, people only infrequently try to learn about a religion that is not their own. People rely instead on their social circle's ingrained judgments, which can easily be wrong.

At this stage, D'Arcy examines what Aquinas has to say about religious freedom. Laudably, Aquinas affirms that Jews should not be compelled to baptize their children.[31] He holds that natural justice must not be violated in Christians' dealings with the Jewish people—even when what is at stake is eternal salvation. Whereas for Aquinas Christian heretics and apostates can justly be compelled by the state, on penalty of death, to return to the practice of the Catholic faith, "unbelievers" or non-Catholics cannot and must not be compelled to believe. Here Aquinas argues on the ground of the act of faith's internal requirements, rather than on the ground of natural justice. He states that it would be unjust to baptize an adult against his or her will.

D'Arcy points out that the question of forced conversion would be better put another way, one that draws upon Aquinas's treatment of conscience in *Summa theologiae* I-II, question 19, article 5. In that article, Aquinas states that if one held *in conscience* that one was doing evil by becoming Christian, then one would commit a mortal sin by converting. It follows, as D'Arcy says, that the question of forced conversion is really the question of whether a person can justly be forced to commit a mortal sin (156). The obvious answer is no.

However, Aquinas does not think that apostate Catholics have any rights in conscience. He argues that their free will to be Catholic (prior to apostasizing) is like a contract to which they can be held, by force if necessary. But an apostate Catholic presumably no longer believes the Catholic faith. How then can it be just for a superior, no matter how legitimately possessed of authority, to compel the apostate Catholic to sin mortally by doing something that the apostate thinks is wrong? Again, D'Arcy appeals to question 19, article 5: people should not be compelled to act against their consciences.

As noted above, in societies where the gospel has been preached, Aquinas does not think that people can non-culpably fail to see the truth of Catholic faith: in such societies, people who deny Catholic faith do so always due to a bad will. But even if this were the case, D'Arcy contends that it would still be wrong to force such people to act as though they believe, when in fact they do not. Pretending under compulsion to believe is a sin. Compelling someone to perform a sin is itself a sin.

D'Arcy recalls Augustine's fateful change of mind about whether heretics (Donatists) could be suppressed by the power of the state. Aquinas concurs that heretics should be punished without leniency, on the ground that it is better for the state to kill the heretic rather than to allow the heretic to imperil the supernatural common good. D'Arcy points out that in Aquinas's day capital punishment was used for many crimes, and so his validation of the state's executing heretics is not surprising. In addition, Aquinas's definition of "heretic" does not apply to established branches of Christianity such as modern Protestantism and Anglicanism.

But leaving these points to the side, D'Arcy appeals to Aquinas's "own principle: No end, however exalted, can justify a violation of natural justice" (169). It follows that, whatever else may be the case, the (supernatural) common good cannot be defended by violating the natural justice due to the unbeliever. In erroneous conscience—often invincibly erroneous conscience—a person may reject Catholicism. To embrace Catholicism would be a mortal sin for a person who sincerely does not believe; and to force this person to embrace Catholicism, on pain of death, would itself be a sin.

D'Arcy also addresses Aquinas's position regarding non-Christian or non-Catholic worship. For Aquinas, unbelievers must not be forced to worship as Catholics. But Aquinas holds that, with the exception of Jews whose worship serves as testimony to aspects of Christianity, the rites of unbelievers must be forbidden by Catholic states, except in situations where there is some strategic reason to allow for the continuance of such rites (for example, if there are large numbers of unbelievers and so toleration serves to avoid civic unrest). In response, D'Arcy argues that the grudging permission that Aquinas gives to some unbelievers' rites does not accord with natural justice. In justice, people who wish to obey their conscience in worshipping God should be supported in so doing. Aquinas has not given adequate credence to the fact that people may sincerely hold that Catholicism is false and some other religion's teachings about God is true, without this necessarily being a culpable error. If in justice Jews should not be forced to baptize their children, so also in justice unbelievers should not be hampered in practicing the faith in God that they sincerely profess.

D'Arcy is aware of Charles Journet's emphasis that Aquinas lived under a "consecrational régime," different from our own experience of secular states.[32] He is also aware that Aquinas's experience of the church, and of non-Catholics, was quite different from ours today. As D'Arcy says, "For our contemporaries, the climate of opinion is unfavourable to belief; for St. Thomas it was so favourable that he apparently finds it difficult to conceive unbelief except as ill-will" (180). But the main point remains: it is a sin to pressure or compel people to sinning against their sincere (even if erroneous) conscience, including in the highly important matter of the worship of God.

Reginald G. Doherty, OP

Another helpful advance is provided by the 1961 published dissertation *The Judgments of Conscience and Prudence* by Reginald Doherty, OP. Doherty's position on these two judgments is close to Labourdette's, but Doherty devotes much more space to explaining why he arrives at this position and what is at stake.

Doherty begins by distinguishing practical and speculative knowledge. We are dealing with practical reason when "knowledge is subordinated and ordered to operation."[33] One of the marks of practical reason is a dynamism toward knowing the object "in its concrete, particular mode of existence" (6). Since this is not possible for "direct intellectual knowledge," the practical reason is served by "indirect intellectual knowledge attained through the estimative sense (*vis cogitativa*), the *particular reason*," which has to do with "the realm of the individual and the contingent" (6).[34]

One can already see how complex these matters are—and matters do not become less complicated when the relation to the will is added, since practical reason is about matters to be done and therefore it is knowledge in relation to the will. The judgment of speculative reason does not have a relation to the will (or affectivity); whereas the judgment of practical reason serves the purpose of prompting the movement of the will toward the object. In the order of execution, practical reason joins together various means to produce the desired end. In the order of intention, practical reason begins with the desired end and reasons back to the means. In a practical syllogism, synderesis provides the major premise: for example, "The good should be done and evil avoided." The minor premise of the practical syllogism consists in "a judgment of the reason that a certain action is a particular good" (11).

On the one hand, the practical reason's truth is measured by its conformity to rectified appetite, and so the practical reason's certitude can be found in conformity to right volition, that is, "to the rules which should govern operation" (14). Yet on the other hand, since the practical reason's object is not something necessary (a universal truth), it can be false. Practical reason is true insofar as it correctly judges "something to be useful to a good end" (14). The certitude of virtuous practical reason involves, Doherty explains, a firm "adherence . . . to the rectitude of something to be done. This involves a firmness of assent to the rectitude of the appetite, to the rectitude of the intention, and to the proper ordination of the act in conformity with the right appetite and the right intention" (15). It is an intellectual certitude, but it is a certitude regarding the "right appetite" of the will in a particular case.

After this opening reflection on practical reason, Doherty devotes a chapter to the psychology of the human act. Here his reflections are instructed by Charles Billuart, John of St. Thomas, Domingo Bañez, Cardinal Cajetan (Thomas de Vio), and others (including a 1955 essay by the young Servais Pinckaers). When a person apprehends a desirable object, the will moves toward this object. Then, "the practical intellect begins to judge the possibility of attaining the object by some means" (19). Once the practical reason judges that the object is attainable, an intention is formed. The intention leads the practical reason to seek a specific means. When the practical reason searches for the means, this is called the act of counsel (assuming there is doubt about the means).

Doherty notes that, for Cajetan and Bañez, counsel includes the judgment or decision about the means. For Aquinas, however, counsel and judgment about the means are distinct: counsel is simply the inquiry into the various possible means to attain the object. Within counsel, there may be various judgments, but not the final election of a particular means as the best one. The will may "consent" or tend toward various means that are proposed as apt for attaining the end. When the practical reason judges which means is the best one here and now, "election" follows upon this practical judgment. The will affects the practical judgment by directing it to consider one or more particular means. But the will inclines toward the means presented by the practical intellect as the best one; the will may choose another option if this option is at least equal in certain respects. Yet, even after the practical judgment is settled on, when the time arrives to perform the action, the will might not do the action, even if the will has already chosen to do it. A "command" of the practical reason is needed. This command is an imperative declaration of practical reason.

Next, Doherty devotes a chapter to Aquinas's understanding of the judgment of conscience, focusing on antecedent conscience. In commenting on the *Sentences*, Aquinas distinguishes conscience from the conclusion of the practical syllogism, and he also distinguishes the (cognitive) judgment of conscience from the (affective) judgment of election. As Doherty remarks, it follows that "there is some formal distinction between the judgment of conscience and that of prudence, the virtue which governs the act of the judgment of election" (40). Doherty also notes that while conscience proceeds from intellective habits—including science, wisdom, and synderesis—prudence is not on this list. He comments, "If prudence were the proximate eliciting principle of the act of conscience, St. Thomas would hardly have passed over this relationship in silence" (40).

Commenting on the treatment of conscience in question 17 of *De veritate*, Doherty argues that the crucial text for the relationship between conscience and prudence is the answer to the fourth objection in article 1. In this passage, Aquinas explicitly distinguishes between the judgment of conscience and the judgment of election. After remarking that the two judgments are similar in certain ways, Aquinas states that "the judgment of conscience consists simply in knowledge, whereas the judgment of free choice consists in the application of knowledge to the inclination of the will."[35] John of St. Thomas's claim that the judgment of conscience *simply is* the judgment of prudence cannot stand up to the evidence of this passage.

In his treatment of the discussion of conscience in the *Summa theologiae*, Doherty highlights the fact that an error of conscience is an error in the practical reason in proposing an object to the will. Such an error differs from an error in prudence (an error in the judgment of election), which is caused by a disordered appetite. Conscience's errors are like the errors found in other kinds of knowledge. They are not errors resulting from bad affectivity. I note that, due to a bad will, one may omit to form one's conscience as one should; but even here the actual error comes about in the practical reason that does not know what it should know. A bad will may be to blame for negligence in forming conscience, but it is not to blame for anything that occurs within the activity of conscience itself. The point for Doherty is that conscience, unlike prudence, "is really the subjective aspect of the law," or "the application of the principles [of law] to something that must be done" (54, 59).

Doherty's next chapter reviews Aquinas's understanding of the virtue of prudence and its potential parts. Prudence is right reason regarding things to be done, a virtue of the practical intellect. Prudence serves the will by proposing the right object. Prudence relies upon synderesis (the habit of the first practical principles) and upon the natural inclination of the will to seek "the reasonable good" (62). In proposing the right object to the will, prudence applies universal moral principles to a particular case, by way of an "operative syllogism" (63). Aquinas defines prudence as follows: "It is necessary that the practical reason be perfected by a habit in order to judge rightly concerning the human good according to the single acts that must be performed. And this virtue . . . is called prudence."[36] In many ways, this certainly sounds like the definition of conscience, namely, the application of moral knowledge to a particular act. Conscience, however, is an act rather than a habit; and conscience (unlike prudence) does not "determine the *medium* of virtue in each case" or move "the appetitive powers to their rational object" with regard to each of the moral virtues (64).

Doherty goes on to reiterate some things he had said about the practical intellect, including that its truth is constituted by conformity with right appetite (tending to the moral end). He also examines how it is that the moral virtues depend upon prudence even while prudence, measured by right appetite, depends upon the moral virtues. In part, this circular relationship comes about because prudence has to do with the means to an end, not with the end itself. If there were no (right) appetitive inclinations toward ends, then there would be no prudence about the means. Practical reason about the means is therefore affected by right appetite toward the end. Such right appetite brings about in the practical reason a connaturality with regard to the judgment about the means (or the particular thing to be done). Thus, as

Doherty puts it, "a rectified appetite can incline the reason to judge how to act in the singular, contingent, existing circumstances" (68). Prudence, in other words, is emphatically not a judgment of "pure" knowledge.

Certainly, both prudence and conscience "apply universal principles to singular acts" and depend upon synderesis for the major premise of their practical syllogism (69). But prudence differs from conscience not only with regard to the role of affectivity but also with regard to the "estimative sense." As noted above, prudence does not end in judgment but rather in command. Aquinas identifies the operations of prudence as counsel (aided by the virtue of *eubulia*), judgment (aided by the virtues of *synesis* and *gnome*[37]), and precept (the *praecipere* that most properly belongs to prudence). Why is it, then, that conscience should not be construed as strictly identical with the judgment elicited through *synesis*?

Doherty explains that *synesis* need not be simply one judgment; it may be a set of judgments. It has to do with what the best means is for attaining the end. The judgment of *synesis* enables one to apprehend a thing as it is, rather than having erroneous ideas about a thing. This is necessary for distinguishing one means from another as better fitted for attaining the end. The judgment of *synesis*, like the virtue of prudence itself, is also shaped by the rectitude of the appetites, which connaturalizes practical reason in relation to the means that befits the good end. Election depends upon the judgment of *synesis* (or, if needed, the judgment of *gnome*) about the most apt means.

Doherty also takes up the question of whether "precept" here is identical with the act of command that follows upon election. Most Thomists think that it is, but others think that "precept" is actually "a judgment included in the act of election" (77). This is not an issue that I need explore here, other than to say that Doherty gives strong reasons for holding that, for Aquinas, "precept" is the act of command following upon election.

The final chapter of Doherty's book focuses upon the relation of the judgment that is conscience to the judgment that belongs to prudence.[38] In his defense of the claim that the judgment of conscience and the judgment of prudence (or *synesis*) are distinct, he identifies four pillars to his argument. The first pillar is historical. Namely, by contrast to prudence, "conscience" as a theologically developed notion did not really emerge until the thirteenth century. Aquinas himself pays a great deal of attention to prudence and relatively little (especially in the *Summa theologiae*) to conscience. If conscience were identical to *synesis*, then Aquinas would have thought it more significant and discussed it within his treatise on prudence. Doherty argues that Aquinas found the concept of conscience to be "inadequate to express the reality involved in the judgment necessary to ensure virtuous action" (93).

The second pillar has to do with the different "formalities" of the two judgments. Namely, the judgment of prudence provides for actual operation (as the judgment from which election and command follow), whereas the judgment of conscience evaluates the moral quality of the action but does not have to do with moving the will to operation.[39]

The third pillar is that the two judgments relate differently to practical truth. Prudence involves the conformity of practical reason to right appetite. Conscience's judgment, by contrast, does not contain a link to right appetite. The prudent person has a connaturality with the means that is apt to attaining the end of right appetite, whereas the exercise of conscience lacks an intrinsic relation to right appetite and therefore is more prone to error in practical truth.

His fourth pillar is that a bad will can pervert election, whereas a bad will does not directly pervert the judgment of conscience. As he says: "As a result, there are two judgments present: the right judgment of conscience, and the judgment of election contrary to that of conscience" (98). A perverted judgment of election, of course, characterizes imprudence rather than prudence.

All this seems quite reasonable. If so, why did John of St. Thomas and the Thomists who followed his position make their error? Doherty speculates that it was because "John of St. Thomas conceives of conscience as being immediately ordered to the production of operation, to execution" (99). This conception shifts conscience in the direction of prudence. In fact, while conscience has to do with things to be done (or things that have been done), Aquinas does not associate it with actual operation or execution. For Aquinas, conscience serves virtue, but conscience does not pertain to the actual exercise of virtue.

Of course, John of St. Thomas recognized that people can act against the judgment of conscience. He explains that the judgment of *synesis* (which he deems to be conscience) can be replaced by a contrary judgment prior to command. Doherty points out that that Aquinas, by contrast, holds that not only synderesis but also the actual judgment of conscience remains in place, condemning the act. Furthermore, Doherty notes that conscience does not presume rectified appetite: many people sin against their conscience, which condemns them. By contrast, prudence presumes rectified appetite; otherwise, a person has imprudence, not prudence.

Nevertheless, Doherty grants that *synesis* has a relation to the judgment that is conscience. Indeed, he considers that in the virtuous act of prudence "the two judgments are numerically the same, while remaining formally different" (102). The same judgment can be considered under two aspects. Doherty argues that in the prudent person *synesis* takes up within itself conscience's evaluation of the moral goodness or badness of the act. To conscience, *synesis* adds the elements of conformity to right appetite and thus of the ordering to actual operation—but the judgment is numerically the same. On this view, in the prudent person *synesis* accomplishes the judgment of conscience within itself, even though the judgment of conscience can be seen to be formally distinct from the judgment of *synesis*.

In contending that in the virtuous person "the judgment of conscience is *formed within* the judgment of prudence," Doherty is not positing two separate judgments in the virtuous person (102). The judgment of *synesis* does not join to itself a separate judgment, that of conscience. Rather, the judgment made by the prudent person can be viewed in two ways. In one way, it can be viewed as pertaining to operation and conformed to rectified appetite, and as such it is *synesis*; in another way, it can be viewed as evaluating the action on the basis of synderesis and moral science, and as such it is conscience. But in the prudent person, the one judgment is properly called *synesis* because, as part of the virtue of prudence, it pertains to operation and rectified appetite. Doherty notes that, as a result, in the prudent person "the problems of the doubtful and the erroneous conscience are solved" (so long as the person is truly being prudent) (103). The formal distinction explains how an imprudent person can still possess right conscience—and be condemned in his or her actions by conscience.

Doherty holds that acting on the basis of a doubtful or erroneous conscience constitutes "a sin against the special virtue of prudence, an act of imprudence or negligence" (104). To act without the approval of conscience in cases of doubtful or vincibly erroneous conscience is to show disregard for the gravity of sin and the necessity of virtuous action. Doherty also thinks that when we are condemned by right conscience this judgment of right conscience can be said to flow "from the virtue of synesis," if only in the sense that right conscience is the same conscience that *would* be present in a virtuous (and thereby prudent) act (104).[40]

Doherty agrees with his fellow Dominican Thomas Deman about the stakes of the debate: "Either conscience is formed within prudence, or conscience is prudently formed" (107). Either conscience has the leading role in moral action and is merely assisted by prudence, or else conscience is integrated within prudence, and prudence has the leading role in moral action. It is quite evident which option was taken by Aquinas. As Doherty says, conscience is "ill-suited" to directing acts; conscience judges acts, but it is not equipped to direct them (107). For virtuous acts to take place, what is needed is prudence, with its grounding in synderesis (through wise counsel) and its conformity to right appetite as well as its ordering to election and command. Doherty recognizes that the position for which he argues is essentially that of Deman. Likewise, Doherty notes that his position on the relationship between the judgment of conscience and the judgment of prudence accords with that of Labourdette, even if Labourdette expresses it slightly differently.[41]

Servais Pinckaers, OP

In the final section of this chapter, I survey two essays that appear in *The Pinckaers Reader*: "Conscience and Christian Tradition" (1990) and "Conscience and the Virtue of Prudence" (1996).[42] The latter essay is more substantial philosophically, while the former lays out Pinckaers's theological perspective in depth.[43] Pinckaers is today widely honored as the most influential Thomist moral theologian of the twentieth century. Alasdair MacIntyre has praised Pinckaers for his "rare ability to know precisely what needs to be said and when and how and to whom to say it."[44] My survey of Pinckaers's perspective will conclude this chapter on twentieth-century Thomist views of conscience (and twentieth-century Thomist moral theology more broadly).

In "Conscience and Christian Tradition," Pinckaers first briefly summarizes St. Paul's understanding of conscience. Like Congar, he focuses on how Paul treats "cases of conscience." He finds such a case in 1 Corinthians 6, for example. Responding to the Corinthian practice of fornication with prostitutes, Paul employs arguments that rely upon reason and arguments that rely upon faith. The arguments that rely upon reason include the point that "he who joins himself to a prostitute becomes one body with her. . . . Every other sin which a man commits is outside the body; but the immoral man sins against his own body" (1 Cor. 6:16, 18). The arguments that rely upon faith include the point that "your bodies are members of Christ" and "your body is a temple of the Holy Spirit within you, which you have from God" (1 Cor. 6:15, 19). Perceiving the integration of faith and reason through Christian prudence, Pinckaers comments, "Reason and faith interact reciprocally in a progressive argument that throws light on the case at a new depth stemming from a relationship with Christ. The rule of conduct thus established is given a richness of content which philosophy alone could not have provided."[45] His suggestion here is that conscience is not an autonomous realm in which God simply speaks to human reason, laying down the moral law so that persons can obey. Instead, cases of conscience require to be inserted within the framework of Christ's body and the outpouring of the Holy Spirit.

Pinckaers notes that the letter to the Romans provides significant resources regarding the Christian moral life. The grace of Jesus Christ has convicted Paul of pride (Rom. 2–3). Wisdom, whether rooted in Torah or in the lesser path of Greco-Roman philosophy, cannot suffice by itself. What is needed instead is for God's love to be "poured into our hearts through the Holy Spirit who has been given to us" (Rom. 5:5), so that we are "dead to sin and alive to God in Christ Jesus" (Rom. 6:11). We need to receive "the law of the Spirit of life in Christ Jesus" (Rom. 8:2) and to be "children of God" and "fellow heirs with Christ" who are aided by the Spirit (Rom. 8:16–17). Pinckaers emphasizes that Paul's understanding of the moral life does not center on the rational dictates of conscience or on moral obligations but rather centers on "the living presence of Christ Jesus . . . as the source of the justice and wisdom of God, that is, of the entire moral life."[46]

On this basis, Pinckaers interprets the moral teaching found in Romans 12–15. His first step is to note that Paul connects the moral life with worship: "Present your bodies as a living sacrifice, holy and acceptable to God, which is your spiritual worship" (Rom. 12:1). It is by understanding our lives as a self-offering to God in Christ and through the Spirit that we can be "transformed" and can make manifest "what is the will of God, what is good and acceptable and perfect" (Rom. 12:2). Pinckaers observes that for Paul there is no speaking of the role of conscience for the Christian without firmly planting it within the context of prayer, the sacraments, Christ, and the Spirit. In this context, there is no danger of an individualistic ethics; instead, Paul emphasizes that "we, though many, are one body in Christ, and individually members one of another" (Rom. 12:5). As such, we must flee from pride and we must "love one another with brotherly affection; outdo one another in showing honor. Never flag in zeal, be aglow with the Spirit, serve the Lord" (Rom. 12:10–11). Paul teaches that the center of the Christian moral life is charity, not simply as a reality for the individual person but also as an ecclesial reality uniting the church.

In Romans 12, Paul goes on to list concrete, embodied virtues by which Christians show charity for God and each other. These virtues and actions include hope, patience, endurance of persecution, constancy, almsgiving, and hospitality (Rom. 12:12–13). In words that echo the Sermon on the Mount, Paul adds that we must avoid vengeance, pray for our persecutors, and care for our enemies. Instead of being proud, we must "associate with the lowly" (Rom. 12:16) and exhibit a peaceable disposition. Pinckaers concludes that what Paul reveals of his own conscience shows that he does not see the moral life as simply a matter of obedience to particular rules known by reason. As Pinckaers states, "Paul's conscience is not static, limited by rational imperatives determining what is allowed and what is forbidden. It is animated by charity's thrust toward what pleases God, toward the perfect. At the center of Paul's conscience dwells the person of Christ."[47]

Before leaving Romans 12–15, he examines how Paul approaches another notable case of conscience, namely, how the believer should relate to the civil authorities. Again Pinckaers finds a mix of arguments from reason and faith. Reason tells us that "there is no authority except from God, and those that exist have been instituted by God" (Rom. 13:1)—thereby calling Christians back from anarchism. In this context, Paul appeals explicitly to believers' consciences: "Therefore one must be subject, not only to avoid God's wrath but also for the sake of conscience" (Rom. 13:5). According to Pinckaers, this understanding of civil authority fits well with how Paul has earlier framed his discussion of charity. Recall that Paul urges believers, as part of practicing charity, to "live in harmony with one another" and insofar as possible to "live peaceably with all" (Rom. 12:16, 18). This peaceableness and willingness to subject oneself humbly to others, with a respectful attitude toward the gifts and vocations that God has given them, is reflected in Paul's exhortation to believers to be subject to civil authority. It follows that the subjection to civil authority advocated by Paul flows not only from reason but also from faith. It is a subjection that has, at its source, the God who "has revealed himself to us in the service and obedience of Christ" and whose Holy Spirit infuses us with charitable desire for the common good.[48] Pinckaers argues therefore that the "conscience" spoken of by Paul is enlivened by the Holy Spirit.[49]

He next turns to Aquinas's theology of conscience. For Aquinas, prudence receives the central place, whereas later moralists give the central place to conscience. As Pinckaers remarks, "St. Thomas's moral teaching is a morality of the virtues, organized around charity and prudence, rather than a morality of commandments and obligations imposed upon conscience."[50] Prudence, or virtuous practical reason, is habitual right reason with respect to matters of action. Pinckaers explains that practical reason has its roots in our rational inclinations or instincts toward the true and the good. These rational inclinations are a created participation in divine truth and goodness.[51] We possess the first principles of practical reason habitually, as a real and unchangeable possession. The habitual possession of these first principles—the "moral light" that we experience in ourselves—is called "synderesis" by Aquinas. As a created moral light, synderesis is the locus of the infusion of supernatural virtues by the Holy Spirit.

Synderesis informs practical reason and is inalienably possessed by each human person. Even those who lack the virtue of prudence possess the habitual moral light of synderesis. What prudence adds is "a clear, active discernment of the conditions for action and of oneself, a discernment gained by personal experience and by the kind of reflection that knows how to profit by the opinions and experience of others as well."[52] Prudence allows us to apply well, in particular circumstances, our knowledge of what is good in matters of action. By perfecting practical reason, prudence ensures that our habitual moral light is able to unfold fully in our action. Pinckaers describes Christian prudence (or the infused virtue of prudence) as "a kind of practical wisdom receiving a new, profound light from faith and a higher strength from charity, which unites it to God and deepens its understanding of the neighbor."[53] Enriched by the Spirit's gifts of counsel, understanding, and wisdom, Christian prudence enables the believer to act virtuously, in accord with the demands of charity and with the freedom of the Holy Spirit.

When we possess Christian prudence, we are able to do the right thing, putting into action the principles known habitually through synderesis. Pinckaers argues that in order to understand Aquinas's teaching on conscience—and in order to avoid the distortion caused by the manuals' conscience-centered morality—we do better to speak of prudence. In light of the gospel (especially the Sermon on the Mount), it is clear that Christian prudence has beatitude as its goal. Thus, among Christians at least, there is no domain of individual conscience separate from the whole dispensation of Christ and his Spirit. Christian prudence is an ecclesial virtue, enabling us to act with the church. Christian prudence also plays a role in strengthening human societies by ensuring that Christians obey the civil law and live in solidarity with their neighbors. The Spirit's gifts of counsel and piety enable Christian prudence and justice to tend toward the kingdom of God.

In light of the above, Pinckaers describes the place of conscience in the post-Tridentine manuals of moral theology. He notes that a standard moral manual had four parts in its first section, which was devoted to fundamental or general moral theology. The four parts covered, respectively, human acts, conscience, laws, and sins. After this first section, the manual turned to "special" moral theology, namely, the commandments of God and of the church followed by particular cases of conscience. The result was that, instead of Aquinas's (and Paul's) focus upon the goal of beatitude, the grace of the Holy Spirit, charity, prudence, and so on, the post-Tridentine moral manuals presented moral theology with conscience at the center and with the goal of showing what is forbidden and what is permitted. Freedom here is seen as *restrained* by conscience and law.

Inevitably, such freedom is "freedom of indifference"—freedom to choose (which is restrained by conscience and law)—as distinct from the "freedom for excellence" (which welcomes conscience and law) that the gospel and virtue ethics presuppose.[54] For the manuals, Pinckaers points out, if an act is obligatory, it is "under the law"; if an act is permitted, then it is "under freedom." In this system, expert moral theologians played a similar casuistical role to that played, according to this system, by conscience. The goal was to figure out what is permitted and to ensure that freedom does not pass the point of no return and fall into sin. Likewise, certain acts are found to be obligatory; one can do more—for example, one can go to daily Mass—but one cannot rightly do less. On this view, doing more is where spiritual theology comes in (prayer, the beatitudes, the Spirit's gifts), whereas moral theology proper has to do with "the determination of the legal minimum."[55] Communicating the obligations of the law to the free will, conscience operates like a great casuist, permitting this and forbidding that.[56]

Not surprisingly, therefore, a battle arises between personal freedom and legalistic obligation. Pinckaers observes that this battle characterized the centuries-long post-Tridentine history of moral probabilism, including the criticisms lodged by the Jansenist rigorist Blaise Pascal against the Jesuit probabilists of his day. In the manuals, conscience stands at the center but has lost touch with beatitude, prayer, the spiritual life, the grace of the Holy Spirit, prudence, charity, and so on. All that is left for conscience is law, freedom, and obligation. There is hardly any real need for Scripture, since once the laws are known, Scripture becomes redundant. There is not much need for the church, since individual morality is the central focus. The church, like the state, now becomes simply a lawmaking and law-interpreting mechanism. The church has value for morality only insofar as it lays down laws and imposes obligations authoritatively. Rather than studying Scripture, moralists studied the magisterium's decrees, as if the magisterium—rather than God, human nature, and human destiny as revealed in Scripture and tradition and as appropriated with the aid of philosophical wisdom—"were the source of moral obligation and doctrine."[57]

Pinckaers finds that the situation at the time of his writing in 1990 still reflects the manualist understanding of moral theology, despite Vatican II's call for a return to moral theology's sources. Prior to the Council, a legalistic conscience reigned; after the Council, conscience still reigns for most moral theologians, but now as a conscience that insists upon its freedom over against law. Thus, today's conscience-centered Catholic moral theology is merely another episode in probabilism.[58]

At the end of his essay, Pinckaers describes the proper task of conscience. He remarks, "Conscience sets us upon an astonishing road. It calls for effort that lifts us high after humbling us in submission to the moral law."[59] This effort is not about rules, duty, and obligation; instead, it is about virtues such as prudence and humility, and the road is the demanding one of love. Pinckaers concludes that the true reality of Christian conscience illustrates "the Gospel principle: he who humbles himself shall be exalted. The key to this paradox is in the hands of love, which finds its joy and fulfillment in the humility of service, after the example of Christ."[60] When we return to the gospel, we can reclaim the truth of a demanding conscience without falling into a conscience-centered morality. The truth about conscience is bearable when one discovers that God, in Christ and through his Spirit, wills to heal and transform us so that we can enjoy true flourishing, the beatitude of everlasting union with God and with the blessed.

What does Pinckaers's 1996 "Conscience and the Virtue of Prudence" add to his 1990 essay? Here he is writing after Pope John Paul II's 1993 encyclical *Veritatis Splendor*, with its appreciation for the natural inclinations (toward the true and the good) at the root of human freedom. Pinckaers appreciates that *Veritatis Splendor* makes clear that the laws or commandments of the Decalogue are a gift of divine love by which God invites his people to draw close to him. This ensures that the commandments are not misunderstood as external or arbitrary laws of an aloof God.

Describing law as "both exterior and interior, superior and immanent," he notes that "law, like conscience which bears it witness, has a spiritual and ecclesial dimension."[61] Both law and conscience are part of God's drawing us to his truth and goodness, in company with others. By means of law,

God is not giving us merely external duties that we obey as individuals; rather, God is establishing our flourishing with him and with our neighbors. Thus understood, law and conscience provide us with a real encounter with Christ, as Pinckaers indicates through a quotation from Newman that he draws from the *Catechism of the Catholic Church*: "Conscience is the ab-original Vicar of Christ."[62]

Pinckaers then turns to the virtues, which perfect our powers of knowing and loving so that we can hear and obey law and conscience and thereby attain the beatitude that God desires for us. Not only the virtues but also the gifts of the Holy Spirit (Isa. 11:2), the beatitudes of the Sermon on the Mount (Matt. 5:3–10), and the fruits of the Spirit (Gal. 5:22–23) have a central place here. The special importance of the virtue of prudence consists in its role in connecting the virtues. Since prudence is wisdom in matters of action, prudence ensures that each virtue is rightly enacted.

Synderesis is our habitual, inalienable, unchanging knowledge of the first principles of practical reason. Conscience assists prudence in applying what is known by the light of synderesis to particular cases. Pinckaers describes the fundamental difference between conscience and prudence according to Aquinas: "The judgment of conscience remains at the level of knowledge, whereas the judgment of the choosing as well as the judgment of prudence includes the involvement of the 'appetite,' that is, of the affective will."[63] Unlike conscience, prudence terminates in a command or decision to act.

A second difference between prudence and conscience is that the latter does in fact create an "obligation" on the part of the will, which is *obligated* to follow conscience. The just will is guided by the conscience's rational perception of a particular action as good or bad. But when taken out of the context of the virtue of prudence, this connection between conscience and obligation can result in our imagining conscience and obligation to be the center of Christian morality.

Pinckaers mentions a third difference between conscience and prudence. Conscience applies itself to past actions (which it excuses or accuses) or to future actions (which it approves or forbids). By contrast, prudence terminates in *present* action, even if prudence first deliberates about a possible future action and reflects upon the experience of past actions.

Despite these differences, conscience serves prudence, and both have to do with the discernment between good and evil in action. Given that conscience can be wrong, revelation and other sources, including virtuous prudence, help to form conscience. The formation of conscience enables "a fruitful application of synderesis, a real participation in its light, a true echo of the voice of God."[64] Once we realize that conscience needs formation, we are unlikely to make the mistake of placing conscience at the helm of the moral life. Far from being a merely automatic tool for judging actions, conscience needs divine revelation in Christ, the enlightening of the Holy Spirit, and the connatural knowledge that prudent and charitable actions bring. A person who repeatedly performs a certain kind of good action comes to know intuitively what pertains to good and well-ordered actions in that domain.

Although Pinckaers is wary of too much talk about conscience, he recognizes that when conscience is rightly understood, its role is important. The main point for Pinckaers is that conscience is not an individualistic or legalistic mechanism for determining what is forbidden and what is permitted. Rather, conscience's indebtedness to synderesis shows that what is at stake is our natural orientation to divine truth and goodness, and the fact that conscience serves prudence shows that moral theology involves the fullness of the interconnected virtues.

Merkelbach deems conscience to be the judgment of prudence; and he holds that a graced conscience is the rule of supernatural acts. He argues that conscience's judgment is practically practical, whereas synderesis communicates speculatively practical truth. Although conscience can err, conscience is binding due to its grounding in synderesis, or, in the case of supernatural conscience, in synderesis being used by the theological virtues. When conscience's judgment is not certain, we should follow the safer path or else, if possible, hold off on acting until we have further formed our conscience. Merkelbach helps to initiate the path toward viewing conscience in light of prudence (rather than the other way around) and toward emphasizing the supernatural life of grace. He remains committed to the Dominican probabiliorist tradition, however.

Labourdette's treatment of conscience offers a detailed analysis of Aquinas's writings on conscience in the *Summa theologiae* and especially in *De veritate*. He notes that the judgment of conscience differs from the judgment of election: unlike conscience, prudence has to do with choice. He cautions that conscience must not be conflated either with prudence or with synderesis's absolute divine voice. Notably, conscience means nothing less than ordering one's life by *truth*. Right conscience alerts us to the dictate of God's eternal law and helps to draw us toward the Good.

Labourdette corrects Merkelbach on some points, but his most notable contribution consists in his devastating critique of the post-Tridentine "morality of conscience," including the Dominican probabiliorist version of this system. In his view, after the Council of Trent (and even before it, due to the work of nominalist theologians), obligation displaced the Good, and freedom was severed from orientation toward the Good. The result was to frame morality as a competition between law and liberty, in which the "goodness" of an act consists not in participating in the Good (or even in human flourishing) but in adherence to obligation and commandment. Worse, the term "probable"—which in Aquinas meant probably *true* as distinct from demonstrably certain—came to be a mere intermediate point between true and false. Thus one might hold equally two completely opposed "probable" opinions.

Labourdette insists that moral theology needs to be reintegrated into theology as a whole, with God as the ultimate end calling humans to beatitude. Conscience needs to be subordinated to prudence, rather than conceiving of conscience as prudently judging between "probable opinions." Memorably, Labourdette denounces the "algebraic mechanism" and "pseudo-universal schematization" of post-Tridentine conscience-centered moral theology.

D'Arcy focuses on the relationship of conscience and religious freedom, with the goal of constructively developing Aquinas's position. He rightly criticizes Aquinas for disallowing invincible ignorance in matters of faith in societies where the gospel has been preached. D'Arcy values Aquinas's insistence that erroneous conscience is binding, and that natural justice should not be violated even to serve the goal of eternal salvation. D'Arcy makes clear that the main question is whether one can rightly seek to compel someone to commit a sin.

Aquinas holds that unbelievers' rites are always sins and that no one in Christian lands can reject Christianity on any other grounds than a bad will. He therefore thinks it is generally legitimate for the state to suppress non-Christian and non-Catholic rites. In response, D'Arcy urges that Aquinas should have allowed for invincible ignorance in religious matters and should have extended the principles that enabled him to apprehend that no one should compel another person to commit a sin.[65] The common good and the truth of Catholicism do not override natural justice, rooted in respect for people's duty to obey even erroneous conscience (especially invincibly ignorant conscience) in matters pertaining to God.

Doherty's contribution pertains to distinguishing conscience and prudence. Here he carries forward the work of Labourdette. Doherty identifies four grounds for distinguishing the judgment of conscience from the judgment that belongs to prudence (*synesis*). Most importantly, conscience and prudence have different formalities—only prudence is involved with moving the will to operation—and prudence alone has a relation to right appetite. The judgment of conscience may be correct even when the judgment of election fails, thereby demonstrating that conscience and prudence must be distinct.

Doherty also demonstrates that in the act of prudence it is correct to identify the judgment of conscience and the judgment of prudence as numerically the same. *Synesis* takes up within itself conscience's task, to which it joins the element of conformity to right appetite. Doherty proposes that this way of viewing conscience's participation in the judgment of prudence solves, for the prudent person, the problem of doubtful conscience.

Like Labourdette, Pinckaers urges a return to the perspective of Aquinas and virtue theory, with the desire for God (beatitude) and Christ's eschatological outpouring of the Holy Spirit at the center, and with the natural inclinations, natural law, new law, virtues, gifts of the Spirit, beatitudes, and fruits as the path. Like Congar, Pinckaers examines how Paul treats "cases of conscience" and shows that Paul inserts them within the framework of the mystical body and the outpouring of the Spirit. Christian moral life must have the personal presence of Christ at its core, and therefore such things as prayer, worship, the sacraments, and charity must be foregrounded. Pinckaers's contribution consists in unfolding the characteristics of supernatural (graced) conscience. Not only reason but also faith informs conscience's judgment.

Pinckaers's critique of the manuals' conscience-centered moral theology is essentially the same as Labourdette's, including with regard to freedom and the Good. He distinguishes conscience and prudence along the lines proposed by Labourdette and developed by Doherty. Conscience's true role consists in passing judgment on past and future acts rather than creatively steering the entire moral organism.

According to Pinckaers, a prudent and charitable Christian will live a self-sacrificial life in all areas of his or her being. Sustained by prayer and the sacraments, he or she will perform the works of mercy and will bear the cross even unto martyrdom.[66] Christian conscience, therefore, can be expected to be a *demanding* voice, calling us upward to the flourishing that consists in sharing in the divine life.

It should be evident that the two giants of twentieth-century Thomistic moral theology, Labourdette and Pinckaers, provide a rich understanding of conscience within prudence and within the Christian moral life as a whole. Labourdette warns that the Catholic moral theology of his day, in the 1950s, is in danger of moving from a mechanistic conscience-centered legalism to a new conscience-centered subjectivism. Pinckaers makes clear that this concern in fact came to pass after the Council. How this happened is the subject of the next chapter.

Chapter 4

Conscience and German Thought

In a study of twentieth-century developments in understanding conscience, German philosophy and theology merit a special place. This is so for two reasons. First, the influence of twentieth-century German philosophers and theologians is difficult to overestimate. In the twenty-first-century church, German-speaking theologians and bishops remain the dominant intellectual leaders, as they largely were in the twentieth century as well.

Second, in the 1920s and 1930s, the existentialist philosophers Martin Heidegger and Karl Jaspers paid significant attention to conscience and thereby paved the way for further developments after the Second World War.[1] As John Gallagher points out, in the years surrounding World War II, "Heidegger's philosophy and situation [or existential] ethics were capturing the minds of intellectuals."[2] In the 1930s and 1940s, German Protestant theologians such as Dietrich Bonhoeffer and Karl Barth developed what became known as "existential ethics" that proved highly influential upon German Catholic theologians in the 1940s and 1950s. Describing his seminary studies in the aftermath of World War II, Joseph Ratzinger has recalled widespread interest in the thought of Heidegger and Jaspers.

In this light, my fourth and final chapter will survey the approaches to conscience found in major twentieth-century German-speaking thinkers. Without being able to be exhaustive or to tie these figures together into a tightly knit history, I examine the perspectives of eight figures, two of whom are philosophers, two Protestant theologians, and four Catholic theologians.[3] I arrange the eight figures chronologically: Martin Heidegger, Karl Jaspers, Dietrich Bonhoeffer, Karl Barth, Karl Rahner, SJ, Josef Fuchs, SJ, Bernard Häring, CSsR, and Joseph Ratzinger. Although Heidegger's breakthrough work is atheistic, his earliest publications exhibit what Edward Baring terms a strong "proximity to the progressive neo-scholastics," and it was not until after 1916 that he separated himself from Catholic faith and began to read heavily in Protestant thought.[4]

As for Jaspers, Baring points out that "by the early 1930s he had risen to become the leading figure of Existenzphilosophie," outpacing Heidegger in certain ways.[5] Jaspers's perspective "allowed Christian existentialists to foreground Heidegger's discussion of the human individual over and against 'scholastic' ontology."[6] The emphasis on the human individual was highly significant for existential ethics in both its Protestant and its Catholic forms. Peter Joseph Fritz comments in his recent study of Rahner, while discussing Heidegger's perspective: "*Dasein*, as conscience, summons itself 'back to the stillness of itself'. . . . The uncanny call of conscience for Heidegger summons *Dasein* to its 'ownmost distinctive possibility.'"[7] Fritz goes on to connect this perspective with Rahner's epistemology, and rightly so, but it could equally be connected with (though not equated with) Rahner's existentialist understanding of conscience, in light of his transcendental anthropology.[8]

Among the German Catholic theologians whose thought bears the imprint of existentialism is Theodor Steinbüchel, who directed the doctoral thesis of Bernard Häring and also had a notable impact upon Servais Pinckaers and Joseph Ratzinger.[9] As Steinbüchel shows in his 1948 *Existenzialismus und christliches Ethos* and his posthumous *Religion und Moral*, existentialist and personalist insights can in fact be helpful in Catholic moral theology.[10] In *Existenzialismus und christliches Ethos* (a short pamphlet rather than a full-scale book), Steinbüchel appreciatively remarks that existentialist philosophy, like Christianity, is concerned with the person's "deeper and valuable self."[11] At the same time, he warns that existentialist philosophy must not reject God as the transcendent ultimate end of the human person.[12] In *Religion und Moral*, Steinbüchel argues that the human person "knows in the depths of his conscience that no one can forgive him his guilt"—no one other than God, whose mercy is paramount for Christian morality.[13] He adds that in the depth of our conscience we make decisions that no general law can govern but that come to us as "a demand of the personal God," requiring our obedience.[14]

The Nazi horror, including the collaboration of so many Christians in Germany and elsewhere, only increased the popularity of existentialism.[15] Jaspers describes the stunning blow that was the National Socialist epoch, during which (in 1937) he was removed from his teaching position and his life was put in danger: "The extent of man's capacity for monstrous deeds, of the intellectually gifted for delusions, of apparently good citizens for perfidy, of the seemingly decent person for malice, what is possible to the mob in the way of thoughtlessness, of selfish short-sighted passivity, all this became real to an extent that the knowledge of man had to undergo a change."[16] For Jaspers, the horrors of the Third Reich were a confirmation of his existentialist philosophical perspective, in which he urged people to live up to the demands of reason and to appreciate the importance of personal decision rather than bowing to mere external authority.[17]

Although existentialism boomed in popularity after the war, it did not emerge fully vindicated. For one thing, Heidegger and Jaspers, while insisting upon personal self-discipline, cast doubt upon moral absolutes. In this regard their approach (especially Heidegger's) fit with the Nazis' rejection of absolute moral norms. In *The Nazi Conscience*, Claudia Koonz remarks: "The popularizers of anti-Semitism and the planners of genocide followed a coherent set of severe ethical maxims derived from broad philosophical concepts. . . . Because they believed that concepts of virtue and vice had evolved according to the needs of particular ethnic communities, they denied the existence of universal moral values."[18] In the early 1930s at least, Heidegger, whose understanding of "conscience" emphasizes authenticity, considered Hitler to be (in Koonz's words) "authenticity personified."[19] Koonz points out that Heidegger, unlike Jaspers, not only publicly supported the call-to-arms of "the Nazi Party's racial expert, Walter Gross," but also "asked his Jewish students to find other mentors and cut off their financial aid."[20] For a number of years, Heidegger was a supporter of the Nazis in significant ways.[21]

Given that many Catholics went along in some way with the Nazis, postwar German theologians argued that if prewar Christians had actually learned to form and follow their consciences in an existentially authentic way, they would never have fallen in line with such an evil external authority.[22] Inspired by Protestant theologians such as Bonhoeffer and Barth, but taking in their own direction the Protestant emphasis on personal encounter with the commanding God, many leading German Catholic moral theologians focused their postwar attention on the personal decision of conscience in concrete situations and on the person's fundamental existential stance.[23] Rahner was already moving firmly in this direction during his wartime years at the Pastoral Institute of Vienna, and Fuchs was not far behind.[24] In the late 1950s and 1960s, as we will see, these theologians shifted further, emphasizing the radical historicity of human nature and downplaying the universality of moral norms.

In the resulting postconciliar Catholic moral theology, a reconceived view of conscience remained at the center. This new conscience-centered Catholic moral theology no longer focused upon receptivity to eternal law and universal moral norms, let alone upon adjudicating "probable opinions" of post-Tridentine casuists. The ongoing centrality of (now radically reconceived) conscience would have surprised earlier reformers such as Fritz Tillmann and Theodor Steinbüchel. Yet, Häring's three-volume work from the early 1950s, *The Law of Christ*, never was "a totally consistent rejection of the manuals."[25] After the Council, the manualist tradition was radically modified but, in terms of the driving role of conscience, continued creatively on in the dominant strand of academic Catholic moral theology.[26]

Martin Heidegger

Few twentieth-century philosophers were as impactful as Martin Heidegger, and his work continues to be widely celebrated today. For many scholars, as Michael Inwood remarks, it is clear that Heidegger "was (with the possible exception of Wittgenstein) the greatest philosopher of the twentieth century."[27] Heidegger's breakthrough book, *Being and Time*, appeared in 1927, and a significant section treats conscience.[28] Paul Strohm observes that for Heidegger, "the call of conscience is inherently empty, more concerned with self-differentiation of the self from the multitude than with any characteristic ethical content."[29] Other scholars are more positive, without disagreeing fundamentally with Strohm's summation. For example, Rafael Winkler holds that for Heidegger the call of conscience enables the person "to be otherwise, to be itself authentically, that is, to be itself self-responsibly."[30] John Caputo argues that Heidegger's understanding of conscience provides for a highly valuable awakening "to the abyss beneath every ground" and thereby should attune us today "to the excluded of every community, to the plurality of ways to be, to the different," through "a profoundly pluralistic, decentered openness to the other."[31]

Both critics and admirers of Heidegger's theory of conscience agree that personal authenticity cannot be specified in moral norms. As Paul Ricoeur says in criticizing Heidegger on conscience: "Cut off from the demands of others and from any properly moral determination, resoluteness remains just as indeterminate as the call to which it seems to reply. . . . It is as though the philosopher were referring his reader to a moral situationism destined to fill the silence of an indeterminate call."[32] For scholars such as Caputo, however, this indeterminacy is a benefit, not a problem.

In *Being and Time*, Heidegger argues that humans are not merely "Sein" (being) but rather are "Dasein." By this term, he means that the kind of being that we are is reflective upon its own being, which is a being-toward-death. Dasein's authentic self-actualization comes through embracing its absolute finitude. Heidegger states, "Dasein always understands itself in terms of its existence, in terms of its possibility to be itself or not to be itself. . . . Existence is decided only by each Dasein itself in the manner of seizing upon or neglecting such possibilities."[33] Heidegger avers that "Dasein exists as thrown being-*toward*-its-end," and the challenge is to give oneself up to this truth without flinching (241).[34]

In this light, Heidegger's treatment of "conscience" is concerned about inauthenticity, which characterizes people who refuse the truth of their being (i.e., being-toward-death or annihilation). To become "*authentic being-one's-self*," a person must freely affirm and embrace the potentiality-of-being that is authentic being-toward-death (258). The manifesting of this potentiality-of-being—the fact that embracing it is a real option for us—is attributed by Heidegger to what he calls "conscience."

Heidegger conceives of conscience as a "phenomenon of Dasein" (259). Conscience calls; conscience summons. Heidegger observes, "The call of conscience has the character of *summoning* Dasein to its ownmost potentiality-of-being-a-self by *summoning* it to its ownmost being-guilty" (259).[35] Those who "hear" the summons show that they want to choose authentic being-a-self by embracing (rather than fleeing from) their being-toward-death. According to Heidegger, however, most people are inauthentic Dasein.

If conscience calls Dasein in its lostness to authenticity, does the call come from the person? Does Dasein call itself? Heidegger suggests that this is so in one sense, but not in another. He states that "ontologically it is not enough to answer that Dasein is the caller and the one summoned *at the same time*" (264). A person's deepest potentiality-of-being differs in a certain sense from the Dasein who is called. This source of the call in our deepest potentiality explains the authority of the call. Rafael Winkler comments: "the call always strikes Dasein as absolutely unfamiliar and strange, uncanny (*Unheimlichkeit*). . . . It unsettles its being-at-home and makes conspicuous its singular being-in-the-world."[36]

Dasein experiences itself as having been thrown into existence. What Heidegger calls "attunement" occurs when Dasein recognizes this thrownness and thereby comes face to face with itself. But it finds itself to be alarming and it experiences "anxiety." Dasein summons itself away from the lostness of its inauthenticity. Dasein calls to itself, to its lost self (caught up in distraction), from the core of its own "being-in-the-world, as not-at-home" (266). Heidegger describes this call of Dasein to itself as rooted in the fact that Dasein is "care" (267). For Heidegger, therefore, it would be a mistake to appeal to a universal conscience or a public conscience, since "conscience" pertains radically and solely to one's uniqueness. The whole point of conscience is to enable the person to turn away from the distraction of the world—including the world's false notions of a universal conscience—and to face the truth of Dasein.

Heidegger affirms that the call of conscience judges us as "guilty." To be "guilty" is the same thing as "being-the-ground for a being [Sein] which is determined by a not" (267). Guilt in this sense is fundamental to Dasein, because a "not" (namely, our *thrownness* into existence, our existential nullity) belongs to the intrinsic core of Dasein. His point here is existential, not moral. He explains, "Dasein exists as thrown, brought into its there *not* of its own accord. It exists as a potentiality-of-being which belongs to itself, and yet has *not* given itself to itself" (267). This existential "not" is the core of Dasein as "guilt." The call of conscience always charges Dasein with this existential guilt, this situation of "being-the-ground of a nullity" (274).[37] Our existential guilt is that we are constantly thrown into situations that we did not choose.

In the face of our uncanniness (inclusive of "guilt" understood in the above sense), conscience calls distracted Dasein to embrace being-toward-death and thereby to acquire authenticity. The alternative is that Dasein will succeed in permanently closing "itself off from itself as thrown," unable to accept itself as being-toward-death and therefore living in a condition of permanent distraction (275).

Heidegger asks whether his reflections can be squared with what he calls the "vulgar" or common understanding of conscience, namely, the idea that conscience is a judgment about the moral goodness or badness of an action. To reiterate, his view is that conscience is an ontological reality, not something that has to do with intellectual judgment: conscience is Dasein's call to authenticity in "being-guilty" by embracing the radically "thrown" character of human existence, which can have no security or permanence whatsoever in the face of death.

In response, Heidegger begins with the experience of a "bad conscience." He strives to show that the "calling back" we experience takes place "in such a way that authentic, existentiell *being*-guilty precisely 'comes after' the call" (279). The guilt is the primal condition of being thrown into existence; and the call of conscience seeks to enable us to embrace this guilt (our "thrown being") rather than distracting ourselves from it.

Summoned by conscience into itself, Dasein becomes "still in the stillness of itself" (284). The result is "resoluteness," Dasein's *disclosedness* at its height, constituted by finally "being-in-the-world" in *truth* (284). As Inwood comments, "Dasein assesses the possibilities implicit in its situation and makes a decisive choice."[38] It is when Dasein stands in the "truth of existence" (of being-toward-death) that Dasein is *"authentic"* (284). Authentic existence opens up the real "relevance" and "significance" of all things, as "the concerned being-with with others is now defined in terms of their ownmost potentiality-of-being-a-self" (285). Note that "resoluteness," in its fundamental choice, does not rely upon and cannot be measured by "any established moral code."[39] No moral rules govern the choice of a resolute person; the choice is simply the decision or fundamental stance of authentic Dasein in light of the whole of its being-toward-death.

Insofar as obeying the call of conscience means determining upon a fundamental existential stance that accepts (without any loopholes) our own mortality, Heidegger thinks it is the root of "care" for others. He states, "It is from the authentic being a self of resoluteness that authentic being-with-one-another first arises" (285). A resolute person, with an authentic existential stance, knows what to do in every situation, without programming this action ahead of time.

In this discussion, Heidegger often comes back to our need to be rescued from the vulgar mass of people who live inauthentically, having distracted themselves from the truth of Dasein (for example, by hope for an afterlife). The person who, living in accord with the call of conscience, has attained to resoluteness is one who no longer lives in the lostness of the vulgar mass of people. Even though the vulgar mass remains predominant, "it cannot challenge resolute existence" (286). This is because only authentic persons, having heard the call of conscience, can rise to the level of each situation. Heidegger claims along these lines that "the call of conscience does not dangle an empty ideal of existence before us when it summons us to our potentiality-of-being, but *calls forth to the situation*" (287). Having embraced Dasein, being-toward-death, a person lives in accord with his or her own existential position and thereby lives authentically and in accord with conscience in every situation. The resolute person does not need to appraise a situation, but rather he or she is already *acting* with existential authenticity and concerned care in the situation.[40]

CHAPTER 4

Karl Jaspers

Heidegger turns conscience into a call from the deepest depths of Dasein to achieve authenticity by embracing being-toward-death, so as to act authentically in each situation without need for moral norms. The existential intensity of this argument is apparent, as is its nihilistic rejection of anything transcendent. Heidegger gets rid of conscience understood as the application of moral knowledge to particular actions.

For many theologians, Karl Jaspers's existentialist approach to conscience was even more influential than Heidegger's. During the same years that Heidegger was writing *Being and Time*, Jaspers was writing his three-volume *Philosophy*, which was published in 1931. Heidegger consistently belittled Jaspers's philosophical work; and Jaspers, in his brief autobiography, does not mention Heidegger.[41] Jaspers explains the purpose of his work: to create "disquiet in the reader by provoking him to his potential *Existenz*, to encourage him in becoming himself, to conjure up in him the possible meaning of Being, and to let his thought founder on the uncomprehended."[42]

In *Philosophy*'s second volume, *Existenzerhellung*, Jaspers reflects at length upon Existenz and upon "absolute consciousness." Just as Heidegger's thought revolves around Dasein, Jaspers's thought revolves around Existenz.[43] Jaspers defines "Existenz" as follows: "there is the being which in the phenomenality of existence *is not* but *can be*, *ought to be*, and therefore decides in time whether it is in eternity. This being is myself as *Existenz*. I am Existenz if I do not become an object for myself."[44] Existenz is just the subject (the self) freely existing, an existential phenomenon rather than an object for intellectual dissection.

Jaspers differentiates between "existential nonbeing" and "vital nonbeing" (198). We exist in a broader current of being that does not depend upon the "vital being" of this or that person; the annihilation of individual persons in death (their "vital nonbeing") does not put an end to the broader current of being. Existential nonbeing would only occur if the broader current (i.e., the evolving cosmos, transcending all individuals) ceased to be. Thus, personal annihilation need not worry us so long as the story of the cosmos continues. On this basis, Jaspers teaches that Existenz, which means living meaningfully "in the *present existential reality of the moment*," requires the context of the broader current of cosmic being and cannot be squared with existential nonbeing per se, i.e., with the annihilation of the cosmos (198). But Existenz *can* be squared with vital nonbeing, i.e., with our own nonbeing. In Jaspers's view, our "empirical" or "vital" existence must not be absolutized, and it need not be absolutized if the continuance of the broader cosmic current of existence is assured and if our Existenz actualizes its potential. He concludes, "*Total nonbeing* will horrify an Existenz to the extent to which in existence it has betrayed its potential. A realized potential, on the other hand, fulfills my life until old age may permit me to tire of living. Lacking a future, I can be at peace in existence, no longer knowing even the question of an existence after death" (199).

Indebted to Friedrich Schleiermacher, Jaspers probes more deeply into Existenz. He proposes that a person who enjoys "absolute consciousness" is one who possesses a true "sense of Existenz, the consciousness of true being from an unconditional source" (225). Dwelling securely in Existenz, one is assured of stability and purpose. Speaking about "absolute consciousness," Jasper comments: "It rests me when I am restless, reconciles me when I am enmeshed in strife and tension, helps me decide when I truly ask" (225). Existenz and absolute consciousness are experienced subjectively but cannot become an object of our intellect. They are the flow of life and communication, which, if we pause to analyze it, slips from our grasp.[45] Jaspers praises absolute consciousness as reflecting "the source of any grasp upon mundane existence in its nonobjective historic depth, the source of the unconditional actions of Existenz and of the manifestations of transcendence" (227). Again, transcendence requires a broader current of cosmic existence transcending the individual's subjective existence but does not require the radical transcendence of a Creator God or eternal life in a personal sense. The key in absolute consciousness is the experienced knowledge that being, including self-being, is not meaningless, so that we are able to be Existenz, living fully "in the *present existential reality of the moment*" (198).

In the midst of his discussion of absolute consciousness—true and secure Existenz—Jaspers reflects upon conscience. The conscience is the self calling to the self at the deepest core of the self. According to Jaspers, in conscience "my empirical existence is addressed by the source of my self-being" (234).[46] Conscience is our deepest self trying to keep us on the right path. At the deepest core of the self, we choose our basic stance: for or against Existenz.

Jaspers explains further: "Conscience is the basis on which I must recognize or reject what is to have being for me, the reality that interposes itself between my existence and my true self-being, which is not yet manifest to me" (234). Conscience challenges us to "soar and seize [our] being and feel it is true" (234). At the very core of our being, conscience presses and challenges us to fully adopt the true existential attitude that is Existenz, so that in absolute consciousness we embrace our self-being in its meaningfulness.

Jaspers does not deny that conscience has to do with good and evil. Good and evil, though, are measured by absolute consciousness, not by moral norms. What is good is absolute consciousness, the enjoyment of Existenz. What is evil is anything that turns us away from absolute consciousness. It is "fulfilled absolute consciousness" that is the standard applied by conscience (235). Jaspers connects this *fulfilled* absolute consciousness with love and faith, although he does not at this stage develop the latter notions.[47] His point is that we only know good and evil, in matters of action, when we are living in absolute consciousness, Existenz. To act in a good way is to enhance Existenz.

Without citing Kant, Jaspers adapts and expands upon Kant's categorical imperative, now grounded by Jaspers's understanding of Existenz. Jaspers affirms, "What I do should be such that, by this standard, I *can will a world* in which it *must* be done everywhere. What conscience shows me is a universal being I can forever affirm. . . . *What I am in my actions I want to be eternally*, says this standard" (235). This does not refer to eternal life as conceived by Christianity, but rather to a positing of eternality. If our lives were to recur eternally in an everlasting cycle, we would still want to do precisely this thing; if we were held responsible for all the consequences, we would still want to do precisely this thing. For Jaspers, we can say such things about an action—and we can say them with conviction—because the action is "a phenomenal manifestation of intrinsic being" (235).

Conscience, therefore, helps us at the core of our being to become the self that we should be. It presses us to choose to *be* in a deeper way, in the fullness of Existenz. The result of attending to conscience, says Jaspers, is self-determination through "an existential decision of absolute consciousness" (235). Conscience requires that we decide in favor of being what we should be; and "resolution"—obeying the voice of conscience—is not based on conditional reasons. It is an existential decision, one that is taken unconditionally because it belongs to our fundamental existential stance for or against absolute consciousness or Existenz. In this existential decision in obedient response to conscience, our whole self is involved, everything that we are and know.

Once we arrive at resolution, we can be said to have arrived at maturity; but maturity is a beginning point rather than an endpoint. In the unfolding of our life, true resolution will be displayed insofar as we remain faithful to the existential decision to be the self that we should be, that our core self calls us to be. Resolution involves the entirety of our self-being and therefore is determinative over the shape of our entire life. Jaspers emphasizes the rigorous "resoluteness of my inmost self-being" in obedience to the self-calling voice of "conscience" (236). When it speaks from the core of human Existenz—from an existential attitude that recognizes the transcendent meaningfulness of being even if one's personal existence is snuffed out by death—conscience is "infallible" and can acknowledge "no superior judgment" (236).

Jaspers emphasizes the autonomy of the self-calling conscience, pressing us toward (fulfilled) absolute consciousness. No external rule or law, however widespread, and no feeling or arbitrary impulse of the will, let alone any self-interest or purposeful goal assisted by a particular means, can govern conscience. Conscience is found only at the existential core of the person in the quest for absolute consciousness, pure Existenz.

Indeed, human conscience is obscured whenever one stays on the surface rather than channeling down to one's existential core. Jaspers warns, "The human conscience is lulled to sleep by all objectivities, by conventions and by moral laws, by institutions and by society" (237). We must break through all of these barriers in order truly to possess conscience, that is to say, to be guided truly by our self-being toward full attainment of Existenz. Jaspers shares Heidegger's negative view of the mass of human beings by contrast to the person who truly has conscience. According to Jaspers, the person who truly has conscience will be misunderstood and persecuted unless he or she stays silent. He remarks in this vein, "The masses recognize only a common conscience—that is to say, none at all. This is why a really original conscience must not show itself in the world" (237). Instead, true conscience will know that what matters is "existential communication between one individual and another," because here the quest for fidelity to one's deepest self-being can be fruitful (237). This is especially so given that conscience will continually press us toward a deeper Existenz, and therefore conscience will always "prick" us (237).

Since Jaspers strongly rules out the notion of conscience as God's voice, it may seem that conscience isolates us in the self. For Jaspers, however, what conscience does is to enable "the factual communication between Existenz and Existenz" (237).[48] What would isolate us in the self would be to hear *God's* voice; this would lock us inward, communing with God, whereas real conscience is invested in communication with other people, since communication belongs to the core of Existenz. Certainly, there is only individual conscience, not a universal conscience. But this is because Existenz, absolute consciousness, involves real communication that must be rooted in individual self-being (and thus the development of self-being through self-questioning). If there were no individuals, there would only be monologue, not communicative dialogue.

It follows that any claim to know in conscience the *divine* will, the divine voice, is false. Such claims distance us from our existential ground, our self-being and our interior call to absolute consciousness, by pressing us to listen to God's voice rather than to our own core being. For Jaspers, too, Jesus's claim to absolute authority must be false because it would separate him from all other humans and would alienate those who obeyed him from their own existential core, their self-being in its deepest form.[49] Jaspers notes that Jesus's followers have in fact, sadly, used their claims about God to justify their own misdeeds and their power over others; many of them have simply deified the church.[50]

What is needed instead is the endless existential quest into one's own self-being, the source of conscience's self-calling. In making this existential quest, people will not be locked in themselves but instead will adopt a stance of continual communication, in accord with the mandate of absolute consciousness. Again, if we deem conscience to be God's voice, then, even if we intend to obey this voice, we have estranged ourselves from true conscience that "is precisely not God's voice but the moved and moving source of the truth of my being" (240).[51] If we hand ourselves over to a voice not our own, we have abandoned the self-being, the true Existenz, that conscience calls us to *be* more and more fully.

Does the movement of conscience, however, end ultimately "in nothingness, with conscience at a standstill before the void" (241)? Jaspers thinks not. Conscience is not the endpoint; being is. The current of being transcends us. A fulfilled absolute consciousness involves "incommunicable mystical union with transcendence" outside this world, by which self-being merges with being and thereby transcends the personal self (241). Existenz, however, is phenomenally in this world, acting and thinking. As Existenz, absolute consciousness is connected by Jaspers with love, faith, and imagination.

What does Jaspers mean by these terms? He states with regard to love: "Conscience remains aimless without love; lacking love, it will lapse into empty stringency and formality" (242). Love allows for not-knowing, and love "restores us to assured being" (242). In love, Existenz stands firmly assured that nothing will be lost or meaningless, because the broader current of being will ensure the significance of self-being. Love reaches out to other persons, seeing "the other's being and originally, groundlessly, and unconditionally [affirming] it as being" by willing it to be (242). Self-being and self-surrendering are revealed by love to be identical. Love grounds the communication between Existenz and Existenz; love reveals that being is not impersonal. Love is infallible because it sees clearly. Jaspers adds that love defines faith: "Faith is love's explicit, conscious certainty of being" (243). Faith is not belief in God but belief in being and the meaningfulness of being. As Jaspers says, "Instead of taking me out of the world by an uncertain knowledge of a beyond, faith keeps me in the world by the mundane perception of what I can transcendently believe in" (244).

Thus, faith possesses a transcendent dimension, but not in the sense of faith in God. Instead, every Existenz has in itself, in its phenomenality, "a sense of transcendence" insofar as it is related to cosmic being (244). This transcendence cannot rightly be objectified, as it is for Jaspers in Christian faith. So long as "God" is not objectified—so long as the term "God" has no clear cognitive content—one can speak of faith without ruling out "God." Certainly, faith believes in being, believes in a "sense of [Existenz's] originating in a transcendent relation" (245). Faith trusts in "the ground of being"; faith is "sure of being" (245).[52] Faith is belief that we can act meaningfully and truly in history. Faith's belief in "being" or being's "ground" is ultimately a stance, in conscience, of self-being toward the cosmic current of being.

Such faith grants that every human person and plan will die and come to nothing in itself. Such faith grants that humans do not exist again in an afterlife, or through descendants, or through their place in a progressive historical unfolding. Yet faith's power consists in never losing touch with the "transcending certainty of being" (246). For Jaspers, our faith consists in perceiving, in everything, "the reality of being," so that concrete existents "seem translucent" to being, which we grasp by imagination (246). The existential stance of Existenz—the core self-being—thus goes beyond the empirical. Jaspers states, "Formative imagination is a life in forms that symbolize being; speculative imagination, a life in thoughts that make sure of being" (247). But what "being" in the transcendent sense means cannot be pinned down intellectually, except to say that we have self-being and it cannot be limited to the empirical.

Jaspers does think there are moral norms, such as "You shall not lie." However, this does not mean that conscience's task is to apply such norms.

On the contrary, Jaspers emphasizes that such moral norms have "an alien objectivity" and that "in some situations lies may be truthful acts although their truth will not be that of an objectively valid law," because objectivity is not everything (313–14). What matters is the concrete situation. In the concrete, Existenz will know what to do, because "the unconditional ought comes from the autonomy of a free Existenz that hears itself and thus relates to its transcendence. What it hears as the right is its self-being" (316).[53] Through the self-call of Existenz, and thus in the freedom of true Existenz, right action will come about. What conscience properly does is to challenge us constantly to deepen our Existenz, to "soar and seize [our] being and feel it is true," in communication with other Existenz (234). The call of self-being to deeper and purer being, as found in Existenz or absolute consciousness moving toward fulfillment in love, is what Jaspers means by "conscience."

Dietrich Bonhoeffer

As we will see, Jaspers's perspective on situation ethics has a large impact on postwar Christian ethics, as does Heidegger's. In a certain sense, however, it would be difficult to find a perspective that diverges more from that of Heidegger and Jaspers than that of Dietrich Bonhoeffer, since he insists upon a God-centered and Christ-centered worldview. Yet Bonhoeffer (among others) helps to develop a Christian situation or existential ethics.

Bonhoeffer's work contains a significant engagement with Heidegger, including in the domain of conscience and the moral life.[54] Recall that for Heidegger, we are "called" from our deepest potentiality, called to become who we truly are, to live a life not of distraction but of "*authentic* being-one's-self."[55] For Jaspers, at our deepest core we must choose our existential stance, and we must heed conscience's call to choose Existenz. Both thinkers hold that in the concrete situation (outside of any universal moral law), the authentic person will know what to do.

Bonhoeffer holds a similar position in certain respects. As Barry Harvey notes, against the existentialist philosophers, Bonhoeffer rejects "the shift from a transcendent to a transcendental locus of authority," in which "the I is now responding not to a You but to its 'higher' self, with the role of the other recast as the occasion of responsibility to one's higher self."[56] But Bonhoeffer also deploys central existentialist elements, such as the view that conscience is a call to self-unity and that personal morality cannot be governed by universal moral norms.

Bonhoeffer's earliest reflections on conscience appear in his *Act and Being*, published in 1931.[57] In *Act and Being*, he offers an extensive summary of Heidegger's *Being and Time*, which he praises as "the most recent and encompassing phenomenological investigation," and in which he finds the important insight that "Dasein is the existence of human beings in their historicity, in the momentariness of the decisions that they, in every instance, have already taken."[58] In a further section of *Act and Being*, he explores the difference between "being in Adam" and "being in Christ." Being in Adam means being in sin. In Scripture, God reveals that humans at the outset tore "themselves loose from community with God and, therefore, also from that with other human beings," so that now humans "stand alone, that is, in untruth" (137).[59]

At this stage, Bonhoeffer argues that invocations of conscience are merely an attempt to be our own judge and therefore are a form of idolatry. Alienated from God, we feel the weight of our alienation. We indict ourselves, using "the language of conscience" and even claiming repentance (138). We imagine that we no longer need God even for judging us. Bonhoeffer concludes that "such conscience is of the devil, who leaves human beings to themselves in untruth"; and he deems that such "conscience must be mortified when Christ comes to human beings" (140).

Having set forth law, next Bonhoeffer sets forth gospel. He explains that when Christ comes to us, we know in faith that we have utterly nothing in ourselves or of ourselves on which to rely. Left to our own devices, even our conscience is put to the service of our miserable pride. Christ reveals our guilt and our spiritual death. Bonhoeffer remarks in this regard, "When conscience is said to be an immediate relation to God, Christ and the church are excluded, because God's having bound the divine self to the mediating word is circumvented" (141).

It follows that conscience cannot pronounce definitive judgment upon the sinner; only Christ can do this. The death of the sinner occurs not in conscience but in Christ, since it is Christ who bears all sins. Can there, then, be a conscience "in Christ"? Yes, but not if conscience is still seen as somehow independent from Christ. Conscience is only beneficial spiritually if it "is the place where Christ, in real temptation, kills human beings in order to give them life or not" (142). All too often, Bonhoeffer reiterates, conscience serves a deadly purpose. In our conscience, we discern our solitude and desperation; but *through* our conscience, using our own resources, we try to overcome our solitude and desperation. In so doing, we show that we have not really grasped the truth of our solitude. Instead, we experience "merely a general consciousness of being-left-alone, and this is what conscience is to eliminate by restoring human beings once again to themselves" (148). Conscience enables us to experience anxiety in the face of "the powers of this world, law and death," which dominate us (148). But this anxiety has the tendency to lock us within ourselves even further, as our conscience attempts to conquer what threatens us.

Fortunately, Christ does not leave us in this condition. He "assails human beings through the law" so that we experience temptation and understand our solitude properly: namely, as guilt (148). In Adam, we use our conscience in order to repel the truth about our solitude by trying to be our own savior. But Christ shows us that we cannot ward off death by any resources of our own. We are truly and inescapably mired in sin and death. This experience is a profound trial for humans, bringing with it "ever anew the horrors of eternal death," since the experience of solitude is now recognized for what it is: we may be eternally cut off from God, and everything depends not on us but on God (149).

Having allowed us to enter into this temptation and experience of death, Christ succeeds in finally turning our eyes away from ourselves and toward God as Savior. Christ thereby makes it possible that, for us, "life should come from death" through "God's free gift" (149). We discover that Christ died for our sins, meeting us in our very death and taking our part, overcoming death once and for all. In faith, we focus no longer on ourselves but now on Christ; we no longer seek salvation through ourselves but only in and through Christ. Again, Bonhoeffer reiterates that the creature simply cannot be known *as creature* (as distinct from *as guilty in Adam* and *as saved in Christ*). He states, "There is no ontological specification of that which is created that is independent of God being reconciler and redeemer, and human beings being sinners and forgiven" (151).[60]

Bonhoeffer goes on to make another striking claim about conscience: it exists only in a state of sin. This means that, in Christ, "conscience is something defined by the past in Adam" (155). We will not have conscience in eternal life. For Bonhoeffer, conscience is primarily our voice, not primarily God's. This is because conscience leads us to reflect upon ourselves, rather than turning outward and reflecting upon Christ.

Does conscience then have any positive role for us in Christ? Certainly not if conscience tries to come between Christ and the believer. Conscience can do this by pointing "relentlessly" to our sinfulness, thereby tempting us to forget about Christ and to fall into despair (155). Such conscience is a tool of the devil, operative against the Christ who wills to offer his mercy to us.

Nevertheless, there is a positive place for conscience when we are in Christ, insofar as conscience perceives our sinfulness but perceives it "within the forgiveness through Christ" (156). Such conscience inspires repentance, not as a human work attempting to save ourselves but rather as part of our belief that Christ has forgiven us on the cross. When conscience does these things in Christ, it helps to keep us in Christ rather than allowing us to return to a life of pride.

Bonhoeffer also treats conscience briefly in his 1937 book *Creation and Fall*. Here he develops his thought as a biblical meditation. He argues that when in Genesis 3:8 the man and woman (having sinned) hide themselves from God, this flight from God is precisely "conscience." He reaffirms that conscience comes into existence only after the fall. The trouble with conscience is that, while rightly condemning us as sinners, it seeks to give the human being a place of security apart from God. In conscience, humans appoint themselves to be their own judges, thereby claiming to know good and evil for themselves and avoiding God's judgment. For Bonhoeffer, therefore, "Conscience is not the voice of God to sinful man; it is man's defence against it, but as this defence it points towards it, contrary to our will and knowledge."[61]

The fact that God does not allow us to hide in our conscience is symbolized by God's calling to Adam in Genesis 3:9. We are tempted to think that by wallowing in remorse and so on we have done what is needful. But what is needful is in fact coming out of ourselves and hearing the divine word of grace in Jesus Christ. Conscience tells us that we cannot stand before God; whereas God commands us to come out and stand before him.

When Adam confesses his sin to God, he shows how persistent we can be in taking refuge in our conscience. Adam admits what he has done, but Adam implies that God is at fault because it was God who gave Adam the woman, Eve. Appealing "to his conscience, to his knowledge of good and evil," Adam "has accused his Creator" and has rejected the grace that God is offering him.[62] This is an all-too-frequent move on our part. When cornered in a sin, we respond by blaming God for putting us into the situation. We use our conscience as a means both of hiding from God and of trying to pin the ultimate blame upon God.

Bonhoeffer did not live to see his *Ethics* published; it remained unfinished at the time of his imprisonment by the Nazis. Between 1940 and

1943, he wrote the text that we now have, which was edited and published by his friend Eberhard Bethge after Bonhoeffer's execution by the Nazis. In this final text, he takes a significantly different view of conscience.[63] So long as conscience is "heard as the call of human existence to unity with itself" and "comes as indictment of the loss of this unity and as a warning against the loss of one's self" (notice the Heideggerian language here) then conscience is positive and valuable.[64] Influenced by Heidegger, he argues that conscience is primarily about integrity of being, not about particular acts except insofar as our acts can jeopardize our integrity of being. When alerted by conscience that a particular act will threaten our self-unity, we must obey conscience on pain of corrupting and destroying our own being. Thus, he states, "Action against one's own conscience runs parallel with suicidal action against one's own life, and it is not by chance that the two often go together" (242).

Yet, on the other hand, the self-unity of a fallen human being is built upon the lie of pride, the desire to be our own God. We have a false, egoistical self-unity that in fact is monstrous. From this angle, conscience must be identified as dangerous. In accord with his earlier discussions of conscience, Bonhoeffer remarks that conscience "presupposes disunion with God and with man and marks only the disunion with himself of the man who is already disunited from the origin" (24). Conscience in this sense is the voice not of God but of "apostate life" (24). Conscience is correct about what actions are not permitted, but conscience fails to alert the sinner that, in the state of sin, even actions that are permitted are still bound up in the state of sin. The very fact that a movement of conscience arises in us indicates that we are sinners in need of the reintegration that can come only from God. By arrogating the place of God, conscience claims that we truly do know good and evil and no longer need God as judge (or, therefore, as Savior). In this state of sin, conscience focuses our life on self-knowledge rather than on knowledge of God. It is as though by knowing and judging ourselves we could reunify our being (25). This claim is a monstrous lie that enables us to hide from Christ. As Bonhoeffer warns, in this sense "the call of conscience has its origin and its goal in the autonomy of a man's own ego" (243).

Through faith in Jesus Christ, says Bonhoeffer, the crimped call of conscience is transcended and, miraculously, the lost unity of the human person is restored—through divine judgment and divine grace. At this stage, however, Bonhoeffer asks a question that differs from anything that he previously had asked. What is the relationship between insisting that the call of conscience is fulfilled only in and through Christ, and seeking the fulfillment of the call of conscience in another man (e.g., Hitler)? If Christians require looking outward to another person (Christ), how is it that this move does not warrant others' looking outward in the same way, though with a different person in view?

Bonhoeffer responds by observing that the person in whom our self-unity is truly found must be no less than our Savior. Conscience calls us to a self-unity that is only realized through Christ. Since self-unity itself is fallen (due to its connection with pride), our true self-unity comes about through union with Christ. We must surrender our ego. We rightly say, "Jesus Christ has become my conscience" (244).

How can we trust Christ so radically? In his life, he gave up everything for the love of God and of his fellow human beings. He did not live by law alone, since he acted to purify all human law and to direct it to the accomplishment of God's love. He freely allowed himself to be counted among the guilty and refused the temptation of power and prestige. He never focused on himself. In this way, he "sets conscience free" even "from the law" (244). Had he followed the law alone, he never would have sinned, but neither would he have allowed himself "to enter into the guilt of another man for the other man's sake" (244).

Bonhoeffer applies this point to our situation: "The conscience which has been set free [from the law, by Christ] is not timid like the conscience which is bound by the law, but it stands wide open for our neighbour and for his concrete distress" (244). In other words, if in conscience we only avoid doing what is wrong, that is not enough. Conscience must be expanded in Christ so as to open us up to the suffering neighbor out of love for God and neighbor. Bonhoeffer's own actions vis-à-vis Hitler exemplify his meaning. Bonhoeffer, imitating Christ, chose to bear guilt because of his love for his guilty Nazi neighbors and (even more so) for those whom they were persecuting. His love led him to determine to break the law against killing the head of the nation, out of love for the people of that nation.

Against Immanuel Kant, Bonhoeffer therefore denies that it is necessary to follow the moral law at all times. For Kant, it is necessary to speak truthfully about the whereabouts of one's friend, even to someone who intends to kill this friend, because conscience demands that we must never lie. Bonhoeffer sees this as a perfect exemplification of the proud, self-focused conscience that is blind to love for neighbor. Violating conscience makes us guilty, but to bear guilt in the name of charity can be the right thing to do.[65] Conscience alone cannot suffice and in fact easily becomes a cover for pride; we must turn to Christ and obey him directly in the particular situation.

While affirming that it is sometimes necessary to bear guilt (by violating conscience) out of love, Bonhoeffer places two limits on this principle. First of all, we should not do anything that violates our true self-unity. Surrendering our ego, even to the point of doing something technically forbidden by conscience (such as lying), differs from *destroying* the ego. When we are considering taking responsibility in Christ along lines that involve violating conscience, this cannot mean that we should do something that is simply too burdensome for us to bear. Second, the moral law that is upheld by conscience is not nothing; we are not free simply to disregard it. Mere disregard for the law upheld by conscience will inevitably result in an irresponsible action. We cannot discard the law "as it is explained in the Decalogue, in the sermon on the mount and in the apostolic parenesis" (247). This law, after all, is the law of love and the law of life. We are free in Christ to violate it in particular instances, but only for the most serious reasons of life and love. We can violate it because it now takes second place to Christ, and so "in the contest between conscience and concrete responsibility, the free decision must be given for Christ" (247). This does not impede self-unity but rather establishes it because Christ is "the Lord of conscience," and it is he who gives us true unity (247).

In Christ, and only in Christ, are we free to go beyond the limits of conscience in responsible action, without destroying that which conscience serves, namely, self-unity. We are free to do this only when our action and our freedom from conscience's limits are "forced" upon us by a necessity of love, and only when in so acting we stand before God not in pride but in a plea for grace and mercy. Bonhoeffer concludes, "It is only when the concrete vocation is fulfilled in responsibility towards the call of Jesus Christ, it is only upon the foundation of the knowledge of the incarnation of Jesus Christ, that conscience can be free in concrete action" (257).[66]

Karl Barth

Writing in response to Karl Jaspers's *Philosophy* and to existentialism in general, Karl Barth observes that existentialist philosophy offers "the picture of a self-enclosed human reality beyond which there is nothing to confront it."[67] Barth firmly rejects such a worldview. As with Bonhoeffer, however, his position also resonates with some elements that we found in

Heidegger and Jaspers. Most importantly, like Bonhoeffer, he questions the application of universal moral law to particular situations faced by persons. In such cases, he affirms that Christ retains the freedom to command whatever Christ determines to be fitting for the person in the situation. He conceives of Christian ethics as a response to a personal divine command and as requiring humans to choose a basic existential stance.

In part due to his correspondence with Bultmann in the 1920s, and also through his brother Heinrich Barth (a philosopher and sharp critic of Heidegger), Barth was well aware of Heidegger's work although he kept his distance from Heidegger.[68] In 1950 he criticized the existentialism of both Heidegger and Jean-Paul Sartre in *Church Dogmatics* III.3, on the grounds that "nothing" plays the central role in both philosophers.[69] Nevertheless, as Edward Baring observes regarding Protestant dialectical theologians in the early 1930s, "Because they dramatized the absolute dependence of man on a divine other, the ontic aspects of Heidegger's thought (his analysis of human existence) seemed promising."[70]

John Webster has observed that in the 1920s Barth gave conscience a central role in ethics, though only as part of his task of "pull[ing] ethics away from its magnetic attraction to moral consciousness, towards an ordering centre in the being and act of God."[71] In Barth's later *Church Dogmatics*, the place of conscience is somewhat reduced, given that the focus is even more firmly on the divine command, which can encounter humans through various venues and not solely through conscience. In both Barth's early and later work, conscience is Christologically defined as a reality of the inaugurated eschatological kingdom, insofar as the one who commands is the God who reigns in Christ and the one who receives the command is known by God as a new creation.[72]

Let me begin with Barth's *Ethics*, a set of lectures written in 1928 but published only after his death.[73] In these lectures, Barth first describes conscience as "our human knowing of what, not merely according to our own presuppositions, God alone can know as he who is good, as the giver of the command and the judge of its fulfillment, namely, of the goodness or badness of the act which I am about to commit or upon which I look back already as committed."[74] We know what God *alone* can know, because God *alone* commands and God alone judges. But how is it that we too can know what God alone knows?

In response, Barth warns: "It is overhasty to call [conscience] part of man's constitution by creation" (475). The problem is that when we appeal to the order of creation, we fail to perceive how radical conscience is. If conscience is our co-knowing of God's command, this is because God's command is an "eschatological determination" (476).[75] As such, conscience involves our own fallenness and fallibility. It is a co-knowledge of not only of our wickedness but of the wickedness of conscience itself. Moreover, as real *co*-knowledge, conscience requires that we be in Christ; it requires faith, hope, and love. It requires "our divine sonship, the reality of our eternal future reaching into our present, i.e., the future of the Lord who, in bringing himself to us, brings our own future" (477). Lacking such fellowship with Christ, no "conscience" can exist. Put another way, "To have a conscience is no more and no less than to have the Holy Spirit. For 'no one knows what is in God except the Spirit of God' (1 Cor. 2:11). To have a conscience is to know what is in God, to know his judgment on our conscience" (477).[76]

Thus, "conscience" for those who are in Christ means two things. It means knowing our own sinfulness and error; and it means knowing (co-knowing) this wickedness of ours by the presence of the indwelling Holy Spirit who enables us to know the judgment of Christ upon us. Conscience simultaneously reflects the fact that we are condemned and the fact that we are redeemed. Absent the indwelling of the Spirit and fellowship with Christ, we have no "conscience"—no way of knowing that we are sinners, no way of co-knowing God's judgments and commands. Barth connects this point with his interpretation of Romans 2:15's reference to the gentiles, "their conscience also bears witness and their conflicting thoughts accuse or perhaps excuse them." In his view, such self-accusing and self-excusing cannot be authoritative; at best such a "conscience" could only be "a witness to and prototype of the judgment of the true conscience that is captive to the Word of God" (477). The only conscience that can tell us the truth (co-knowledge) and that can be authoritative is the conscience of the person united to Christ and participating in Truth incarnate.

The true conscience, then, is never independent or autonomous vis-à-vis Christ, but rather it is our hearing of Christ's judgment and command. The Christ whose commands we know in conscience, furthermore, is the coming Christ who has inaugurated his kingdom in the Spirit. This requires prayer, begging God for the gift of the Spirit and of adoption as sons in the Son. Conscience is not neutral with respect to the distinctive elements of Christian life; instead, conscience is possessed in the mode of prayer.

On this basis, Barth firmly "reject[s] all more primitive ideas of conscience, the idea of a voice of truth immanent in man by nature, or that of a voice of humanity which sums up supposedly individual voices of conscience" (478). Naturalism and idealism cannot give us a true understanding of conscience. We can never possess God's judgment and command as our own (non-eschatological) possession. We should not imagine that there is a neutral domain in which we know good and evil abstracted from the actual historical reality of sin and redemption, or abstracted from Christ and the Spirit. Far from being natural, neutral, or within our control, conscience is an eschatological reality. Barth argues that if there really were an authoritative natural answer book available in conscience, ethics would be incontrovertible—whereas in fact "if we let people tell us what their conscience is saying to them," conscience "can have almost any concrete content" (479).

As a co-knowing, conscience truly is the person's own voice—not the voice of the person's fallen self but rather the voice of the eschatologically new self in Christ. Conscience is also God's voice, since co-knowledge means precisely that "God speaks to us through ourselves" (481). Thus, conscience is indeed (as Friedrich Schleiermacher thinks) "a God-consciousness immanent in human self-consciousness," but not in the way that Schleiermacher supposes (481).

In conscience, we present ourselves with an authoritative commandment that must be obeyed. We do so as our eschatological self, co-knowing with Christ. But we *receive* the command of conscience as our fallen self. It is therefore difficult to hear the command of conscience as it really is. In fact, conscience is a *"final* judgment" upon us (482). In Christ, we find ourselves free to act upon this judgment, through our freedom as God's adopted sons, a freedom that also binds us. As Barth puts it, "the child of God recognizes in the voice of genuine authority the voice of his father which he obeys spontaneously and in freedom. 'My sheep hear my voice' [John 10:27]—because they are my sheep" (483). Only in Christ do we have freedom; only in Christ do we have true conscience; and only in Christ can we truly obey God. Barth adds that the "education" of conscience makes no sense given that what is truly at issue is whether we have become God's children.

Quoting Karl Adam and Robert Bellarmine, Barth observes that for Catholic theologians the voice of conscience in every person has binding force, even if one's conscience decrees (for example) that one must not belong to the church. For Protestant theologians, says Barth, conscience likewise has binding status—but only so long as the conscience stands bound to God's word. Insofar as it does so, then it will truly be free with the freedom of the children of God. However, Barth reiterates that the hearer of conscience is a sinner. Even if the voice of conscience (the voice of our eschatological self in Christ) resounds in us, we may obscure or distort it in our hearing of it. Christians therefore do not possess conscience in a triumphalistic way. On the contrary, "Even as the children of God we tell ourselves something very different from what we learn from it. Our self-dialogue is undoubtedly a constant self-misunderstanding" (485). Barth warns against the abuse of conscience that he considers to be afflicting both Protestants and Catholics, who use a de-eschatologized notion of conscience to uphold a "mad autonomism [self-law]" (485). When heard rightly, conscience is our co-knowing of God's absolute reign, and conscience propels us forward toward this eschatological perfection.[77]

All depends, then, upon whether our conduct (as commanded by conscience) advances us toward the promised future in which God will reign perfectly. In this sense, "conscience is the living and present message of the coming kingdom of God" (487).[78] Conscience requires that we live entirely in accordance with God's promises, so that God alone secures our future. Conscience does not allow us to rest content in any present, whether of the world or of the church. Conscience makes of us radical pilgrims who, in active prayer, await God's action rather than trying to be God for ourselves. In conscience, our life "is hid with Christ in God [cf. Col. 3:3]" (489).[79]

Thus, part of conscience's content is that we must wait upon the God of the promise. But another part consists in the fact that we must hasten to obey God's call. Awaiting the coming Christ, we must act; we cannot build the kingdom, but we must work toward it. This does not mean that the fullness of the kingdom of the Holy Spirit can be found anywhere, whether in the Roman Catholic Church or in an earthly millennium or kingdom of the Spirit. But it does mean that we cannot shy away from committing ourselves, through action, to the promised future.

Of course, even though conscience is always primarily God's word and not under our control, the fact that we can hear it in a distorted form means that we must always listen for the Spirit's confirmation and never become arrogant or imperious in our obedience. After all, any absolute "triumph" of conscience's voice can only take place at the eschaton, the full establishment of God's reign. We need to be modest; we should speak to others out of the commands of conscience that we have received, but without commanding others as though we (not God) were the ones who could establish unity in Christ. Barth states in this regard: "The greater the urgency with which we address others in the name of conscience, the more we have to consider the alternative that, while this might be an appeal to the miracle of God, it might also be the illegitimate expansion of a decidedly human reality" (494). Instead of pressuring others in conscience, we must be willing to stand alone if need be and thereby to allow God to bring others in conscience to our side—if we have rightly heard God's judgment and command.

Barth considers, too, that what God commands in conscience here and now may change later. Again, conscience is an eschatological event; and God speaks his Word at each moment rather than allowing his command to become our enduring possession. We cannot "store up" conscience's commands, no matter how true they are, for later use. We do not "possess a store of verdicts of conscience on which we need only draw industriously to be obedient to conscience" (495). No matter how good our moral principles are, they are not God's commands. We must be open to new commands of God; we must be open to being obedient to what God says in each new day. Otherwise, our security would come from ourselves rather than from the living God.

Agreeing with Ritschl, Barth makes a final point in his *Ethics*: there is not a "good conscience" that is parallel to a "bad conscience." Rather, conscience simply has to do with accusation; and a "good conscience" would be merely the absence of such an accusation. Conscience disrupts us by calling us to order, as measured against the absolute perfection of the kingdom of God. Thus, in reality, we will always have a bad conscience if we are being faithful to God, or at least our "good conscience" will be hidden in Christ, as part of losing our life in Christ.

Barth discusses conscience at various points in his *Church Dogmatics*, but I will focus here upon two instances. In his discussion of the doctrine of God in volume two (part two) of *Church Dogmatics*, published in 1942, Barth examines the nature of a divine command. A command of God, he says, "is a claim addressed to man in such a way that it is given integrally, so that he cannot control its content or decide its concrete implication. . . . It comes to us, therefore, with a specific content, embracing the whole outer and inner substance of each momentary decision and epitomising the totality of each momentary requirement."[80] One can see how this fits with the understanding of conscience described above, and so it is not surprising that Barth at this juncture offers at short excursus on conscience. I note that in the *Church Dogmatics*, as Gerald McKenny remarks, "Barth begins with the bold and rather startling claims that God alone knows and judges good and evil and that God accomplishes the good in our place."[81]

The excursus begins by comparing the "idea of the good" with the "idea of God's command" (666). Both the good and the divine command can be understood to be God, but the difference between the two notions is that the good is our own idea, whereas a divine command—if it is truly such—comes to us from outside ourselves. Barth briefly treats Kant's categorical imperative, and he argues that the problem with it is that, as a formula, it cannot really be a command. All such formulae are at best only a sign or remembrance of an actual command, and therefore in practice they tend to "minister to the illusion in which man wills to be good of himself and to impute the good to himself" (667).

The notion of conscience, Barth fears, falls into the same trap. When conscience is thought to be the supreme judge to which we are accountable morally, we set ourselves up as our own autonomous judge. Properly understood, "conscience is the totality of our self-consciousness in so far as it can receive and proclaim the Word and therefore the command of God as it comes to us, in so far as we can be participants in the divine knowledge . . . because God Himself wills to speak with us" (667).[82] Again, this means that conscience is not an anthropological possession, but an eschatological one. It requires our union with Christ and the Spirit in order to exist. It looks to the future perfection of the kingdom of God, which only Christ and the Spirit can bring about. Outside of union with Christ by faith, we do not have conscience, because outside of Christ our knowledge or self-consciousness cannot be "claimed as the organ of the divine will and claim and judgment confronting our will" (668). Moreover, even when we do possess conscience in Christ, we do so without claiming any primacy or independence for our conscience. The primacy always belongs to Christ, and nothing that is our own can be "ranked above or even alongside the Word and command of God" (668).

Barth is even more insistent upon this latter point than he was in his *Ethics*, where he spoke about "co-knowledge" and about "our" voice. Now he emphasizes instead that God's "command is not revealed and given *by* conscience but *to* conscience," and conscience functions *solely* to hear and bear witness to God's command (668). Conscience does not serve to make intelligible what would otherwise be unclear and indefinite. God's command does not come to us in a formless way. Conscience does not play the role of shaping or interpreting or applying God's command so that we can thereby understand what God wills to say. Rather, conscience has a witnessing function: it reminds us of God's command, and it testifies that God's command is directly addressed to us. The key point is that there is nothing lacking in God's command per se.[83] In fact, God's command serves to awaken conscience in the first place, assuming that conscience does awake.

In its task of witnessing, conscience alerts us that we may not diminish God's command by subordinating it to ourselves. Conscience helps us to stand "against every perversion of the divine command into the dictates of our self-will" (668). Thus, a properly functioning conscience will assist us in appreciating that our will is not God's will, and that God's command has free charge over "the totality of our life" (668). God does not need our conscience's help in order to speak personally, freely, authoritatively, and directly. Still, conscience has a role, namely, bearing witness to God's commands precisely in their sovereignty over any human volition.

The second brief discussion of conscience in the *Church Dogmatics* that I will examine comes from the third volume (part four) on the doctrine of creation, originally published in German in 1951. Remarking that Christian dogmatics treats the word of God, and Christian ethics treats this Word as *command*, Barth states, "Man's action is good in so far as he is the obedient hearer of the Word and command of God."[84] This point leads Barth into his distinction between "general ethics" and "special ethics." General ethics explores God's command as God's claim upon human beings through the power of his merciful grace in Jesus Christ. In general ethics, God's sovereign decision to redeem humankind stands at the center. The purpose is to show that "good human action is action set free by the command of God, by His claim and decision and judgment" (5). Special ethics, by contrast, focuses upon human action under God's gracious command. Special ethics therefore treats concrete acts. It has to do with the acting person in the complexities of history. As Barth puts it, special ethics "follows the work of grace and the Word and command of God into the distinctive lowlands of real human action and therefore into the sphere of concrete human volition, decision, action and abstention, into the events in which this particular man realises this particular condition and possibility and therefore himself" (6).

Barth does not conceive of special ethics as guided by universal moral norms drawn from natural law, Scripture, and church tradition. He does not think of God's commands as cognitively or textually present in this way. He denies that the task of special ethics is to take divinely ordained laws and to apply them to individual cases, building up a set of prohibitions and permissions regarding what should or should not be done in particular circumstances. In short, Barth denies that special ethics is ultimately about making determinations in cases of conscience.

He portrays the casuistic ethicist as rushing "to the help of doubtful and groping consciences in their individual decisions" and offering "precise and detailed information about good and evil in relation to what man has done or intends doing" (7). Barth holds that while such an approach to special ethics may sound tempting, it is rooted in a longstanding (dating, he suggests, to the early second century) "lack of confidence in the Spirit (who is the Lord) as the Guide, Lawgiver and Judge in respect of Christian action" (7). It misreads Scripture as a legal text. Although Tertullian and Ambrose are implicated in this Ciceronian misreading, the real impulse for casuistic ethics comes from the development of the sacrament of penance and the confessional in the early medieval period, as can be seen in the tradition of medieval penitential manuals treating a vast variety of cases of conscience.

According to Barth, the Reformation sought to reclaim the freedom of the Christian, the fact that Christian Scripture is not a legal text, and the fact that natural law is not the basis for Christian ethics. But in the second half of the sixteenth century, Protestants failed to carry forward their breakthrough—and in the meantime the Jesuits perfected the casuistic art. Barth bemoans that "by the end of the 16th century matters had gone so far that the Puritan William Perkins was willing and able to write a book, *De casibus conscientiae*, in which he gave a systematic account of the correct individual decisions enjoined upon a Christian. This was followed in 1630 by the even more famous work of Wilhelm Amesius, *De conscientia*" (8). Further work along the same lines continued in the Reformed and Lutheran world. Barth considers that more recent Protestant ethics, informed by Pietism and idealism, has not resolved the problem, even though it has placed more emphasis on purity of intention and less on law and external action.

He does not wish to dismiss casuistic ethics without granting its strengths. Although he rejects it, he appreciates its recognition of the decisive significance of human choices, each of which takes place under a concrete command of God. God claims and judges the person in light of each specific action's positive or negative relation to his specific command. Barth allows that "conscience" may mean the encounter, in specific cases, of God's command and a person's specific action, and this encounter really is describable as a case of conscience.

Individual humans are never alone but always exist in relation to others. Humans have duties toward each other, including the duty to warn each other about particular courses of conduct or to encourage each other in particular courses of conduct. In every case of conscience, we are called to listen to the judgments of our friends and to the judgments of the wise—even if the action is ultimately up to the individual. Casuistic ethics, therefore, has this dimension also in its favor, since it brings the judgments of wise fellow Christians to our attention and does so for our good in specific questions about how to act. As a practical matter, casuistry is frankly unavoidable, nor would we wish to avoid it. Barth fully grants that we have to make the effort "of understanding God's concrete specific command here and now in this particular way, of making a corresponding decision in this particular way, and of summoning others to such a concrete and specific decision" (9).[85]

But he still rules out "casuistical ethics." This is because he denies that God's command can be universalized in such a way as to be trotted out and applied in cases. Christianity is not a set of legal texts, and God confronts each person at each moment in a radically distinct way. No ethicist can determine for God what is good for a particular person at a particular moment. Only God can determine this; and only the particular person— and certainly not the universalizing ethicist who attempts to sit in God's throne—can know God's command.

Barth maintains that his position accords with that of John Calvin. We require a "practical casuistry" in lived Christian experience as we seek to obey God's command in a specific circumstance, but we cannot trade the actual encounter with God for a moral guidebook drawn up by humans.[86] We cannot place God's commanding will under the control of human ethicists. The relation of every human to God must be that of a recipient and beneficiary, not that of an expert who knows what God must will. God's free grace must be left to work freely at each and every moment in each and every life.

Barth points out that although the Decalogue and the Sermon on the Mount (among other texts) are often put forward by theologians as the ground and justification for casuistry's universal laws, in fact these teachings have a specific context, and God (or Christ) addresses himself to a quite specific people.[87] When theologians treat these teachings as universal truths, cut off from their context, then the same theologians have to go to great lengths to apply here and now the supposed universal truths, employing "all kinds of amplifications and additions drawn from the treasures of natural law and tradition" and thereby revealing that the teachings are being misunderstood and misused (13).

Barth also bemoans what casuistic ethics does to Christian freedom, which consists in the freedom to obey God's specific command in a particular choice or action. God's grace is at the heart of God's command, and it is grace that frees us for obedience to God's command. Without Christian freedom, God's command cannot hit its target, because God wants our free obedience. God desires not merely our external accordance with rules but our interior, free appropriation of God's command. Without this interior assent and self-offering in response to God, there can be no "good conscience" or "clear conscience" (13–14). This interior assent must respond to God rather than merely to a human casuistic rule. Conscience is only good when our action involves the gift of our whole self precisely to God, in the willing of a particular action.

The fundamental problem with casuistic ethics, says Barth, consists in its asking too little of human beings. In making this point, Barth quotes Bonhoeffer saying the same thing about the historical and personal specificity of God's commandments. Casuistic principles, no matter how seemingly salutary, cannot stand in for the living God's concrete encounter with Christians in their freedom. Ethics must trust "the authority, guidance and judgment of the Holy Spirit" in the life of the Christian who faces a decision, as each of us constantly does, of "practical casuistry" in cases of conscience (16).

Barth is not saying that God is continually issuing a (barely intelligible) stream of commands to each individual. On the contrary, Barth remarks that "we do not have a disconnected multiplicity of individual demands, claims, directions and prohibitions"; rather, what we encounter is "a single and unitary command," even though every encounter with the living God is unique and context specific (16). In history, God works out his plan, and this plan is not fragmentary. Human lives, too, are not fragmentary, as though each action or decision arises without any context. It is the same human subject who acts in the course of many individual actions and decisions. The God who commands is the providential Creator, Reconciler, and Redeemer. The root of truly fruitful special ethics, then, will not be the universalizing casuistry of the ethicist but the constancy of the God who commands. This divine constancy can be known by attending to God's "Word revealed in Jesus Christ."[88]

In the encounter in which God commands the free human being, God will not be other than who he is as revealed in Christ, namely, "Creator, Reconciler and Redeemer," and so "wherever and whenever the command of God encounters a man, it is always determined by the fact that He is this

God" (25). God is no arbitrary, inconstant, or fragmented commander, but rather he is the one whose commands will never be in contradiction with the gracious, holy, covenanting, faithful God whom he has revealed himself to be. Likewise, the ethical event is not mere randomness or arbitrariness, because the human person who receives the divine command is always "God's creature and covenant-partner, the pardoned sinner, the child of God" (26).

Special ethics should be developed from within these divine constancies, which ground the true reality of each and every historical moment. Within these constancies, we are able to recognize that the only true joys— the only things good for us, the only things that accord in truth with "our conscience, our *syneidēsis* or agreement with God"—are actions that reflect our commitment, in faith's freedom, "to rejoice in God Himself as the Creator and Lord of life, as the Giver and Revealer of all its provisional fulfillments" (382).[89] Barth's ethics is an existentialist or situation ethics, therefore, insofar as it rules out the discernment and application of universal moral norms, but not insofar as it is anthropocentric or lacking in any consistent content.

Karl Rahner, SJ

In his *Twentieth-Century Catholic Theologians*, Fergus Kerr, OP, includes Karl Rahner among the ten most important Catholic theologians of the century.[90] Rahner's influence was equaled after the Council only by that of Joseph Ratzinger, whose impact on academic theology was comparatively minimal prior to his election as pope. Like Ratzinger, Rahner served as a *peritus* or theological advisor to the German bishops at Vatican II. After the Council, a steady stream of publications that combine scholarly depth with an unusual pastoral range enabled him to have an enormous impact upon the theology taught in Catholic seminaries and universities worldwide.

As a doctoral student in philosophy in 1934–35, Rahner studied under Heidegger for four semesters, attending his lectures assiduously.[91] The result—in conjunction with the influence of the writings of Joseph Maréchal—was what Hue Woodson calls Rahner's "existential theology of experience," even if neither Rahner nor Heidegger thought of himself as an "existentialist."[92] Vincent Holzer has shown how strongly Rahner's work resonates with Heidegger's in the 1930s, so that, metaphysically speaking, "Rahner is closer to Heidegger's meditations on Being than to Kantian analytic," even if "the Heideggerian source of Rahner's thought is at times quite neglected."[93]

In the 1930s, numerous German-speaking Jesuits engaged at length with Heidegger's thought. In addition to Rahner, the list includes Erich Przywara, Alfred Delp, Hans Urs von Balthasar, Caspar Nink, August Brunner, and J. B. Lotz, among many others. In 1940, while serving during the war at the Jesuits' Pastoral Institute in Vienna, Rahner published an instructive essay on Heidegger, "Introduction au concept de philosophie existentiale chez Heidegger," which anticipates his influential 1941 book (based on lectures given in 1937) *Hearer of the Word*.[94] Rahner's essay is both critical and appreciative, and he proposes that Heidegger's thought could be profitably developed in light of transcendental anthropology—which is in fact what he himself strove to accomplish.[95]

In 1944 the American Catholic philosopher James Collins remarked that in Germany "the enthusiastic support of a majority of young thinkers and of the thinking laity has been enlisted in favor of the philosophy of existence as expounded by its chief representatives, Heidegger, Jaspers and Heyse."[96] Collins argues that German Catholic scholars have done crucial work by drawing out the good aspects of existentialist philosophy while criticizing its bad aspects. For Collins, the work of Alfred Delp was particularly significant. Imprisoned by the Nazis in July 1944 and executed by them in February 1945, Delp—with whom Rahner had hoped to collaborate on scholarly projects—urged from prison: "The Society [of Jesus] must again become a source for springs of creativity. I hope very much Karl Rahner manages that for theology."[97]

Rahner made contributions to Catholic moral theology that arose from his appreciation for existentialism. During the war, Rahner and other young German Jesuits began to explore and address the "personalistic and voluntaristic conception of ethics" or existential ethics that we found in Barth and Bonhoeffer (and Bultmann) and that is also present in Emil Brunner, Helmut Thielicke, and other Protestants from this period.[98] Representative of the Jesuit reception of existential ethics is Hans Wulf's 1949 "Gesetz und Liebe in der Ordnung des Heils," in which he describes the existential-ethic position of the German Catholic layman Ernst Michel. Wulf held that the casuistic manuals were responsible for some of the moral disorientation of German Catholics because they produced an existentially impoverished laity. Mark Graham summarizes Wulf's argument: "Instead of fostering the skills and insights necessary to solve new and complex moral issues, the Catholic Church's practice of handing down moral laws to the faithful had dulled their moral decision-making skills and left them unable to deal effectively with emerging moral issues."[99]

Rahner agreed with this charge, and, beginning in 1946 with his essay "The Individual in the Church," he labored steadily, joined by other German Jesuits such as Hans Hirschmann and Josef Fuchs, to reconfigure the Catholic Church's moral theology along existentialist lines.[100] In 1946, against the notion that the application of universal moral norms can suffice for Catholic moral theology, he suggested that "within the Church he [every human being] has a truly private sphere, in the sense that this cannot be immediately reached by the Church as a lawgiving society."[101] Rahner deemed that existential ethics was correct to posit a personal domain of action that moral norms cannot regulate. As we will see, in the late 1950s and 1960s Rahner moved toward a more fully existentialist position, reconceived in light of transcendental anthropology, with regard to such themes as conscience as the self calling to the self, the choice of a fundamental existential stance, and the inapplicability of universal moral norms.[102] Like other Christian thinkers of this period, he highlights what Heidegger in 1947 termed "the abode (*ēthos*)" of the human being, "the human being's essential abode from being and toward being"—in Christian terms, ethics as encounter with God in the deepest core of the person's being.[103]

Let me begin by surveying "Principles and Prescriptions," published in 1957. Here Rahner has in view "ethically important precepts, addressed to the conscience and the practical creative power of an individual, a nation or an age."[104] His argument is that universal "principles" have bearing upon human nature, whereas "prescriptions" have bearing upon individual human beings. Like Barth and Bonhoeffer, but without their insistent Christocentricism, he suggests that we need to think of the individual human being as "the object and goal of a moral demand which is not identical with the validity of general principles, but is a concrete, particular, individual obligation."[105] Such a particular obligation is a "prescription." Indeed, Rahner indicates that any time one has in view something more than universal human nature, one will be dealing not with a general principle but with a particular, individual prescription, although he assumes that the prescriptions will not be in contradiction to the principles.

On the one hand, in 1957 Rahner affirms a universal natural law and universal moral principles. Natural law follows from the fact that each human being has a human nature. On the other hand, distinct human persons have a particularity and a personality that go beyond generalized human nature. This means that even after applying universal moral principles, there are often various licit possibilities for action. It is up to personal discernment to determine what is the right path for the individual person, a discernment whose outcome is not determined by any universally applicable law.

Rahner here mentions prudence, which, as he notes, is a virtue neglected in the moral manuals. His understanding of prudence is largely what Aquinas would have deemed to be conscience. He states, "prudence first envisages the full range of general principles, then the concrete circumstances and inquires what principle or combination of principles is to be actually applied in precisely these circumstances."[106] In Rahner's view, prudence operates on the level of general principles, even though it has in view the application of these principles to a concrete case. Likewise, the church's teaching office remains on the level of promulgating general principles, normative though they are.

When it comes to the individual person, therefore, the power to discern what Rahner calls *prescriptions* will be required. In actual human life, the decisions that individuals make (or that collectives such as the church make) cannot be reduced to an application of general principles. An individual does not merely obey or disobey general rules; rather, guided by the Spirit, the individual truly discerns what is right for him or her as a uniquely existing human person.[107]

Applying this argument to the situation of Germany, he notes (surely with the Nazi era in mind, though not only the Nazi era) that German Catholicism possesses many true principles, but the question is "why these principles when preached are so little heeded."[108] His answer is that the German church lacks, and has lacked, "a statement of prescriptions"— not universal moral precepts but concrete summons to specific actions, to existential decision, in the actual and uniquely personal life of individual human beings and of the church.[109] He warns that if the church and its preachers speak simply at the level of general principles, people will not connect existentially to this teaching. As a result, they will turn away and, "from sheer boredom," they will "submit to the yoke of men who possess prescriptions even if they are false and short-sighted ones."[110] Existential prescriptions are what interest persons. These prescriptions must come not from the church's magisterium, but from preachers united closely to the people or, better, from individual persons themselves, in accord with the proper freedom of the lay apostolate and with true spiritual discernment. Here probabilism can be put to use, if simply to underscore that "a prescription based on probability is better and surer than a merely correct abstract principle from which no action springs."[111] The point is that if

Christianity lacks existential purchase, its moral principles will come to nothing; and appeals to universal moral principles are not what is needed when speaking to concrete persons.

In "On the Question of a Formal Existential Ethics," published in 1955 in the second volume of his *Theological Investigations*, Rahner evaluates "situation ethics" or "existential ethics." On the one hand, he rejects the subjectivism of much Protestant situation ethics; but on the other hand, he notes that existentialism has already been shown to be of significant value for ethics, including by many trusted Catholic moral theologians such as Josef Fuchs and Theodor Steinbüchel (and by Rahner himself in earlier essays). Against subjectivism, Rahner deplores "the explicit or implicit denial of the absolute validity of material norms for the human person as such," including "in the concrete situation."[112] Although Rahner does not mention Barth and Bonhoeffer, one can see connections with their perspective in the following definition of "situation ethics," which Rahner criticizes: "Norms are universal, but man as an existent is the individual and unique in each case, and hence he cannot be regulated in his actions by material norms of a universal kind. Man is the believer; and faith sets free from the Law. There remains then as 'norm' of action only the call of each particular unique situation . . . be it before the inappellable judgement of his free decision as a person, or be it before God" (218). Having rejected this position as a nominalist denial of universal knowledge and of human nature, Rahner then asks why it attracts people. He identifies the attraction as rooted in two issues: it seems difficult to know what pertains to the "universal and unchanging nature of man" and it seems difficult to explain why humans cannot morally change some aspect of previously unchanged human nature, as part of self-actualizing freedom (219). He finds that at present, these questions lack good answers.

He next inquires into the adequacy of the moral manuals' understanding of how universal moral norms are applied to concrete situations, leading to a specific command about what should be done. According to the standard view, he says, "whoever knows the universal laws exactly and comprehends the given situation to the last detail, knows also clearly what he must or may do here" (222). Ethics, in this view, is syllogistic and deductive. Rahner's question, however, is whether ethics really reduces to universal laws as realized in particular situations. He argues that the answer is no.

As he says, it is hard to define the character of particular situations in their actual existential reality. Their complexity is not expressible by a general summative proposition; nor are we able to perceive them in all their depth. Even if we *could* do so, perhaps by the virtue of prudence—and even if we fully grasped all the applicable universal laws—we could at best come up with an imperative. But we could not show that this imperative is necessarily "identical in the concrete with what we are morally obliged to do here and now" (224). Of course, we cannot violate a universal moral law; but equally we cannot rely simply upon the universal law or our knowledge of the situation to formulate what we must do. Perhaps there are ways of acting that have not been identified but would nevertheless be permissible. Or perhaps some of the ways that, in the syllogism, appear to be permissible are actually not acceptable in reality, since in fact it may happen that only one specific action is truly suitable.

Putting the matter more strongly, Rahner avers that a person's "spiritual individuality cannot be (at least not in his acts) merely the circumscription of an in itself universal nature through the negativity of the *materia prima*, understood as the mere repetition of the same thing at different points in space-time" (226). This is because individuality or personhood must add something significant. What the personal action of a spiritual being should be in a concrete instance cannot be determined on the basis of knowledge about nature. A person is utterly unique and unrepeatable, by contrast to a nature; and the same holds for personal freedom.

If so, then of what use are universal moral norms? Can they really govern the actions of a spiritual, free, unique person? Rahner argues that we must presume that the spiritual person's decisions take place within a domain regulated by the universal norms (or the universal moral good), so that violating these norms remains out of bounds. His emphasis is on the achievement, through a moral decision, of personal "moral individuality" (227). In this uniquely individual decision, the person identifies God's authoritative will for the person. God has a particular will for the person that comes to light through individual decision, and not through the mere application of universal norms. In this sense, "there is an individual ethical reality of a positive kind which is untranslatable into a material universal ethics" (229).[113]

Again, if this is so, how do we know that universal ethics—pertaining to universal human nature—holds for individual personal determinations? Can there really be a "formal existential-ethics" rather than simply individual, singular cases (229)? Here he argues that, properly understood, conscience not only applies universal norms to particular situations but also apprehends what I, as an utterly *unique* person, must do here and now.[114] At issue is how the "I" apprehends its unique individuality in a future action. Rahner notes that an answer would require—among other things—discussing "the fundamental option of the total . . . basic decision about himself, in which the person, when he begins to reflect about himself, always finds himself already there" (230).[115] An answer would also require reflecting upon the connaturality of the spiritual person to the divine Spirit. To know our existential uniqueness as related to existentially binding action requires reflecting upon our (transcendental) interiority.

Having suggested that this can be done through appeal to conscience, he proposes that in some moral cases—and he pauses to affirm his general appreciation for "traditional casuistry"—no unambiguous universal determination can be made as to the choice of action (231). In such cases, an existential ethics is needed, as opposed to the usual "essentialist ethics" that builds upon universal human nature. Indeed, he remarks that an existentialist approach must be the starting point for all ethics, given that we are in fact persons. He comments that Ignatius of Loyola's teaching on "choice" in his *Spiritual Exercises* is a model for a truly existential ethics, rooted in spiritual discernment and awareness of our personal uniqueness rather than reliance upon universal norms.

Here again, the question is what role *"essentialist* ethics" (or the application of universal norms) can truly play.[116] Rahner makes this issue clearer by arguing that sin (without ceasing to be a violation of God's law) is above all a violation of "an utterly individual imperative of the individual will of God, which is the basis of uniqueness" (232).[117] Love of God, after all, is profoundly relational and personal, grounded in personal encounter with God. Ethics should therefore be equally personal and existential. This means that rather than simply obeying the church's universal moral norms, the ethical individual must freely come to a personal (and unique) determination. The church's pastoral practice, then, is no mere application of the dictates of the church's universal (and hierarchical) teaching office. Instead, the pastoral domain, which is firmly tied to the personal (and to unique charisms), has its own integrity. Existentially speaking, persons are not called to simple obedience to the hierarchy's determinations.

How does Rahner's position unfold and develop during and after the Council? In his 1964 essay "Guilt—Responsibility—Punishment within the View of Catholic Theology," Rahner proposes that "man disposes over the totality of his being and existence before God and this either towards Him or away from Him."[118] Here he develops more fully his account of the "fundamental option."

Rahner maintains that the key to freedom and responsibility is the relation of the human person to himself or herself. Freedom of choice is fundamentally "the freedom of self-understanding, the possibility of saying yes or no to oneself, the possibility of deciding for or against oneself."[119] In other words, freedom and responsibility have to do with one's fundamental existential stance, and whether that fundamental stance will be self-constituting or, rather, will be a disastrous turning away from the truth about the self. Human freedom and responsibility have the moral depth they do because human decisions, in conscience, always involve "a self-realisation towards God or a radical self-refusal with regard to God."[120]

Rahner focuses his attention here upon the person's fundamental existential stance, which he terms a person's "total project of existence, one's own total self-understanding, the *'option fondamentale.'*"[121] It is not only that free choices shape one's fundamental existential stance; the latter itself functions as an overarching and determinative reality. One's fundamental existential stance, therefore, can be described as "a basic act of freedom which embraces and moulds the whole of existence."[122] This basic act is not easily dislodged. Rahner grants that a person's fundamental option is actualized and achieved through individual actions, but he urges that the fundamental option cannot be "simply identified with the moral quality of the last of these posited free acts."[123] If one's freely determined fundamental existential stance is toward God (consciously or unconsciously) and thus toward the fulfillment of one's own being, a sinful act that cuts against this fundamental existential stance will rarely overthrow it. In seeing one's life as a whole, one makes a "total decision" about one's life in its totality, in such a way that this decision can hardly be cast aside by a mere individual act, especially given that a bad act of freedom is not, given God's will to save, "an equal realisation of freedom and responsibility on the same plane as the free decision for good."[124]

After the Council, Rahner took a newly firm line of opposition to the now-defunct moral manuals. Regarding the problems with the moral manuals, he made this observation in his 1972 book *The Shape of the Church to Come*: "When modern man gets the impression that the Church's morality is a matter of inculcating laws which are not the concrete expression of the impulse of the Spirit liberating man from within, it is evident that we are moralizing and not really proclaiming Christian morality as it must be proclaimed."[125] Emphasizing interior freedom from extrinsic law, he adds that it is of the utmost necessity that all moral principles be "traced back to that innermost core of the Christian message which is the message of the living Spirit, the message of freedom from merely external law, the message of love which is no longer subject to any law when it prevails" (66). In his view, as of 1972 the Catholic Church had put forward far too many concrete norms in cases of conscience, when in truth the church lacks the means to defend such norms. Although he grants that people may appeal to conscience in an overly subjectivist way, he urges that this is not the pressing problem today. Instead, the real problem is that the church has exaggerated its competence in evaluating human actions.[126]

From this perspective, Rahner deems that the church must give up the casuistic effort to set forth applicable norms in all domains and must now turn to forming and trusting the consciences of Christian believers. Thus, he calls for "a very important change of emphasis in Christian [moral] proclamation: consciences must be formed, not primarily by way of a casuistic instruction, going into more and more concrete details, but by being roused and trained for autonomous and responsible decisions in the concrete, complex situations of human life" (68).[127] In the past, when life was simpler, casuistic moral instruction may have served a purpose. At its best, probabilism recognized the limits of the church's competence vis-à-vis consciences. But modern life has grown too complex for casuistic moral theology. It is evident that "many things which cannot be covered at all by moral theory or casuistry . . . nevertheless may be matters of conscience of the greatest moment" (68–69).

In Rahner's view, the problem is not simply the growing complexity of modern life. A deeper problem is that post-Tridentine Catholic moral theology did not recognize the depths of "moral decision" or "existential decision" (69). In the past, Rahner says, it was thought that decisions of conscience in which believers could validly choose either alternative had to do with morally indifferent (even if personally consequential) matters. A main purpose of casuistry was to ensure that all morally controverted decisions were the domain of well-studied cases of conscience. By contrast, he thinks, today we have realized that casuistic instruction does not and cannot suffice for truly personal moral decision-making.

In the postconciliar church, Rahner identifies "an urgent desideratum for a real training of conscience, which today can no longer be accomplished merely by purifying the relevant moral norms" (69). He calls for a significantly increased scope for conscience in the moral life. As noted above, he urges the church to reorient its moral instruction to forming consciences. Rahner thinks that, thanks to well-formed consciences, the result will be an increase in "genuine morality" and a strengthening of rightly ordered "responsibility before God and before man's dignity in justice and love" (69). In his view, a new focus on forming and freeing consciences will produce a significant advance over the preconciliar conscience-centered Catholic morality, which relied upon "an ever more exact and detailed casuistry supposedly universally applicable" (69).

By encouraging Catholics to understand the dignity of existential decision and their responsibility for this task, the church will enable Catholics to live out "a genuine relationship with God," now with a due modesty about moral truth claims—since in the presence of God we can only surrender with a "radical helplessness" to his incomprehensible mystery (69–70). Instead of forming conscience through emphasizing divine and natural law and the corresponding obligations, conscience will now be formed by emphasizing the believer's obligation to attain perfect Christlike love.

Rahner holds that the new vision of Christian moral life will continue to allow amply for human weakness and moral development, indeed even more fully than did the probabilist moral manuals. Conscience will not need to feel guilty or troubled if it discerns that at present it cannot yet achieve the moral ideal but can only attain a lesser stage. Rahner explains, "it cannot be said that this absolute obligation [to perfect love] binds us at every moment to the most perfect realization then possible in a concrete deed: man is therefore also permitted and simultaneously required to remain open to a further evolution of his own reality and to a higher actualization of his moral consciousness" (65).[128] In the new conscience-centered morality, both individual and communal moral progress will be expected.

Furthermore, as the believer and the church (and the world) proceed along the path of conscience in attunement with historically developing human nature, new moral norms will come into view. Affirming that human nature is historically contextualized and changes over time both individually and societally, Rahner argues that many "concrete moral norms which were formerly and quite rightly proclaimed as binding, because they corresponded to man's concrete nature at the time," today no longer apply (65).[129] The church's formation of conscience will enable Spirit-filled believers to make these judgments, in accord with their experience.

The future morality of Christianity, he predicts, will accord with that of the enlightened secular opinion of the early 1970s. Well-formed Christian consciences will no longer devote so much attention to agonizing over the difficult personal cases that so exercised the moral manualists. Instead, Christians will join in conscience with others of good will to seek solutions to economic, political, and environmental problems. He names "such concrete problems as the population explosion, hunger in the world, the structure of a future society offering more freedom and justice" (69).[130] He thinks that the church's prophetic voice in such matters will be welcomed as arising from the depths of Christian conscience, even if particular actions will not be dictated by the church but instead will come forth from the consciences of believers.

A decade later, in 1983, Rahner delivered a lecture on conscience that, the next year, appeared in a volume of his *Theological Investigations*. The fact that Rahner, almost eighty and nearing the end of his life, chose to write about this theme indicates his estimation of its importance. As a final step in my survey of Rahner, I will set forth the argument of this lecture on conscience.

He begins by very briefly noting the many aspects of the problem of determining the meaning of conscience, including the difficulties with respect to the Old Testament and New Testament data—as well as the complex reception of the theme by the church Fathers and especially by the medievals, with their misinterpretation of a text by Jerome (leading to the distinction between *synderesis* and *conscientia*). He also points out that contemporary secular understandings of conscience highlight its autonomy rather than, as Christians believe, its theonomy. He deems the approval of religious freedom in *Dignitatis Humanae* to be a new and deeper "admission of freedom of conscience."[131] He affirms that conscience develops historically in certain ways, due to its biological, social, and cultural conditioning. Clearly, conscience is formed differently in different cultures.

Having briefly mentioned this background, his focus turns to conscience's relation to God. Certainly, he says, there are objective moral norms, which are absolute. But such norms have to be known and grasped freely by the human subject. Their character as binding upon human freedom only succeeds when humans freely accept the norms as binding. He quickly clarifies that this does not mean that humans merely invent their own norms rather than receiving them from objective reality. Since there is an "objective morality," people know that "not every opinion, every preference, every arbitrary prejudice can claim to be a real dictate of conscience" (6). Nonetheless, people are obliged to follow the dictates of conscience, assuming that they have reflected responsibly upon the matter. Rahner is aware of doubtful or perplexed conscience, and he considers that in such cases, normally speaking, "either of the two possibilities is morally acceptable" (6).

When we obey a dictate of conscience (as we are required to do), it can happen that our conscience is wrong. This can happen in matters of religion, and it is the basis for a legitimate freedom of religion. A dictate of conscience has the authority of "a command of God" for the one who receives it (7). But how does it retain this dignity when it is wrong? Put otherwise, from where does the dignity of conscience come?

In Rahner's view, it does not come from the "world of concrete realities and values"; it does not come from outside us, from the objective moral order (8). This can be seen in the fact that conscience retains its dignity even when unconsciously contradicting the objective moral order. In a certain sense, he notes, the dictates of conscience cannot be "erroneous." This is because even if the conscience errs vis-à-vis the actual moral order, the conscience itself retains the power to bestow "absolute obligation," and therefore in this latter regard the conscience cannot be merely dismissed, as the word "erroneous" too easily implies (8).

What Rahner is working toward here involves a distinction between the transcendental and the categorial, in Kant's sense of these terms. At the transcendental level, every "dictate of conscience that refers to a free action asserts the transcendental necessity of the distinction between good and evil" (9). Since this distinction is fundamental and permanent, the conscience may be wrong in its judgment at the categorial level but not at the transcendental level. The transcendental distinction between good and evil is rooted in a transcendental experience or consciousness of "freedom and responsibility," prior to and not dependent upon any empirical engagement with the world (9). This knowledge of our freedom and responsibility cannot be proven from empirical data, but it grounds all our engagement with the world, even when we try to deny the very existence of human freedom and responsibility. Even such a denial arises as the free act of a responsible self.

Rahner is not here saying that our transcendental consciousness of freedom and responsibility (and thus good and evil in human action) is ever unmediated by the categorial world. His point is simply that it does not depend upon the categorial world. To call conscience "erroneous" misses this deeper transcendental level. The dignity of conscience consists in the fact that "every real decision of conscience is to be accepted as an absolute summons to freedom and responsibility" (10).

Rahner continues by observing that the human person experiences a "transcendental self-givenness" in discovering freedom and responsibility (10).[132] The human spirit has its deepest existence on this transcendental plane, in which its freedom, as an intrinsically unlimited dynamism, reaches out toward the good. Rahner terms this the human spirit's "un-limited transcendentality," and he suggests that it is here that the human person discovers both the dignity of conscience and its relation to God (10). In this sense, it is not wrong to think of conscience as the "voice of God." Conscience is fully human and can be erroneous. But in the discovery of freedom and responsibility, of absolute obligation, a person cannot do other than affirm "God" even without knowing God.[133] The transcendental dynamism of the conscience only makes sense in light of an infinite, utterly absolute freedom.

It is in the light of this implicit relation of conscience to God that Rahner proceeds to interpret what the Second Vatican Council's *Gaudium et Spes* has to say, in paragraph sixteen, about conscience. His main interest consists in religious freedom because he sees this as a major breakthrough for the Catholic understanding of conscience. He emphasizes that a certain sense of religious freedom applies also to Catholics *within the church* as well as to non-Catholics. As he says, "Conscience must be respected by all social and ecclesiastical authorities, since their immediate function concerns the objective structures of reality" (11). Certainly, the church may and should teach moral norms. But these norms should not be taught by the church as though the structures of reality were simple. Given the difficulty of concrete cases of conscience, the church should be modest in pressing its claims. Rather than seeking to propose (let alone insist upon) universal moral norms, the church would do better to go to the very root of conscience.[134] The church should awaken believers to their transcendental dignity by "point[ing] out more clearly that humanity strives irresistibly for God and that, in this striving, human morality becomes theonomous and, as a result, really autonomous" (12).

Such a church would firmly trust the consciences of believers as realized in their transcendental striving in responsible freedom. Rahner grants, of course, that society could not function without basic moral norms being articulated and obeyed. But far greater than such legalistic obedience is the interior discovery of the greatness of the conscience that, knowingly or not, manifests our "irresistible yearning for God," the transcendentality of the human person in its unrestricted dynamism toward the good (12). Even when Catholics disagree with each other (or with non-Catholics) about the commands of conscience, we should rejoice in finding the powerful action of conscience at work.

Thus, Rahner exhibits great trust in conscience, and he has a serene and joyful sense of the bonding power of the discovery of transcendental striving as the core of human dignity. He is less worried about dis-agreements about the content of conscience's dictates. Such disagree-ments are bound to occur, but when they occur within an arena where conscience is respected and understood in its true dignity, he believes that people will attain to a unity and peace rooted in the upward move-ment of human transcendental striving, explicitly or implicitly affirming the infinite mystery of God.[135] Rahner thereby parts ways with the old conscience-centered morality, rooted in God's law, and embraces the new conscience-centered morality, rooted in transcendental freedom and in an emphasis on the difficulty of arriving at and rightly applying universal moral norms.

Josef Fuchs, SJ

Josef Fuchs, whose work bears a close relation to Rahner's, was a preem-inent Catholic moral theologian both before and after the Council.[136] A professor at the Gregorian University in Rome, prior to the Council he authored influential works on natural law, situation ethics, and chastity that reflected and deepened the perspective of the moral manuals. He also published a Latin manual, *Theologia Moralis Generalis*, written for the sem-inarians he taught at the Gregorian.[137] Mark Graham describes Fuchs's 1955 *Natural Law* as a "*magnum opus*" that "immediately distinguished Fuchs as one of the premier figures in Roman Catholic natural law theory and was hailed as a 'radical', landmark work."[138]

In his preconciliar writings, Fuchs insists upon the reality of universal human nature, natural law, and the Creator God's eternal law against the viewpoints of Barth, Bultmann, Bonhoeffer, and others, while at the same time affirming existential ethics' emphasis on personal norms as distinct from norms of nature and on the Spirit's concrete movement of the per-son to right action.[139] In *Natural Law*, he develops "a natural law theory grounded in metaphysical human nature, and therefore universally applica-ble, while rendering it capable of attending to the manifold ways human na-ture is realized in diverse historical situations, particularly different epochs in salvation history."[140] He distinguishes between "relative" and "absolute" natural law, with the latter being grounded in God's creation of human nature as a metaphysical universal that undergirds actual human existence in every era, and the former having to do with the application of "absolute" natural law in particular historical eras.[141]

In the midst of the Council, Fuchs underwent a thoroughgoing change of perspective, which "dramatically altered his notion of natural law and culminated in an explicit repudiation of most of his earlier positions."[142] Fuchs came to affirm the radical historicity of human nature (as actualized by the creative freedom of persons) and therefore about the weakness of moral norms traditionally drawn from natural law. The influence of Pierre Teilhard de Chardin, SJ's 1955 book *The Phenomenon of Man* should be noted here, including Teilhard's remark about evolving human nature: "Being a collective reality, and therefore *sui generis*, mankind can only be understood to the extent that, leaving behind its body of tangible constructions, we try to determine the particular type of conscious synthesis emerging from its laborious and industrious concentration. It is in the last resort only definable as mind."[143] Prior to the Council Rahner had taught a doctoral seminar on Teilhard at the University of Innsbruck, and Teilhard's vision of human nature was making a considerable impact on moral theology by the late 1950s, as the work of the Belgian Jesuit Louis Monden also shows.[144] In 1966 Jacques Maritain noted the widespread popularity of "Teilhardism," pointing out that it offers a *"purely evolutive* conception where being is replaced by becoming and every essence or nature stably constituted in itself vanishes."[145]

Graham sums up Fuchs's position in the 1950s, which was largely also Rahner's position in that period: "On the first, the plane of 'universal essences,' human nature grounds universal moral norms. . . . The second supernatural plane, on which 'the absolute originality of each individual' comes to expression, is the forum for the moral agent's personal response to the call of God that determines her or his existence."[146] With regard to his shift in the early 1960s, Fuchs's doctoral student James Keenan describes the change thusly: "Whereas earlier he believed that the way to apply church teachings was simply to obey them, now he realized that genuine application required adults to relate church teaching conscientiously to their personal responsibilities," thereby displaying "the competency of a mature moral conscience."[147] I will focus here on setting forth Fuchs's *postconciliar* perspective.

Let me begin with his essay "The Absoluteness of Behavioral Moral Norms," originally published in 1971. In this essay, Fuchs argues that there are no absolute moral norms. He grants that "the believing-loving Christian must concern himself with recognizing the absolutely valid, or that which always corresponds objectively to the concrete human (Christian) reality in a moral matter."[148] In concrete action, there are absolutely valid decisions; but there are no universalizable moral norms that apply always and everywhere.[149] He goes on to distinguish between "norms" and "models" for Christian behavior. The latter can be absolutely valid, even if they are applied differently in accord with different situations. The key point is that every life situation is personally and culturally conditioned, and so is every moral norm, including those found in Scripture. The moral norms taught in Scripture can be universal or absolute in the sense of "objectivity," as *models* taking account of cultural context.

Fuchs recognizes that the church has taught moral norms and has defended their universal application. He argues that in so doing, the church did not adequately take into account the changing concrete contexts of human life. According to Fuchs, the fact is that even "a strict behavioral norm, stated as a universal, contains unexpressed conditions and qualifications which as such limit its universality."[150] In part, this is because human nature is an evolving rather than static reality, and in part it is because human life situations are so varied.[151] Fuchs describes the implications of human historicity: "Morality would have him live rightly the actual man, i.e., the man (humanity) of each actual moment, the present with the past enfolded within it and the projective future: that is, starting from each present reality he should 'humanize' himself and his world. Whatever leads to our unfolding, in the fullest and best sense of the word, is good."[152] Morality is creative self-actualization, unfolding and evolving in individual and communal existence over time.

Fuchs briefly explains the place of conscience in this perspective. He begins with the traditional view, found in the moral manuals, that conscience applies the universal norms of the moral law to concrete cases. Suggesting that this view contains at best a partial truth, he argues that in fact conscience's role is to ensure that human action is "authentic" or "self-realizing," through a conformity of the "concrete human reality" with truth or "objectivity."[153] The key is learning to assess the interpersonal consequences of a concrete action. Fuchs holds that we must weigh different values or benefits procured by the action for the individual (in his or her interpersonal context) and for the society, in light of the cultural matrix.[154] He asserts, "The critical question . . . is not one of relativism but of objectivity, or the 'truth' of the action which must be in conformity with the whole concrete reality of man (of society)."[155]

Reflecting further upon the "situation-conscience," Fuchs emphasizes the interpersonal and social dimensions of moral evaluation. The moral norms that conscience recognizes will be accepted and acceptable in one context but not in another. Faith, too, may play a shaping role, especially with regard to "responsible discernment of spirits."[156] In each situation, we should actualize human reality in a way that is most expressive and worthy of human values and therefore of the purposes of humanity's Creator and Redeemer.[157]

In the same year (1971), in "Vocation and Hope: Conciliar Orientations for a Christian Morality," Fuchs sets forth more fully his understanding of conscience. His intention is to clarify the meaning of *Gaudium et Spes* §16. Regarding the intention of the Council, he remarks, "It is first of all important to conceive of conscience as the most intimate experience-knowledge of man's total state of dependence and submissiveness in the face of the Absolute and thus, ultimately, in the face of God."[158] He then compares this experience-knowledge with the subjective reality of Christian existence. He states, "For the believing Christian, this fundamental experience has the same character of absolute submissiveness as that formed in faith, in love, and in following Christ."[159] Just as Christ calls us and we must obey, so also conscience calls us and we must obey. Fuchs inquires into whether conscience's judgment constitutes the moral norm or whether conscience receives the norm (from synderesis and natural law) and then applies it to a particular action. He argues that no norms are revealed by God; rather, all norms are derived from natural law and are therefore *human* norms.[160] In his view, in making its judgments, conscience must recognize that previously formulated norms will not suffice, given that new problems are arising in modern society for which no concrete norms have previously been formulated. Even when there are previously formulated norms, the radically new context of modern society means that many of these prior norms will have to be reformulated.

Let me now turn to Fuchs's 1979 essay "The Question Addressed to Conscience." He begins by contrasting the traditional approach, namely, cases of conscience governed by a set of universal norms, with the situation of "contemporary man" who "understands himself to a greater extent and in a more profound way as a person; he is given and is responsible for an 'I' unique to him, which possesses a dynamism proper to itself and which is to actualize itself through the exercise of personal conscience."[161] In Fuchs's view, for both traditional and contemporary man, conscience is the key to the moral life.

Fuchs emphasizes the developmental growth of persons to maturity within a web of social relations and also in the context of the natural world. Humans actualize their freedom in self-determination or "transcendental self-disposition"; and humans either alienate themselves by claiming self-sufficiency or realize themselves by receiving their self as gift (216–17).[162] Freedom itself, alongside the sense of moral duty or responsibility, "attests to an originative and self-sufficient Absolute," God (217).

Freedom is only conceivable in light of conscience. Fuchs describes conscience as the inner core of the person in which the person is "totally present to himself" and experiences himself (or herself) as marked by "the inner demand to realize the self" through free action (218). Conscience is more than a power or an operation; it is "a total experience" of the self, self-presence in the deepest manner, that becomes clearer to those who believe "in God and in the importance of the Christ-event" (218).[163] Self-presence, freedom, and responsibility for self-realization characterize the interior domain of conscience.

On this basis, Fuchs addresses the question of how we know and do our moral duty (what God wills) in particular, complex situations. As he puts the question, How do we use our freedom to attain self-realization rather than self-alienation, in the context of interpersonal and social relations? He affirms that conscience contains moral knowledge that we receive as an "absolute demand" (219). How does this knowledge reach us through conscience? He rejects the traditional view, which he deems "legalistic and static," that conscience applies universal norms to concrete instances (220). Such norms, anyway, will not be universal. Instead, therefore, what conscience must do is interpret the self (the personal "I") in "its actual situation with a view to genuine self-fulfillment" (220).[164] Conscience has to do with the inner push toward self-realization in and through freely chosen actions. This inner push requires judgments of value, which draw upon various norms, whether inherited or developed through life experience, including faith. In conscience, the deepest interior of the personal "I" functions as a light showing the way; and when the decision of conscience makes itself apparent, it "compels us from the very depths of our being" (221).

Objectively, the person who has decided in his or her totality, from his or her innermost core, has acted correctly, even if true self-realization later shows the decision of conscience to have been incorrect in some way. Fuchs reiterates that conscience arrives at its decision aided by norms, about which it has to make judgments (due to the limitations of every norm) but which nonetheless are helpful in guiding conscience. In this sense, conscience has to be *formed*. The formation of conscience can involve rejecting a norm's application in today's situation. We can learn from wise members of the community who have either affirmed or rejected specific norms. We can realize that certain norms, while formally true, are insufficient to guide action in given situations without being adapted, or without having their underlying "horizons of understanding and social conditions" illuminated (224).[165] Norms must be subjectively engaged and critiqued. Since objectivity comes about through subjective inquiry, Fuchs finds simplistic the notion that the conscience is subjective and the norms objective. Thus, the binding character of conscience relates to the significance of its work in seeking to arrive at an objectively valid judgment.

In concluding his essay, Fuchs observes that conscience has to do not only with personal self-realization but also with decisions made by persons on behalf of the whole society. Such decision-makers seek to arrive at a decision that "correspond[s] to the nature and dignity of man and of society in their situation as it now is, insofar as this 'now' leads to a future" (226). There is no simple solution presented to decision-makers by norms. Instead, decision-makers must act in a truly human way and with an adequate knowledge of "human goods and values, their hierarchy and urgency" (226). Ethicists can contribute the latter knowledge to decision-makers. The needs of the common good, sensitivity to a pluralistic society, and the counsel of other people in authority should influence how a society's decision-makers act vis-à-vis moral questions. But ultimately decision-makers have to consult their own consciences, since acting on behalf of the public is still a personal action.

For Fuchs, then, the moral norms are what need to be called into question; the ability of humans to act toward self-realization or for the public good is less in doubt. At the core of personal freedom and responsibility, the person's mature conscience undertakes an arduous labor in light of the person's "total experience," drawing upon an array of resources, both internal and external. Persons can be counted upon to move in the direction of humanization, or at least to realize when they have failed to do so. Since moral norms are provisional and context-bound, conscience does not apply secure and stable moral norms to ever-changing situations; rather, conscience is the work of the personal "I" in coming to a hard-won and deeply interior moral maturity. Public action, too, requires this deeply personal probing, informed by ethical and interdisciplinary perspectives and weighing various values in seeking the most humane decision. The dynamism of freedom in self-realization points to Absolute Freedom (God), whether or not God or Christ is explicitly affirmed. Self-alienation always is as a possibility, insofar as the person may claim self-sufficiency. But Fuchs is optimistic about the potential of conscience in its personal, non-legalistic form to achieve authenticity for persons and societies. For Fuchs, the post-Tridentine conscience-centered morality was built upon faulty assumptions, but the post-Vatican II conscience-centered morality will work well.[166]

Bernard Häring, CSsR

Born in the same year as Fuchs (1912), Bernard Häring equaled or surpassed Fuchs's broad impact on twentieth-century Catholic moral theology—and he shared Fuchs's strong optimism about postconciliar conscience-centered morality.[167] Unlike Fuchs, Häring was a critic of the moral manuals prior to the Council. According to Raphael Gallagher, it was Häring's *The Law of Christ* in 1954 that decisively exposed to a wide audience the deficiencies of the moral manuals.[168] Charles Curran echoes Gallagher's assessment of the impact of Häring's three-volume work, pointing out that within a few years it had been translated into fifteen languages.[169] In the late 1970s Häring published a postconciliar trilogy, *Free and Faithful in Christ*, which likewise had significant influence on the teaching of Catholic moral theology.

Most scholars today assume that Häring's *The Law of Christ* broke sharply from the moral manuals.[170] In some notable respects, this is true. For example, Häring draws heavily upon existentialist and personalist philosophy—this is evident in his understanding of charity and justice as "types of values" (rather than virtues) and in his strong distinction between nature and personhood, with moral theology being about concrete human persons summoned by Christ.[171] Dietrich von Hildebrand, Karol Wojtyła, and others were following similar paths in the same time period, influenced by Max Scheler.[172] In his foreword to the work's three volumes, Häring proclaims along Fritz Tillmann's lines: "The principle, the norm, the center, and the goal of Christian Moral Theology is Christ. The law of the Christian is Christ Himself in Person. . . . We are created in the eternal image of the Logos, the Word of God, and re-created by the Redemption through Christ Jesus. Christian morality is life flowing from the victory of Christ."[173] This foregrounding of Christ, along with the emphasis on Christ as the law in Person, differs from what one finds in traditional moral manuals. In addition, Häring emphasizes that he has "abstained from including the materials of ecclesiastical law and civil law in the content of this text, in order to avoid all semblance of equating law and morals or of reducing moral theology to forms of law."[174]

The Law of Christ was greeted with acclaim by those who were seeking to reform or do away with the moral manuals. In *The Sources of Christian Ethics*, Servais Pinckaers includes Häring's *The Law of Christ* among the major sources of inspiration in the early development of his own approach to moral theology.[175] For his part, Häring credits the impact of numerous scholars, including the nineteenth-century moralists John Michael Sailer and Johann Baptist von Hirscher, who "felt the urgent need of shaping— over and above the casuistic moral of the age—a moral theology whose primary concern should be to restate the perfect ideal of the whole Christian life and to underline the means of attaining it."[176] Häring appreciatively describes Christ-centered works by Ferdinand Probst, Franz Xavier Linsenmann, and other nineteenth-century thinkers; and he commends Antony Koch, one of the moral manualists whom I study in chapter 2, for adhering "to the patristic and scholastic tradition."[177] He gives special credit to his teacher Theodor Steinbüchel, as well as to Fritz Tillmann's emphasis on the imitation of Christ.

Against "legal minimalism," Häring urges in passing that "the Sermon on the Mount and the counsels" should be "accorded their rightful place of honor in moral theology as such."[178] Yet, *The Law of Christ* remains profoundly conscience-centered, notwithstanding the presence of other points of emphasis. Häring begins with a short first chapter on the history of moral theology and a short second chapter focusing on the category of "responsibility" in a moderately personalist or existentialist vein, in which "commandment and law" are presented as characterizing a theocentric dialogue.[179] He then treats theological anthropology in a short third chapter emphasizing personhood, community, historicity, and Christian worship.

In a lengthy and decisive fourth chapter, however, he explores freedom, the Good, and the moral faculty: conscience. The section on conscience runs for more than fifty dense pages. After a short section on human acts, Häring then moves in the fifth chapter to a sixty-page discussion of norm and law, with ten of those pages treating the law of Christ (the new law). After three short chapters on the moral object, intention, and circumstances, the ninth and tenth chapters take up sins, and the tenth through twelfth chapters have to do with elements of the sacrament of penance. Finally, the last two chapters treat the virtues in general and the cardinal virtues, with fourteen pages devoted to the virtue of prudence. In this section on prudence, he underscores its connection to conscience: "It is the exalted task of prudence to provide that man, through his conscience, hear the voice of

God, speaking in and through rightly understood reality. . . . Conscience throughout impregnates with its dynamism the acts of prudence."[180]

In the expansive section he devotes to conscience in *The Law of Christ*, Häring shows that he thinks of prudence mainly as the prudent application of conscience. His lengthy treatment of the post-Tridentine probabilist controversies shows him to be a convinced equiprobabilist of the Redemptorist school. In a traditional manner, he connects conscience firmly with divine and natural law, not least by emphasizing that "only one with a totally perverted concept of the real nature and function of conscience could repudiate the infallible *magisterium* of the Church in the name of conscience."[181] His portrait of conscience's role in the moral life is ample indeed. He describes conscience as "man's moral faculty," "the inmost center of the soul," the soul's "spiritual instinct for self-preservation arising from the urge for complete unity and harmony," and the principle of "the inner unity and completeness of the psychic powers."[182]

Thus far Häring's perspective in 1954. Now let me turn to his postconciliar work, influenced by Rahner, Fuchs, and others.[183] Although many of his viewpoints changed radically, the postconciliar Häring not only continued to perceive the conscience as the center of the Christian moral life but even significantly expanded his vision of conscience's centrality and role.

In the first volume of his three-volume *Free and Faithful in Christ*, originally published in 1978, he offers a study of "general moral theology."[184] Here he devotes twenty pages to the Old and New Testament frameworks for Christian ethics; thirty pages to the history of the church's moral theologians from the Fathers onward; forty-five pages to creative liberty, creative fidelity, and creative co-responsibility; sixty pages to creation, Christ, the Holy Spirit, personal freedom, and the church; sixty pages to the fundamental option; eighty pages to conscience; seventy-five pages to law and liberty; and ninety pages to mortal and venial sins and the sacraments. The number of pages he devotes to conscience has notably increased, especially given that he reduces his earlier lengthy discussion of the probabilist controversies to a mere few pages. The basic structure of the book still follows that of the moral manuals, though with some new sections added to introduce what remains the heart of the matter—human action, conscience, law, and sin. Naturally, he is much less confident about the magisterium of the church, arguing that the breakthrough accomplished by the postconciliar church is or should be "a liberation from scrupulosity and from all too many doctrines about absolutes that can be imposed and are fit for control" (284).

At the outset of his book, Häring proclaims the *postconciliar* era to be the great era of conscience. He states: "I am convinced that we have moved into a new era that will be determined by people who live by their own conscience and are particularly qualified to act as discerning members of community and society" (4). He bemoans the fact that the preconciliar (post-Tridentine) emphasis "was no longer on the law inborn in man and discovered by conscience in the reciprocity of consciences, but rather on the authoritative decision of what natural law prescribes for people of all times" (46–47).[185] In his view, this situation has now changed and a new, vibrant period marked by responsible and reciprocal consciences has emerged for Catholics.

In place of the language of virtue, Häring relies upon the notions of "fundamental option" and "fundamental dispositions."[186] He argues that "the fundamental option gives unity, integration and final firmness to attitudes, sentiments and emotions" (91). In his view, Christian freedom is the central element of gospel morality. He states, "The Synoptics present the eruption of freedom, above all, under the paradigm of God's kingdom" (118). Jesus frees us from hatred, from legalism, from overscrupulosity, from alienation, from egoism, from the fear of death, from the desire for power and wealth for their own sake, from patriarchy, from ideology, and from "the powers of oppression, greed, racism, sexism, [and the] cult of violence" (122).

He notes that the church, which ought "to be a sacrament of the history of liberation," has often failed to mirror Christ the Liberator and instead has shown "a defensive, intolerant attitude towards others," not least by burning heretics and showing no respect for freedom of conscience (158–59). Häring conceives of Jesus's relationship to his past—Israel's past—as marked most centrally by a critique of Jewish legalism, for the purposes of liberating God's people.[187] He concludes that today "a common profound devotion to responsible freedom and unconditional respect for the dignity and conscience of all people help more than anything else to lead us to Christ the Liberator" (160).

For one's fundamental option to be good and ordered to salvation, it cannot be egoistical; it must be cooperative and open to others, above all, God. It can be weakened, but not destroyed, by "superficial inconsistencies" at the level of action (167). Gradually, as we become mature adults, our fundamental option will manifest itself in "fundamental attitudes" that will show whether we have chosen for or against God and neighbor (193–95). Ultimately, the necessary thing is constant "renewal of the all-embracing intention" and "vigilance to keep the fundamental intention alive and to relate it vitally to one's activities and decisions" (197). A mortal sin is any act or decision that completely destroys "the fundamental option for the good self-commitment to the service of God and love of neighbour," but this is rare (211).[188] According to Häring, the work of the Holy Spirit in us is most clearly found in the realm of the fundamental option.

Häring locates his lengthy chapter entitled "Conscience: The Sanctuary of Creative Fidelity and Liberty" directly after his discussion of the fundamental option (and immediately prior to his chapter on law). He argues at the outset of the chapter that "conscience makes us aware that our true self is linked with Christ," and he notes that "the sensitivity and truthfulness of our conscience grow in the light of the divine Master who teaches us not only from without but also from within by sending us the Spirit of truth" (224). Similarly, he suggests that the truth that comes to us through conscience is the truth of the divine Word, the same Word who became incarnate for our sake and to whom we are expected "to listen with all our being" (224).

Reaching back to the prophets of Israel, Häring holds that the prophets' sense of hearing God's voice was an experience of conscience. Conscience here is "a person's innermost being" and "the spirit within the person who guides him if he is willing to open himself to it" (225). Conscience functions as a divine guide. It does not simply pass judgment on the morality of past or future acts, though it does this. Rather, conscience is the place where an extensive dialogue with God occurs. Conscience is the very deepest core, the "heart," of the person. At this core, we must "listen to the prompting of the Spirit" (226). This listening involves a creative path, an invitation to journeying with God and neighbor.

When the prophets promise that God will give his people a new heart in which the law is interiorly inscribed, this new heart is the Spirit's renewal of conscience. Häring maintains that when Paul mentions "conscience," Paul has in view the Old Testament's "heart." According to Häring, Paul "explicitly broadens the understanding of conscience in the light of the prophetic tradition," and thus he goes well beyond the Stoic view of conscience as that which interiorly identifies a particular action as evil (228).[189] Even if conscience is what interiorly judges the goodness or wickedness of our action, conscience is also "constructive" and "creative" in its search for the truth (228).

On the one hand, Häring holds that a Christian understanding of conscience must come from Scripture as interpreted in the church. But on the other hand, he notes that, in the history of the church, a presupposed philosophical anthropology inevitably shaped how theologians understood conscience. For that reason, we cannot simply reiterate what past theologians have said about conscience, given that their anthropological presuppositions reflected their context, not ours. He praises Aquinas's account of conscience, with its relationship to synderesis and prudence, including practical reason's ordering to goodness and truth and including the role of the gifts of the Holy Spirit in producing connaturality to the good (231). He finds the thirteenth-century Franciscan conception of synderesis as primarily involving the will (rather than the intellect) to be complementary to the thirteenth-century Dominican view, but he considers that "as soon as the two schools became antagonistic [beginning in the fourteenth century], there was a militant emphasis on one aspect as against the other, and thus the wholeness was shattered" (232).

In his view, the retrieval of the wholeness requires maximizing the place of conscience in moral theology, though now on new grounds. We must recognize that "conscience has to do with man's total selfhood as a moral agent" (235). Conscience is not merely the means by which synderesis's first principles are applied to past and future actions, in service of practical reason (or the virtue of prudence). Instead, a healthy conscience involves the emotions, intellectual powers, and volitional energies all "functioning in a profound harmony in the depth of one's being" (235). In addition to being the place of harmonious union of all human powers, conscience is where the Spirit's creativity touches and perfects us. It is where God's word speaks to us; and it is where we respond in the wholeness, the totality, of our personhood. Conscience is powerfully present in both the intellect and the will because it is located "in the deepest reaches of our psychic and spiritual life," "the deepest part of our being," where "intellectual, volitional and emotional dynamics are not separated; they mutually compenetrate in the very depth where the person is person to himself" (234–35). Conscience takes on a maximal role because it involves a coming together of the key human dynamisms and because it is the place where personhood is located.

Conscience, therefore, can judge what is life-giving and what is not, when presented not only with our actions but also with teachings and experiences that come to us from the church or from the depths of other consciences. Häring observes that "the deepest part of our being"—namely, conscience—"is keenly sensitive to what can promote and what can threaten our wholeness and integrity" (234). A healthy conscience ensures the "wholeness and integrity" of the person by affirming what contributes to such integrity and rejecting what does not contribute. Häring does not leave out prudence entirely, but he makes clear that conscience is in the driver's seat as we "dynamically decipher and experience the good to which God calls us in the particular situation" (235).

The Christian is called to stand forth boldly upon the ground of a free and healthy conscience, where intellectual, volitional, and emotional energies join together in harmony at the core of the person's being. Häring states, "In the wholeness and openness of our conscience we are a real sign of the promptings of the Spirit who renews our heart and, through us, the earth" (235). The fullness of Christian life, obedient to Word and Spirit, shines forth in those whose consciences are whole, integrated, healthy, open, and free. Certainly, as fallen creatures, we can experience opposition between intellect and will at the depth of our being. When this happens, the Spirit reaches to the rift in our conscience (our deepest personhood) and brings healing. Conscience's work ensures the integration of our powers, not least because it is our conscience that leads us to hear the truth and to love God and neighbor. As Häring puts it, "The call to unity and wholeness pervades our conscience. It is a longing for integration of all the powers of our being that, at the same time, guides us towards the Other and the others" (236).

In guiding us toward union with God and neighbor, the key aspect of the conscience—according to Häring—is openness. This openness is first and foremost openness to the light of the Word. It is also openness to the insights of our fellow human beings, as these insights have developed in the great cultures of the world. Our conscience sees in others' consciences the "same longing for dignity and wholeness" (236). We ask others to respect and love us "as persons with consciences," and when they do so, we open ourselves and our conscience creatively to their consciences in a fashion that reveals more clearly the "depth and dynamics of our conscience" (236).

In Jeremiah, the promise of the new covenant entails a new heart in which the law is written. Häring argues that this is quite simply a renewed conscience, now enabled to know and love the Word. The golden rule and the new commandment of love that we find in the New Testament are further expressions of a renewed conscience. Perfect love is made possible when in our conscience/heart "we receive the Spirit and are open to him," and when we give ourselves (in Christ) in perfect openness and service to others, thereby reaching "wholeness in our conscience and unity with our fellowmen" (237).

According to Häring, the primary task of conscience is to choose our fundamental option, for or against God. When this has been rightly chosen (in the Spirit), we can trust "the creative judgment of conscience," in which conscience's intrinsic yearning for wholeness is confirmed (238). Häring also recognizes the value for a healthy conscience of "the dispositions toward vigilance and prudence and all the other dispositions that embody a deep and good fundamental option" (238). No conscience, moreover, is an island, and so each conscience must rely upon its openness to "the mutuality of consciences in a milieu where creative freedom and fidelity are embodied and there is active and grateful dedication to them" (238). In addition, the conscience must never rest statically on a set of truths but must constantly renew its "actual fidelity, creativity and generosity in the search for truth in readiness to 'act on the word'" (238). Häring emphasizes the creativity and freedom of conscience in its connatural or intuitive knowledge born of love. With respect to conscience's dynamic creativity, he states, "It is the conscience itself that teaches the person to overcome the present stage of development and to integrate it into a higher one," so that the conscience grows "into new dimensions" (239).

Häring accepts, of course, that a sincere conscience can err. Drawing upon John Henry Newman and Alphonsus de Liguori, he adds that when a sincere conscience does so, it does so in the quest for truth and thus without personal culpability. In directing the person's quest, the sincere conscience is always journeying "towards ever fuller light," even when the conscience is in error due to defective knowledge (240). There can be deviations on the path, but so long as the conscience is sincerely open, the path is oriented toward the increasing light of truth and goodness. Häring notes that, for Aquinas, a person is bound to obey an erring conscience, even though such obedience—due to the objective error—will result objectively in a sin and even though the person must always pursue the formation of conscience.[190] Häring emphasizes that there is no sin or personal culpability, so long as "the person is sincerely seeking the truth and is ready to revise the decision as soon as he realizes that new pertinent questions call for his consideration" (242).

Christian faith marks the Christian conscience in distinctive ways. Häring states, "A salvific knowledge of Christ"—a knowledge that "is a gift of the Holy Spirit who reaches into the innermost depths of our soul"—"includes confirmation of our fundamental option that gives us wholeness of conscience and a knowledge by connaturality" (247). In faith, we receive Christ as the one sent by the Father, and we surrender ourselves in friendship to him. Faith gives firmness to Christian conscience. As Häring observes, "St. Paul sees the human conscience and the conviction of conscience illumined and confirmed by faith. Especially in his Pastoral Epistles, 'faith' and 'conscience' have almost the same meaning" (248).[191]

Häring adds that it is a mistake to think of either faith or conscience as simply entailing propositional knowledge. On the contrary, "A mature Christian conscience will not think of faith as a catalogue of things and formulations" (248). Indeed, merely communicating doctrines to conscience does not help to form Christian conscience at all. Overemphasizing doctrine actually obstructs the formation of mature conscience and faith. What is needed instead is an attitude of openness, the attitude that characterizes the integrity of conscience and that corresponds to conscience's (and faith's) longing for wholeness and relationship with God and neighbor. Häring comments, "What shapes all the moral dispositions, gives wholeness to the conscience and firmness to the Christian's fundamental option is the profound *attitude* of faith and its responsiveness" (248). Not a carefully controlled cognitive content but rather the stance of responsive openness is what mature conscience and faith require. Similarly, law and obligation are not central to authentic Christian conscience; what is central is Christ's grace and our gratitude for what he has given us, including his renewal of our hearts/consciences by his Spirit.

In identifying conscience as the animating center of Christian life and personhood, whose wholeness and integrity are the true marks of the interior presence of the Word and Spirit, Häring offers a critique of legalism, both in its laxist and its rigorist forms. It is only when we are moved by love rather than by legalism that we can truly live for Christ and our neighbor. He remarks that "to live under grace means a shift from the prohibitive laws [i.e., the Decalogue] to the orientations of the goal-commandments, the affirmatives presented in the whole gospel, in the words of Christ and the Letters of St. Paul" (250). He warns against what he sees as the preconciliar split between "a static moral theology" and "a lofty ascetical and mystical theology," and he finds that in the preconciliar period "the beatitudes, all the goal-commandments and the 'harvest of the Spirit' were considered as a mere ideal or as *parenesis* and, therefore, not as a part of normative Christian ethics" (252).

Among the major "sins against liberty and sanity," Häring lists first the sin of not overcoming "a static view of life, norms, rules and conscience" (263). He condemns supporting "centralism and authoritarian forms of government that stifle subsidiarity and collegiality, and favour uncritical obedience"; he warns against dividing "religion into a separated dogmatic (abstract doctrines not concerned with man's wholeness and salvation) and morals proposed without a convincing value system"; and he rejects "an ethics of prohibitions and controls to the detriment of an ethics of creative liberty and fidelity" (263).

Exploring the reciprocity of consciences, Häring underlines the profound respect we owe to another person's conscience. He examines Paul's account of such respect in Romans 14 and 1 Corinthians 10. He also provides a short history of debates over freedom of conscience in religious matters, culminating in Vatican II's *Dignitatis Humanae*. He emphasizes the need for the state to "protect and promote people's right and readiness to search freely for truth and thus become capable of genuine cooperation" (274).[192]

In accord with his vision of the role of the state, he sees the church's role vis-à-vis theologians as one of protecting freedom to search for truth. In no case, however, is this a matter of "indifference in matters of morality or truth" (277). Rather, it is about recognizing that Christian freedom is opposed to an atmosphere of manipulation. Häring argues that there has been a "paralysis of theology since the seventeenth century," due to "the oppressive spirit of the Inquisition that expected the Catholic theologian to commit no error in the search for truth" (277). As a result, hidden and unconscious errors built up without being "creatively corrected" (277).[193] He expresses the hope that the church will today embrace a newly prophetic morality that will enable people, in the context of our "new historical situation (*kairos*)" and without turning to individualism, "to realize something new, to grow in liberty, in goodness and truthfulness" (278–79). In accord with true reciprocity of consciences, there must now be "freedom of inquiry and freedom to speak out even in dissent from official documents," a freedom exercised precisely in service to the church (281). The result, says Häring, will be a deepening and renewing of the church's faith as we encourage "each other to ever greater depth of conscience" and as we listen to "the prophetic people who are always vigilant for the coming of the Lord and can communicate to our conscience their experience" (282).[194]

Häring reflects briefly on the controversies surrounding probabilism in the sixteenth through eighteenth centuries. He thinks that the present controversies over moral issues are indeed in certain ways a return of the probabilist controversies, but he is sanguine about this situation. For Häring, the probabilists had the correct side of the argument then, and their heirs are even better positioned today when legalistic assumptions no longer need set the terms for the debate. On the one side are those who cling to law, authority, tradition, past documents, and control; on the other side are those who respect the creative freedom of conscience and who understand that new historical contexts require new norms. Häring considers his postconciliar perspective on conscience to be what the Jesuit probabilists *would* have said had they not been themselves "partially caught in the system of conventional morality, at least regarding the methods by which they wanted to free the overburdened conscience" (287).[195]

Joseph Ratzinger

The final word in this chapter will go to Joseph Ratzinger, who in certain respects moves away from the conscience-centered morality that has been the focus of the chapter to this point, even as he retains some existentialist elements. In summarizing Ratzinger's perspective on conscience, I will rely on two essays, the first originally published in 1972 and the second originally published in 1991. The first essay bears the title "Conscience in Time"; the second, "Conscience and Truth."[196]

In "Conscience in Time," Ratzinger opens with a question that cuts against the grain of the postconciliar celebration of conscience: "Is conscience really a power we can count on?"[197] After all, conscience can seem quite abstract and hardly particularly forceful. He describes a novel by Reinhold Schneider in which conscience is represented by a frail young girl among a group of Spanish conquistadores. Even if conscience exists, it can hardly do much against the powers of this world, as history shows over and over again—despite the noble witness to conscience that we see in a few persons.

Besides, what is the evidence that conscience really exists? Education, cultural prejudices, and the norms enforced by the state shape what people say that they hear (and do not hear) their consciences telling them. People can also appeal to conscience merely out of the will-to-power, the will to be a law unto themselves.

Yet, if conscience did not exist, on what basis could we know whether, for example, murder is wrong? It seems clear to Ratzinger that to deny the existence of conscience would be to play into the hands of totalitarian, murderous states. Conscience can be easily abused, but it can also be sorely missed.

Ratzinger proposes a definition of conscience that he thinks grounds it in reality and shields it from being abused. He states, "Conscience, to put it quite simply, means acknowledging man, oneself and others, as created, and respecting the Creator in his creation."[198] To live according to the voice of conscience means to live as a creature among God's other beloved creatures and thus to give honor to the Creator in his creation. Such conscience involves humility, rather than arrogating godlike power over oneself or others. When power is exercised in conscience, power does not become arrogant but rather recognizes a supreme power over it. By contrast, when power is exercised without attending to the "innermost core" of conscience where we recognize our creatureliness, power becomes the ultimate reality. At best, we rely upon an unstable human "balance of power"; at worst, tyranny reigns. Humans become measured not by the shared dignity of creatureliness but by their degree of value in the scales of power. The latter situation destroys the true dignity of human persons. If no one is courageous enough to suffer for the sake of conscience, Ratzinger suggests, unjust power will have no check and tyranny will not be overcome.

He tests this argument by applying it to the case of the discovery of the Americas by the Spaniards and specifically to the mid-sixteenth-century situation of the Native Americans and the protests of conscience launched by the Dominican priest Bartolomé de las Casas. Ratzinger asks whether conscience truly served to check the abuse of power on the part of priests and soldiers: Was anyone "proclaiming the absolute character of the Creator in the absolute dignity of the powerless"?[199] In his 1542 *Brevísima relación de la destrucción de las Indias Occidentales*, Las Casas demonstrated the brutality of the conquistadores vis-à-vis the native population, whom they enslaved, exploited, and decimated. In response to Las Casas's indictment, the Spanish government passed laws liberating the Native Americans and ensuring them the protection of the law. Some of these laws involved instruction in the Catholic faith, which Ratzinger argues was intended to establish the Native Americans on equal footing with the Spanish. Of course, these laws had little impact. But Ratzinger identifies them as at least evidence of the light of conscience, its ability to function as a check over tyranny by affirming the equal human dignity of all people. For Ratzinger, the weakness and failure of conscience, in practical terms, does not discredit it. Its witness remains crucially important.

According to Ratzinger, a distinguishing mark of conscience's testimony to creatureliness is the fact that "the power of conscience consists in suffering, in the power of the Crucified."[200] Conscience acts as itself when it acts in accord with Jesus Christ. Conscience meets power with humility; it does not meet power with power. This stance generally entails suffering. If conscience has the backing of worldly power or depends upon this backing, then conscience will become merely another form of worldly power. It cannot judge or check the ambitions of worldly power if it has capitulated to worldly power by becoming simply another approved tool of the powerful.

Ratzinger suggests that this understanding of conscience—as a testimony to creatureliness and thus intrinsically as a refusal to exercise power in the way that the world does—reflects the moral teaching of the New Testament. Conscience stands at the heart of Christian ethics if what is meant by conscience is the courageous humility that testifies to truth by being willing to suffer. Here conscience is intimately bound up with the cross of Christ and with such texts as Romans 13:1–7, 1 Peter 2:13–25, and Mark 12:17, each of which demonstrates that Jesus's path was and is not the path of a political revolutionary. Rather, he was a witness to the distinction of God's power from Caesar's power; he was a witness to the limits of human power. He witnessed to this in his willingness to suffer and die. Politically speaking, the sign of conscience's presence is martyrdom, which is not a form of worldly power but which serves true human freedom. Conscience clings not to the power of this world but to the power of God.

Yet, is conscience limited solely to passive suffering? According to Ratzinger (indebted to Schneider), in its testimony to creatureliness, conscience also possesses a prophetic role. Not only martyrs but also prophets (who can easily become martyrs) testify in conscience against corrupt worldly power that imagines it has no limits. There are also people who exercise power in this world but who seek to do it in conscience, under God's judgment and recognizing due human limits. For such persons, power is a burden and a responsibility, not a matter of personal ambition or glorification. This is "healed power," in which conscience's witness of suffering (against abusive power) becomes the interior suffering of the ruler who pours himself out for his people in seeking the common good. Thus Ratzinger connects conscience with the core of Christian ethics, with the recognition of creatureliness and the imitation of Christ. Conscience is most clearly found in the martyr and the prophet who protest abuse of power peacefully. Yet, conscience can also be found in every human being who takes on responsibilities of care for others, measured not by self-interest but by what one owes in justice and charity to other creatures of God.

What does "Conscience and Truth" add to this portrait? Here Ratzinger has in view the condition of Catholic moral theology and the place of conscience therein. He frames his essay by a discussion of how and why "the question of conscience has become paramount" among postconciliar moral theologians.[201] Namely, the centering of conscience upon personal freedom aims to correct preconciliar Catholic moral theology. On this view, the church previously sought control over its members, and now what is needed is an insistence upon the primacy of conscience as a principle of freedom, including freedom against the heavy hand of the church. Conscience has the task of deliberating upon the church's moral teachings and determining whether or not they should be obeyed. A person who obeys his conscience does not sin in so doing, and thus a person's conscience ultimately has greater authority than any church teaching about morality.[202]

A problem with this view, as Ratzinger notes, is that conscience's dictate in one person can contradict conscience's dictate in another person. As a result, one can easily move from insisting upon absolute freedom of conscience to denying that conscience has any authority whatsoever. Ratzinger suggests that there must be a middle position, one that does not rely upon framing conscience merely in terms of freedom versus authority.

Inquiring into what this middle position might be, Ratzinger begins by telling a story from his time as a professor. Ratzinger recalls a colleague who reasoned that since Christianity is so challenging, God generously allows most people to gain salvation by obeying erroneous conscience and rejecting Christianity. For Ratzinger's colleague, it seemed that faith and truth, far from making us happier, make salvation more difficult by asking for heroic moral behavior that really is not feasible for most people. No doubt, some people experienced preconciliar Catholicism in this way, namely, as a miserable moral burden that nonetheless had to be borne. No wonder such people desire to cast off all authority!

In response, Ratzinger proposes that conscience is "man's openness to the ground of his being" and is "the power of perception for what is highest and most essential."[203] Conscience opens us to truth, which comes to us from God, truth which is most fully found in Christ. Otherwise, we may find ourselves in the dreadful situation of no longer having a functional conscience and of not having sufficient guilt to prompt us to change our ways. We can become stuck in self-righteousness, lacking an opening to God and Christ. In Jesus's parable of the Pharisee and the Tax Collector, for instance, "The Pharisee no longer knows that he too has guilt. He has a completely clear conscience. But this silence of conscience makes him impenetrable to God and men, while the cry of conscience which plagues the tax collector makes him capable of truth and love."[204]

In this context, Ratzinger again discusses conscience in terms of creaturehood. He points to Romans 2:1–16, where Paul describes gentiles who have humility and who model "patience in well-doing" (Rom. 2:7) rather than worldly wickedness. Such persons, Ratzinger suggests, are living truly as creatures and therefore have a saving conscience. His main point is that conscience cannot be a box that locks us in ourselves, in our own subjective certitude. If it did so, it could hardly fight against our disinclination for self-criticism and our tendency toward self-interest. Conscience must instead be an openness to God (and Christ). When God is suppressed, as in totalitarian systems, many people lose a sense of conscience. Ratzinger notes that this is what happened in the Soviet Union, according to testimony given after the fall of Communism in 1989. The most important definition of conscience, then, is "the transparency of the subject for the divine," which differs radically from any "reduction to subjective certitude."[205]

Ratzinger next examines what John Henry Newman contributes to the discussion of conscience. It is a mistake to associate Newman with the valorization of subjectivity over against objective truth, or with the polarity of freedom versus authority. Newman rejected religious liberalism and subjectivism. What conscience meant for Newman is that human beings truly have access to God's challenging and correcting truth. In seeking to hear and obey this truth, Newman was willing to sacrifice worldly trappings that meant a good deal to him.

Today, says Ratzinger, a notion of historical progress has generally replaced the notion of ontologically grounded truth. It may seem that truth is static; progress is dynamic. Truth claims are arrogant; progress consists in deconstructing them. If this were so, Ratzinger observes, then belief in conscience could hardly be more than a pretense. There would be no "co-knowing" of truth (divine truth); rather, there would only be what seems good to people at a particular time and place.[206] In this regard, Ratzinger refers to the debate between Socrates and Plato, on the one side, and the Sophists on the other. The former believed in truth. Their view fits with that of Christians who believe in the Logos and in healing and liberation through divine Truth. Without truth, power stands unopposed at the center of life. It is truth alone, perceivable by humans, that places a limit upon power.

Ratzinger next inquires into conscience's "two levels," traditionally called synderesis and *conscientia*. Instead of using the word "synderesis," he employs "anamnesis."[207] He means by this the "spark" or "basic understanding," given to us in our created nature by God, that enables us to know the true and the good and to be inclined toward it. In our created nature, we are not self-enclosed but rather are open to God and able to hear God's truth. The gospel itself answers to this yearning, even while exceeding it. When the gentiles "are a law to themselves" (Rom. 2:14), it is not because they are lucky not to have the burden of God's law but rather because they yearn or incline toward God's truth through "anamnesis" (or synderesis). Through anamnesis, humans possess "an antecedent basic knowledge of the essential constants of the will of God."[208] This basic moral knowledge is found in the Decalogue, whose precepts find an echo in other cultures, even if without the same clarity. Seeking God's presence opens us up ever more clearly to the content known through anamnesis.

It follows that we should not frame conscience in terms of a contrast or contradiction between authority and freedom. Rather, freedom itself is not autonomous, and the truth that speaks to us in "anamnesis" is not external to us in the sense of being foreign to our yearning for fulfillment and happiness. The reality of anamnesis shows that we are created for divine truth and can know it, although we need "assistance from without so that it [anamnesis] can become aware of itself."[209] Faith's moral teaching fulfills the yearning and, in part, the content that we know in anamnesis. The authority of the church, insofar as it is communicating God's word, is not in opposition to this interior freedom and fulfillment. Ratzinger speaks of "the new *anamnesis* of faith which unfolds, similarly to the *anamnesis* of creation, in constant dialogue between within and without."[210] Just as we have access to God's truth through anamnesis (or synderesis), so too the church has a dynamism that enables it to hear and know God's truth. This magisterial "Christian memory" secures the truth of the church's moral teaching.[211] Otherwise, Christians would be threatened by moral enslavement to their own subjectivity in conformity with the wider culture(s) in which they live.

Anamnesis is the first, ontological level where we hear God's truth; *conscientia* is the second level. This second level involves judgment and decision, the application of God's truth to particular situations. Anamnesis is the habitus, while *conscientia* is the act. Ratzinger notes that when stripped of its grounding in anamnesis or synderesis, conscience becomes a shell of itself. For Thomas Aquinas, Ratzinger says, conscience is grounded upon synderesis and consists in three steps: recognizing, testifying, and judging. The judgment of conscience can be erroneous if one of the first two steps is incorrect. Much depends, therefore, upon our moral character, which can obscure our reception of God's truth in anamnesis or synderesis. The judgment of conscience is binding, but the problem is that our will may impede the communication of the content of synderesis. We err in conscience culpably when, due to a bad will, we choose to become "deaf to the internal promptings of truth."[212]

Christian moral truth will be difficult, but it will also make us happy. The key is that hearing the divine truth given through anamnesis or synderesis opens us not merely to the voice of our Creator and Judge but also to the merciful voice of our Redeemer whose word fulfills our deepest yearning for truth. In conflicts of conscience, we are not simply doomed to guilt. In Christ, grace comes to justify us, to unite us to Christ's expiation of our sin, so that divine truth does not crush us as a burden from which we would wish to flee. We encounter divine truth not solely through anamnesis (or synderesis) and conscience, but through the Word incarnate.

Christ is the source of the church's "Christian memory" that fulfills "what the *anamnesis* of the creator expects of us."[213] If Christ and his merciful truth are not at the center, then truth becomes too much of a burden for us. The answer is not to flee to an autonomous freedom that will destroy us but to turn to the fulfillment of freedom—true freedom—in Christ who loved us and died for us so that we might live in his glorious truth. Ratzinger concludes, "Only when we know and experience this from within will we be free to hear the message of conscience with joy and without fear."[214]

Today, Christian morality faces a sharp challenge: do traditional Christian moral teachings truly have a divine source? In responding to this question, Christian ethics has to deal with the problem that conscience often fails to show up when cultural pressures incline toward wicked behavior or toward complicity in evil. From a perspective suspicious of the claims of conscience, Timothy Gorringe has remarked: "Is it really the case that human beings live only in an 'echo chamber', or might it be the case . . . that humans are addressed from beyond themselves, so that they are not simply left to the mercy of their own conscience (which, as the experience of National Socialism showed, is extremely malleable)?"[215]

In this chapter, we have seen that Catholic theologians moved away from the moral manuals—with their emphasis on teleology and natural and divine law—and instead focused on forming conscience in existential authenticity. In "Moral Theology since Vatican II: Clarity or Chaos?," Richard A. McCormick, SJ, describes the shift in postconciliar moral theology as toward "a pedagogy of personal responsibility," so that we now recognize that "the articulated wisdom of the community—the teaching of the magisterium—*enlightens* conscience; it does not *replace* it."[216] As a prominent twentieth-century representative of the new conscience-centered morality, McCormick can help us to understand how the new conscience-centered morality became so popular throughout the world after the Council.[217]

McCormick maintains that Vatican II accomplished many things in moral theology, including the rejection of legalism, the discovery of transcendental freedom (or the fundamental option), the option for the poor and oppressed, the new centrality of the person's overall good (or the overall consequences of an action), and a new tentativeness regarding moral norms and magisterial authority.[218] He assures us that postconciliar conscience must continue to seek formation; the new conscience-centered morality does not mean that "we decide by ourselves what is right and wrong."[219] In our transcendental freedom, no longer burdened by legalism or by strictly authoritative judgments of natural or divine law that we must obey, "we form our consciences in a community, a community of experience, reflection and memory" (21).

McCormick grants the danger of "a rationalistic secularism which ignores the deep influences of Christian realities on our moral sensitivities and imaginations" (23). For warding off this danger, he exhorts us to "trust in the Spirit" who will see us through (23). The key is that in our deepest core the grace of the Spirit enables us to make a "*total self-commitment of the person.*"[220] Transcendental freedom, he says, is "the capacity to decide about oneself," and the decision about the self—about one's self-disposition—is for or against "grace."[221] At this deepest level of the fundamental option, conscience and the Holy Spirit converge and self-actualizing moral determinations are made.[222]

McCormick's perspective reflects that of his mentors. Rahner argues that the Catholic Church should focus her moral teaching on proclaiming the transcendental truth, actualized in responsible and free conscience, that "humanity strives irresistibly for God and that, in this striving, human morality becomes theonomous and, as a result, really autonomous."[223] Fuchs speaks of conscience as "an experience of coming to a position in which insight is guaranteed, accepted and absolutely compelling," and he emphasizes our freedom from any absolute moral norm in the historically evolving human quest for transcendental self-realization through action.[224] Häring identifies conscience as the very heart of personal freedom, the place where the person determines his or her fundamental option, and the center of everything Christian.

In my view, these Catholic theologians' expansion of conscience's place and function—now distanced from natural and divine law—exhibits an inappropriate optimism about what happens when such conscience is at the helm of the moral life of fallen human beings. Before the Council, Catholic moralists sought to identify the universal moral norms or laws that bound conscience and then, in difficult cases of conscience, to identify the limits within which people could exercise their liberty without sinning. Natural and divine law played a constraining role, as did authority—even if probabilist authorities often sought to reduce the pressure of the law's constraints. After the Council, as Mark Graham says with regard to Fuchs, those who continued to discuss natural law did so "by wedding a notion of universal human nature with contemporary personalism emphasizing historicity, mutability, personal development, and concrete, integral flourishing."[225]

In this way, postconciliar conscience-centered Catholic moral theology experimented with the idea that too much law was the problem and that Catholic consciences can now be liberated in order to act responsibly for the good that humans transcendentally desire. The results have not been promising. Looking back on the 1970s and 1980s from the perspective of the sexual abuse scandals, Bishop Robert Barron notes that "a moral relativism, especially in regard to matters sexual, came to be taken for granted in the years following the Second Vatican Council, and this attitude was adopted by too many within the priesthood itself."[226] Even more tellingly, he observes that Catholics at present seem to be profoundly morally adrift: at the very time that "our society seems, more and more, to run on purely materialist and egotistic principles . . . , poll after poll reveals that, on the major moral issues under discussion today, Catholics more or less track with the secularist consensus."[227]

What can be done? Philosophically and theologically, a retrieval of human nature and its flourishing—and thus of natural law, virtue, and, correspondingly, sin—is needed, and so also is a renewed acknowledgment of divinely revealed moral norms.[228] In this task, moral philosophers and theologians can benefit not only from the work of Pinckaers, Labourdette, and others treated above, but also from additional twentieth-century classics as Hannah Arendt's 1958 *The Human Condition* and Alasdair MacIntyre's 1999 *Dependent Rational Animals: Why Human Beings Need the Virtues*.[229]

Early in his pontificate, Pope Benedict XVI urged just such a recovery of the reality of human nature and universal moral norms. Recognizing that such things may sound reactionary to postmodern ears, he pointed out their connection with true liberation. Natural law is "the true guarantee offered to each one in order that he may live in freedom, have his dignity respected and be protected from all ideological manipulation and every kind of arbitrary use or abuse by the stronger."[230] It is no secret that in the contemporary world—as so often in human history—political life is often deeply dysfunctional. Indeed, the ugly manifestations of political life today reflect the very opposite of the post-World War II optimism about the liberating potential of freeing human relationships from the constraints of law.

Fortunately, it is precisely sinners whom Christ came to save. The church's role is to diagnose our condition in light of God's law of love and to apply the healing and elevating balm of Christ. As we have seen, Ratzinger appreciates "the human longing that conscience's objectively just indictment . . . not be the last word."[231] Ratzinger finds in Jesus Christ the Truth that both judges *and* forgives. Christ thereby enables conscience to speak "of an authority of grace, a power of expiation which allows the guilt to vanish and makes truth at least truly redemptive."[232] Moreover, by recalling the habitus of synderesis or anamnesis, Ratzinger affirms that the judgment of conscience—conscience's application of the moral norm—is grounded both in God's eternal law and in the church's "memory" mediated by the magisterium. On the path to human beatitude, Christ sends his Spirit to heal our rational and emotional life and to perfect our conscience.

In an essay on Ratzinger's theology of conscience in relation to the healing and elevating of culture, Peter Casarella concludes: "The full interior connection between culture and conscience can be found in Benedict's retrieval of the Pauline notion of *logike latreia* (Rom. 12:1, 'spiritual worship'). . . . Paul is exhorting us to see that when Christian living is offered in the one Body and in the one living Christ, then it becomes its own kind of Eucharist for the world."[233] In the Christian moral life, supernatural love—sharing in Christ's eucharistic self-offering—is the very center, but conscience, within the matrix of the virtues (especially prudence), has an important place in orienting us toward God's Word. Both through the demands of conscience and through the demands of Christ, the Word of God challenges us to a holiness that is countercultural in every age. No wonder, then, that Paul urges believers not to rely upon themselves but to be transformed: "Do not be conformed to this world but be transformed by the renewal of your mind, that you may prove what is the will of God, what is good and acceptable and perfect" (Rom. 12:2).

Conclusion

The Path Forward

The twentieth century was a century of horrific carnage, with two World Wars, the Holocaust, the mass death caused by Stalin and Mao and others, and countless smaller wars and atrocities. Arguably, it was also a century of more change in Catholic moral theology than in any century since the fourteenth. Unfortunately, at the end of the century, just as at the beginning, conscience—though now radically reconceived—reigned supreme in the dominant academic strand of Catholic moral theology. In this book, I have sought to trace the paths taken by twentieth-century thinkers on conscience with the goal of offering a preliminary window into how this happened.

My first chapter showed that conscience, biblically speaking, is a significant reality for the Christian moral life but not the central one. More important are realities such as adoptive sonship, the grace of the Holy Spirit, cruciform love, apostolic teaching, and the new creation. Believers are the temples of the Spirit; we must live according to the spirit rather than according to the flesh. The Christian moral life involves governing our passions and living in accord with God's law. When we do not resist the Spirit of Jesus Christ, we can be transformed so as to live truly self-sacrificial lives, guided by the beatitudes and by the life of prayer.

My second chapter showed that the preconciliar moral manuals were better than one would suppose from today's stereotypical portrait of them. They generally offer a rich account of human nature, human action, and natural law. They contain nuanced and profound engagements with ancient and modern thinkers. Their account of conscience, too, is in certain ways a valuable one. In the varieties of probabilism, we can see a noble attempt to help Christians facing difficult decisions in their work, their family, and their society. The moral manuals seek to support the laudable Christian desire to perform every action in accord with God's law. The manuals assume that the motivation for morally good action is a devout desire to avoid sin and to participate fully (eucharistically) in Christ's self-offering in love to the Father through the Spirit. The manuals were not rigorist—even if they were demanding, just as Christ is demanding.

Nevertheless, we saw that the moral manuals and the ethical system they sustained were deficient. By heavily foregrounding conscience, the manuals turned Christian ethics into a quest for the legal minimum, focused on fulfilling legal obligations. Moreover, conscience, as the act that applies moral knowledge to particular cases, has its place within the broader task of prudence. It is prudence that issues the command to perform a particular action. For the Christian, the end or goal of the virtues is not merely earthly flourishing or obedience to law but rather is everlasting sharing in the divine beatitude as members of the family of God. The supernatural virtue of charity is the "form" of all the virtues, including prudence, insofar as prudence directs everything to this supernatural end. The path to the joy of everlasting beatitude is cruciform love, along with faith, hope, the infused moral virtues, and the gifts of the Spirit.[1] Conscience retains its important role in the supernaturalized moral life, but it is not the center of that life.

In chapter 3, we encountered some significant advances. Early twentieth-century Thomists such as Merkelbach continued to accept the probabilist system, while insisting that prudence be given its due. In the work of Labourdette, we found a brilliant elucidation of why the probabilist system cannot suffice. A further advance was made by D'Arcy, who perceived that traditional defenses of the suppression or persecution of "unbelievers" (or apostates or heretics) are at odds with principles regarding conscience that Aquinas himself articulated. It is a sin to compel people to undertake religious practices that violate their (erroneous) consciences and force them to sin (by lying, for example) on pain of death or other severe penalties.

The advances made by preconciliar readers of Scripture and Thomistic moral theologians prepared a fertile ground for advancing beyond the moral manuals. A third element for advancement became evident in chapter 4, namely, existentialist insights. The treatment of conscience and obligation certainly feels legalistic in some moral manuals. Existentialism, with its emphasis on personal responsibility and communication, provides a way to exhibit the dynamic character of the moral life and the unity of moral and mystical theology, in accord with the virtue of prudence. Personalist philosophy, grounded in phenomenology, can contribute in a similar way.[2] In the early 1930s, as Edward Baring has shown, "[Jacques] Maritain was able to use the language of existence to both associate his work with and distinguish it from other existentialisms."[3] So-called existential Thomism made helpful contributions to all branches of Catholic theology.[4]

After the Council, however, these preconciliar biblical, Thomistic, and existentialist advances toward a richer Catholic moral theology were carried forward only by a minority of moral theologians. Instead, the mainstream of postconciliar Catholic moral theology followed Rahner, Fuchs, and Häring in advancing a conscience-centered morality resituated within a transcendental anthropology. In chapter 4, I presented this development, in accord with David Kelly's and Ronald Modras's recognition that "Rahner's significance for moral theology has often been overlooked."[5] These thinkers argued that the preconciliar reformers were right about the deficiencies of the moral manuals but wrong in supposing that the solution was to remove conscience from the center. In the moral theology advanced by these theologians, newly conceived "conscience" became even more central than it was before, though now within a framework of transcendental freedom, existential decision, and human liberation.[6]

In his 1987 book *The Making of Catholic Moral Theology*, John Mahoney, SJ, argues that postconciliar Catholic moral theology has made significant advances with regard to what he calls "totality, diversity, and mystery."[7] By this phrase, he means three things: the critique of moral absolutes, the pluralistic valuation of different cultural standpoints and modes of discourse, and the movement away from deductive logic toward embrace of "the sheer wonder of man's being as it responds in freedom to the design of God."[8] Each of these developments, I observe, sheds light on the increasing irrelevance of moral theology (as such) to Catholic decision-making. No wonder Mahoney concludes his section on "mystery" by stating that in moral "matters, as the Second Vatican Council observed, man is ultimately 'alone with God' in the 'sanctuary' of his conscience."[9]

The ongoing relevance of the twentieth century can be seen in what two prominent twenty-first-century Catholic moral theologians have to say about conscience. The first theologian follows in the tradition of Rahner, Fuchs, and Häring[10]; the second in the tradition of Labourdette and Pinckaers. These two theologians—James Keenan and Reinhard Hütter—illustrate the significance of the history I have examined. Let me begin with Keenan.

James F. Keenan, SJ

Although James Keenan's writings span the whole spectrum of Catholic moral theology, including biblical ethics and virtue theory, nothing has characterized Keenan's work more decisively than his advocacy of the centrality of conscience.[11] As a doctoral student of Fuchs in the 1980s who was influenced also by the later Rahner and Häring, Keenan's approach exemplifies postconciliar conscience-centered morality.[12]

According to Keenan, Pope John Paul II's 1993 encyclical *Veritatis Splendor*—praised by Thomistic opponents of the moral manuals such as Pinckaers[13]—is in fact "a contemporary expression of neo-manualism."[14] Perhaps by this statement Keenan means simply that *Veritatis Splendor* defends universal moral norms as well as the ability of the magisterium to authoritatively teach these norms, and it also contains teachings on the structure of human action, natural law, conscience, and sin. Otherwise, it is hard to square Keenan's claim with the notable differences between the moral manuals and the encyclical, most prominently the encyclical's biblical and existentialist emphases.

Indeed, the opponents of *Veritatis Splendor* tend to sympathize with the probabilism of the moral manuals. Häring, for instance, remained to his dying day a defender of probabilism, so long as it is separated from the preconciliar emphasis on law and absolute moral norms. Häring explains, "The purpose of probabilism is to allow a careful evaluation of the present opportunities, of the needs of fellowmen and community in view of God's gifts, and always in the light of our vocation to holiness," in order to produce a "sincere judgment of conscience."[15] In his view, the manuals are still acceptable in their method, once their legalism has been corrected. He concludes, "Classical probabilism is still of great actuality."[16]

In various publications, Keenan himself has registered his agreement with this point. But his main task has involved highlighting the absolute centrality of conscience. In a 2015 essay entitled "Redeeming Conscience," he reflects upon the purpose of the church's moral teaching, and he underscores that the very heart of the matter is conscience. Recalling the counsel of his teacher Klaus Demmer, Keenan holds that the most important thing is that "bishops should attend to their primary charge: to remind all Christians that they each have a conscience to be followed. If bishops spent their moral energy on this, then maybe the people of God would get somewhere."[17] From this perspective, the proclamation of the moral content of the gospel can be summed up, by and large, as the commandment to form and follow one's conscience. For Keenan, the crucial thing is that the church "be a respecter of consciences."[18]

Much like George Tyrrell and Bernard Häring, Keenan highlights the central importance of the collective conscience of Christians. He thinks that this collective conscience today requires reversing much of the church's sexual teaching. He places "conscience" at the very heart of the *sensus fidelium*: "Conscience is what makes for the credibility of *sensus fidelium*. Sensus fidelium* is not some poll-taking of what Catholics believe, but rather is what they hold in conscience. *Sensus fidelium* is about the laity's beliefs as a faith lived in conscience."[19] These beliefs could indeed be ascertained by a poll, but Keenan's point is that they are not superficial beliefs, even if they are in many cases beliefs that contradict both Scripture and tradition. On moral matters, the majority of Catholics believe today whatever the wider culture around them believes. In Keenan's view, this is generally (though certainly not always) a good thing. He values the fact that the wider culture reflects a growing appreciation of the various forms of human sexual expression. He observes, "Like the young gay man searching for God's will, the laity's struggle to arrive at their positions on homosexuality, divorce and remarriage, cohabitation, and a host of other matters did not come overnight."[20]

On this view, now that the New Testament's teachings on sexual matters are no longer acceptable to the majority of Catholics, bishops need to appreciate the developing witness of the *sensus fidelium* that is found in "the laity's consciences" and in every "socially informed and collectively engaged conscience."[21] Once the church accepts the "primacy of conscience" for the moral life, the church will be able to acknowledge the history of the "horrific lack of moral agency" among Christians and to overcome this history by collectively facing up to the errors of the past.[22] Keenan agrees with the Catholic moral theologian Margaret Farley, who affirms in her 2007 book *Just Love: A Framework for Christian Sexual Ethics* that the Bible's teachings must be measured by our consciences, since the biblical texts (and Jesus) aim to "free us, not enslave us to what violates our very sense of truth and justice."[23]

Keenan concludes his *A History of Catholic Moral Theology in the Twentieth Century* by praising "Farley's universally oriented guidance for sexual conduct" and by summing up his vision of postconciliar conscience-centered Catholic morality: "As we conclude our study of the incredible twentieth century, we can now, in our own time and place, most likely in our communities of faith, recognize God's call to discipleship. As we listen to the summons, we should be able to hear the will of God in the sanctuary of our consciences calling us to just love."[24] On this view, conscience-centered morality, rooted in an existential summons at the core of our freedom as followers of Christ, will liberate Catholics from any static vision of the word of God as mediated by the church over the centuries and thereby will become a force for the spread of liberative love and grace in the world.

But on what grounds are Catholics to believe that God now reveals himself in a set of consciences that the church must obey, over against the consistent teachings of Scripture and tradition? Keenan's answer involves the historicity of human nature. In *A History of Catholic Moral Theology in the Twentieth Century*, Keenan appreciatively cites a number of "European theological ethicists who have for the past twenty years been developing a deep and abiding interest in the hermeneutical compatibility of reason, tradition, and the evolutionary nature of creation."[25] No doubt Keenan knows that this development goes much further back than merely twenty years—although perhaps he has in view John Mahoney, SJ's *Christianity in Evolution*.[26] As Karl Rahner puts the point in his book written fifty years ago, "concrete human nature has itself a real history and is subject to an internal and social mutation. Such a change, however, can render no longer binding many a feature of the concrete moral norms which were formerly and quite rightly proclaimed as binding, because they corresponded to man's concrete nature at the time."[27] Although Rahner affirms the "ultimate, essential consistency" of humankind, he holds that it is very difficult to know in the course of history itself what truly pertains to the essence of human nature, since human nature is spiritual.[28] He insists, "Man is therefore also permitted and simultaneously required to remain open to a further evolution of his own reality and to a higher actualization of his moral consciousness."[29]

How is it that theologians can know that there exists a universal "conscience" or "moral consciousness" that, as the one constant element in the midst of evolving and fluid human nature, merits credence in moral matters? In addition, how is it that theologians can suppose that evolutionary theory or the events of the twentieth century warrant the supposition of a moral evolution of humankind, a progressively "higher actualization" of human moral consciousness?

Aware of such concerns, Keenan warns against the "classicist" temptation, borrowing this term from Bernard Lonergan. He explains, "For classicists, the world is a finished product and truth has already been revealed, expressed, taught and known. In order to be a truth it must be universal and unchanging."[30] Rejecting what he considers to be the straightjacket imposed by many claims about universal and unchanging truth, Keenan turns still more firmly to conscience as the universal human moral ground, the core of our being where we make our act of faith and take our fundamental stance. Conscience is where we commit ourselves to Christ: "When we say 'Amen,' we say it in conscience. There we testify to the Lordship of Jesus and there we stand in solidarity with him."[31]

To be in "solidarity" with the Lord Jesus "in conscience" does not carry with it any firm moral content other than "love and justice."[32] But our evolving understanding of this love and justice is continually informed by "the teachings and stories from the sacred Scriptures" and from "the church's tradition," and also by "the wisdom of parents, elders, and teachers, as well as friends and mentors," the insights of "our local culture," and "the lessons learned in our own life experience."[33] The above-named wisdom, insights, and lessons may potentially reverse any specific moral teaching of Scripture and tradition, but for Keenan this situation is fine so long as conscience stands firm, since in conscience we find an ever-present union with Christ.

Keenan regularly discusses the moral manuals in his writings. Like Häring, he argues that their deficiency was legalistic rigorism. Failing to trust the consciences of the laity, they imprisoned the laity within an outdated morality. In addition, their emphasis on the "probable opinions" of authorities allowed believers to develop habits of docility toward authority, thereby impeding the true development of conscience. Keenan contends, "The evident failure of the moral manuals in shaping Catholic consciences to resist rather than to participate in the barbarism of Fascism and Nazism led Catholic moral theologians throughout Europe to a complete repudiation of the manuals immediately after the war."[34] According to Keenan, therefore, the best preconciliar Catholic moral theologians were committed to strengthening the place of conscience. They defended a "more robust notion of conscience that requires more from the ordinary Christian and that sees the conscience as the source of moral agency"; and they located their understanding of conscience "in the pursuit of the good, animated by the call to love God, self, and neighbor."[35] For Keenan, the great advance in Catholic moral theology after World War II, and especially after the Council, has consisted in enhancing and refining the manuals' emphasis on conscience.[36]

Reinhard Hütter

Reinhard Hütter's perspective is quite different.[37] In his 2004 *Bound to Be Free*, written as a Lutheran ethicist, he argues that if Christian freedom obeys no universal moral norms, then such freedom is a mere sham. He cannot accept that Christ merely sets us "free to do what we want, as long as we have a 'good will' (are motivated by the 'gospel') and thereby intend 'something good' in what we do."[38] He is concerned to counter the modern understanding of "freedom" as lawless and therefore inevitably as "the law of our unexamined desires."[39] If we simply are called in Christ to follow wherever our hearts lead, then there is no need for a theological discipline of "ethics"; "moral theology" as such becomes impossible except as a rubber stamp to whatever the Zeitgeist or our personal desire proposes. Such antinomianism ends by becoming a strict legalism, though now a legalism based upon the unlawfulness of criticizing whatever desires happen to be culturally approved.

According to Hütter, anthropocentric ethics cuts against Scripture and the tradition's theocentric, teleological ethics. Moral theology properly has at its center God, active in the creative and redemptive past, in the ecclesial and sacramental present, and in the eschatological future. In fact, freedom and moral flourishing are ordered to God and enabled by God. Such freedom takes shape in virtues and is impeded by vices. Furthermore, it is God's law—God's commandments—that instructs us in the path of true (relational) freedom; law and love are correlative.

Hütter became a Catholic in December 2004, and his first book as a Catholic appeared in early 2012, titled *Dust Bound for Heaven*. Here, he defends Thomistic hylomorphism as a biblically faithful path between the extremes of angelism and animalism. The key is Aquinas's awareness that "the passions do not act exclusively on the soul, but rather on the whole human composite."[40] According to angelism, the passions merely distract the immaterial intellect's life; whereas according to animalism (grounded in Epicureanism, Thomas Hobbes, and David Hume), the intellect—here simply material—exists to express and serve the passions. For Aquinas, by contrast, the intellective power governs the passions, making it possible for the passions to offer their proper contribution to the true flourishing "of the whole human being" under the healing and elevating grace of the Holy Spirit.[41]

In *Bound for Beatitude* (2019), Hütter examines Aquinas's theocentric understanding of conscience and prudence. Hütter integrates these topics into the fuller framework of the Christian moral life, including nature and grace, eternal law and natural law, the saving power of Christ's cross, charity, faith, hope, the virtue of religion, the virtue of chastity, and our hope for resurrection and eternal life.[42] He emphasizes that sinners, headed toward death, need the redemption that Christ brings and the transformative faith, hope, and love that his Spirit imparts.

Notably, he warns that absent a proper understanding of human "finality" or body-soul ordering toward beatitude, "the late-modern person vacillates between the self-image of an essentially disembodied sovereign will that submits all exteriority, including the body, to its imperious dictates, and the self-image of a super-primate . . . gifted or cursed with a developed consciousness that is driven by instincts, passions, and desires beyond its control."[43] Real conscience has no place in either of these distorted self-images. Real conscience, after all, judges our actions and often condemns them. Real conscience does not give free rein to a person's desires.

What is needed, Hütter says, is for Catholic moral theology to move away from "the denial of the finality of nature and the consequent metaphysical evacuation of nature itself."[44] By "finality" he means theocentric teleology, our ordering toward the Good, toward God as our ultimate end who brings to fulfillment our body-soul creaturehood by accomplishing in us the real truth of our being. Universal human nature derives from the Creator. Insofar as the human race is a unity, God has given us a nature, whose natural flourishing has distinctive exigencies. The same is true for the "supernatural new nature" that we receive through grace. On the path of beatitude, conscience helps us to recognize our fallenness, to hear God's moral law regarding our true flourishing, and to pursue this practical truth through the virtue of prudence.

As Hütter observes, the "typically modern crisis of moral motivation" involves the question: "Why should I pursue the good? Why should I be moral in the first place?"[45] When beatitude is not foregrounded, human beings can feel trapped by human nature and embrace the supposed freedom of either angelism or animalism. Hütter terms this situation "subjective sovereignty."[46] By contrast, when the Good is firmly at the center, we can see the proper value of synderesis (especially when illuminated by faith) and conscience in communicating to us the eternal law.[47] We can recognize that conscience's judgments are not mere condemnations but rather are an opening to repentance and hope. The reason to do the good is that God wants us to share in his joy everlastingly. Christ reveals this to us, but we need conscience to help lead us toward it as a real possibility.

This work takes place through supernatural prudence, which the act of conscience serves.

Treating synderesis, which he calls "the primordial conscience," Hütter remarks that it enables practical reason to pursue and achieve its end, namely, truth in matters of action. The principles contained in the habitus of synderesis enable us to know that the "end" or goal of action is the good. If there were no universal human nature and no theocentric teleology rooted in the attraction of the Good, then there would be no "conscience" worthy of the name. In such a situation, one might still appeal to "conscience," but it would be only the demands made by the person based upon perceived desires. There would be no way to measure the demands of such conscience against the objective reality of true human flourishing.

In this light, Hütter addresses the problem of "counterfeit" conscience. He states, "Turning away from the primordial conscience [synderesis] and . . . from the teleological order of reality and embracing instead the negative freedom of sovereign self-determination, the anthropocentric turn and the consequent sovereign subjectivity give rise to a pervasive counterfeit of conscience, the presumptuous 'authenticity' of self-will."[48] Such "conscience" is not ruled by law as expressive of God's teleological ordering for our flourishing. Its demands are arbitrary and express merely the fact that the person has a strong desire or viewpoint. It does not place the person's actions under the judgment of God the lawgiver. Instead, it asserts the person's own will or desire as the source of law. It may be instructed by biblical stories, ecclesiastical advice, personal experience, and so on; but it is not grounded in a recognized divinely established ordering for human flourishing to which we are accountable. Whatever it is, therefore, it is not "conscience." At best it is a "counterfeit" conscience that reflects the strong impulses or notions of our culture or of our personal experience. Such conscience will be on the alert not to be overrun by "extrinsic" authorities such as God or Scripture or church, on the grounds that ultimately only the self can determine for the self what is good.[49]

If conscience were really about following our own path rather than any path "imposed" upon us, however, then the problem of human fallenness would simply be exacerbated. Many Nazis, for example, claimed to be following "conscience." If there is no cognitively knowable human nature and natural law, no theocentric teleology governing human action toward the Good, who is to say that these Nazis were *not* following real conscience? Without a moral measure, conscience can mean anything.

What is the difference between counterfeit conscience (i.e., self-will making its demands in accord with our desires and the standards of our culture) and sincere but erroneous conscience? Aquinas insists that erroneous conscience must always be obeyed. Can the same be said for what Hütter calls "counterfeit" conscience?

The difference is that a person acting out of erroneous conscience is not denying the reality of "an objective moral order and reliable knowledge of it."[50] Erroneous conscience presupposes, and indeed insists upon, just such an order. The contrary is the case with counterfeit conscience. Conscience as self-will rejects universal human nature and a knowable natural law. Counterfeit conscience is therefore not erroneous conscience.

How do we know when we are dealing with counterfeit conscience rather than with erroneous conscience? Hütter offers a test: "In the wake of the anthropocentric turn, 'sincerity,' 'authenticity,' and 'being at peace with oneself' become the new criteria of a radically subjectivist conception of moral judgment in service of the sovereign self."[51] If conscience simply appeals to its own existential authenticity, and justifies itself simply on the basis of a feeling of interior peace, then we know we are not dealing with conscience as it actually is but rather with counterfeit conscience. Again, real conscience involves the imperious moral law; real conscience is a rational judgment whose dictate is not measured simply by how the (fallen) self feels. The person who asserts self-will as "conscience" has fallen into self-deception. Though the person thinks he or she is free, the person has become a slave to his or her passions. Often such persons turn to "three versions of self-justification: moral nihilism ('There is neither good nor evil,' 'Good and evil are strictly subjective success terms'), moral skepticism ('Human beings are inherently incapable of discerning reliably moral good and evil'), and moral sovereignty ('I am the creator and arbiter of my own moral code')."[52]

As Hütter points out, persons who take this stand live in performative self-contradiction because they still act for ends that they perceive as goods. To this degree, they recognize the truth of teleology even while attempting to deny it. In fact, despite their skepticism about natural teleology and natural law, they "*de facto* display the first principle of practical reason, follow the first precept of the natural law, and for the most part also acknowledge an at least tacit knowledge of some of the secondary precepts of the natural law."[53] Since synderesis cannot be suppressed, real conscience makes itself known even in persons who deny it and substitute in its place sovereign self-will.

Is there a solution to this mess? Hütter finds the solution to be Jesus Christ, who reveals that "the first truth and the sovereign good are at hand in the utter humility and vulnerability of the human nature that the incarnate Logos assumed from among a people God created for that purpose."[54] To receive this Logos we have to relinquish our sovereign self-will. Christ offers us beatitude, but on the path of cruciform love, in obedience to the God who is both love and lawgiver. Christ, who is Good, is also the Truth (John 14:6)—and he is so as cruciform love. Christ thereby confirms the fundamental dictate of synderesis: "To be good is to do the truth."[55]

Hütter's position accords with the place given to conscience in the New Testament. Conscience is not the center of the moral life, but conscience has a crucial role in moral judgment, applying the natural law to particular actions. Conscience does not command or perfect actions; this requires not only right exercise of practical reason (prudence) but also the virtues of faith, hope, love, humility, temperance, and indeed the entirety of the Christian moral organism, including the gifts of the Holy Spirit. The Holy Spirit enables believers—at least those who do not resist the Spirit—to live in cruciform love, rather than living according to the flesh. In this way, believers can be truly free, truly self-integrated, truly creaturely.

By contrast, Keenan places a reconceived conscience at the center, and he exceeds the place of conscience in the New Testament. He does not integrate conscience with prudence in a detailed way; nor does he link conscience to the theocentric and teleological structure of the moral life, or to eternal law as known in natural law and through divine revelation. The weight that he gives to conscience as responsible freedom cannot sustain Christian moral theology.[56]

Keenan's perspective conforms to the way in which most contemporary people actually live. In this sense, Keenan's project can be understood—to quote what Jean-Pascal Gay says of the seventeenth-century probabilist debates—as an attempt to solve "a wider crisis regarding the capacity of theology and theologians to contribute to the social construction of truth."[57] It is an effort to enable the Catholic Church to remain relevant and attractive in the contemporary world.

Rahner had the same goal in view. Hütter articulates Rahner's guiding hope: "according to Rahner, theonomy is realized by way of autonomy. Conscience is fundamentally the self-awareness of transcendental subjectivity arising from the experience of being handed over to oneself, the experience of a primordial freedom and responsibility that *qua* creatureliness is essentially, though unthematically, oriented to the theonomic truth."[58] The problem is that this effort to ground everything in transcendental subjectivity, and thus in existential authenticity at the core of one's being, slides almost inevitably into sovereign subjectivity. Hütter shows that, for Rahner, "the first and constitutive moment of the human spirit is the freedom of self-possession and not the innate habitual presence of the theonomic first principle and first precept of moral truth."[59] The result is to ground the moral law not upon the gift of truth (received in synderesis) but upon the "transcendental experience of freedom."[60] It is a very small step to construing conscience, with its creative responsible freedom, as self-determination. This step becomes inevitable when the notion of universal human nature is undermined. The human person is conceived as evolving toward his or her own perfection by creating, in authentic freedom, ever new norms that allow for fuller expression of transcendental freedom.

The tragedy of twentieth-century Catholic moral theology, in its academically dominant strands, is that it ultimately lacked the strength to overcome the strong cultural push toward sovereign subjectivity. For the manualists, the directive role of conscience was to determine how the law applied to a particular case and therefore what one was at liberty to do. The probabilist system expanded this field of liberty as much as possible within the limits of law. The moral ideal here was to remain in "good faith." This same ideal was taken up by the postconciliar moral theologians, but without the limits of universally valid moral norms grounded in eternal law. Conscience became not only the "proximate rule of human action" but now even the very "source of moral agency." This strains biblical and Catholic morality to the breaking point, since conscience, in reality, cannot credibly claim such a role.[61]

Today, conscience-centered morality is largely a program of individual and collective liberation from universal moral norms and systems, in hopes that this will bring about sexual, social, and ecological justice.[62] But there is a better, truly liberative path. Christian ethics should not be conscience centered. Rather, Christian ethics depends upon the exigencies of human nature—and thus upon the framework of the virtues—and also upon the power of the grace of the Holy Spirit. It is an "eschatological" ethics, rooted in Christ's kingdom-inauguration. Conscience has its proper place within this eschatological ethics.

Drawing upon Paul Lehmann's work, the late John Webster remarked that "the tortuous history of the notion of conscience forces theologians to choose between two simple alternatives: '[E]ither "do the conscience over" or "do the conscience in"!'"[63] Webster admits that the latter path—eliminating any further discussion of conscience—is tempting because of the present "anthropological captivity of the church and its moral theology."[64] But he resists this solution. Instead, he seeks to retrieve the doctrine of conscience for contemporary theology. In so doing, he begins with an important question: "What kind of repair work is needed to accomplish the theological renovation of conscience?"[65]

He and I agree on the answer. The "repair work" must consist in reintegrating conscience into the broader framework of the Christian moral organism—in which, I note, conscience serves prudence and thereby serves the other virtues as well—with God and beatitude at the center, and thus with Christ and the grace of the Holy Spirit at the center, healing and elevating the powers of human nature in accord with God's law. This approach refuses to allow conscience to exceed its important, but limited, place and function. Webster observes that "we best articulate a Christian theology of conscience when we refuse to isolate it and treat it as a phenomenon in itself. Instead, we need to expound it as one feature within a larger moral landscape."[66]

In the present book—focused almost entirely on conscience—I seem to have done the very thing he warns against! But my purpose has been one of repair. In surveying twentieth-century discussions of conscience and in identifying the ongoing problem of conscience-centered Catholic morality in academic theology, I hope to have contributed to making repair possible, despite my own need of the repairing power of Christ's grace. "Help us, O God of our salvation, for the glory of your name" (Ps. 79:9).

Notes

Introduction

1. See Matthew Levering, *Aquinas's Eschatological Ethics and the Virtue of Temperance* (Notre Dame: University of Notre Dame Press, 2019); see also my *Engaging the Doctrine of Marriage: Human Marriage as the Image and Sacrament of the Marriage of God and Creation* (Eugene, OR: Cascade, 2020). For another constructive path forward, see Ezra Sullivan, OP's strikingly original *Habits and Holiness: Ethics, Theology, and Biological Psychology* (Washington, DC: Catholic University of America Press, 2021).

2. See Alphonsus de Liguori, *Moral Theology*, vol. 1, *Books I-III: On Conscience, Law, Sin and the Theological Virtues*, trans. Ryan Grant (Post Falls, ID: Mediatrix, 2006).

3. Gerald W. Healy, SJ, "Recent Moral Theology," *Philippine Studies* 9 (1961): 311.

4. Vatican Council II, *Optatam Totius*, §16, in *The Conciliar and Post Conciliar Documents*, rev. ed., ed. Austin Flannery, OP, vol. 1 of *Vatican Council II* (Northport, NY: Costello, 1996), 720.

5. Raphael Gallagher, CSsR, "Interpreting Thomas Aquinas: Aspects of the Redemptorist and Jesuit Schools in the Twentieth Century," in *The Ethics of Aquinas*, ed. Stephen J. Pope (Washington, DC: Georgetown University Press, 2002), 376.

6. Gallagher, "Interpreting Thomas Aquinas," 376. In Gallagher's view, "It was the contact with experience that forced theologians to develop the manual as a tradition within a tradition; it is the contact with a new experience that can revive that tradition in a theologically credible way" (381). See also Raphael Gallagher, CSsR., "L'actualité de la théologie morale de saint Alphonse de Liguori," *Revue d'Éthique et de Théologie Morale* 268 (2012): 35–57.

7. I value a number of the ways in which existentialist philosophy influenced twentieth-century Catholic thought. For example, Matthew J. Ramage is surely right to describe Joseph Ratzinger/Pope Benedict XVI's thought as "existentialist." Ratzinger, like many German seminarians in the immediate aftermath of World War II, was highly influenced by certain aspects of Jaspers's and Heidegger's philosophy, especially through the writings of Theodor Steinbüchel: see Ratzinger, *Salt of the Earth: Christianity and the Catholic Church at the End of the Millennium: An Interview with Peter Seewald*, trans. Adrian Walker (San Francisco: Ignatius, 1997), 59–60. For discussion, see Ramage, *The Experiment of Faith: Pope Benedict XVI on Living the Theological Virtues in a Secular Age* (Washington, DC: Catholic University of America Press, 2020), 11–14. Similarly,

Jon Kirwan has shown "how dominant existentialism was in post-war [i.e., post-World War II] France." Kirwan, *An Avant-garde Theological Generation: The* Nouvelle Théologie *and the French Crisis of Modernity* (Oxford: Oxford University Press, 2018), 236. It is in this context that one thinks of the Christian existentialist philosophy of Gabriel Marcel, who was influenced by Karl Jaspers. For discussion of Marcel and his reaction against the Thomism of Jacques Maritain, see Edward Baring, *Converts to the Real: Catholicism and the Making of Continental Philosophy* (Cambridge, MA: Harvard University Press, 2019), 153–65. See also the essays in Carl Michalson, ed., *Christianity and the Existentialists* (New York: Scribner's Sons, 1956). For an effort to separate the good elements of existentialist ethics (or situation ethics) from its bad elements, see Dietrich von Hildebrand and Alice Jourdain, *True Morality and Its Counterfeits* (New York: David McKay, 1955).

8. William A. Wallace, OP, "Existential Ethics: A Thomistic Appraisal," *Thomist* 27 (1963): 513. See also Wallace, *The Role of Demonstration in Moral Theology: A Study of Methodology in St. Thomas Aquinas* (Washington, DC: Thomist, 1962), 203–8.

9. For postconciliar American developments, see John Giles Milhaven, SJ, and David J. Casey, SJ, "Introduction to the Theological Background of the New Morality," *Theological Studies* 28 (1967): 213–44; Thomas Wassmer, SJ, "Contemporary Situational Morality and the Catholic Christian," in *To Be a Man*, ed. George Devine (Englewood Cliffs, NJ: Prentice Hall, 1969), 93–106; Wassmer, *Christian Ethics for Today* (Milwaukee, WI: Bruce, 1969); and John Giles Milhaven, SJ, *Toward a New Catholic Morality* (Garden City, NY: Doubleday, 1970). Further sense of the direction in which things headed immediately after the Council can be gleaned from Wassmer, "Is Intrinsic Evil a Viable Term?," *Chicago Studies* 5 (1966): 307–14; and Milhaven, "Objective Moral Evaluation of Circumstances," *Theological Studies* 32 (1971): 407–30. The work of the Americans Milhaven and Wassmer is explored in John A. Gallagher, *Time Past, Time Future: An Historical Study of Catholic Moral Theology* (Mahwah, NJ: Paulist, 1990), 237–39, where Gallagher notes that both scholars were "concerned to dislodge the notion of moral absolutes from their dominant place in Catholic thought. Neither the theology of the new morality nor its method of determining moral obligation could provide a basis for moral absolutes" (239). In the American context, they were influenced by Protestant theologians such as Joseph Fletcher, Reinhold Niebuhr, and H. Richard Niebuhr—with H. Richard Niebuhr's *The Responsible Self: An Essay in Christian Moral Philosophy* (Louisville, KY: Westminster John Knox, 1999) deserving special notice due to its wide influence. In "Contemporary Situational Morality and the Catholic Christian," Wassmer concludes: "My expectation . . . is that a serious re-examination of the notion of intrinsic evil will demonstrate that it is no longer a viable element of contemporary ethical discourse" (106).

10. Although I disagree with conscience-centered moral theology, I agree with Kathryn Lilla Cox when she makes this observation in *Water Shaping Stone: Faith, Relationships, and Conscience Formation* (Collegeville, MN: Liturgical Press, 2015), 120: "We must not treat others with malice or demonize those with whom we disagree. There cannot be a caricature of another's arguments or magisterial teaching." I note that Cox's book begins with three lengthy chapters on conscience: "Conscience in Late Twentieth-Century Magisterial Texts," "Conscience through the Ages: An Overview of Its Intellectual History" (ending with Bernard Häring and Anne Patrick), and "Conscience Formation" (engaging appreciatively with Sidney Callahan and Richard Gula). Cox then concludes the book with two chapters that apply her understanding of conscience to the contemporary divided situation of the Catholic Church, in which she

and many others disagree sharply with magisterial teachings. The chapters are titled "Rethinking Dissent" and "Scandal, Discipleship, and the Cross." Note that, in Cox's view, indebted to Anne Patrick and others, "conscience functions as a metaphor for the whole person and their formation" (162). She concludes, "Realizing that conscience's judgments encompass more than assessments regarding an individual action's 'rightness or wrongness' means recognizing that considering conscience profoundly implies considerations about relationality. One criterion for evaluating the accuracy and validity of conscience's judgments will be the fruitfulness resulting from those judgments and the moral agent's growth in virtue or holiness as a disciple. As a result, conscience's judgments need assessment before and after action. Therefore, ongoing examination of conscience (our emotions, thoughts, reactions, and motivations) is vital" (164). Here "conscience" names a wide array of human realities.

11. James F. Keenan, SJ, *A History of Catholic Moral Theology in the Twentieth Century: From Confessing Sins to Liberating Consciences* (New York: Continuum, 2010). For theological analysis of postconciliar moral theology (from a Protestant perspective, focused on German thinkers), see Wolfgang Nethöfel, *Moraltheologie nach dem Konzil: Personen, Programme, Positionem* (Göttingen: Vandenhoeck & Ruprecht, 1987). See also Nicholas Crotty, "Conscience and Conflict," *Theological Studies* 32 (1971): 208–32.

12. See also Livio Melina, *Sharing in Christ's Virtues: For a Renewal of Moral Theology in Light of "Veritatis Splendor,"* trans. William E. May (Washington, DC: Catholic University of America Press, 2001), inclusive of an excellent chapter on conscience; as well as Romanus Cessario, OP, *Introduction to Moral Theology* (Washington, DC: Catholic University of America Press, 2001); and Cessario, *The Moral Virtues and Theological Ethics* (Notre Dame: University of Notre Dame Press, 1991). For an Eastern Orthodox perspective, see Stanley Samuel Harakas's argument that at the core of the image of God are "freedom, moral law and conscience." Harakas, *Toward Transfigured Life: The Theoria of Eastern Orthodox Ethics* (Minneapolis: Light and Life, 1983), 101. He devotes extensive attention to modern, scriptural, and patristic views of conscience, and he affirms that "the cultivation and development of the conscience is a requirement for our spiritual and moral growth," grounded in the need for discernment (113). He pushes a bit further and insists upon conscience's ethical centrality, naming it "the agent for what we have called *theanthroponomy*"—the synergy of divine and human lawmaking (114). However, he also discusses at length the Trinity and the Good, sin and grace, the natural law and the new law, the virtues and the imitation of Christ, and individual and communal *theosis*. His perspective is similar to Pope John Paul II's.

13. See also the essays in Bruno-Marie Duffé, ed., *La conscience morale: Questions pour aujourd'hui* (Lyon: Profac, 1994).

14. Sidney Callahan, *In Good Conscience: Reason and Emotion in Moral Decision-Making* (San Francisco: HarperSanFrancisco, 1991), 11.

15. Anthony J. Marinelli, *Conscience and Catholic Faith: Love and Fidelity* (Mahwah, NJ: Paulist, 1991), 66.

16. Marinelli, *Conscience and Catholic Faith*, 6–7.

17. Marinelli, *Conscience and Catholic Faith*, 29.

18. See Richard M. Gula, SS, *Moral Discernment* (New York: Paulist, 1997), 2.

19. See Gula, *Moral Discernment*, 26–27. Gula does devote a chapter to practical reasoning, developed along the lines of learning how to act in accord with "our fundamental commitment to God" (47). Similarly, Kenneth R. Overberg, SJ, has published

three editions of his *Conscience in Conflict: How to Make Moral Choices*, most recently in 2006. He urges an embrace of mainstream Western cultural shifts in various domains (sexual, political, and economic) while taking a somewhat countercultural line with regard to abortion and euthanasia. See Overberg, *Conscience in Conflict: How to Make Moral Choices*, 3rd ed. (Cincinnati, OH: St. Anthony Messenger, 2006).

20. In this regard, see also chapter 5 of Dietrich von Hildebrand's 1969 book *The Encyclical "Humanae Vitae": A Sign of Contradiction*, trans. Damian Fedoryka and John Crosby (Chicago: Franciscan Herald, 1969), republished in 1998 as *Love, Marriage, and the Catholic Conscience* (Manchester, NH: Sophia Institute, 1998). Von Hildebrand argues that "the true cooperation of conscience, whose voice admonishes us to full responsibility, presupposes a knowledge of what is fundamentally good or evil, pleasing to God or sinful, allowed or not allowed. And in the case of a Catholic, only he who humbly and gratefully accepts the moral law revealed by God and the definition of what is morally good or not good as explicitly proclaimed by the Church is truly conscientious and truly responsible. The voice of the Holy Church, however, *does not replace conscience*, does not stifle it or call upon us to renounce responsibility, but rather offers conscience the indispensable information about what is good or evil. It protects and supports our conscience against all the tendencies of our fallen nature that try to drown out its voice" (*Encyclical "Humanae Vitae,"* 96–97).

21. David E. DeCosse and Kristin E. Heyer, "Introduction," in *Conscience and Catholicism: Rights, Responsibilities, and Institutional Responses*, ed. David E. DeCosse and Kristin E. Heyer (Maryknoll, NY: Orbis, 2015), xv.

22. DeCosse and Heyer, "Introduction," xxiii. See also, among many others, the 2004 volume edited by Charles E. Curran, *Conscience* (Mahwah, NJ: Paulist, 2004); as well the 1996 volume—whose essays (by contrast to the other volumes discussed above) carefully limit conscience's function and place in the moral life—edited by John M. Haas, *Crisis of Conscience* (New York: Crossroad, 1996).

23. DeCosse and Heyer, "Introduction," xv-xvi. For an essay running counter to this narrative of disjunction between Popes John Paul II and Benedict XVI, on the one hand, and Pope Francis on the other, see Romanus Cessario, OP, "Religion and the Gifts of the Holy Spirit," *Nova et Vetera* 15 (2017): 996–98.

24. Charles E. Curran, *The Development of Moral Theology: Five Strands* (Washington, DC: Georgetown University Press, 2013), 261.

25. Curran, *Development of Moral Theology*, 261. For a summary of Curran's perspective (a summary published in 1990, indicative of the general consistency of Curran's perspective over the years), see Gallagher, *Time Past, Time Future*, 217–19.

26. From a different perspective—grounded in Thomistic moral philosophy and drawing upon Aristotle—Martin Rhonheimer correctly remarks, "A completely virtuous or prudent man . . . is someone who can live at peace with himself: he possesses that freedom or inner calm that results from the harmony of conscience with judgment about actions and with the accomplishment of actions." Rhonheimer, *The Perspective of Morality: Philosophical Foundations of Thomistic Virtue Ethics*, trans. Gerald Malsbury (Washington, DC: Catholic University of America Press, 2011), 322.

27. In his *Catholic Moral Theology in the United States: A History* (Washington, DC: Georgetown University Press, 2008), Curran praises other exemplars of postconciliar conscience-centered moral theology. He appreciatively notes Timothy O'Connell's

emphasis on "conscience as capacity, as process, and as judgment. Conscience on the first level is the unfolding capacity of the human individual for moral goodness; on the second level, conscience is the process we go through in trying to arrive at our decisions; on the third level, conscience is the judgment about what is to be done in a particular situation" (182). Here Curran cites O'Connell, *Principles for a Catholic Morality*, rev. ed. (San Francisco: Harper & Row, 1990), 88–97. He also appreciatively describes Walter Conn's view of "the growth of conscience" through the threefold conversion of the "self-transcending subject"; Sidney Callahan's insistence upon "the importance of the emotions, affectivity, and intuition in the role of conscience" and "broad understanding of conscience as a self-conscious activity of a person who is thinking, feeling, imagining, and willing action on behalf of moral standards of worth"; and Richard Gula's development of "a holistic understanding of conscience as an expression of the whole self as a thinking, feeling, intuiting, and willing person" (Curran, *Catholic Moral Theology*, 182–83). Curran cites Conn, *Conscience: Development and Self-Transcendence* (Birmingham, AL: Religious Education, 1981); Conn, *Christian Conversion: A Developmental Interpretation of Autonomy and Surrender* (New York: Paulist, 1986); Callahan, *In Good Conscience*; and Gula, *Moral Discernment*, 100.

28. Robert J. Smith, *Conscience and Catholicism: The Nature and Function of Conscience in Contemporary Roman Catholic Moral Theology* (Lanham, MD: University Press of America, 1998), 130.

29. Smith, *Conscience and Catholicism*, 131–32.

30. David E. DeCosse, "The Primacy of Conscience, Vatican II, and Pope Francis: The Opportunity to Renew a Tradition," in *From Vatican II to Pope Francis: Charting a Catholic Future*, ed. Paul Crowley, SJ (Maryknoll, NY: Orbis, 2014), 156. See also Joseph Ratzinger, "The Dignity of the Human Person," in *Pastoral Constitution on the Church in the Modern World*, ed. Herbert Vorgrimler, vol. 5 of *Commentary on the Documents of Vatican II* (New York: Herder & Herder, 1969), 134–36; as well as Ratzinger, "Conscience and Truth," in *Crisis of Conscience*, ed. John M. Haas (New York: Crossroad, 1996), 1–20.

31. DeCosse, "Primacy of Conscience," 166–67.

32. See also Anne E. Patrick, *Liberating Conscience: Feminist Explorations in Catholic Moral Theology* (New York: Continuum, 1997); and James Bretzke, SJ, *A Morally Complex World: Engaging Contemporary Moral Theology* (Collegeville, MN: Liturgical Press, 2004). Patrick's book urges Catholics to "grow to new levels of confidence and competence as moral agents" and to free themselves in conscience from "all that inhibits a generous response to the ethical challenges we face" (*Liberating Conscience*, x). She suggests that we now face "conscience at the crossroads" and must work toward "liberating conscience" by following the path of "conscience as process" (3, quoting the chapter titles). Bretzke's book begins with a chapter on natural law and moral norms, then turns to Scripture and ethics, and finally arrives in the decisive third chapter: "The Sanctuary of Conscience: Where the Axes Intersect" (*Morally Complex World*, 141). Bretzke's book does not pulse with the missional energy of Patrick's work, but he too holds up "conscience-based moral living" as *the* Catholic path, grounded in spiritual discernment so that, in conscience, "we seek to do not just our will, but . . . try to be open and sensitive to God's own Spirit present in our world" (141).

33. William C. Mattison III, *Introducing Moral Theology: True Happiness and the Virtues* (Grand Rapids, MI: Brazos, 2008). See also Andrew Kim's excellent book *An In-*

troduction to Catholic Ethics since Vatican II (Cambridge: Cambridge University Press, 2015); as well as David Matzo McCarthy and James Donahue, CR, *Moral Vision: Seeing the World with Love and Justice* (Grand Rapids, MI: Eerdmans, 2018). In his deeply scriptural and broadly Thomistic study, which is intended to serve as an introduction to Catholic moral theology for undergraduate and graduate courses, Kim treats natural law (in relation to divine revelation), the cardinal virtues, the theological virtues and infused moral virtues, justice, Catholic social teaching, just war, the dignity of the human person, and bioethical decision-making. Conscience does not appear in his book's index. Mattison and Kim follow in the line of Pinckaers and Pope John Paul II, which is an important postconciliar perspective but not the predominant one in postconciliar Catholic academic and popular writings in moral theology.

34. William C. Mattison III, *The Sermon on the Mount and Moral Theology: A Virtue Perspective* (Cambridge: Cambridge University Press, 2017).

35. The bishop was speaking specifically about James F. Keenan, SJ's "Redeeming Conscience," *Theological Studies* 76 (2015): 129–47. More broadly, he may have had in view paragraph 303 of Pope Francis's apostolic exhortation *Amoris Laetitia* (Frederick, MD: The Word Among Us, 2016). See my book *The Indissolubility of Marriage: "Amoris Laetitia" in Context* (San Francisco: Ignatius, 2019).

36. For further background to Tillmann, see Gerhard Höver and Andrea Schaeffer, "Fritz Tillmann (1873–1953)," in *Christliche Ethik im Porträt: Leben und Werk bedeutender Moraltheologen*, ed. Konrad Hilpert (Freiburg im Breisgau: Herder, 2012), 599–624.

37. Joseph Ratzinger, *Milestones: Memoirs 1927–1977*, trans. Erasmo Leiva-Merikakis (San Francisco: Ignatius, 1998), 43. For further discussion, see Peter Seewald, *Benedict XVI: A Life*, vol. 1, *Youth in Nazi Germany to the Second Vatican Council, 1927–1965* (London: Bloomsbury, 2020).

38. Fritz Tillmann, *The Master Calls: A Handbook of Christian Living*, trans. Gregory Roettger, OSB (Baltimore, MD: Helicon, 1960), 38. Originally published as *Der Meister ruft: Die katholische Sittenlehre gemeinverständlich dargestellt* (Düsseldorf: Patmos, 1948).

39. Tillmann, *The Master Calls*, 39.

40. See, for example, Mark E. Graham, *Josef Fuchs on Natural Law* (Washington, DC: Georgetown University Press, 2002), 203–4; and Keenan, *History of Catholic Moral Theology*, 60–69. Graham presents Tillmann as rejecting "the presentation of Christian morality portrayed by the neo-Thomist manualists" and as proposing "an entirely different basis for the Christian moral life: following Christ" (*Josef Fuchs on Natural Law*, 203).

41. See Gérard Gilleman, SJ, *The Primacy of Charity in Moral Theology*, trans. William F. Ryan, SJ, and André Vachon, SJ (Westminster, MD: Newman, 1959). Other books from the 1940s and 1950s could be mentioned, such as Gustav Thils, *Tendances actuelles en théologie morale* (Gembloux: J. Duclot, 1940), which adopts a Christian personalist perspective centered upon life in union with Christ; and Jacques Leclercq, *L'enseignement de la morale chrétienne* (Paris: Vitrail, 1949).

42. This is the title of the third part of Gilleman's book. After he completed this book as his dissertation, the Jesuit order sent him to teach in their theological faculty in Kurseong, India, where he still was as of 1959. Given that his teaching responsibilities made it impossible for him to revise his work, the two French editions and

the English edition were overseen by René Carpentier, SJ. In Josef Fuchs, SJ's 1965 book *Natural Law: A Theological Investigation*, trans. Helmut Reckter, SJ, and John A. Dowling (New York: Sheed and Ward, 1965), which he later repudiated, Fuchs draws appreciatively upon Gilleman (see 140–41). For the relation between Gilleman's book and Carpentier's essay "Conscience," in *Dictionnaire de spiritualité: Ascétique et mystique, doctrine et histoire*, vol. 2, bk. 2 (Paris: Beauchesne, 1949–53), 1547–75, see the study by Vincent Leclercq, AA, "Le *Primat de la charité* de Gilleman et la *Conscience* de Carpentier: Le renouveau théologal de la vie morale," *Studia Moralia* 44 (2006): 353–75. Carpentier's moral theology was conscience-centered, but he was a critic of the moral manuals.

43. Gilleman, *Primacy of Charity*, xxi.

44. Gilleman, *Primacy of Charity*, xxi.

45. Gilleman, *Primacy of Charity*, xxii.

46. See Fritz Tillmann, *Die Idee der Nachfolge Christi*, vol. 3 of *Handbuch der katholischen Sittenlehre* (Düsseldorf: L. Schwann, 1934). Tillmann edited this *Handbuch* and wrote two of its four volumes, the second being titled *Der Verwirklichung der Nachfolge Christi*. Vincent Leclercq notes that around the same time as Tillmann, the Belgian Jesuit Arthur Vermeersch advocated an analogous renewal of moral theology: see Vermeersch, "Soixante ans de théologie morale," *Nouvelle Revue de Théologie* 56 (1929): 863–84, cited in Leclercq, "Le *Primat de la charité* de Gilleman et la *Conscience* de Carpentier," 364, 370. In *Time Past, Time Future*, Gallagher praises Tillmann as a successor of the nineteenth-century Tübingen German moral theologian Johann Baptist von Hirscher, who died in the 1860s. Gallagher describes Tillmann's approach in a manner that sounds far more wooden (and far more like the dominant stream of postconciliar Catholic moral theology) than it actually is in *The Master Calls*: "The person of Christ presented in the scriptures was the norm of morality to be imitated by all who would follow him. The kingdom of God was central to Christ's preaching, and its realization was the goal of Christian striving. From the outset, Tillmann's vision of Christian ethics required a social context for personal moral agency. Individuals were thought of as planned and designed for a social, communal existence within the kingdom and were the product of historical and cultural development. Moral theology was a science because it not only identified the source and goal of Christian morality, but also sought to understand the relationship between the distinct elements within the system" (*Time Past, Time Future*, 163). I agree, however, with Gallagher's concluding point: "The most distinctive feature of Tillmann's theology was his attempt to establish all of his theology in direct relation to scriptural themes" (166).

47. Gilleman, *Primacy of Charity*, xxxii.

48. Gilleman, *Primacy of Charity*, xxx.

49. He warns that, lacking in interiority, "supernaturalism can very well engender naturalism; a body abandoned by its spirit can fall very low indeed, and give itself over to the fatal influence of a mechanical, materialistic civilization" (Gilleman, *Primacy of Charity*, xxxiii). He also credits existentialism, with attention to the warning given by Pope Pius XII's *Humani Generis*: "Might not the recent trends of existentialism and the philosophy of value be able to contribute some help to our research? Evidently we are referring to an existentialism which admits the reality of essence and of God. For an existentialism which denies Supreme Existence can only see moral effort as a tendency

to self-annihilation, thus effectively killing the love for the last end which is the soul of moral life" (xxxiv).

50. Gilleman, *Primacy of Charity*, xxxiii. This was a strong concern of both Ambroise Gardeil, OP, and Réginald Garrigou-Lagrange, OP, as well as of another teacher of Garrigou-Lagrange, Juan G. Arintero, OP, who died in 1928. See, for example, Arintero, *The Mystical Evolution in the Development and Vitality of the Church*, 2 vols., trans. Jordan Aumann, OP (St. Louis, MO: B. Herder, 1949–51); and Gardeil, *La vraie vie chrétienne*, ed. H.-D. Gardeil (Paris: Desclée, 1935).

51. For Gilleman's debt to Mersch, see Leclercq, "Le *Primat de la charité* de Gilleman et la *Conscience* de Carpentier," 373–74.

52. Emile Mersch, SJ, *Morality and the Mystical Body*, trans. Daniel F. Ryan, SJ (New York: P. J. Kennedy & Sons, 1939), 33.

53. Mersch, *Morality and the Mystical Body*, 96.

54. Mersch, *Morality and the Mystical Body*, 97.

55. Mersch, *Morality and the Mystical Body*, 99.

56. He emphasizes against Nazism and Bolshevism: "For it is love which is the authentic mark of Christ, and which ought to be, in the Church, the converting sign. She is, it is her primordial mission, the school of charity. And this lesson for our epoch, is the most necessary of all. Making plain to men, and that in acts, in devotion, in self-sacrifice, in the giving of self to all, how, in fact, they are all one in Christ, and one with a unity at once divine and human, marvellously human and veritably divine, one with a unity far superior to the unities which they seek by their revolutions, alas, and by their murders—it is this which will convert the world. Only let the salt not lose its savor! Let Christians who live by this unity, who ought to make it shine before the eyes of men, not hide it under their egoisms of class, of race or of persons, under theories of massacre and of hostilities, of reprisals and of parties. They would be responsible before Him Who died that we might be one, for the loss of their brothers and for the exhaustion of humanity in death" (Mersch, *Morality and the Mystical Body*, 176).

57. See also Mersch's *L'obligation moral principe de liberté: Étude de philosophie morale* (Paris: Alcan, 1927). Here Mersch notes that the search for God is obligatory, and yet this search does not impinge upon our liberty. In reality, we become free by adhering to the constraints of moral obligation because, in this way, we escape enslavement to our passions and become free to attain the one thing necessary. For Mersch, "obligation" is rooted in the will's natural tendency toward the Good. Admittedly, in his review of this book, Pierre Harmignie cautions that Mersch "conflates obligation with the obligatory ultimate end or with the necessary desire for the good in general." Harmignie, "Review of Emile Mersch, S. J., *L'obligation morale principe de liberté*," *Revue Néo-scholastique de Philosophie* 29 (1927): 355. But Harmignie adds that Mersch offers an excellent view "of the splendor of the moral order" (355), and he concludes with praise for Mersch's work. Notably, Mersch roots "obligation" very clearly in the good and roots liberty in the obligation of love.

58. See also such books as Romano Guardini, *The Virtues: On Forms of Moral Life* (New York: Regnery, 1967); and Josef Pieper, *The Four Cardinal Virtues*, trans. Richard Winston and Clara Winston et al. (Notre Dame: University of Notre Dame Press, 1966).

59. See Maria C. Morrow, *Sin in the Sixties: Catholics and Confession, 1955–1975* (Washington, DC: Catholic University of America Press, 2016).

60. Gallagher, *Time Past, Time Future*, 223. Gallagher here is somewhat correcting the perspective of John Mahoney, SJ, *The Making of Moral Theology: A Study of the Roman Catholic Tradition* (Oxford: Oxford University Press, 1987), 259–301, although he agrees with Mahoney that *Humanae Vitae* was a watershed in terms of revealing the (already present) fundamental divide.

61. Gallagher rightly comments: "Much remains to be learned concerning the emergence of situation ethics [existentialist ethics] among Catholic intellectuals in post-World War II Germany. Men and women were questioning the morality which had permitted or at least tolerated the atrocities and evils of the war. How could so many Germans have complied with the demands of such an unjust regime? . . . Precisely what the issues were for Germans of the late 1940s and early 1950s, and the manner in which a growing number of philosophers and theologians were being swayed in the direction of situation ethics, remains a largely untold story" (*Time Past, Time Future*, 226).

62. Erich Przywara, SJ, *Analogia Entis: Metaphysics; Original Structure and Universal Rhythm*, trans. John R. Betz and David Bentley Hart (Grand Rapids, MI: Eerdmans, 2014), xxi. For discussion of Przywara's firm critique of Heidegger, see John R. Betz, "Translator's Introduction," in *Analogia Entis*, 78–80. See also Cyril O'Regan, "Heidegger and Christian Wisdom," in *Christian Wisdom Meets Modernity*, ed. Kenneth Oakes (London: Bloomsbury, 2016), 45–48; Philip John Paul Gonzales, *Reimagining the "Analogia Entis": The Future of Erich Przywara's Christian Vision* (Grand Rapids, MI: Eerdmans, 2019).

63. See Erich Przywara, SJ, *Christliche Existenz* (Leipzig: Hegner, 1934); and Alfred Delp, *Tragische Existenz: Zur Philosophie Martin Heideggers* (Freiburg: Herder, 1935). I note that Przywara's book, while beginning with a nod to the existentialists ("Existence is the word of our time" [*Christliche Existenz*, 13]), focuses upon developing his own vision through careful readings of Scripture, Aquinas, and other Christian sources rather than upon directly responding to contemporary existentialism. For extensive engagement with Jaspers's work (and Blondel's), see Przywara, "Sein im Scheitern—Sein im Aufgang," *Stimmen der Zeit* 123 (1932): 152–61. In this essay, Przywara links Heidegger, Jaspers, and Paul Tillich (with Jaspers situated philosophically in the middle); he much prefers Blondel to any of them. Elsewhere, in an essay originally published in 1941, Przywara comments on conscience: "As consciousness essentially beholds the 'thing,' so is conscience essentially the being-toward [*das Hin zum*] objective law. . . . [Likewise] the authoritative Church is grounded not in Corpus Christi Mysticum, but the latter in the former." Przywara, "Alter und Neuer Katholizismus," in *Katholische Krise*, ed. Berhard Gertz (Düsseldorf: Patmos, 1967): 188–89n3, my translation.

64. Eberhard Schockenhoff, *Wie Gewiss ist das Gewissen? Eine ethische Orientierung* (Freiburg: Herder, 2003). Schockenhoff's recent work in moral theology is more closely connected to the new movement of conscience-centered morality. For the beginnings of this transition, see Eberhard Schockenhoff and Christiane Florin, *Gewissen—eine Gebrauchsanweisung* (Freiburg: Herder, 2009).

65. See, for example—to name some recent books—Paul Strohm, *Conscience: A Very Short Introduction* (Oxford: Oxford University Press, 2011); Richard Sorabji, *Moral Conscience through the Ages: Fifth Century BCE to the Present* (Chicago: University of Chicago Press, 2014); Martin van Creveld, *Conscience: A Biography* (London: Reaktion, 2015); and Mika Ojakangas, *The Voice of Conscience: A Political Genealogy of Western*

Ethical Experience (London: Bloomsbury, 2013). For more specialized studies, see, for instance, Timothy C. Potts, *Conscience in Medieval Philosophy* (Cambridge: Cambridge University Press, 1980); Emre Kazim, *Kant on Conscience: A Unified Approach to Moral Self-Consciousness* (Leiden: Brill, 2017); Gerald J. Hughes, "Conscience," in *The Cambridge Companion to John Henry Newman*, ed. Ian Ker and Terrence Merrigan (Cambridge: Cambridge University Press, 2009), 189–220; Geertjan Zuijdwegt and Terrence Merrigan, "Conscience," in *The Oxford Handbook of John Henry Newman*, ed. Frederick D. Aquino and Benjamin J. King (Oxford: Oxford University Press, 2018), 434–53; and Charlotte Hansen, "Newman, Conscience and Authority," *New Blackfriars* 92 (2011): 209–23.

66. Vatican Council II, *Gaudium et Spes*, in *The Conciliar and Postconciliar Documents*, rev. ed., ed. Austin Flannery, vol. 1 of *Vatican Council II: Constitutions, Decrees, Declarations* (Northport, NY: Costello, 1996), §16, p. 916.

67. *Gaudium et Spes*, §16, p. 917.

68. See Mattison, *Introducing Moral Theology*, 109–10: "This discussion of slavery and the question of vincible/invincible ignorance prompts two observations. . . . First, the fact that slave owners several centuries ago seem to have genuinely thought they were acting rightly raises some humbling questions about our own contemporary societal practices. What are the things we do today that instrumentalize and victimize people—ourselves included—even though we do not see it? . . . Even if slaveowners in the year 1700 were not blameworthy [because of invincible ignorance due to cultural prejudice], they would still be inflicting enormous harm on other people (the slaves), themselves (by being deprived of seeing, serving, and enjoying the dignity of these people right before their eyes), and society."

69. *Gaudium et Spes*, §17, p. 917. Michael S. Sherwin, OP, makes the important point—against the position of James Keenan and others—that Aquinas does not present "charity's act [as] antecedent to and independent of the conceptual knowledge proper to practical reason." Sherwin, *By Knowledge and By Love: Charity and Knowledge in the Moral Theology of St. Thomas Aquinas* (Washington, DC: Catholic University of America Press, 2005), ix.

70. Richard B. Hays, *The Moral Vision of the New Testament: Community, Cross, New Creation; A Contemporary Introduction to New Testament Ethics* (New York: HarperCollins, 1996).

71. For a fruitful insistence upon universal human nature and natural law, well integrated into the fullness of the Christian moral life, see Paulinus Ikechukwu Odozor, CSSp, *Morality Truly Christian, Truly African: Foundational, Methodological, and Theological Considerations* (Notre Dame: University of Notre Dame Press, 2014).

72. H. Richard Niebuhr comments: "At all times . . . , but particularly among the German interpreters in whom the Kantian symbolism holds sway, the deontological interpretation of man the obedient legislator has been used not only as the key to Biblical interpretation but for the definition of the true Christian life. For Barth and Bultmann in our times, not to speak of most interpreters of the Old Testament, the ethics of the Bible, and Christian ethics too, is the ethics of obedience. How to interpret Christian freedom and what to make of eschatology within this framework has taxed the ingenuity of the interpreters severely. Bultmann has transformed eschatology into existentialism in order to maintain an ethics of radical obedience; Barth has had to transform the law

into a form of the gospel and the commandment into permission in order to reconcile the particularity of gospel ethos with deontological thinking" (Niebuhr, *The Responsible Self*, 66).

73. See Philippe Delhaye, "La théologie morale d'hier et d'aujourd'hui," *Revue des Sciences Religieuses* 27 (1953): 112–30.

74. John Gallagher comments, "The importance of the treatise on conscience in the manuals of moral theology in general and the neo-Thomist manuals in particular cannot be overemphasized" (Gallagher, *Time Past, Time Future*, 81). Without himself distinguishing here between conscience and prudence, Gallagher makes apparent how the two were generally conflated in the moral manuals: "Conscience was understood as the ability of practical reason—the use of intelligence with regard to act—to move from the abstract, theoretical notions of the natural law, or from general principles of faith, to a concrete determination of what was to be done here and now" (82).

75. Johann Theiner, *Die Entwicklung der Moraltheologie zur eigenständigen Disziplin* (Regensburg: Friedrich Pustet, 1970).

76. At times I find Gallagher's handling of difficult issues to be inadequate. For example, he defines the natural inclinations as "pre-moral dispositions embedded in human nature as spontaneous sensitive inclinations to the proximate and ultimate ends of human existence" (Gallagher, *Time Past, Time Future*, 89), which strikes me as misleading. Likewise, his judgment upon the manualists' treatment of sexuality is too harsh: "they utterly failed to grasp its interpersonal aspects, nor did they sufficiently perceive its human and Christian dimensions" (118). Yet, his knowledge of the manuals is quite rich. The moral manuals discussed conscience under "general moral theology," while they presented "their concrete moral teaching, usually called special moral theology, in relation to the decalogue or to the theological (faith, hope, and charity) and cardinal (prudence, justice, temperance, and fortitude) virtues. . . . The followers of St. Alphonsus Liguori generally presented their special moral theology in relationship to the Decalogue. The Dominicans and many Jesuits used the schema of the virtues. Others combined the two approaches, presenting first the theological virtues and then turning their attention to the decalogue. Whatever the framework, the neo-Thomist manuals provided their students with an exhaustive treatment of the moral requirements incumbent upon members of the Christian community" (106).

77. Keenan, *History of Catholic Moral Theology*, 9–34. In a more summary fashion, Charles E. Curran describes the early twentieth-century moral manuals in his *Catholic Moral Theology in the United States*, 35–82. Curran pays attention especially to medical ethics and social ethics and thus focuses more on special topics (rather than fundamental ethics).

78. Julia Fleming, *Defending Probabilism: The Moral Theology of Juan Caramuel* (Washington, DC: Georgetown University Press, 2006). See also Nicole Reinhardt, "How Individual Was Conscience in the Early-Modern Period? Observations on the Development of Catholic Moral Theology," *Religion* 45 (2015): 409–28.

79. Stefania Tutino, *Uncertainty in Post-Reformation Catholicism: A History of Probabilism* (Oxford: Oxford University Press, 2018), 355–56. For earlier analysis, critical of probabilism, see Miriam Turrini, *La coscienza e le leggi: Morale e diritto nei testi per la confessione della prima età moderna* (Bologna: Il Mulino, 1991). See also such recent magisterial works as Rudolf Schuessler, *The Debate on Probable Opinions in the Scho-*

lastic Tradition (Leiden: Brill, 2019); Schuessler, "Scholastic Social Epistemology in the Baroque Era," *American Catholic Philosophical Quarterly* 93 (2019): 335–60; Schuessler, *Moral im Zweifel*, vol. 2, *Die Herausforderung des Probabilismus* (Paderborn: Mentis Verlag, 2006); Pierre Hurtubise, *La casuistique dans tous ses états: De Martin Azpilcueta à Alphonse de Liguori* (Ottawa: Novalis, 2005); Jean-Pascal Gay, *Morales in conflit: Théologie et polémique au Grand Siècle (1640–1700)* (Paris: Cerf, 2011); and Paul Valadier, *Rigorisme contre liberté morale: Les Provinciales; Actualité d'une polémique antijésuite* (Brussels: Lessius, 2013). See the brief sketch provided by Éric Gaziaux, "Les conflits de la conscience dans la tradition catholique: Retour sur l'histoire et les différentes écoles," *Revue d'Éthique et de Théologie Morale*, no. 293 (2017): 11–24.

80. Albert R. Jonsen and Stephen Toulmin, *The Abuse of Casuistry: A History of Moral Reasoning* (Berkeley: University of California Press, 1988), 334. They go on to make a helpful clarification, noting that for many people today, "the intensely personal and existential character of moral choice represents 'the centrality of informed conscience.' For the casuists, by contrast, informed conscience might be intensely personal, but its primary concern was to place the individual agent's decision into the larger context at the level of actual choice: namely, the moral dialogue and debate of a community. . . . So 'liberty of conscience' never meant the right to take up a personal moral position that ran in the face of the general agreement of reflective scholars and doctors" (335). For studies of particular casuistic moralists and further defenses of casuistry, see the essays in James F. Keenan, SJ, and Thomas A. Shannon, eds., *The Context of Casuistry* (Washington, DC: Georgetown University Press, 1995), including Keenan and Shannon's defense of conscience-centered moral theology as offering a "wholeness that centered authority in the individual's conscience" and that provided "greater freedom for the individual to resolve doubts and to determine right conduct" (Keenan and Shannon, "Contexts of Casuistry: Historical and Contemporary," 224). Keenan is influenced by his teacher Klaus Demmer, MSC, in this regard. As Keenan remarks in light of Jonsen and Toulmin's book, "Both Jean-Marie Aubert and Klaus Demmer explored the foundations of casuistry as germane to the revisionist project. Aubert saw casuistry as providing the mediation between law and liberty; Demmer noted that casuistry calls us to recognize the historicity of truth in moral reasoning. For Demmer, every time a principle was applied to a new case, the principle itself was being reinterpreted: the hermeneutics of the application of casuistic principles to cases was a sure guarantee for the historical development of doctrine. Later, Demmer's student Thomas Kopfensteiner advanced the position that casuistry was used to liberate institutions from normative determinations that did not keep pace with other developments" (Keenan, *History of Catholic Moral Theology*, 159, citing Aubert, "Morale et Casuistique," *Recherches de Science Religieuse* 68 [1980]: 167–204; Demmer, "Erwägungen über den Segen der Kasuistik," *Gregorianum* 63 [1982]: 133–40; and Thomas Kopfensteiner, "Science, Metaphor and Moral Casuistry," in Keenan and Shannon, *The Context of Casuistry*, 207–20). See also—for historical analyses that press forward into seventeenth-century skepticism (particularly Thomas Hobbes)—Edmund Leites, ed., *Conscience and Casuistry in Early Modern Europe* (Cambridge: Cambridge University Press, 1988).

81. For a study of Labourdette's viewpoint, see Carlos-Josephat Pinto de Oliveira, OP, "La prudence, concept clé de la morale du P. Labourdette," *Revue Thomiste* 92 (1992): 267–92, which draws also upon Thomas Deman, OP, and M.-D. Chenu.

82. For a recent discussion of this topic, see Pius Mary Noonan, OSB, "*Auriga et Genetrix*: Le role de la prudence dans le jugement de la conscience (I)," *Revue Thomiste* 114 (2014): 355–77; and Noonan, "*Auriga et Genetrix*: Le role de la prudence dans le jugement de la conscience (II)," *Revue Thomiste* 114 (2014): 531–68. Noonan shows that Aquinas differentiated between conscience and prudence but did not explain their precise relations, leading later Thomistic commentators to arrive at a variety of positions. He treats the position of Reginald G. Doherty, OP, along with a wide variety of commentators including John of St. Thomas, Charles-René Billuart, Benoît-Henri Merkelbach, Réginald Garrigou-Lagrange, Dominic Prümmer, Henri-Dominique Noble, Antonin-Dalmace Sertillanges, Odon Lottin, Thomas Deman, Philippe Delhaye, Jacques Maritain, Michel Labourdette, Servais Pinckaers, and Leo Elders. Noonan lavishes praise upon Doherty's solution and notes that his own position largely follows Doherty. See also the debate between Ralph McInerny and Théo G. Belmans, OPraem, in which McInerny distinguishes the two judgments and Belmans argues they are the same: Belmans, "Au croisement des chemins en morale fondamentale," *Revue Thomiste* 89 (1989): 246–78; McInerny, "The Right Deed for the Wrong Reason: Comments on Theo Belmans," in *Aquinas on Human Action: A Theory of Practice* (Washington, DC: Catholic University of America Press, 1992), 220–39; Belmans, "Le 'jugement prudentiel' chez saint Thomas. Réponse à R. McInerny," *Revue Thomiste* 91 (1991): 414–20.

83. For discussion of Luther's perspective on conscience, which influences Bonhoeffer, see Paul Althaus, *The Ethics of Martin Luther*, trans. Robert C. Schultz (Minneapolis: Fortress, 2007), 5–6: "What the Christian does is never so good as to be right and acceptable in the sight of God, for man's sinful nature continues to contaminate everything he does. Nevertheless, the deeds are right in the sight of God because in his grace he approves them—even as he approves the man who in faith lays hold of his wondrous grace and favor. It is by virtue of this justifying 'yes' of God that the Christian is given, through faith, a good conscience about his works. In and of itself, in an immanent sense, his conscience is not good; it only becomes a good conscience in a paradoxical way—through the word of forgiveness, God's act of justification."

84. As Dietrich von Hildebrand cautioned in 1955, "conscience . . . plays such a predominant role in circumstance [existentialist] ethics" (von Hildebrand and Jourdain, *True Morality and Its Counterfeits*, 138). Von Hildebrand and Jourdain add, "we must stress that conscience is *not* the organ with which we grasp morally relevant or moral values. The goodness of justice, the evil of injustice, the intrinsic beauty of purity, the horror of impurity are perceived and understood by something other than conscience. The value of a human person, the sacredness of man's life, the dignity of truth are not grasped by conscience. Conscience presupposes the knowledge of these values. It is not through conscience that we discover moral values, morally relevant values, and divine commandments" (139). Louis Dupré's "Situation Ethics and Objective Morality," in *Situationism and the New Morality*, ed. Robert L. Cunningham (New York: Meredith, 1970), 90–102—originally published in *Theological Studies* 28 (1967): 245–57— sums up the position advocated by Bonhoeffer, Barth, and others: "If God's demands in the order of salvation would constantly be in conflict with the objective requirements of human nature, they would obviously jeopardize His creation. But the Protestant situationist does not hold such a position. He does not even deny the existence of some sort of ob-

jective moral law. He merely says that this law is insufficient to express man's personal relationship with God in Christ" (99).

85. James F. Bresnahan, "Rahner's Ethics: Critical Natural Law in Relation to Contemporary Ethical Methodology," *Journal of Religion* 56 (1976): 39n11. In *The Incarnate Lord: A Thomistic Study in Christology* (Washington, DC: Catholic University of America Press, 2015), Thomas Joseph White, OP, offers the following salient reflection upon human historicity: "Over against Lessing, we must insist that the human being is a composite being having an individualized body that enroots him or her in time, place, and culture. So it is of the 'universal essence' of the human being to be immersed in history. Essence and individuality should not be played off against one another by undue emphasis on the abstract knowledge of essences. Every concrete essence is individuated. Over against [Edward] Schillebeeckx, the search for an analogous interpretation of the message of the Gospel across the ages logically presupposes the affirmation of a common core of human nature that remains identical over time, albeit realized in differing modes and in analogously similar conditions. So it is not feasible to seek to attain to a scientific universality of the meaning of human existence devoid of reference to man's concrete historicity. But it is also impossible to undertake a historical-hermeneutical study of the development of culture without grounding this study in the knowledge of the *essential form* of human nature" (501).

86. Dupré's "Situation Ethics and Objective Morality" has its finger on the German pulse on this topic. The key idea for Rahner, Fuchs, and Häring is that (as Dupré puts it, though without reference to their views) "the moral law is the law of a dynamic, self-creating being," defined by personhood rather than by nature—even if, as Dupré says, we may posit that "human nature remains *basically* identical" ("Situation Ethics and Objective Morality," 96). Once one takes this view of human nature, it is difficult to make an (a priori) claim that a particular moral norm is *universal*, even if one can suppose that the norm will generally hold or even will hold in all presently conceivable circumstances. For Dupré, the solution is to distinguish "between universal principles and less universal applications of these principles," while also affirming that "some acts are always and under any circumstances destructive of an essential human value. An act of adultery, for instance, cannot but violate the universal precept of justice and is therefore always wrong" (97). Dupré concludes that "no fixed norms can adequately determine the course of human freedom. Since freedom is an inventive and creative forward surge, human nature—that is, what is given originally and what has been acquired through past decisions—can never provide a definitive rule of action. But this does not mean that freedom determines itself in a vacuum. Freedom can exercise itself only *within* the objectivity of nature," which constitutes a "given part of the self" (100).

87. For Emmanuel Levinas, somewhat similarly, conscience entails a recognition of one's being limited by the divine Other. Levinas explains: "The disproportion between the Other and the self is precisely conscience [*la conscience morale*]. Conscience is not an experience of values, but an access to external being: eternal being is, par excellence, the Other." Levinas, *Difficult Freedom: Essays on Judaism*, trans. S. Hand (Baltimore, MD: Johns Hopkins University Press, 1997), 293.

88. Douglas C. Langston, *Conscience and Other Virtues: From Bonaventure to MacIntyre* (University Park: Pennsylvania State University Press, 2001), 1.

89. For the danger, today and in earlier eras, of "the boundless enthusiasm for ex-

plaining away all moral reservations in the name of ideology," see Patricia S. Churchland, *Conscience: The Origins of Moral Intuition* (New York: W. W. Norton, 2019), 192. As a physicalist, Churchland considers conscience a solely neurobiological reality, but a meaningful and helpful one nonetheless. The voice of conscience can be obscured and silenced. For the absence of the voice of conscience among certain individuals, see Robert D. Hare, *Without Conscience: The Disturbing World of the Psychopaths* (New York: Guilford, 1993).

90. Langston, *Conscience and Other Virtues*, 174. Thus far, Langston's call has gone unheeded. In recent philosophical works such as *The Cambridge Companion to Virtue Ethics* (2013) and *Virtues and Their Vices* (2014), conscience continues to be ignored. See Daniel C. Russell, ed., *The Cambridge Companion to Virtue Ethics* (Cambridge: Cambridge University Press, 2013); and Kevin Timpe and Craig A. Boyd, eds., *Virtues and Their Vices* (Oxford: Oxford University Press, 2014). Virtue ethics also now tends to be unmoored from (natural and eternal) law, much to the detriment of virtue ethics. Gerald P. McKenny comments with regard to contemporary virtue ethics: "Much of virtue ethics appeals to the same phenomenon that motivated the turn to responsibility [in mid-twentieth-century existentialist or situation ethics]: namely, the recognition that certain areas of life (or perhaps the whole of it) are not easily brought under determinate norms, yet are still morally significant. The appeal to responsibility was useful for reining in the exaggerated claims on behalf of freedom that sometimes accompanied this recognition (the first purpose), but it proved less fruitful in articulating the morally significant features of the area of life that is declared free of such norms (the second purpose). The older language of virtue provides a much richer moral vocabulary for discharging the latter task. It is now *phronēsis* or *prudentia* in conjunction with a virtuous character that identifies and weighs the morally relevant features of situations." McKenny, "Responsibility," in *The Oxford Handbook of Theological Ethics*, ed. Gilbert Meilaender and William Werpehowski (Oxford: Oxford University Press, 2005), 239. McKenny directs attention to William Schweiker, *Responsibility and Christian Ethics* (Cambridge: Cambridge University Press, 1995), and Kathryn Tanner, "A Theological Case for Human Responsibility in Moral Choice," *Journal of Religion* 73 (1993): 592–612.

Chapter 1

1. For background, see Eugene Thomas Long, *Jaspers and Bultmann: A Dialogue between Philosophy and Theology in the Existentialist Tradition* (Durham, NC: Duke University Press, 1968).

2. See Raphael Gallagher, CSsR, "Interpreting Thomas Aquinas: Aspects of the Redemptorist and Jesuit Schools in the Twentieth Century," in *The Ethics of Aquinas*, ed. Stephen J. Pope (Washington, DC: Georgetown University Press, 2002), 376: "The organizing principle of the whole of moral theology (not just the manuals) was radically questioned by Fritz Tillmann and, later, by Theodor Steinbüchel and Johannes Stelzenberger, among others. Their criticisms were based on biblical grounds and personalist philosophy." Steinbüchel died in 1949, Tillmann in 1953.

3. Pope Pius X, *Pascendi Dominici Gregis*, §23, available at www.vatican.va. For Tyrrell's efforts to discredit John Henry Newman in the wake of *Pascendi*, see Stephen

Bullivant, "Newman and Modernism: The *Pascendi* Crisis and Its Wider Significance," *New Blackfriars* 92 (2011): 189–208.

4. George Tyrrell, *Essays on Faith and Immortality*, ed. M. D. Petre (New York: Longmans, Green & Co., 1914), 22, cited in Hastings Rashdall, *Conscience and Christ: Six Lectures on Christian Ethics* (London: Duckworth, 1916), 167n1. The first essay in *Essays on Faith and Immortality* is titled "The Doctrinal Authority of Conscience."

5. George Tyrrell, *Through Scylla and Charybdis; or, The Old Theology and the New* (London: Longmans, Green, and Co., 1907), 381. Pope Pius X describes this viewpoint: "in the same way as the Church is a vital emanation of the collectivity of consciences, so too authority emanates vitally from the Church itself. Authority, therefore, like the Church, has its origin in the religious conscience, and, that being so, is subject to it" (*Pascendi Dominici Gregis*, §23).

6. Tyrrell, *Through Scylla and Charybdis*, 383. For Tyrrell's only partly successful efforts to distinguish his theological positions from Liberal Protestantism, see Anthony M. Maher, *The Forgotten Jesuit of Catholic Modernism: George Tyrrell's Prophetic Theology* (Minneapolis: Fortress, 2018), 132–34 (although Maher thinks Tyrrell succeeded). David G. Schultenover, SJ, argues that Vatican II vindicated Tyrrell, but in my view this claim is demonstrably inaccurate with regard to the actual teachings of the Council. See Schultenover, *George Tyrrell: In Search of Catholicism* (Shepherdstown: Patmos, 1981), 360: "the modernism for which Tyrrell stood and gave his life merely went underground for a time. Anyone who has studied both him and the documents of Vatican II will recognize his principles reborn on nearly every page."

7. Tyrrell, *Essays on Faith and Immortality*, 10.

8. Tyrrell, *Essays on Faith and Immortality*, 12.

9. Tyrrell, *Essays on Faith and Immortality*, 12.

10. Tyrrell, *Essays on Faith and Immortality*, 13.

11. Tyrrell, *Essays on Faith and Immortality*, 14. Tyrrell goes on to say, "As men grew better, more spiritual and moral, they realised that first-power and brain-power were not really worthy of their deepest reverence; they felt that the commands of a Nature-God or of a Philosophy-God were subject to and conditioned by the approval of conscience; that God's absolute claim to obedience and adoration could rest only on His Righteousness. It was left for Christ to subject the physical and metaphysical to the moral, and to purify the conception of God from the last alloy of materialism and idolatry" (16–17).

12. Tyrrell, *Through Scylla and Charybdis*, 370.

13. Tyrrell, *Essays on Faith and Immortality*, 18.

14. Tyrrell, *Essays on Faith and Immortality*, 19.

15. Tyrrell, *Essays on Faith and Immortality*, 19. Since this is so, it follows for Tyrrell that "the Catholic and Christian tradition is given us on the Church's testimony as her authorised expression (however inadequate) of what she has experienced; of what has been revealed to her in Christ and in the prophets and Saints of the Old and New Law. But it does not thereby become an expression of my experience; of what *I* know and have seen. It is but an instrument, a standard of my spiritual self-education, whose value and meaning becomes real for me in the measure that my own experience is developed by its aid on the same lines" (21). As an instrument, it is potentially faulty: "we find that it is verified here and falsified there" (20). A similar point holds for the Scriptures, which Tyrrell describes as "approved as Sacred, not by my isolated and unformed conscience,

but by that of the whole Christian people—'sacred,' namely, as exhibiting the workings of God's Spirit in the process of the Church's genesis, the gradual transition by which a chosen people were led from the childish religious fancies of semi-savagery and barbarism up to the pure religion of Spirit and Truth, from the worship of God in Nature to the worship of God in Conscience" (23). The Scriptures are "Sacred" in this sense, but they are not thereby a stopping point. Tyrrell observes in this regard that "the Scriptures only stereotype the self-consciousness of the Church up to the sub-apostolic age; they are but a part, however central and important, of her present self-utterance" (23). Neither, however, are the dogmas and practices of Catholic tradition a stopping point. Faith rests not in dogmas or Scriptures but in the living church (Christ and his saints), in which we see "the extension, the complement, the development of that revelation of Himself which God makes in our own individual conscience" (24).

16. Ernst Troeltsch, *The Christian Faith: Based on Lectures Delivered at the University of Heidelberg in 1912 and 1913*, ed. Gertrud von le Fort, trans. Garrett E. Paul (Minneapolis: Fortress, 1991), 166. Troeltsch grants that there are "requirements for stringent self-surrender before God, separation from the entanglements of the world, and, most emphatically, love of the brother. So there *is* a content to be discovered. By no means do we hold that there are no restraints whatsoever. Jesus' demands are to be taken as revelation. Purity of heart that achieves what is needful, love which is not mere helpfulness but rather a genuine bond in and through God—these are absolute requirements. They define both the starting point and the ending point. But both the goal and the beginning lie in God. He himself constitutes the freedom of the conscience" (167). Or, as Tyrrell says: "When the term faith is given to mere orthodoxy, to a mental assent to the authorised formulation of Faith's object; or, in other words, when that formulation is substituted for the reality which it symbolises, a like unreality is imparted into our devotion and love. These affections are then directed, not to a God who is given us in immediate experience, not to a Spirit in felt conflict with our own, but to the fictitious, absent and distant original of the representations of our mind" (*Essays on Faith and Immortality*, 25).

17. Pope Pius X, *Pascendi Dominici Gregis*, §24. Pius X goes on to describe the position of Tyrrell and his supporters more fully: "As this [ecclesiastical] magisterium springs, in the last analysis, from the individual consciences and possesses its mandate of public utility for their benefit, it necessarily follows that the ecclesiastical magisterium must be dependent upon them, and should therefore be made to bow to the popular ideals" (*Pascendi*, §25).

18. Hastings Rashdall, *Conscience and Christ: Six Lectures on Christian Ethics* (London: Duckworth, 1916), 167. Hereafter, page references from this work will be given in parentheses in the text.

19. Although Jesus's preaching of the imminent Kingdom might have made "all other occupations, interests, aims in life [seem] *comparatively* unimportant beside that of announcing that the Judgement was at hand," in fact, "the essential principle even of such sayings does, however, remain eternally true. 'Seek ye first the Kingdom of God and His righteousness'" (Rashdall, *Conscience and Christ*, 63–64). Rashdall adds, "No doubt . . . we must to some extent translate the conception of the Kingdom into terms of modern life. For us the light of Science and the course of History have dispelled the dream of a speedy return of Jesus upon the clouds of Heaven" (65–66). But this "trans-

lation" need not be as radical as may seem necessary at first glance, since "Jesus did also in all probability speak of a Kingdom which should come gradually, which was actually coming gradually in a quiet, unobtrusive, uncatastrophic development, as individual souls listened to His message, and as a little society formed around Him in which God's will was being already done. If this meaning of the Kingdom was for Him, in a sense, a secondary meaning, it is clear that to us it must be the primary one. The Kingdom of God, after all, means only the reign of God. To bring about a reign of God in human society is surely the true conception of the supreme end of human life" (66). Rashdall firmly rejects the claim that "the Christian idea of the Kingdom of God has absolutely nothing in common with that hope of a gradual improvement in the social and spiritual condition of Humanity in which Protestant Liberal Theology has been disposed to find its deepest meaning" (67).

20. Rashdall adds, "He [Christ] did not ask men to obey his precepts except in so far as their Consciences bore independent witness to their truth. . . . It was a voice within, not merely an external voice, to which he appealed in confirmation of the claim which He made upon their allegiance" (*Conscience and Christ*, 35).

21. This is the standard Liberal Protestant position. Rashdall argues that from this principle flow the following, all taught by Christ: love of enemies, forgiveness of injuries, self-sacrifice, the danger of riches, humility, the "Christian Good" or the duty to extend the Kingdom by teaching love, sexual purity that flows from the principle that every human should be treated with love, the duty of making others better, repentance, the sin of casting stumbling-blocks, and the danger of hypocrisy (*Conscience and Christ*, 120–33). These teachings, however, do not convey a code of conduct or a set of precepts. Rashdall responds to an argument frequently made against positions such as his: "It will no doubt be thought by some that the element of Christ's teaching which we have left standing, if we fully accept this principle of Development, is a very small one. It comes, it may be said, to little more than this—that Morality consists in the unselfish pursuit of the good for all men, and in the recognition of the supreme value of moral goodness as the highest and most important element of that good. And that, it may be urged, is a very small element in a moral system—one which might be equally accepted by those who in practice would adopt very different maxims of conduct and recognize very different ideals of life. I should reply, Yes, if you compare the sheer bulk of these precepts with the mass of detailed rules which are required in practice for the guidance of our complicated modern life, their bulk is, indeed, small; but ethically speaking it is the one thing needful" (220–21).

22. Rashdall comments that "the teaching of Jesus Christ presupposes a morality of a very advanced and developed order" (*Conscience and Christ*, 79). See also Adolf von Harnack's praise of the first Christians for taking "purity in the deepest and most comprehensive sense of the word, as the horror of everything that is unholy, and as the inner pleasure in everything that is upright and true, lovely and of good report. They also meant purity in regard to the body: 'Know ye not that your body is the temple of the Holy Ghost which is in you? therefore glorify God in your body.' In this sublime consciousness the earliest Christians took up the struggle against the sins of impurity, which in the heathen world were not accounted sins at all." von Harnack, *What Is Christianity?*, trans. Thomas Bailey Saunders (New York: Harper & Brothers, 1957), 167–68. For von Harnack, "the Gospel is the knowledge and recognition of

God as the Father, the certainty of redemption, humility and joy in God, energy and brotherly love" (299).

23. Rashdall considers, "The great defect of the Christian ideal as it has commonly been understood in all past times, whether we think of the Apostolic Church, of the patristic Church, of medieval Christendom, or modern Protestantism, is this—that Christian Charity has contented itself far too much with curing sin, with relieving suffering, with removing injustices, with mitigating poverty, instead of trying so systematically to organize human society that suffering and injustice shall, as far as possible, not arise, and that undeserved poverty shall altogether cease. We have only just begun to recognize this as the true aim of Christian morality" (*Conscience and Christ*, 224).

24. The kerygma calls forth not a judgment about historical facts, but faith. Eugene Thomas Long sums up: "It is a decision in which man understands himself free from past bondage to the world and living out of God's future. Man acknowledges himself as a recipient of that gift in which he understands himself anew, and in this way faith takes on the character of confession from within a particular historical tradition" (Long, *Jaspers and Bultmann*, 23). Later, Long expands upon this description by stating, "Bultmann's exposition of the Christian revelation brings together two factors which he considers to be inseparable. First, there is the present encounter with God in which my understanding of myself in relation to God is altered. . . . But second, this present encounter is, according to Bultmann, bound up in an indissoluble way to the past event in which Jesus of Nazareth is understood as the eschatological event in faith. . . . It is not that the facts of the past are recalled in their worldly actuality or that one encounters human existence and its interpretation in the past. Rather, in the recollection of the kerygma, the events of the past are represented in such a way that within them God's Word may encounter me, demanding a decision from me" (46–47). Put another way: "According to Bultmann it is not the historical Jesus but the Christ of the kerygma who is the object of faith, and man who is addressed by the kerygma may not go behind it seeking to verify it by historical investigation. The proclamation that God has acted in Jesus as the Christ can neither be affirmed nor denied by historical investigation because it is beyond the sphere of historical investigation to say that God has acted here" (138). For the common criticism that Bultmann's position does not give sufficient weight to the actual historical persons and events, see, for example, H. P. Owen, *Revelation and Existence: A Study in the Theology of Rudolf Bultmann* (Cardiff: University of Wales Press, 1957); Ian Henderson, *Myth in the New Testament* (London: SCM, 1952); and Gerhard Ebeling, *Theologie und Verkündigung: Ein Gespräch mit Rudolf Bultmann* (Tübingen: J. C. B. Mohr, 1962).

25. For discussion of this early interaction between Heidegger and Bultmann, see Hue Woodson, *Heideggerian Theologies: The Pathmarks of John Macquarrie, Rudolf Bultmann, Paul Tillich, and Karl Rahner* (Eugene, OR: Wipf & Stock, 2018), 60–80. See also William D. Dennison, *The Young Bultmann: Context for His Understanding of God, 1884–1925* (New York: Peter Lang, 2008); as well as John Van Buren, *The Young Heidegger: Rumor of the Hidden King* (Bloomington: Indiana University Press, 1994). Heidegger contributed lectures to Bultmann's Winter 1923/1924 seminar on Paul's ethics. For Bultmann's extensive and enduring debt to Heidegger's existential analysis, see Woodson, *Heideggerian Theologies*, 79–91, citing especially Bultmann, "The Historicity of Man and Faith," in *Existence and Faith: Shorter Writings of Rudolf Bultmann*, ed. and trans. Schubert M. Ogden (New York: The World Publishing Company, 1966), 92,

and Bultmann, "New Testament and Mythology," in *Kerygma and Myth: A Theological Debate*, ed. Hans W. Bartsch (New York: Harper & Row, 1961), 25. See also John C. Staten, *Conscience and the Reality of God: An Essay on the Experiential Foundations of Religious Knowledge* (Berlin: Mouton de Gruyter, 1988). Staten ties together Bultmann, Heidegger, and Rahner. He argues that through the experiential reality that Heidegger calls "conscience," we possess "ontological grounding for understanding the reality deemed 'God'" (24; cf. 127–29).

26. Rudolf Bultmann, *Theology of the New Testament*, 2 vols., trans. Kendrick Grobel (Waco, TX: Baylor University Press, 2007), 212.

27. Bultmann, *Theology of the New Testament*, 212.

28. Bultmann, *Theology of the New Testament*, 215.

29. Bultmann, *Theology of the New Testament*, 216.

30. Bultmann, *Theology of the New Testament*, 217.

31. Bultmann, *Theology of the New Testament*, 218.

32. For Bultmannian "faith" as a new "self-understanding" through God's action, see Long, *Jaspers and Bultmann*, 19. For Bultmann, "personal or 'existentiell' understanding is realized only here and now as my self-understanding. . . . Faith is a new self-understanding which is never a possession of mine and must be renewed in every moment of concrete encounter. And this existentiell self-understanding of faith for Bultmann is a response to the encounter with God's Word as proclaimed in the kerygma" (Long, *Jaspers and Bultmann*, 20).

33. Bultmann, *Theology of the New Testament*, 220.

34. C. A. Pierce, *Conscience in the New Testament* (Chicago: Alec R. Allenson, 1955), 40.

35. Pierce, *Conscience in the New Testament*, 57. Pierce argues that the concept of conscience in the New Testament does not have a specifically "Stoic" background, as some have thought. Instead, he identifies the relevant background as ancient Greek and Roman literature and philosophy more broadly, beginning with Plato. He also treats the contribution of the Jewish thinker Philo, who frequently refers to conscience. Pierce states, "*Conscience* is one of the few important Greek words of the N. T. that have not had imported into them, through use by the LXX, a colouring from the Hebrew experience and outlook of the O. T." (60).

36. Pierce, *Conscience in the New Testament*, 83.

37. The Catholic biblical scholar Frank J. Matera interprets *syneidēsis* here as "moral consciousness": in 2 Cor. 4:2, Paul "commends himself in full disclosure of the truth to everyone's moral consciousness, as he will also do in 5:11. And whereas earlier he called upon the witness of his own conscience (1:12), now he commends himself to the conscience of others. Thus, if they allow their moral consciousness to bear witness, it will acknowledge his apostolic integrity." Matera, *II Corinthians: A Commentary* (Louisville, KY: Westminster John Knox, 2003), 100. Similarly, Ernest Best interprets *syneidēsis* in 2 Cor. 4:2 and 5:11 to mean the ability of Christians "to judge for themselves." Best, *Second Corinthians* (Louisville, KY: Westminster John Knox, 1987), 50.

38. Pierce, *Conscience in the New Testament*, 88.

39. Pierce, *Conscience in the New Testament*, 88–89.

40. Pierce, *Conscience in the New Testament*, 102.

41. Pierce, *Conscience in the New Testament*, 110.

42. Pierce, *Conscience in the New Testament*, 115, paraphrasing Rashdall, *Conscience and Christ*, 30.

43. Pierce, *Conscience in the New Testament*, 117.

44. Pierce, *Conscience in the New Testament*, 122.

45. Pierce, *Conscience in the New Testament*, 123, referring to J. B. Lightfoot, "Dissertation [or Appendix] II: St. Paul and Seneca," in *Saint Paul's Epistle to the Philippians: A Revised Text with Introduction, Notes and Dissertations*, 12th ed. (Peabody, MA: Hendrickson, 1995), 303. Augustine and Jerome believed that Paul and Seneca had exchanged letters, and Jerome claimed to have seen these (spurious) fourteen letters. Lightfoot believes that Paul's understanding of conscience derives from Stoicism and that Christian moral teachings echo the ethical teachings of great non-Christian moralists. Lightfoot states, "The mere ethical teaching, however important, is the least important, because the least distinctive part of Christianity. . . . The moral teaching and the moral example of the Lord will ever have the highest value in their own province; but the core of the Gospel does not lie here. Its distinctive character is, that in revealing a Person it reveals also a principle of life—the union with God in Christ, apprehended by faith in the present and assured to us hereafter by the Resurrection" ("Dissertation [or Appendix] II," 328).

46. Yves Congar, OP, "St. Paul's Casuistry," in *A Gospel Priesthood*, trans. P. J. Hepburne-Scott (New York: Herder and Herder, 1967), 49. His lengthy footnotes to this short essay display his erudition. In a note added after the original publication, he directs the reader's attention to a book (unknown to him previously) that shows—much as Congar does in this essay—how Paul's casuistry is guided by the church's faith: Hans von Campenhausen, *Die Bergründung kirchlicher Entscheidungen beim Apostel Paulus: Zur Grundlegung des Kirchenrechts* (Heidelberg: Carl Winter, 1957). He also refers to the three volumes of Bernard Häring, translated into English as *The Law of Christ*, 3 vols., trans. Edwin G. Kaiser, CPPS (Westminster, MD: Newman, 1961–66).

47. Congar, "St. Paul's Casuistry," 62. Underestimating the richness of Rabbinic Judaism, he adds, "as rabbinical casuistry did and still does."

48. Congar, "St. Paul's Casuistry," 64. He assumes mistakenly that the Mosaic law, or the Torah as practiced in ongoing Judaism, is not understood as a gift of divine love to which Jews are supposed to respond in obedient love.

49. Congar, "St. Paul's Casuistry," 62.

50. Congar, "St. Paul's Casuistry," 62.

51. Congar, "St. Paul's Casuistry," 62.

52. Congar, "St. Paul's Casuistry," 64.

53. With regard to the latter, Congar quotes a warning provided by Karl Rahner in 1950, as well as Pope Pius XII's two speeches in 1952 (also, as we will see, referenced positively by Michel Labourdette) and the condemnation issued in 1956 by the Holy Office. See Karl Rahner, SJ, "Der Appell an das Gewissen: Situationsethik und Sündenmystik," *Wort und Wahrheit* 4 (1949): 721–34; Rahner, *Gefahren im heutigen Katholizismus* (Einsiedeln: Benzinger, 1950). Note that Rahner's word of warning was combined with a highly positive appraisal of certain elements of "situation ethics" or "existential ethics," as I will discuss below. For Pope Pius XII's teaching, see his "Address to the World Federation of Catholic Young Women," *Catholic Documents* 8 (1952): 15–20; Pius XII, "The Christian Conscience as an Object of Education," *Catholic Documents* 8 (1952):

1–7. See also the concerns expressed by Kenneth A. Moore, OCarm, "Situational Ethics," *American Ecclesiastical Review* 135 (1956): 29–38.

54. Congar, "St. Paul's Casuistry," 65.

55. This point is important because interpreters, pointing to Paul's timebound casuistic dictates (for example, about slavery), sometimes assume that *none* of his moral teachings are binding and authoritative in every time and place.

56. Congar, "St. Paul's Casuistry," 50.

57. Congar, "St. Paul's Casuistry," 50.

58. Paul states his concern clearly: "For even when we were with you, we gave you this command: If any one will not work, let him not eat. For we hear that some of you are walking in idleness, mere busybodies, not doing any work. Now such persons we command and exhort in the Lord Jesus Christ to do their work in quietness and to earn their own living" (2 Thess. 3:10–12).

59. Congar, "St. Paul's Casuistry," 53.

60. Congar, "St. Paul's Casuistry," 52.

61. Congar, "St. Paul's Casuistry," 53.

62. Congar, "St. Paul's Casuistry," 54.

63. Congar, "St. Paul's Casuistry," 56. Along similar lines, see Richard B. Hays, *First Corinthians* (Louisville, KY: Westminster John Knox Press, 1997), 145, with regard to 1 Corinthians 8: "The central message of this chapter is a simple one: Love is more important than knowledge. Paul calls for a shift from *gnōsis* to *agapē* as the ordering principle for Christian discernment and conduct. Rather than asserting rights and privileges, we are to shape our actions toward edification of our brothers and sisters in the community of faith. In so doing, we will be following the example of Christ, who died for the weak (v. 11), and also the example of Paul, who is willing to renounce all meat in order to keep his brothers and sisters from stumbling (v. 13). The *gnōsis*-boasters frame their decisions and actions in terms of their own *exousia*, looking to the cultivation of their own spiritual freedom and sophistication as their highest end; Paul calls them instead to look to the cultivation of loving community as the goal of Christian action."

64. Congar, "St. Paul's Casuistry," 57.

65. Congar, "St. Paul's Casuistry," 59.

66. Congar, "St. Paul's Casuistry," 61.

67. Congar, "St. Paul's Casuistry," 63.

68. Congar, "St. Paul's Casuistry," 64. As Congar states in his final paragraph, "In the *theo*-logy of Aquinas the fulfilment of man is wholly relative to God, humanism is wholly theological. This humanism has two poles: charity, the virtue of the divine purpose, and prudence, the virtue of the means, wholly 'informed' by charity. Casuistry has no place in the setting of a prudent life, seeking to respond to the demands of charity. Not a casuistry which claims to give, ready-made, the solution to 'cases' by pure deduction from general principles, or so-called principles: that would be to ignore the specificality of the practical order, as Aquinas sees it, and to betray the lessons of Paul. Nor yet a casuistry limited to the legal or juridical aspect of things. But rather, in the line of Paul and even, we hope, in his school, an attempt, pursued in the communion of the Church, to respond to the intentions of God, who is *agape*, in the situation in which we are placed" (65).

69. See Johannes Stelzenberger, *Syneidesis im Neuen Testament* (Paderborn: Ferdinand Schöningh, 1961). Hereafter, page references from this work will be given in

parentheses in the text. In what follows, I employ David Augustine's unpublished translation of Stelzenberger's text. See also Stelzenberger, *Lehrbuch der Moraltheologie: Die Sittlichkeitslehre der Konigherrschaft Gottes* (Paderborn: Ferdinand Schöningh, 1953); Stelzenberger, *"Conscientia" bei Augustinus: Studie zur Geschichte der Moraltheologie* (Paderborn: Ferdinand Schöningh, 1959); and Stelzenberger, *Syneidesis bei Origenes: Studie zur Geschichte der Moraltheologie* (Paderborn: Ferdinand Schöningh, 1963).

70. See Rudolf Schnackenburg, *The Moral Teaching of the New Testament*, trans. J. Holland-Smith and W. J. O'Hara (New York: Herder and Herder, 1965), 287–96.

71. Schnackenburg, *Moral Teaching*, 288.

72. Schnackenburg, *Moral Teaching*, 293–94.

73. Schnackenburg, *Moral Teaching*, 296.

74. Philippe Delhaye, *The Christian Conscience*, trans. Charles Underhill Quinn (New York: Desclée, 1968), 19; originally published as *La conscience morale du chrétien* (Tournai: Desclée, 1964). Hereafter, page references from this work will be given in parentheses in the text. Delhaye chaired the International Theological Commission from 1972 to 1989. For further background to Delhaye—including his extensive postconciliar writings—see Éric Gaziaux, "Philippe Delhaye (1912–1990)," in *Christliche Ethik im Porträt: Leben und Werk bedeutender Moraltheologen*, ed. Konrad Hilpert (Freiburg im Breisgau: Herder, 2012), 729–58.

75. Regarding the value of law, I note the following remark of Bernard Häring, CSsR: "The protection of life and the problems raised by suicide and euthanasia impose great responsibility on legislators. I am thoroughly against any form of legalization of euthanasia. . . . Legalization of euthanasia would all too easily tempt weak families to suggest to their burdensome members that they choose euthanasia and thus leave the theatre of life. If it were to become a legal right even under limited circumstances, it would turn into an explicit and implicit public appeal to the sick and the aged to consider whether the hour had come to request the 'service' of euthanasia." Häring, *Free and Faithful in Christ: Moral Theology for Clergy and Laity*, vol. 3, *Light to the World* (New York: Crossroad, 1981), 88.

76. See also Stefania Tutino, *Uncertainty in Post-Reformation Catholicism: A History of Probabilism* (Oxford: Oxford University Press, 2018), 5–25.

77. Delhaye, *Christian Conscience*, 32; referring to René Le Senne, *Traité de morale générale*, 3rd ed. (Paris: Presses Universitaires de France, 1949), 307–73. Le Senne, influenced by Maurice Blondel, plays a noteworthy though secondary role in Edward Baring's survey of European Catholic conduits of phenomenological and existentialist currents: see Baring, *Converts to the Real: Catholicism and the Making of Continental Philosophy* (Cambridge, MA: Harvard University Press, 2019). See also Le Senne's existentialist-inflected *Obstacle et valeur* (Paris: Aubier, 1934), about which Baring states, "Little read today, the book's publication was a major event in French philosophy. In a review, [Gabriel] Marcel declared Le Senne to be the 'most authentic' philosopher in France, and suggested that it was a scandal that he had not been offered a chair at the Sorbonne. Le Senne presented himself as an idealist, and yet by appealing to existence he could extend an olive branch to the Thomists" (*Converts to the Real*, 167–68). For discussion of Le Senne as an influence on Gérard Gilleman, SJ, see Vincent Leclercq, AA, "Le *Primat de la charité* de Gilleman et la *Conscience* de Carpentier: Le renouveau théologal de la vie morale," *Studia Moralia* 44 (2006): 371–73.

78. See Ceslas Spicq, OP, "La conscience dans le Nouveau Testament," *Revue Biblique* 47 (1938): 50–80. See also Spicq's commentary on Paul's pastoral letters in *Les épitres pastorales* (Paris: Gabalda, 1947), 29–38, and the bibliographical references listed therein.

79. The RSV translation reads: "happy is he who has no reason to judge himself for what he approves."

80. Richard B. Hays, *The Moral Vision of the New Testament: Community, Cross, New Creation; A Contemporary Introduction to New Testament Ethics* (New York: Harper-Collins, 1996), 19. Hereafter, page references from this work will be given in parentheses in the text. Of course, Hays is not alone among twentieth-century biblical scholars in entirely excluding conscience from his presentation of New Testament ethics. See, for example, L. H. Marshall, *The Challenge of New Testament Ethics* (London: Macmillan, 1946).

81. See also Michael J. Gorman, *Cruciformity: Paul's Narrative Spirituality of the Cross* (Grand Rapids, MI: Eerdmans, 2001).

82. Andrew David Naselli and J. D. Crowley have recently sought to fill the gap in Evangelical Protestant understandings of conscience, in their *Conscience: What It Is, How to Train It, and Loving Those Who Differ* (Wheaton, IL: Crossway, 2016). Treating every verse in Scripture in which the term "conscience" (*syneidēisis*) appears, they seek "to show from Scripture what God intended and did not intend conscience to do," as well as to explain how "conscience works, how to care for it, and how not to damage it" (17). They argue that Scripture teaches that "everyone . . . has a conscience, an imperfect-but-accurate-enough version of God's will" and that "conscience is all about right or wrong, black or white. It doesn't do gray scale very well" (24–25). They hold that if a dictate given by conscience "contradicts Scripture," then it arises from a "wrongly calibrated conscience" (29; cf. 65–68). As they observe, conscience can be weak, wounded, defiled, guilty, and deadened; and conscience can also be cleansed and blameless. Conscience can bear witness, judge (including the action of another person), and "lead one to act a certain way" (42). They direct attention to an earlier Evangelical (Reformed) book on conscience, John MacArthur's *The Vanishing Conscience* (Dallas, TX: Word, 1994), as well as to a more recent book similar to theirs, Christopher Ash's *Pure Joy: Rediscover Your Conscience* (Downers Grove, IL: InterVarsity, 2012).

83. Tyrrell, *Through Scylla and Charybdis*, 381.

84. Tyrrell, *Through Scylla and Charybdis*, 370.

85. See Frank J. Matera, *New Testament Ethics: The Legacies of Jesus and Paul* (Louisville, KY: Westminster John Knox, 1996). Matera quotes Paul (in passing) five times with reference to conscience, but never discusses the meaning or significance of Pauline conscience except to say, in a footnote, that "for Paul, conscience (*syneidēsis*) refers to a moral awareness or consciousness of good and evil" (285n34).

86. See Ralph McInerny, *Aquinas on Human Action: A Theory of Practice* (Washington, DC: Catholic University of America Press, 1992), 93: "Note how Thomas retains the notion of what is good or bad in itself. Without that point of reference, there would be no way to speak of the conscience as erroneous, of course. But the one with the erroneous conscience is unaware of the discrepancy between what he thinks good or bad and what is good or bad, so he is unaware that his conscience is erroneous. But what if his reason should tell him to do something against divine law? If he himself is aware of this

conflict, then his conscience is not completely erroneous, and he is obliged to follow divine law, not his own defective judgment. The same would be true of a Catholic who thinks he ought to do something he knows is contrary to Church teaching. To be aware of the discrepancy is to know that he ought to follow Church teaching"—presuming it is a teaching that belongs to the consistent ordinary magisterium.

87. Brendan Byrne, SJ, *Romans* (Collegeville, MN: Liturgical Press, 1996), 94.

Chapter 2

1. For example, see Brian Van Hove, SJ, "Looking Back at *Humani Generis*," *Homiletic and Pastoral Review*, December 23, 2013, https://www.hprweb.com/2013/12/looking-back-at-humani-generis/.

2. See Réginald Garrigou-Lagrange, "Remarks Concerning the Metaphysical Character of St. Thomas's Moral Theology, in Particular as It Is Related to Prudence and Conscience," trans. Matthew K. Minerd, *Nova et Vetera* 17, no. 1 (2019): 247. This is a translation of Garrigou-Lagrange, "Du charactère métaphysique de la théologie morale de saint Thomas, en particulier dans ses rapports avec la prudence et la conscience," *Revue Thomiste* 30 (1925): 341–55.

3. Thus in his article "St. Thomas's Moral Theology," Garrigou-Lagrange adds, "Nobody can have a profound knowledge of moral theology without being an expert in dogmatic theology" (249). See also Frederick Christian Bauerschmidt's observation: "For Thomas, perfect possession of any moral virtue requires the possession of all the other moral virtues, in particular prudence, which itself is something of a hybrid between a moral and an intellectual virtue. And the moral virtues themselves are not truly and perfectly virtuous apart from the infused gift of charity, which in turn cannot exist apart from faith, which is a virtue perfecting the intellect. . . . Our views on homosexuality [to name a "moral theology" issue] imply and should be informed by our convictions concerning theological anthropology, or the nature of the authority of Scripture, or whether we believe there is a natural law and how we understand it in relation to culture. The doctrinal and the moral are simply inseparable because what we believe to be true is but the flip side of how we believe we should act, and vice versa." Bauerschmidt, "Doctrine: Knowing and Doing," in *The Morally Divided Body: Ethical Disagreement and the Disunity of the Church*, ed. Michael Root and James J. Buckley (Eugene, OR: Cascade, 2012), 31, 41.

4. Garrigou-Lagrange, "St. Thomas's Moral Theology," 248. He also observes, "If moral theology were reduced to casuistry, as all too often happens, it would become the science of sins to avoid rather than the science of the virtues to be exercised and perfected—as if optics were the science of shadows instead of the science of luminous phenomena! Moral theology would thus lack the ability and impulse for directing men in the practice of lofty and solid virtues" (249). See also Sylvio Hermann De Franceschi, "La défense doctrinale du système thomiste de la mystique étendue: Le P. Réginald Garrigou-Lagrange et la construction d'une école dominicaine de spiritualité," *Revue des Sciences Philosophiques et Théologiques* 103 (2019): 113–43. Notably, too, this was the era of the Liturgical Movement—which was not separate from the reform of moral theology and the desire to get beyond the casuist manuals.

5. Garrigou-Lagrange, "St. Thomas's Moral Theology," 249. I note that anyone who dips into Garrigou-Lagrange's *The Three Ages of the Interior Life* will find therein a profound integration—even if in the name of mystical or ascetical theology rather than moral theology—between Christian spiritual experience and moral theology. In this masterwork, Garrigou-Lagrange writes extensively on prudence, justice, patience, meekness, chastity, humility, faith, charity, and so on. See Réginald Garrigou-Lagrange, OP, *The Three Ages of the Interior Life*, 2 vols., trans. M. Timothea Doyle (St. Louis, MO: Herder, 1948).

6. Garrigou-Lagrange, "St. Thomas's Moral Theology," 250–51.

7. Garrigou-Lagrange, "St. Thomas's Moral Theology," 251.

8. Garrigou-Lagrange, "St. Thomas's Moral Theology," 254.

9. Garrigou-Lagrange, "St. Thomas's Moral Theology," 258. See also Réginald Garrigou-Lagrange, OP, *The Order of Things: The Realism of the Principle of Finality*, trans. Matthew K. Minerd (Steubenville, OH: Emmaus Academic, 2020), chapter 6: "Moral Realism: Finality and the Formation of Conscience." Garrigou-Lagrange sets forth the problems that troubled post-Tridentine moral theology: "How can we arrive at a *certain judgment of conscience* despite the fact that we experience invincible ignorance concerning many of the circumstances of human acts . . . ? Likewise, how can I determine with certitude, *here and now*, in matters that directly concern *me* (and not you) the *golden mean* to preserve in matters of temperance, meekness, humility, courage, patience—all while this golden mean depends on many particular circumstances that are still known only in a vague manner (or, even at times are unknown), such circumstances as my temperament (be it high-strung, sanguine, or phlegmatic), my age, the season (be it summer or winter), my social status, etc. . . . ?" (*Order of Things*, 274–75). He answers: "St. Thomas provides a more profound solution to this question [than that offered by the manualist tradition]. He does not disdain the consideration of probabilities for and against a course of action. Nor does he disdain commonly received reflexive principles. However, he insists before all else on a *formal principle* spoken of by few modern theologians even though it can be found even in Aristotle. This principle can be expressed: '*The truth of the practical intellect* (or, prudence) *is found in conformity with right appetite*,' for, '*According to the way that a man is well or poorly disposed* (in his will and his sensibility), *so does the end appear suitable or not suitable to him*'" (*Order of Things*, 275). For further background to conscience as understood by Garrigou-Lagrange, see his "De conscientia secundum principia sancti Thomae. Supplementum quaestionis XIX et XX," in *De beatitudine de actibus humanis et habitibus: Commentarius in Summam theologicam S. Thomae Ia–IIa qq. 1-54* (Turin: Berutti, 1951), 373–96.

10. Servais Pinckaers, OP, "Dominican Moral Theology in the 20th Century," trans. Mary Thomas Noble, OP, in *The Pinckaers Reader: Renewing Thomistic Moral Theology*, ed. John Berkman and Craig Steven Titus (Washington, DC: Catholic University of America Press, 2005), 76. For further background to Pinckaers's perspective as a preconciliar critic of the moral manuals—and to his debt to the "school" of M.-D. Chenu—see Pinckaers, *Le renouveau de la morale: Études pour une morale fidèle à ses sources et à sa mission présente* (Paris: Casterman, 1964).

11. Pinckaers, "Dominican Moral Theology," 77.

12. See for example Thomas Deman, OP, "Probabilisme," in *Dictionnaire de théologie catholique*, vol. 13 (Paris: Librairie Letouzey et Ané, 1936), cols. 417–619; Deman,

Aux origines de la théologie morale (Paris: Vrin, 1951). For a Redemptorist response to Deman's article, arguing that Alphonsus de Liguori's system was prudence-based, see C. A. Damen, "S. Alfonsus Doctor Prudentiae," *Rassegna di Morale e Diritto* 5–6 (1939–40): 1–27. For discussion, see Raphael Gallagher, CSsR, "Interpreting Thomas Aquinas: Aspects of the Redemptorist and Jesuit Schools in the Twentieth Century," in *The Ethics of Aquinas*, ed. Stephen J. Pope (Washington, DC: Georgetown University Press, 2002), 376. See also the Redemptorist moral manual of Joseph Aertnys and C. A. Damen, *Theologia moralis secundum doctrinam S. Alfonsi de Ligorio Doctoris Ecclesiae*, 16th ed. (Turin: Marietti, 1950).

13. Pinckaers, "Dominican Moral Theology," 80. I note that Pinckaers's schematization is not reflective of all the streams of moral manuals, not even necessarily the major ones coming down out of St. Alphonsus.

14. Pinckaers, "Dominican Moral Theology," 80. Pinckaers partly exculpates the authors of the moral manuals: "I should add that these moralists had basically carried out the task entrusted to them by the Council of Trent, to give a moral foundation to the faithful through their parish priests according to the intention of the *Roman Catechism*. But, aiming at simplification, they had narrowed the field of morality, thereby limiting the horizon of the Christian life too much" (80).

15. Pinckaers, "Dominican Moral Theology," 81.

16. For discussion, see especially Servais Pinckaers, OP, *The Sources of Christian Ethics*, trans. Mary Thomas Noble, OP (Washington, DC: Catholic University of America Press, 1995), chapters 14 and 15. Pinckaers does not advert to the distinction between "passive indifference" and the "dominating indifference" of the will (namely, the fact that the human will is not determined by any finite good *precisely because of its "over-ordination"* in relation to the good as such). See Jacques Maritain, *Bergsonian Philosophy and Thomism*, trans. Mabel L. Andison and J. Gordon Andison (New York: The Philosophical Library, 1955), 272n4: The will "triumphs, 1) over the indetermination of the object (both good and not good, because it is not the Good itself, 2) over the passive indetermination which affects it itself (and which is a sign of imperfection: it is not always in act like the will of God). It triumphs over this double determination by exerting its *active and dominating indetermination or indifference*, which is the very essence of freedom. It is because they have not distinguished between passive indifference and active or dominating indifference in our will that many authors have so completely misunderstood the Thomist doctrine of Free will." This issue concerning two kinds of indifference is also explained by Maritain's collaborator Yves Simon in his *Freedom of Choice*, trans. and ed. Peter Wolff (New York: Fordham University Press, 1969).

17. See Tom Angier, "Quaestiones Disputatae de Pinckaers," *Journal of Moral Theology* 8, Special Issue 2 (2019): 166–87.

18. See my "Supplementing Pinckaers: The Old Testament in Aquinas's Ethics," in *Reading Sacred Scripture with Thomas Aquinas: Hermeneutical Tools, Theological Questions and New Perspectives*, ed. Piotr Roszak and Jörgen Vijgen (Turnhout: Brepols, 2015), 349–73. See also John Cuddeback, "Law, Pinckaers, and the Definition of Christian Ethics," *Nova et Vetera* 7 (2009): 301–26.

19. On this point, see the discussion of Pinckaers in my *Biblical Natural Law: A Theocentric and Teleological Approach* (Oxford: Oxford University Press, 2008), chapter 3.

20. Angier, "Quaestiones Disputatae de Pinckaers," 169. Angier does not recognize how deeply Pinckaers grasps this coordination.

21. Angier has the misimpression that Pinckaers is following a modern philosophical path. He explains that "the idea of a moral 'foundation' is a distinctly modern one. As Julia Annas maintains, there is among modern thinkers 'the common assumption that the model for an ethical theory must be a scientific one, with basic and derived concepts, and with reduction and theoretical simplicity seen as major aims.' On what she calls this 'hierarchical and complete' model of ethics, it makes perfect sense to identify virtue (or law) as explanatorily basic or ultimate, thereby reducing other moral notions, so far as possible, to their alleged monistic foundation. But it is very far from obvious that ancient or medieval thinkers were moral foundationalists. Although Aristotle tends to *focus* on the virtues, they are not *foundational* for him in the way they are, arguably, for modern 'virtue ethicists.' They are, rather, coordinate with other notions: notions such as nature, law, function and fulfillment. Such conceptual coordination (as opposed to superordination) holds *a fortiori*, I will argue, for Aquinas, who inherits not only the Aristotelian conceptual scheme, but also the biblical one, with its comparatively strong emphasis on law. For Aquinas, as for Aristotle, neither virtue nor law plays the role of a moral foundation" ("Quaestiones Disputatae de Pinckaers," 168–69). To all of this, Pinckaers would simply reply: Of course. Angier has read Pinckaers in the context of Julia Annas and her opponents rather than in the context of the twentieth-century Dominican polemic against the moral manuals. See Annas, *The Morality of Happiness* (Oxford: Oxford University Press, 1993), 11; Rosalind Hursthouse, *Virtue Ethics* (Oxford: Oxford University Press, 1999); and Christine Swanton, *Virtue Ethics: A Pluralistic View* (Oxford: Oxford University Press, 2005).

22. On this point, see also the discussion of how to understand the notion of "norm" in Jacques Maritain, *An Introduction to the Basic Problems of Moral Philosophy*, trans. Ornelia N. Borgerhoff (New York: Magi, 1990), 141–57.

23. Lacking appreciation for the context of Pinckaers's concerns, Angier misunderstands what Pinckaers intends when he criticizes an ethics of obligation or duty. Angier comments: "For Pinckaers, an 'ethics of law' is synonymous with an 'ethics of obligation.' But . . . this is conceptually imprecise. Properly speaking, commandments or divine laws constitute a *species* of obligation. We thus find Aristotle referring to acting *hōs dei*, 'as one must' or 'as one should'—i.e. acting as one is obliged to do—but we never find him appealing to the notion of divine laws or commandments. This conceptual disparity between obligations and commandments or laws has important theoretical repercussions. For the modern understanding of obligation is typically that of a moral requirement or duty which is minimal in nature. Often negative or prohibitory in content, it designates a moral threshold below which we must not fall. By contrast, and as I shall argue, biblical commandments or divine laws need not have such a minimal or threshold nature. *Contra* Pinckaers's essentially modern construal of them, they can and do accommodate morally very ambitious content" ("Quaestiones Disputatae de Pinckaers," 169). Again, Pinckaers would answer: Of course. But Pinckaers is not fighting against the Decalogue or the Torah or Christ's new commandment (let alone the many moral commandments one finds in Paul's letters and in the Sermon on the Mount) but rather against the moral manuals.

24. Pinckaers, *Sources of Christian Ethics*, 277.

25. Pinckaers, *Sources of Christian Ethics*, 277.

26. Pinckaers's critique of Protestant ethics is sharp, and it is not applicable to all Protestant moral theology by any means: see *Sources of Christian Ethics*, 282–86. At the same time, he warns that the Catholic moral manuals possess a negative, reactionary "Anti-Protestant Conditioning" (287). He concludes, "Protestants inclined to the side of faith and were prepared to abandon ethics based on law. Catholics favored morality in its relationship to law and weakened its bonds with faith. Casuists even asked, How many times in a lifetime is one bound to make an act of faith?—as if the faith of a Christian should not be active throughout life" (288). Even worse, "The absolute priority given by Protestantism to Scripture, according to its principle of 'Scripture alone,' '*Scriptura sola*,' and its rejection of tradition, led Catholic theologians to emphasize the teaching of tradition and to keep their distance from Scripture" (288). See also his observations on page 293 in light of the Second Vatican Council's decree on ecumenism, *Unitatis Redintegratio*.

27. See Pinckaers, *Sources of Christian Ethics*, 293–94. For contemporary studies influenced by Pinckaers, see for example William C. Mattison III, *The Sermon on the Mount and Moral Theology: A Virtue Perspective* (Cambridge: Cambridge University Press, 2017); and Jonathan T. Pennington, *The Sermon on the Mount and Human Flourishing: A Theological Commentary* (Grand Rapids, MI: Baker Academic, 2017). See also the summary of Catholic moral thinking in Andrew Kim, *An Introduction to Catholic Ethics since Vatican II* (Cambridge: Cambridge University Press, 2015), especially chapters 1–2.

28. Brian Besong, "Reappraising the Manual Tradition," *American Catholic Philosophical Quarterly* 89 (2015): 578.

29. Besong, "Reappraising the Manual Tradition," 580. I agree, too, with Besong when he comments that "it is an error to see a strong division between the new law of grace and 'the old law of written precepts.' . . . The precepts of the new law are all virtually contained in the old; yet in the new law, these precepts are set out more explicitly and with greater firmness of codification than in the old, and thus in no way are abolished as superfluous to those under the guidance of the Holy Spirit" (582–83). On the place of casuistry in the overall structure of moral theology, see William Wallace, OP, *The Role of Demonstration in Moral Theology: A Study of Methodology in St. Thomas Aquinas* (Washington, DC: Thomist, 1962), 189–217.

30. See also Paul Rambert, "Conscience et loi naturelle dans les manuels d'avant Vatican II," *Revue Thomiste* 119 (2019): 397–448. Rambert treats fifty-six preconciliar manuals, though he counts works that I have treated outside my moral-manual chapter—for instance, works by Michel Labourdette, Johannes Stelzenberger, and Bernard Häring. Rambert argues in favor of adopting the manuals' distinction between "habitual conscience" (inclusive of synderesis, the natural law or moral knowledge, experience, and even the virtue of prudence) and "actual conscience" (the specific act of applying the moral law to a particular action). He thinks that "habitual" and "actual" conscience would today be a suitable substitute for the concept of "natural law" in moral theology, in part because this would clearly emphasize the perspective of the acting subject. In my view, removing the clear reference to "natural law" would be a serious mistake, because of the centrality of law (in conjunction with the virtues), including natural law, for biblically informed Christian moral theology. See also Rambert, "L'articulation entre

la loi éternelle et la loi naturelle dans les manuels thomistes d'avant Vatican II," *Revue Thomiste* 113 (2013): 47–82; and Rambert, "La loi comme ordination rationis dans les manuels d'avant Vatican II," *Revue Thomiste* 109 (2009): 531–88.

31. Austin Fagothey, SJ, *Right and Reason: Ethics in Theory and Practice*, 2nd ed. (Charlotte, NC: TAN, 2000), 5. Hereafter, page references from this work will be given in parentheses in the text.

32. Writing as a philosopher inquiring into the "natural end" of human beings, Fagothey states: "St. Thomas is primarily a theologian and only secondarily a philosopher. He nowhere makes a complete study of the end of man explicitly undertaken from the standpoint of pure reason alone. But he gives the groundwork for such a study, which we can carry on by abstracting from the data of Christian revelation and from the concept of the supernatural" (Fagothey, *Right and Reason*, 51). Fagothey goes on to reason, "If the human soul is naturally immortal, obviously even its natural demands and capacities cannot be satisfied by the transitory goods of this life. If the Beatific Vision, as supernatural, transcends the demands and capacities of man's nature, there must be some absolutely last end to which man would be destined were he left on the purely natural plane. This is the end of man and the kind of happiness that philosophy is chiefly interested in and that ethics must determine. It is objected that such a study is purely hypothetical, that man is not and never was in such a state of pure nature. Granted, but that does not in any way make our study useless or impractical. The supernatural should not be thought of as opposing the natural, but rather as presupposing the natural and adding to it" (53). This may sound like a two-tier system wherein grace is merely an addition, but Fagothey makes clear that he sees the integration of nature and grace as more complex than would be implied by the notion of grace as an addition to nature.

33. Against the claim that only the supernatural beatific vision is "sufficient" for our happiness—and thus there is not even the possibility of a natural ultimate end—Fagothey makes some cogent remarks. He terms natural happiness a "*relatively perfect happiness*," and he explains: "The natural order of things, far from excluding the possibility of elevation to a higher plane, is open to the supernatural in the sense of having an *obediential potency* toward it. An obediential potency, which is a potency only in an extended sense, is merely negative and does not call for fulfillment" (Fagothey, *Right and Reason*, 79). Yet: "*If man's happiness is to be but an actually finite possession of the Infinite, man will know that a higher degree of happiness is possible and will not be satisfied with what he has; how then can there be such a thing as actually finite happiness?* Each soul possessing God to the fullness of its proximate capacity, will be as happy as it can be; but, since these capacities differ according to the good and evil done during life, each soul will recognize that other souls with higher proximate capacities are enjoying greater degrees of happiness. We may think that they will be envious of others or dissatisfied with their own actual limitations. But neither of these is possible in a state of entire happiness, which supposes complete conformity of the created will with the divine will. Knowledge of God implies that what God has approved is best, and love of God implies whole-hearted submission to the scheme of things ordered by divine providence. This whole objection, if carried to its logical extreme, would mean that man cannot be happy without being God. But the desire to be God [i.e., to have exactly the infinite happiness that God possesses precisely as God possesses it] is satanic pride, the essence of all sin, the very opposite pole to happiness" (81–82; italics in the original).

34. He adds an important clarification: "None of these writers says that God actually is arbitrary or capricious in His willing" (Fagothey, *Right and Reason*, 122–23). His further remarks are worth quoting here: "René Descartes goes to a further extreme when he declares that even mathematical truths depend on God's free choice; if so, moral truths likewise would be no more than divine whimsies. . . . We must not imagine God looking over the catalogue of possible human acts and arbitrarily picking out some which He determined to designate as wrong, but might just as well have picked out others. It is true that God commands good acts and forbids evil ones, but this will of His is not arbitrary or capricious; His will depends on His intellect and both His intellect and will depend on His essence. There can be no contradiction in God. He cannot command man to perform the kind of act His own holiness makes impossible for Him, and He cannot forbid man to perform the kind of act His own holiness requires of Him" (123).

35. Likewise, in 1960, Louis Monden, SJ—responding to "situation ethics" from a perspective in accord with Rahner's and Fuchs's at that time—proposes that the solution to this "situation ethics" is first to realize that human freedom "is never only a freedom 'from' every coercion, but is always also a freedom 'towards' an intended fullness of possible self-realization." Monden, *Sin, Liberty and Law*, trans. Joseph Donceel, SJ (New York: Sheed and Ward, 1965), 88.

36. Addressing a related aspect of Kant's thought, he notes: "Kant correctly argues that there can be no morality without free will. But in his discussion of freedom there is always a confusion between freedom of choice and freedom of independence, as if one could not retain free will and still be under the command of another's law" (Fagothey, *Right and Reason*, 196).

37. He adds, "The human will is not free to seek or not seek happiness, but must of its very nature seek it. . . . The human intellect perceives this design of his Creator impressed on man's very nature not merely as the offer of a reward which may be sought if one wishes but as the objective order inherent in creation itself and enacted by man's being the kind of being God made him to be" (Fagothey, *Right and Reason*, 199–200). It follows that "sanction" (reward and punishment) is nothing other, ultimately, than the gain or loss of everlasting beatitude.

38. Thomas J. Higgins, SJ, *Man as Man: The Science and Art of Ethics* (Milwaukee, WI: Bruce Publishing Co., 1949), 27.

39. Higgins, *Man as Man*, 137.

40. Higgins, *Man as Man*, 137.

41. Higgins, *Man as Man*, 137.

42. Michael Cronin, *The Science of Ethics*, vol. 1, *General Ethics* (New York: Benziger, 1909), vii. Hereafter, page references from this work will be given in parentheses in the text.

43. He emphasizes that "the will must in every action desire the 'good,'" even if the will is indeterminate with regard to particular finite goods known by the intellect (Cronin, *Science of Ethics*, 175).

44. In making this case, Cronin engages various eighteenth- and nineteenth-century thinkers. For example, he states, "[Francis] Hutcheson goes even farther than Hume in this matter, and declares that not only is Conscience an impulse—that is, a spring of action—but that it is supreme amongst all impulses commanding and overruling all the rest, so that we have but to follow this impulse to be sure we are doing the right. Wundt

also insists that no intellectual faculty could be a *motive* of action, and that consequently Conscience could not be the ordinary intellectual faculty" (*Science of Ethics*, 452). In addition to Hutcheson and Hume, Cronin ably canvasses and critiques the viewpoints of John Stuart Mill, Leslie Stephen, Johann Gottlieb Fichte, Josiah Royce, Thomas Reid, G. W. F. Hegel, and others.

45. What follows is Cronin's summary of Butler's viewpoint, in Butler, *The Works of Joseph Butler, Containing "The Analogy of Religion" and Sixteen Celebrated Sermons* (London: William Tegg, 1867).

46. Against many secular thinkers of his day, Cronin argues forcefully that "savages" (i.e., those people who until very recently, or even now, do not have written language and other elements found in the world's major civilizations) have a high moral code. At times, the way that he writes about African or Native American tribes is embarrassing due to its stereotypes, but his constant concern is to insist upon the full humanity and ethical standards of the tribal peoples that he treats. He grants, "The old and infirm were, in the case of some savage tribes, often freely done away with, and deformed and illegitimate children were strangled at birth. Now, these are cases of the complicated Ethical problem of which we have spoken, which only the trained mind may be trusted to solve aright. Take, first, the killing of aged parents. The savage finds himself here confronted with two or three powerful moral principles. The first is the principle that the killing of a relation is a very great evil. In that conviction all savage tribes agree, and the most stringent laws are enacted against the killing of a member of one's own family. Secondly, there is the principle of affection for an aged and infirm parent, who must be protected from pain. Now, in the cases under discussion, it seems to us that this principle of affection was itself the actuating force that gave rise to this apparently cruel custom of patricide, because in cases of patricide death seemed to be the only source of relief for the aged and infirm. . . . Thirdly, there was question here of a principle so difficult of solution even for us civilized men, as to how far the private good must be subjected to the necessities of the State. To the savage, the nomadic tribe was the State, and if the tribe was to maintain its existence, it was necessary that its movements should not be impeded in any way in case of flight" (*Science of Ethics*, 536). Cronin also treats the case of the "wild man of the woods" who has grown up without human contact and without language: such a person shows that "Reason, absolutely unaided, and especially unaided by Speech, is incapable of exercise except in the crudest possible way" (*Science of Ethics*, 539).

47. Antony Koch, *A Handbook of Moral Theology*, ed. Arthur Preuss, vol. 1, *Introduction: Morality, Its Subject, Norm, and Object* (St. Louis, MO: Herder, 1918). Hereafter, page references from this work will be given in parentheses in the text.

48. His approach to freedom involves a misapprehension of the impact of sexual difference. He remarks, "The male sex, generally speaking, possesses greater spontaneity, energy, and strength than the female. These advantages are counterbalanced by certain defects, *e.g.*, lack of delicacy and sentiment. The female sex, on the other hand, enjoys greater receptivity, a more delicate sense of modesty, a more intense religious sentiment and greater patience, but is less strong in resisting evil, and more prone to fall" (Koch, *Handbook of Moral Theology*, 91). Fortunately, at least he goes on to say that with regard to men and women, "the assumption of a so-called double standard of morals is unchristian" (92).

49. Of course, it is longer in his multi-volume manual, as distinct from his one-volume summary that I am treating here.

50. Dominic M. Prümmer, OP, *Handbook of Moral Theology*, trans. Gerald W. Shelton (Harrison, NY: Roman Catholic Books, 1957), 7. In Prümmer's text this proposition is italicized. Hereafter, page references from this work will be given in parentheses in the text.

51. Besong, "Reappraising the Manual Tradition," 584.

52. Pinckaers, *Sources of Christian Ethics*, 272.

53. Pinckaers, *Sources of Christian Ethics*, 272.

54. James F. Keenan, SJ, "To Follow and to Form over Time: A Phenomenology of Conscience," in *Conscience and Catholicism: Rights, Responsibilities, and Institutional Responses*, ed. David E. DeCosse and Kristin E. Heyer (Maryknoll, NY: Orbis, 2015), 14.

55. Kevin L. Flannery, SJ, *Christian and Moral Action* (Arlington, VA: The Institute for the Psychological Sciences, 2012), 75.

56. See Flannery, *Christian and Moral Action*, 1–6.

Chapter 3

1. Jean-Pierre Torrell, OP, *Saint Thomas Aquinas*, vol. 2, *Spiritual Master*, trans. Robert Royal (Washington, DC: Catholic University of America Press, 2003), 314–22.

2. Martin Rhonheimer explains further with regard to synderesis: "Thomas calls this habitus a 'natural habit.' It is not inborn, but it takes shape with a natural spontaneity. . . . The habitus of the first principles is, in a way, the 'law of our intellect,' and it contains the 'precepts of the natural law, which are the first principles of human actions.' The function of this most fundamental habit of practical reason consists in 'urging to the good and dissuading against evil, to the extent that we proceed on the basis of the first principles to discover what is to be done and to judge what we discover.'" Rhonheimer, *The Perspective of Morality: Philosophical Foundations of Thomistic Virtue Ethics*, trans. Gerald Malsbury (Washington, DC: Catholic University of America Press, 2011), 310, citing *Summa theologiae* I-II, q. 94, a. 1, ad 2 and I, q. 79, a. 12.

3. Leo J. Elders, SVD, *The Ethics of St. Thomas Aquinas: Happiness, Natural Law and the Virtues* (Washington, DC: Catholic University of America Press, 2019), 84.

4. See Denys Turner, *Thomas Aquinas: A Portrait* (New Haven, CT: Yale University Press, 2013).

5. See Bernard McGinn, *Thomas Aquinas's "Summa theologiae": A Biography* (Princeton, NJ: Princeton University Press, 2014).

6. Daniel McInerny, *The Difficult Good: A Thomistic Approach to Moral Conflict and Human Happiness* (New York: Fordham University Press, 2006), 142.

7. See John Rziha, *Perfecting Human Actions: St. Thomas Aquinas on Human Participation in Eternal Law* (Washington, DC: Catholic University of America Press, 2009).

8. See Thomas S. Hibbs, *Virtue's Splendor: Wisdom, Prudence, and the Human Good* (New York: Fordham University Press, 2001).

9. Romanus Cessario, OP, *Introduction to Moral Theology* (Washington, DC: Catholic University of America Press, 2001), 122. See also Cessario, *The Moral Virtues and Theological Ethics* (Notre Dame: University of Notre Dame Press, 1991), 86: "Three

distinct acts embody prudence's principal working. These are counsel, judgment, and command. Counsel, shaped by the special virtue of *eubulia*, supplies a rational deliberation about means which ensures that the prudent person solicits whatever established moral wisdom provides for a certain matter. Judgment makes a decision about what one is going to do now; it follows the settling onto concrete means. The practical judgment of conscience applies this particularized wisdom to the actual circumstances of a given case. If a poorly informed conscience makes a faulty judgment about particulars, no virtue can develop; the question of culpability, however, raises other questions. Because of the importance the act of judgment holds in the moral life, two special virtues aid its formation: *synesis* ensures sound judgment in ordinary matters and *gnome* provides the wit to judge the exceptional cases. Finally, command supplies the efficacious imperative note in the act of prudence. To command remains the principal act of prudence which gives to the judgment of conscience its imperative value. By this, prudence enters into the formal act of the moral virtues, i.e., the choosing of the good as such."

10. Cessario, *Introduction to Moral Theology*, 129. Cessario comments further, "Recall that accounts of the moral life from the patristic and high medieval periods located conscience under prudence and thereby in conjunction with the other moral virtues. But reductionist views of prudence, such as one that identifies *tout court* moral judgment with rational conscience disembodied from virtue, overlook the important role that the development of moral virtue plays in directing human affairs. Theorists who argue that conscience plays an autonomous role in the moral life depreciate the importance of a rational measure to direct and shape the movement of *appetite* toward good ends. Even when this emphasis is accompanied by insistence on the obligation to have an informed conscience, the presentation of the Christian moral life is truncated" (131). See also Cessario's sharp critique of the casuist moral system in his "Appendix: Flight from Virtue; The Outlook of the Casuist Systems," in *Introduction to Moral Theology*, 229–42. In my view, despite the noble efforts of many theologians during the period of probabilist or casuist ethics, Cessario is correct to warn: "The casuist view of individual conscience and responsibility seems to encourage a line of demarcation between maximal exercise of free will and adherence to the divine will. . . . Conscience comes to be preoccupied with arbitrating human freedom and establishing the frontiers of human autonomy" (240).

11. For more recent valuable Thomistic discussions of conscience, see Cajetan Cuddy, OP, "St. Thomas Aquinas on Conscience," in *Christianity and the Laws of Conscience: An Introduction*, ed. Helen M. Alvaré and Jeffrey B. Hammond (Cambridge: Cambridge University Press, forthcoming); Tobias Hoffmann, "Conscience and Synderesis," in *The Oxford Handbook of Aquinas*, ed. Brian Davies and Eleanore Stump (Oxford: Oxford University Press, 2008), 255–64.

12. Benoît-Henri Merkelbach, OP, *Summa Theologiae Moralis*, 3 vols. (Paris: Desclée de Brouwer, 1931–40). For background to Merkelbach, see Réginald Beaudouin, OP, *Tractatus de Conscientia*, ed. Ambroise Gardeil, OP (Tournai: Desclée, 1911)—a work that is much indebted to Charles Billuart. See also Ambroise Gardeil, OP, "La certitude probable," *Revue des Sciences Philosophiques et Théologiques* 5 (1911): 237–66, 441–85; Gardeil, "La topicité," *Revue des Sciences Philosophiques et Théologiques* 5 (1911): 750–57. Beaudouin influenced numerous other eminent Thomists of Gardeil's generation, including Pierre Mandonnet, OP. See Mandonnet, "Le décret d'Innocent XI et le Probabilisme," *Revue Thomiste* 9 (1901): 460–81, 520–39, 652–73; 10 (1902): 676–98;

Mandonnet, "La position du Probabilisme dans l'Eglise catholique," *Revue Thomiste* 10 (1902): 5–20; Mandonnet, "De la valeur des theories sur la probabilité morale," *Revue Thomiste* 10 (1902): 314–35.

13. I am quoting from Matthew K. Minerd's unpublished translation of Merkelbach, *Summa Theologiae Moralis*, 155. Hereafter, page references from this work will be given in parentheses in the text. My thanks to Professor Minerd for permission to use his translation.

14. For basic information about this somewhat forgotten point of terminology, see "Appendix 2: On the Speculative, the Speculatively-Practical, and the Practically-Practical," in Réginald Garrigou-Lagrange, OP, "Remarks Concerning the Metaphysical Character of St. Thomas's Moral Theology, in Particular as It Is Related to Prudence and Conscience," trans. Matthew K. Minerd, *Nova et Vetera* 17 (2019): 266–70.

15. For criticism of this position (also found in Henri-Dominique Noble, OP), see Paul Rambert, "Conscience et loi naturelle dans les manuels d'avant Vatican II," *Revue Thomiste* 119 (2019): 428–29.

16. More attention to the possibility of implicit faith is needed here.

17. Benoît-Henri Merkelbach, OP, "Where Should We Place the Treatise on Conscience in Moral Theology?," trans. Matthew K. Minerd, *Nova et Vetera* 18, no. 3 (2020): 1032.

18. Merkelbach, "Conscience in Moral Theology," 1032.

19. Michel Labourdette, OP, *Les actes humains*, vol. 2 of *"Grand cours" de théologie morale*, Latin passages translated by a Benedictine of l'Abbaye Notre-Dame du Pesquié (Paris: Parole et Silence, 2016), 204. Hereafter, page references from this work will be given in parentheses in the text. All English translations from this text are my own. See also Labourdette, "Connaissance pratique et savoir morale," *Revue Thomiste* 48 (1948): 142–79; Labourdette, "Théologie morale," *Revue Thomiste* 50 (1950): 192–230.

20. See Thomas Aquinas, *Truth*, vol. 2, *Questions X-XX*, trans. James V. McGlynn, SJ (Indianapolis, IN: Hackett, 1994), 314–37.

21. Aquinas, *Truth*, 2:336.

22. Aquinas, *Truth*, 2:336.

23. By contrast, for Labourdette's contemporary, the influential Catholic moralist and personalist Louis Janssens, even when a person is objectively acting against God's will, so long as he or she is following conscience then "it is the love of moral good which animates what he does, and it is precisely the maintenance of this love which promotes his moral perfection." Janssens, *Freedom of Conscience and Religious Freedom*, trans. Brother Lorenzo, CFX (Staten Island, NY: Alba House, 1965), 81. On this view, everything depends upon "the fundamental judgment of conscience," or what Janssens—like many others—calls the person's "fundamental option" or "fundamental choice" (59).

24. See also Labourdette's critique of "situation ethics" in Labourdette, *Foi catholique et problèmes modernes* (Tournai: Desclée & Cie, 1953).

25. For Anscombe on conscience, treating issues discussed by D'Arcy (including reflection on Aquinas on erroneous conscience), see G. E. M. Anscombe's essays "Authority in Morals" and especially "On Being in Good Faith," in *Faith in a Hard Ground: Essays on Religion, Philosophy and Ethics by G. E. M. Anscombe*, ed. Mary Geach and Luke Gormally (Exeter: Imprint Academic, 2008), 92–100 and 101–12, respectively. See also, in the same volume, her "Sin," 117–56, especially 127–38. A very brief, previously

unpublished consideration of the problem of "false conscience" appears as "Must One Obey One's Conscience?," in *Human Life, Action and Ethics: Essays by G. E. M. Anscombe*, ed. Mary Geach and Luke Gormally (Exeter: Imprint Academic, 2005), 237–41.

26. Eric D'Arcy, *Conscience and Its Right to Freedom* (New York: Sheed and Ward, 1961), 37. Hereafter, page references from this work will be given in parentheses in the text.

27. Regarding "Good should be done and evil avoided," D'Arcy considers that this is "a purely formal principle, providing the rule that governs all our moral reasoning, rather than its universal premiss" (50, 52). I disagree with D'Arcy in this respect.

28. Aquinas, *In II Sent.*, dist. 22, q. 2, a. 1; quoted in Labourdette, *Conscience and Its Right to Freedom*, 92.

29. In Alphonsus de Liguori's *Theologia Moralis*, vol. 1, ed. Léonard. Gaudé (Rome: Typographia Vaticana, 1905), 1.1.6, Alphonsus writes: "Not only does one who acts with an invincibly erroneous conscience not sin, but even more probably he acquires merit." On this point, see also Louis Vereecke, "La conscience selon saint Alphonse Liguori," *Studia Moralia* 21 (1983): 263.

30. Martin Rhonheimer aptly comments: "Sticking to an erroneous conscience *without blame* is unthinkable, at least in the case of fundamental moral principles and norms [assuming, of course, that a person is not mentally incapacitated in some way]. We do not think it credible that, say, a Nazi like Adolf Eichmann acted well and was really a good human being when he defended himself before the court through his subjective conviction, his conscience, and his consciousness of duty, just because he always followed this conviction and his conscience and always did what he thought was his duty. 'To be a good person' is not the same as 'following one's conscience.' Rather, we believe that subjectively convinced Nazis would be especially despicable human beings *because of* their malformed consciences, that this malformed conscience was blameworthy, and that the actions that followed upon this conscience were not only not right, but also made them into evil persons and drove them ever more deeply into guilt" (Rhonheimer, *Perspective of Morality*, 319). I agree with this point with regard to Nazis who were intimately involved in planning and executing the Holocaust. In situations where grave cultural blinders are in force, such as Nazi Germany or the American South in the time of slavery, I would not wish to suggest that *all* persons involved in the sinful societal structure (that is, all persons other than the victims) are in a condition of mortal sin, though their consciences are tragically blinded by their cultural prejudices and it may well be that most of them are mortally culpable for their erroneous consciences. See also Edward Zukowski, "The Good Conscience of Nazi Doctors," *The Annual of the Society of Christian Ethics* 14 (1994): 53–82.

31. For discussion of various medieval viewpoints in this regard, see Marcia L. Colish, *Faith, Fiction, and Force in Medieval Baptismal Debates* (Washington, DC: Catholic University of America Press, 2014).

32. D'Arcy, *Conscience and Its Right to Freedom*, 179; citing Charles Journet, *The Church of the Word Incarnate* (London: Sheed and Ward, 1955), 285.

33. Reginald G. Doherty, OP, *The Judgments of Conscience and Prudence in the Doctrine of St. Thomas Aquinas* (River Forest, IL: The Aquinas Library, 1961), 1. Hereafter, page references from this work will be given in parentheses in the text.

34. For discussion, see Daniel D. De Haan, "Moral Perception and the Function of

the *Vis Cogitativa* in Thomas Aquinas's Doctrine of Antecedent and Consequent Passions," *Documenti e Studi sulla Traditione Filosofica Medievale* 25 (2014): 289–330; De Haan, "Perception and the Vis Cogitativa: A Thomistic Analysis of Aspectual, Actional, and Affectional Percepts," *American Catholic Philosophical Quarterly* 88, no. 3 (2014): 397–437. See also George Klubertanz, *The Discursive Power: Sources and Doctrine of the* Vis cogitativa *according to St. Thomas Aquinas* (St. Louis, MO: The Modern Schoolman, 1952); Julien Peghaire, "A Forgotten Sense: The Cogitative according to St. Thomas Aquinas," *Modern Schoolman* 20 (1943): 123–40, 210–29.

35. Thomas Aquinas, *De veritate*, q. 17, a. 1, ad 4; English translation in Aquinas, *Truth*, 2:320.

36. Thomas Aquinas, *De virtutibus in communi*, q. un, a. 6; quoted in Doherty, *Judgments of Conscience and Prudence*, 64.

37. Although both are "judgment," *gnome* differs from *synesis*: *gnome* has to do with judgment "according to higher principles than the common laws" (*Summa theologiae*, II-II, q. 54, a. 4). For my purposes, it suffices to discuss *synesis*.

38. He notes that the identification of the judgment of conscience with the judgment that precedes election (the judgment of prudence) is upheld by John of St. Thomas, Charles Billuart, Benoît-Henri Merkelbach, Réginald Garrigou-Lagrange, and many others. Among those distinguishing between the two judgments, he names Leonard Lehu, Thomas Deman, and Michel Labourdette.

39. This point is expressed well by William A. Wallace, OP, in his book *The Role of Demonstration in Moral Theology: A Study of Methodology in St. Thomas Aquinas* (Washington, DC: Thomist, 1962). The judgment of conscience is not concerned with the self *precisely as this unique self with his or her own character, circumstances, etc.* Such a judgment falls to prudence (and the annexed virtues that assist it in counsel and judgment). Rather, the judgment of conscience is concerned with an *individuum vagum*, a universalized X who is considered in particular circumstances, though without a full, personal accounting of the details. See Wallace, *Demonstration in Moral Theology*, 199–202.

40. Doherty goes on to compare his position to that of Henri-Dominique Noble, OP, who wrote extensively on conscience in the early twentieth century and whose position is in certain respects quite similar to Doherty's. See Noble, *La conscience morale* (Paris: Lethielleux, 1923); Noble, *Le discernment de la conscience* (Paris: Lethielleux, 1934). Doherty states: "While we agree with P. [Père] Noble in finding a formal difference between the judgments of conscience and of prudence, it does not seem necessary that they be separated in the virtuous act. In fact, he uses the same terms that we have used: materially the act approved by the judgment of conscience is that which is chosen, but formally a difference exists between the two judgments. However, closer examination shows that he has placed the identity in the act which is the object of the judgments and not in the judgments themselves. In this supposition the judgment of conscience still precedes that of prudence, and therefore prudence can in no way guarantee the rectitude of the judgment of conscience" (Doherty, *Judgments of Conscience and Prudence*, 106).

41. Doherty explains: "Labourdette, while generally agreeing with the opinion we have expressed, prefers to see in the two judgments of conscience and of prudence not merely two aspects of the same judgment, but two moments of a movement which accomplishes its full rectification by means of prudence. It seems to us that this is a

mere dispute over the manner of expressing the reality. It does not seem that P. [Père] Labourdette means to imply two moments of time, but it is rather an accentuation of the fact that as the act actually occurs in *actu exercito* without reflexion, the one same judgment is realized first as proceeding from synderesis, and afterwards as attaining the singular act in conformity with the inclination of right appetite. Thus there are two formally distinct aspects of the numerically same judgment, realized at two *moments* of the virtuous act" (*Judgments of Conscience and Prudence*, 108).

42. Servais Pinckaers, OP, "Conscience and Christian Tradition," trans. Mary Thomas Noble, OP, in *The Pinckaers Reader: Renewing Thomistic Moral Theology*, ed. John Berkman and Craig Steven Titus (Washington, DC: Catholic University of America Press, 2005), 321–41; Pinckaers, "Conscience and the Virtue of Prudence," trans. Mary Thomas Noble, OP, in *The Pinckaers Reader*, 342–55.

43. For background to Pinckaers's thought, see also the perspective of his teacher Louis-Bertrand Gillon, OP, as found in Gillon, *Christo e la teologia morale* (Rome: Edizioni Romae Mame, 1961); Gillon, "L'imitation du Christ et la morale de saint Thomas," *Angelicum* 36 (1959): 263–86; as well as Gérard Gilleman, SJ, *The Primacy of Charity in Moral Theology*, trans. William F. Ryan, SJ, and André Vachon, SJ (Westminster, MD: Newman, 1959), originally published as *Le primat de la charité en théologie morale* (Paris: Desclée, 1954). For reflection on his impact, see Craig Steven Titus, "Servais Pinckaers and the Renewal of Catholic Moral Theology," *Journal of Moral Theology* 1 (2012): 43–68; Thomas F. O'Meara, OP, "Interpreting Thomas Aquinas: Aspects of the Dominican School of Moral Theology in the Twentieth Century," in *The Ethics of Aquinas*, ed. Stephen J. Pope (Washington, DC: Georgetown University Press, 2002), 355–73; Michael S. Sherwin, OP, and Craig Steven Titus, eds., *Renouveler toutes choses en Christ: Vers un renouveau thomiste de la théologie morale* (Fribourg: Fribourg University Press, 2009); Dominique Khoury-Hélou, "Servais Pinckaers et le renouveau de la théologie morale," PhD Diss., Universidad de Navarra, 2009; Patrick Clark, "Servais Pinckaers's Retrieval of Martyrdom as the Culmination of the Christian Life," *Josephinum Journal of Theology* 17 (2010): 1–27; William C. Mattison III, "Beatitude and Beatitudes in the *Summa theologiae* of St. Thomas Aquinas," *Josephinum Journal of Theology* 17 (2010): 233–49; John Cuddeback, "Law, Pinckaers, and the Definition of Christian Ethics," *Nova et Vetera* 7 (2009): 301–26; Matthew Levering, *Biblical Natural Law: A Theocentric and Teleological Approach* (Oxford: Oxford University Press, 2008), chapter 3; Levering, "Supplementing Pinckaers: The Old Testament in Aquinas's Ethics," in *Reading Sacred Scripture with Thomas Aquinas: Hermeneutical Tools, Theological Questions and New Perspectives*, ed. Piotr Roszak and Jörgen Vijgen (Turnhout: Brepols, 2015), 349–73.

44. Alasdair MacIntyre, "Preface," in Servais Pinckaers, OP, *Morality: The Catholic View*, trans. Michael Sherwin, OP (South Bend, IN: St. Augustine's Press, 2001), vii.

45. Pinckaers, "Conscience and Christian Tradition," 322.

46. Pinckaers, "Conscience and Christian Tradition," 324.

47. Pinckaers, "Conscience and Christian Tradition," 327.

48. Pinckaers, "Conscience and Christian Tradition," 328.

49. Pinckaers's treatment of conscience in Romans oddly does not mention the difficult text of Romans 2:1–16, much discussed by the Fathers. Paul's teaching in Romans 2:13–15 contains an explicit reference to conscience, and conscience does not here seem to be limited to a Spirit-enlivened conscience, because Paul indicates that

conscience is present in gentiles who are outside a covenantal relationship with God (though some Fathers understood these gentiles to be Christian gentiles). For further discussion of Romans 2:13–15 in light of its patristic reception, see my "Christians and Natural Law," in Anver M. Emon, Matthew Levering, and David Novak, *Natural Law: A Jewish, Christian, and Islamic Trialogue* (Oxford: Oxford University Press, 2014), 66–110.

50. Pinckaers, "Conscience and Christian Tradition," 330. Pinckaers's point is that Aquinas organizes his moral teaching around the virtues, not that Aquinas gives no value to the divine commandments (eternal law, natural law, and divinely revealed law) and to our obligation to know and obey these commandments. This is a clarification that Pinckaers does not make in this essay, however.

51. Pinckaers observes that, for Aquinas, our created light of truth and our attraction to the good are the ground of our freedom. Aquinas identifies these dynamisms as the *imago Dei*.

52. Pinckaers, "Conscience and Christian Tradition," 332.

53. Pinckaers, "Conscience and Christian Tradition," 332.

54. Pinckaers, "Conscience and Christian Tradition," 335.

55. Pinckaers, "Conscience and Christian Tradition," 336.

56. Pinckaers briefly pauses to absolve John Henry Newman's understanding of conscience from the charge of moral reductionism. Newman's understanding of conscience cannot be separated from "the entire spiritual life"; it is not simply about navigating legalistic obligations, and it appeals directly to the heart that yearns for God ("Conscience and Christian Tradition," 337).

57. Pinckaers, "Conscience and Christian Tradition," 339.

58. Pinckaers, "Conscience and Christian Tradition," 340.

59. Pinckaers, "Conscience and Christian Tradition," 340.

60. Pinckaers, "Conscience and the Virtue of Prudence," 343.

61. Pinckaers, "Conscience and the Virtue of Prudence," 347.

62. See John Henry Newman, "Letter to the Duke of Norfolk," in *Certain Difficulties Felt by Anglicans in Catholic Teaching*, vol. 2 (London: Longmans Green, 1885), 248; cited in *Catechism of the Catholic Church*, 2nd ed. (Vatican City: Libreria Editrice Vaticana, 1997), §1778.

63. Pinckaers, "Conscience and the Virtue of Prudence," 352.

64. Pinckaers, "Conscience and the Virtue of Prudence," 354–55.

65. Jacques Maritain puts the matter this way: "Charity has to do with persons; truth, with ideas and with reality attained through them. Perfect charity toward our neighbor and complete fidelity to the truth are not only compatible; they call for one another.... And the more freely I affirm what I hold as true, the more I should love whoever denies it—I don't have toward my neighbor the tolerance demanded by brotherly love unless his right to *exist*, to seek truth, and to express it according to his lights, and never to act or speak against his conscience is recognized and respected." Maritain, *The Peasant of the Garonne: An Old Layman Questions Himself about the Present Time*, trans. Michael Cuddihy and Elizabeth Hughes (Eugene, OR: Wipf & Stock, 2011), 90–91. Of course, simply ignoring religious questions of truth, as many people do today, does not count as true religious freedom, let alone as conscience.

66. See Servais Pinckaers, OP, *The Spirituality of Martyrdom: To the Limits of Love*,

trans. Patrick M. Clark and Annie Hounsokou (Washington, DC: Catholic University of America Press, 2016).

Chapter 4

1. For French developments in this regard, see Jacques Maritain's chapter on action in his 1947 *Existence and the Existent: An Essay on Christian Existentialism*, trans. Lewis Galantiere and Gerald B. Phelan (Garden City, NY: Doubleday, 1956). Maritain contrasts authentic (Thomistic) existentialism with an "apocryphal existentialism" that "affirm[s] the primacy of existence, but as destroying or abolishing essences or natures and as manifesting the supreme defeat of the intellect and of intelligibility" (*Existence and the Existent*, 13). See also Jean-Paul Sartre's 1943 *Being and Nothingness: A Phenomenological Essay on Ontology*, trans. Hazel E. Barnes (New York: Philosophical Library, 1956), which mentions conscience very rarely, yet holds that all ethics is subjective, as well as his 1945 lecture *Existentialism Is a Humanism*, trans. Carol Macomber (New Haven, CT: Yale University Press, 2007) and Simone de Beauvoir's 1947 *The Ethics of Ambiguity*, trans. Bernard Frechtman (New York: Philosophical Library, 1948). See also the Thomistic criticisms lodged by Maurice Corvez, OP, *L'être et la conscience morale* (Paris: Béatrice-Nauwelaerts, 1968); and Gaven Kerr's remark that Sartre's "project is not so much a metaphysics but a philosophy of life, such that one exists but one is not an existing essence. Hence one's existence is not limited to a particular essence; one must make a choice, a fundamental project, to determine one's existence accordingly." Kerr, *Aquinas and the Metaphysics of Creation* (Oxford: Oxford University Press, 2019), 9. For extensive background to the French reception of German phenomenology and existentialism, see Edward Baring, *Converts to the Real: Catholicism and the Making of Continental Philosophy* (Cambridge, MA: Harvard University Press, 2019).

2. John A. Gallagher, *Time Past, Time Future: An Historical Study of Catholic Moral Theology* (Mahwah, NJ: Paulist, 1990), 170.

3. Among significant figures absent in this chapter, I should draw attention to Romano Guardini, *Das Gute, das Gewissen und die Sammlung* (Mainz: Matthias-Grünewald, 1929). Guardini focuses his attention on the Good and examines conscience in this light. He identifies conscience as "the place where the eternal enters time" (*Das Gute*, 30, my translation; cf. 34–35 for a valuable discussion of the "eternal demand of the good").

4. Baring, *Converts to the Real*, 92. Baring explains further: "The young Heidegger was a progressive neo-scholastic, in Mercier's mold, and took a similar position in the broader debates over the future of Catholic philosophy. . . . This orientation also lends context to his medieval sources: an appeal, not to the strict Dominican Thomists, but instead to the progressive Franciscan school. . . . Heidegger's connection to progressive neo-scholasticism makes sense of what otherwise might seem a confused stance with respect to modernism. As we saw, progressives criticized modernism while remaining concerned that the deployment of Church authority to crush it would undermine their efforts to renew the scholastic tradition. Heidegger likewise agreed that modernism was philosophically misguided and damaging. He presented himself as a resolute antimodernist in many early articles, such as those he wrote for the ultramontanist *Heuberger*

Volksblatt from 1909–1910. In the short pieces he published in the Catholic journal *Der Akademiker* over the next few years, we see a familiar criticism: modernity led to the fragmentation of philosophy into subjective worldviews" (*Converts to the Real*, 91–92).

5. Baring, *Converts to the Real*, 230.

6. Baring, *Converts to the Real*, 231. Baring directs attention to the existentialist work of the Catholic thinker Louis Lavelle, who considered Maurice Blondel a mentor: see Lavelle, *Le moi et son destin* (Paris: Aubier, 1936); and Lavelle, *De l'acte* (Paris: Aubier, 1937). As Baring says, "Lavelle agreed with the neo-scholastics that Heidegger had reduced the question of being to the being of the individual. But in contrast to them, Lavelle saw Heidegger's emphasis on human subjectivity as the most valuable part of his work. . . . Given their emphasis on the self, the [radical] Christian existentialists were not willing to adopt the neo-scholastics' proposed corrective to Heidegger's thought: that his ontology needed to be released from the constraints of the human starting point. Instead they doubled down on his subjective analysis, arguing that if it were carried through to its ultimate end, it would confirm our personal spiritual connection to God" (*Converts to the Real*, 231). Here Baring also cites Luigi Pareyson's exemplification of Catholic existentialist ethics, *Studi sull'esistenzialismo* (Florence: Sansoni, 1943), 171, where Pareyson praises "the profound connection that exists between the relations between man and God and the assumption of the situation . . . existence must seek itself in the intimacy of the singular, at that point where its relationship to itself coincides with its relationship to God" (cited and translated in *Converts to the Real*, 231–32). Pareyson's first book focused on Jaspers, as Baring notes on 180: see Pareyson, *La filosofia dell'esistenza e Carlo Jaspers* (Naples: Loffredo, 1940).

7. Peter Joseph Fritz, *Karl Rahner's Theological Aesthetics* (Washington, DC: Catholic University of America Press, 2014), 102.

8. As James F. Bresnahan observes, "human nature for Rahner consists of nothing more nor less than the conditions of possibility of conscious freedom by which the 'spirit/person' shapes himself in time and history." Bresnahan, "Rahner's Ethics: Critical Natural Law in Relation to Contemporary Ethical Methodology," *Journal of Religion* 56 (1976): 41; cited in Gallagher, *Time Past, Time Future*, 207.

9. For further discussion, see Andreas Lienkamp, "Theodor Steinbüchel (1888–1949)," in *Christliche Ethik im Porträt: Leben und Werk bedeutender Moraltheologen*, ed. Konrad Hilpert (Freiburg im Breisgau: Herder, 2012), 659–78.

10. Theodor Steinbüchel, *Existenzialismus und christliches Ethos* (Heidelberg: F. H. Kerle, 1948); Steinbüchel, *Religion und Moral: Im Lichte personaler christlicher Existenz* (Frankfurt am Main: Josef Knecht, 1951). Tracey Rowland has an excellent chapter on Steinbüchel in her forthcoming book, which she generously shared with me as an unpublished manuscript. The word "ethos" in Steinbüchel's title calls to mind Heidegger's distinction, in his 1947 "Letter on 'Humanism,'" between "ethos" and "ethics"—with the latter having a negative connotation and the former a positive one. As is often the case in Heidegger, Aristotle plays a negative role: "The tragedies of Sophocles—provided such a comparison is at all permissible—preserve the *ēthos* in their sayings more primordially than Aristotle's lectures on 'ethics.' . . . *Ēthos* means abode, dwelling place. The word names the open region in which the human being dwells. The open region of his abode allows what pertains to the essence of the human being, and what in thus arriving resides in nearness to him, to appear. The abode of the human being contains and preserves

the advent of what belongs to the human being in his essence." Heidegger, "Letter on 'Humanism,'" trans. Frank A. Capuzzi, in Heidegger, *Pathmarks*, ed. William McNeill (Cambridge: Cambridge University Press, 1998), 269. Heidegger applies this point to the project of *Being and Time*: "If the name 'ethics,' in keeping with the basic meaning of the word *ēthos*, should now say that ethics ponders the abode of the human being, then that thinking which thinks the truth of being as the primordial element of the human being, as one who eksists, is in itself originary ethics" ("Letter on 'Humanism,'" 271).

11. Steinbüchel, *Existenzialismus und christliches Ethos*, 47. See also the comments on existentialism in Roger Aubert, *La théologie catholique au milieu du XXᵉ siècle* (Tournai: Casterman, 1953).

12. In this regard, Pope Pius XII cautioned against "the new erroneous philosophy which, rivaling idealism, immanentism and pragmatism, has assumed the name of existentialism, since it concerns itself only with existence of individual things and neglects all consideration of their immutable essences." *Humani Generis, Acta Apostolica Sedis* 42 (1950): §6, at www.vatican.va). He condemns "existentialism, whether atheistic or simply the type that denies the validity of reason in the field of metaphysics" (*Humani Generis*, §32). The aspects of existentialism condemned in the ethical realm by Pius XII are summed up (in a quite different context) by Jan Szmyd: "On the ethical level, it [existentialism] undertook a heroic attempt of constructing radically autonomous ethics of subjective existence and self-creation" through "responsibility for autonomous choice and conscience." Szmyd, "Post-Modernism and the Ethics of Conscience: Various 'Interpretations' of the Morality of the Post-Modern World. Role of A. T. Tymieniecka's Phenomenology of Life," in *Phenomenology and Existentialism in the Twentieth Century. Book Three: Heralding the New Enlightenment*, ed. A.-T. Tymieniecka (Dordrecht: Springer, 2010), 117.

13. Steinbüchel, *Religion und Moral*, 191.

14. Steinbüchel, *Religion und Moral*, 201. See also Max Scheler, *Formalism in Ethics and Non-Formal Ethics of Values: A New Attempt toward the Foundation of an Ethical Personalism*, trans. from the 5th rev. ed. (1966) by Manfred S. Frings and Roger L. Funk (Evanston, IL: Northwestern University Press, 1973), 318–28.

15. William Franke observes: "After the Second World War, the horror of capitulation and connivance with the evil of the Nazi concentration camps could not be overlooked. Existentialism as a philosophy of inescapable freedom [albeit freedom that many people reject, preferring to blend into the crowd], even in the midst of the most sinister and constraining conditions, emerged as the philosophy of the moment." Franke, "Existentialism: An Atheistic or a Christian Philosophy?," in *Phenomenology and Existentialism in the Twentieth Century. Book One: New Waves of Philosophical Inspirations*, ed. A.-T. Tymieniecka (Dordrecht: Springer, 2009), 374.

16. Karl Jaspers, "Philosophical Autobiography," in *The Philosophy of Karl Jaspers*, ed. Paul Arthur Schilpp (La Salle, IL: Open Court, 1957), 60. See also the reflections in Hannah Arendt, "Karl Jaspers: A Laudatio," in *Men in Dark Times* (New York: Harcourt Brace & Co., 1968), 71–80.

17. See also Jaspers's nuanced discussion of collective guilt, published in German in 1946, in which he affirms that he experiences himself to be a member of the German people (and thus experiences guilt for what Germany did under Nazi rule) while also firmly rejecting the notion that a whole people can be "guilty" in the sense that an in-

dividual can be: Jaspers, *The Question of German Guilt*, trans. E. B. Ashton (New York: Doubleday, 1947). See also the discussion in Ronny Miron, "The Guilt Which We Are: An Ontological Approach to Jaspers' Idea of Guilt," in *Phenomenology and Existentialism in the Twentieth Century. Book Three: Heralding the New Enlightenment*, ed. A.-T. Tymieniecka (Hanover, NH: Springer, 2010), 229–51.

18. Claudia Koonz, *The Nazi Conscience* (Cambridge, MA: Harvard University Press, 2003), 1.

19. Koonz, *Nazi Conscience*, 48. Koonz further describes the situation: "Within weeks of Hitler's appointment as chancellor, Heidegger joined a committee formed by Ernst Krieck, the ardently anti-intellectual Nazi educational theorist. Shortly afterward, Heidegger spoke out forcefully against the 'homelessness of blind relativism' and called for 'German scholarship that was informed by its ethical responsibility for truth.' To Jaspers he wrote, 'One must involve oneself . . . A philosopher's duty is to act as a participant in history.' In April Heidegger was nominated for the post of rector of Freiburg University, an honor for which he campaigned with the approval of local Nazi leaders. . . . Jaspers asked Heidegger how he could put up with the Nazis' antisemitism. Wasn't *The Protocols of the Elders of Zion* sheer nonsense? Evasively, Heidegger spoke about a 'dangerous international conspiracy.' Jaspers concluded sadly, 'Heidegger himself appeared to have undergone a complete transformation'" (52–55). As Mika Ojakangas has pointed out, "Heidegger did not see any contradiction between his meta-ethics of conscience and the National Socialist movement. In fact, he saw in the movement the very promise of a new awakening of conscience," as he understood the term. Ojakangas, *The Voice of Conscience: A Political Genealogy of Western Ethical Experience* (London: Bloomsbury, 2013), 21.

20. Koonz, *Nazi Conscience*, 55. Koonz notes that "orderly expulsion [of more than 675,000 German Jewish citizens] required hundreds of thousands of compliant ordinary citizens" (271).

21. See, for example, Rüdiger Safranski, *Martin Heidegger: Between Good and Evil*, trans. Ewald Osers (Cambridge, MA: Harvard University Press, 1998); and the essays in *Heidegger's Black Notebooks: Responses to Anti-Semitism*, ed. Andrew J. Mitchell and Peter Trawny (New York: Columbia University Press, 2017). For a defense of Heidegger's *Black Notebooks*, see Friedrich-Wilhelm von Herrmann and Francesco Alfieri, *Martin Heidegger: La verità sui "Quaderni neri"* (Brescia: Morcelliana, 2016).

22. See, for example, James F. Keenan, SJ, "Bernard Häring's Influence on American Catholic Moral Theology," *Journal of Moral Theology* 1 (2012): 38.

23. See, more broadly, the discussion in Jeremiah Newman, "The Ethics of Existentialism," *Irish Ecclesiastical Record* 77 (1952): 321–32, 421–31. As noted above, Pope Pius XII spoke out against "situation ethics" in 1952, devoting two addresses to the topic. Mark E. Graham summarizes Pius XII's concerns: "According to Pius, situationists treat the conscience as a self-sufficient originator of moral laws capable of generating moral criteria in isolation from any external referents (divine law, natural law)." Graham, *Josef Fuchs on Natural Law* (Washington, DC: Georgetown University Press, 2002), 10. Graham notes Pius XII's view that "situationists . . . refuse to acknowledge the obligatory nature of moral norms and consider them simply as indicators that may be dismissed if an individual judges them inappropriate in a concrete situation. As a consequence, situationism relegates moral norms to the periphery of moral deliberation. . . . The

primary reason why situationists regard the obligatoriness of moral norms as limited, Pius stated, arises from the uniqueness and originality of each concrete situation that cannot be captured fully by moral norms. . . . Pius responded that situationism had conflated the sphere of moral norms with that of their prudent application. Because moral norms arise from human nature, which is present wherever humans are found and independent of changing circumstances, they can be applied across a diverse range of concrete situations" (11). In 1956 the Sacred Congregation of the Holy Office banned "situation ethics" from being taught in Catholic institutions, on the grounds that it undermined unchanging human nature and exaggerated the competence of individual moral judgment. Graham comments: "Throughout his [preconciliar] writings on situation ethics Fuchs was highly critical of the dangers the situationist conception of God posed to absolutely binding moral norms, while simultaneously being sympathetic to the personalistic understanding of the God-human relationship prevalent in the writings of the situationists" (14). The "situationists" whom Fuchs names are Barth, Brunner, and Thielicke. See Pope Pius XII, "Address to the World Federation of Catholic Young Women," *Catholic Documents* 8 (1952): 15–20; Pius XII, "The Christian Conscience as an Object of Education," *Catholic Documents* 8 (1952): 1–7.

24. For the importance of the wartime years in Rahner's overall development— though the cornerstones had been laid earlier, under the influence of Maréchal and Heidegger (among others)—see Karl Heinz Neufeld, SJ, *Die Brüder Rahner: Eine Biographie* (Freiburg im Breisgau: Herder, 1994), chapters 16–17; Christoph Theobald, SJ, "Karl Rahner—La puissance d'engendrement d'une pensée," *Recherches de Science Religieuse* 108 (2020): 451–81.

25. Raphael Gallagher, CSsR, "Interpreting Thomas Aquinas: Aspects of the Redemptorist and Jesuit Schools in the Twentieth Century," in *The Ethics of Aquinas*, ed. Stephen J. Pope (Washington, DC: Georgetown University Press, 2002), 376. Graham states the widely presumed view, which I will show is somewhat inaccurate upon closer inspection: "Häring's insistence on the priority of Scripture in moral theology leads to a presentation of Christian morality markedly at odds with the dominant neo-Thomist manuals" (*Josef Fuchs on Natural Law*, 205). See Bernard Häring, CSsR, *The Law of Christ*, 3 vols., trans. Edwin G. Kaiser, CPPS (Westminster, MD: Newman, 1961–66), originally published a decade previously in German. See also Raphael Gallagher, CSsR, "Bernard Häring's *The Law of Christ*: Reassessing Its Contribution to the Renewal of Moral Theology in Its Era," *Studia Moralia* 44 (2006): 317–51; Eberhard Schockenhoff, "Pater Bernard Häring als Wegbereiter einer konziliaren Moraltheologie," in *50 Jahre "Das Gesetz Christi": Der Beitrag Bernhard Härings zur Erneuerung der Moraltheologie*, ed. Augustin Schmied, CSsR, and Josef Römelt, CSsR (Münster: LIT, 2005), 43–68.

26. This dominant strand opposed the moral teachings of Popes Paul VI and John Paul II. Thus Brennan R. Hill contends: "Häring's mission [during the Council] was to center moral theology on Jesus Christ, make the Holy Scripture the primary resource, and focus on the search for holiness to which all Christians are called. . . . It did not take long after the council for Häring to realize that Pope John's plea for 'the medicine of mercy rather than that of severity, the demonstration of the truth rather than condemnations' was not heeded, and that rigid absolutism and legalism were still operative in the Vatican." Hill, "Bernard Häring and the Second Vatican Council," *Horizons* 33 (2006):

94. Between 1975 and 1979, the Congregation for the Doctrine of the Faith formally investigated Häring's views.

27. Michael Inwood, *Heidegger: A Very Short Introduction* (Oxford: Oxford University Press, 1997), 1. See also Judith Wolfe, *Heidegger and Theology* (London: Bloomsbury, 2014).

28. For treatments of this section in *Being and Time*, see Hannes Nykänen, "Heidegger's Conscience," *Nordic Journal of Philosophy* 6 (2005): 40–65; Ingeborg Schüssler, "Conscience et vérité: L'interpretation existentiale de la conscience chez Martin Heidegger (Être et Temps §§54–62)," *Revista Portuguesa de Filosofia* 59 (2003): 1051–78; Francoise Dastur, "Conscience: The Most Intimate Alterity," in *Heidegger and Practical Philosophy*, ed. F. Raffoul and D. Pettigrew (Albany: State University of New York Press, 2002), 87–98; and Rafael Winkler, "Alterity and the Call of Conscience: Heidegger, Levinas, and Ricoeur," *International Journal of Philosophical Studies* 24 (2016): 219–33. Although I do not agree with Nykänen's interpretation of Heidegger on conscience, I agree with her that "Heidegger misrepresents conscience for, whether we like it or not, our neighbour *is* present in our conscience, and she is there as an experience, which is to say: as something which is not produced by my thoughts" ("Heidegger's Conscience," 62).

29. Paul Strohm, *Conscience: A Very Short Introduction* (Oxford: Oxford University Press, 2011), 104. Inwood puts the matter more positively: "The problem is this. If Dasein runs ahead to its own death, then it can escape the clutches of the 'they' and make an authentic choice about its own way of being, not simply accept the limited range of possibilities allowed it by 'them'. But how can it do that? 'They' already cater for death. *They* tell me not to worry about it, it's a remote possibility. So Dasein remains in the embrace of the 'they'. In this condition Dasein does not really have a conscience, it is not responsible for what it is and does, and it is not guilty of anything. . . . Conscience in the traditional sense commands or forbids certain actions on moral grounds. Often it is regarded as voice that calls to one, sometimes, though not invariably, the voice of God. In this sense of 'conscience', someone mired in the they-self lacks a conscience. Conscience tells *me* what to do and what not to do, me as an individual self, not the they-self. If I have not eluded the they-self, I cannot have a conscience in this sense: I do not view myself as an individual distinct from others, making choices on his own account" (*Heidegger*, 78–79). But even when one does respond to Dasein's call of conscience and begins to choose for oneself—even when one can be said on Heidegger's terms truly to have a "conscience"—it calls us simply to be "authentic" in our action rather than to live in accord with "characteristic ethical content."

30. Winkler, "Alterity and the Call of Conscience," 222. Winkler goes on to observe that "inauthenticity is at bottom a failure to hear (*hören*), a failure to belong (*gehören*), a failure to choose and be decisive (*Entscheidung*). It is an irresponsible, vacillating because not an explicitly owned, self-chosen life, and existence that avoids the moment of *krisis* by avoiding going to the limit of what it can be. . . . Conscience calls Dasein *to* become itself authentically and calls it back *from* the inauthenticity of its lostness in the public world of *das Man*" (222–23).

31. John D. Caputo, *Demythologizing Heidegger* (Bloomington: Indiana University Press, 1993), 99.

32. Paul Ricoeur, *Oneself as Another*, trans. Kathleen Blamey (Chicago: University of Chicago Press, 1995), 350–51. I find Ricoeur's own view of conscience to be somewhat

too critical of law, and his approach also tends toward a conscience-centered morality. Responding to Heidegger, Ricoeur proposes his own view: "To this demoralization of conscience, I would oppose a conception that closely associates the phenomenon of *injunction* to that of *attestation*. Being-enjoined would then constitute the moment of otherness proper to the phenomenon of conscience, in accordance with the metaphor of the voice. Listening to the voice of conscience would signify being-enjoined by the Other. In this way, the rightful place of the notion of *debt* would be acknowledged, a notion that was too hastily ontologized by Heidegger at the expense of the ethical dimension of indebtedness. But how are we to avoid falling back into the trap of 'bad' and 'good' conscience . . . ? A remark made earlier with respect to the metaphor of the *court* put us on the right path. Is it not because the stage of morality has been dissociated from the triad ethics-morality-conviction, then hypostatized because of this dissociation, that the phenomenon of conscience has been correlatively impoverished and that the revealing metaphor of the voice has been eclipsed by the stifling voice of the court?" (351). Note that Ricoeur, while dissociating conscience from the application of law to a particular situation, does not wish to reject law. He thinks that the judgment of conscience in a particular situation arises out of "the end of a conflict, which is a conflict of duties"—and he argues that the law (e.g., the Decalogue) fits into this process: "To find oneself called upon in the second person at the very core of the optative of living well, then of the prohibition to kill, then of the search for the choice appropriate to the situation, is to recognize oneself as being enjoined to *live well with and for others in just institutions and to esteem oneself as the bearer of this wish*" (352). It seems that this view of conscience conflates it with prudence. In Ricoeur's view (which Winkler finds problematic), it is not possible to determine philosophically whether the "Other" is simply "other people" or includes God. For Ricoeur on conscience (in relation to Heidegger and Emmanuel Levinas), see Winkler, "Alterity and the Call of Conscience," 227–33.

33. Martin Heidegger, *Being and Time*, trans. from the 7th German edition (1953) by Joan Stambaugh, rev. trans. Dennis J. Schmidt (Albany: State University of New York Press, 2010), 11. Hereafter, page references from this work will be given in parentheses in the text

34. Heidegger goes on to say: "Entangled, everyday being-toward-death is a constant *flight from death*. Being *toward* the end has the mode of *evading that end*—reinterpreting it, understanding it inauthentically, and veiling it. Factically one's own Dasein is always already dying, that is, it is in a being-toward-its-end" (*Being and Time*, 244). Heidegger's solution is accepting our being as being-toward-its-end, rather than fleeing from this or veiling it: "Can Dasein *authentically understand* its ownmost, nonrelational, insuperable, certain possibility that is, as such, indefinite? That is, can it maintain itself in an authentic being-toward-its-end? . . . Authentic being-toward-death signifies an existentiell possibility of Dasein. . . . Being toward this possibility lets Dasein understand that the most extreme possibility of existence, that of giving itself up, is imminent. But anticipation does not evade the impossibility of bypassing death, as does inauthentic being-toward-death, but *frees* itself *for* it. Becoming free *for* one's own death in anticipation liberates one from one's lostness in chance possibilities urging themselves upon us, so that the factical possibilities lying before the insuperable possibility can first be authentically understood and chosen" (*Being and Time*, 249, 252–53). Discussing Edith Stein's critique of Heidegger, Judith Wolfe observes that even if Heidegger says that his

analysis "implies no judgement on the question whether or not there is life after death," in fact "Heidegger's analysis cannot be said to leave open the possibility of life after death . . . if it is already defined as the end of existence or Dasein" (Wolfe, *Heidegger and Theology*, 190). See also Francesca Brencio, "Heidegger, Catholicism and the History of Being," *Journal of the British Society for Phenomenology* 51, no. 2 (2020): 137-50, DOI: 10.1080/00071173.2019.1703509. Brencio argues that in Heidegger, who rejects all doctrines and dogmas but wishes to retain a sense of the holy, "we encounter a *pious atheism*" ("Heidegger, Catholicism," 12).

35. Winkler comments that for Heidegger, "Choosing to be guilty is the condition for action. I am guilty not because of what I have done. Being-guilty precedes acting. It antedates my freedom and responsibility (in the ordinary sense of being the author or cause of an action). I am guilty because I am not the ground of my being but am rather given over to it from the start. I am guilty because I have not posited my existence but have been consigned to it always already. There is no sense of the 'ought' (*Sollen*) here, as if Heidegger was saying that I should have been the author of my existence but have failed in that respect. . . . Being-guilty, being-the-ground of a nullity, is a value neutral existential" ("Alterity and the Call of Conscience," 228).

36. Winkler, "Alterity and the Call of Conscience," 225. In Winkler's view, there is a logical gap in Heidegger's analysis: "if the caller is absolutely unidentifiable, being indefinite and indeterminate, doesn't Heidegger go beyond the phenomenal findings when he identifies it with Dasein?" (226).

37. Heidegger rules out the possibility of "understanding the existential phenomenon of guilt by taking our orientation toward the idea of evil, the *malum* as *privatio boni*. The *bonum* and the *privatio* have the same ontological provenance in the ontology of *objective presence* which also characterizes the idea of 'value' derived from that" (*Being and Time*, 274). This ontology is, for Heidegger's existentialism, not an option.

38. Inwood, *Heidegger*, 82.

39. Inwood, *Heidegger*, 83. Inwood continues, along lines that show a similarity between Heidegger's approach and Hannah Arendt's: "There are no objectively correct answers to life's basic problems nor any decision procedure for discerning them. The best one can do is to be resolute, to withdraw from the crowd, and to make one's decision in view of one's life as a whole" (83). But, unlike Arendt's focus on self-reflection, for Heidegger, "resoluteness is not *morally* better than irresoluteness. It does not guarantee or even make it more likely that we shall behave in a morally better way. (Hitler was no less resolute than Christ or Socrates.) Nor is resoluteness intrinsically morally superior to irresoluteness. The advantage of resoluteness is that resolute Dasein discloses itself, its possibilities, and its wholeness, in a way that irresolute Dasein does not" (84).

40. Heidegger adds that "*resoluteness is only the authenticity of care itself, cared for in care and possible as care*" (*Being and Time*, 288). Inwood downplays the moral superiority (though not moral in the "vulgar" or commonplace sense of the term) that I think Heidegger associates with resoluteness. For Inwood, "Both resoluteness and irresoluteness, both authenticity and inauthenticity, are ways of Dasein's being. In this respect neither has priority over the other. But irresolute, inauthentic Dasein cannot give an adequate interpretation of its own condition or of resoluteness" (Inwood, *Heidegger*, 85).

41. Little has been written in recent years on the philosophy of Jaspers, in contrast to the continued growth of Heidegger scholarship. I have consulted Chris Thornhill

and Ronny Miron, "Karl Jaspers," in *Stanford Encyclopedia of Philosophy*, ed. Edward N. Zalta (Stanford University, 1997-), last modified July 17, 2018, https://plato.stanford .edu/archives/spr2020/entries/jaspers/. See also the twenty-four scholarly essays about Jaspers's work collected in *The Philosophy of Karl Jaspers*, ed. Paul Arthur Schilpp (La Salle, IL: Open Court, 1957), especially the essay by Jean Wahl, "Notes on Some Relations of Jaspers to Kierkegaard and Heidegger," trans. Forrest W. Williams, 393–406.

42. Jaspers, "Philosophical Autobiography," 93. Jaspers continues by observing that in his "writings there is no presupposition to the effect that somehow truth will assert itself or that the world, from its inception, is guided by reason. The experience both of history as well as in the present [i.e., the post-Holocaust years] bears witness rather to the contrary, in so far as we take our measurement on humanly accessible reason—and only this can we call reason. This is why so much depends upon what the individual is willing to live and work for. He must know where he stands. His own essence and the turn of events depends upon his finding important even his tiniest decisions. He is of eternal significance in the face of that Transcendence, which makes him really become himself if he gives himself to it, where he is no longer threatened either by success or by foundering" (93–94). For discussion of these concepts in Jaspers's writings, see Johannes Thyssen, "The Concept of 'Foundering' in Jaspers' Philosophy," in *The Philosophy of Karl Jaspers*, ed. Paul Arthur Schilpp (La Salle, IL: Open Court, 1957), 297–335; and in the same volume Hans Kunz, "Critique of Jaspers' Concept of 'Transcendence,'" 499–522.

43. John Hennig remarks, "Nowhere . . . has Jaspers explained why the word *Dasein* (existence), traditionally at least one of the attempts to render the word *existentia*, has been used by him for the very opposite of what in his philosophy has been termed *Existenz*" (Hennig, "Karl Jaspers' Attitude towards History," in *The Philosophy of Karl Jaspers*, ed. Paul Arthur Schilpp (La Salle, IL: Open Court, 1957), 565).

44. Karl Jaspers, *Philosophy*, vol. 2, trans. E. B. Ashton (Chicago: University of Chicago Press, 1970), 3. Hereafter, page references from this work will be given in parentheses in the text.

45. See Fritz Kaufmann, "Karl Jaspers and a Philosophy of Communication," in *The Philosophy of Karl Jaspers*, ed. Paul Arthur Schilpp (La Salle, IL: Open Court, 1957), 210–95. Jaspers is aware that his position seems to suggest that philosophizing, as a movement away from Existenz, may be counterproductive. He responds as follows: "What we seek in all philosophizing is to be sure of being—though we cannot know, and though the form of our statements can therefore be only oblique. The reason why we seek this assurance is the incompleteness of any Existenz. An Existenz fulfilled to the point of clear realization would not philosophize; the impulse to do so comes from the tension between absolute consciousness and the consciousness of mere existence, between truth—which ought to be, but is not—and extant cogent accuracy" (Jaspers, *Philosophy*, 2:226). See also the helpful summary of Jaspers's viewpoint offered by Hannah Arendt (his good friend and former student): "The principle itself is communication; truth, which can never be grasped as dogmatic content, emerges as 'existential' substance clarified and articulated by reason, communicating itself and appealing to the reasonable existing of the other, comprehensible and capable of comprehending everything else. '*Existenz* only becomes clear through reason; reason only has content through *Existenz*.'" Arendt, "Karl Jaspers: Citizen of the World?," in *Men in Dark Times*

(New York: Harcourt Brace & Co., 1968), 85, citing Jaspers's *Reason and Existenz: Five Lectures*, trans. William Earle (New York: Noonday, 1955), 67.

46. Kurt Hoffman points out: "*Existenz* . . . is not thinkable conceptually by means of clear and distinct ideas. While discurse thought separates *Existenz* from its proper situation, this situation is in fact the mode of appearance of *Existenz*." Hoffman, "The Basic Concepts of Jaspers' Philosophy," in *The Philosophy of Karl Jaspers*, ed. Paul Arthur Schilpp (La Salle, IL: Open Court, 1957), 102.

47. Eugene Thomas Long comments that Jaspers advocates "philosophical faith as the meaning of philosophical doctrine, and through it he has sought to communicate with those who no longer find ecclesiastical faith illuminating." Long, *Jaspers and Bultmann: A Dialogue between Philosophy and Theology in the Existentialist Tradition* (Durham, NC: Duke University Press, 1968), 3. This philosophical faith is a trust in Existenz and its meaningfulness. Long explains, "Existenz is the Encompassing-that-we-are as Transcendence. It is the source from which all other modes of the Encompassing-that-we-are receive animation and from which they speak. . . . It is in Existenz that Being is present as Transcendence, as that through which I am genuinely myself. And this occurs as Existenz breaks through its objectivity, which is the tangible presence of Transcendence in myth. While no one of these dimensions of human experience is separated from the other and while all modes of the Encompassing-that-we-are make up man, it is nevertheless in Existenz that Transcendence is 'known' to me in such a way that I am aware of a real relation. . . . Existenz is not something to be grasped within the limits of finite explanation but presupposes the leap to Transcendence in which one does not prove but experiences one's freedom from the limits of immanence" (9–10). Long then applies this background to defining philosophical faith: "Freedom and Existenz then are not directly known but are encountered in the act of existing. Yet neither is real apart from Transcendence, which is disclosed to me as I leap from the dimension of immanence to that of freedom and Existenz. This leap is affirmed in philosophical faith, faith which is never sure of itself and is always striving to elucidate itself" (11).

48. Commenting on Jaspers, John Hennig remarks (along lines that point forward to Rahner), "The historical force of '*existential*' philosophy cannot be understood without reference to the tradition, now come into the foreground, of the conception of man's being himself. Distinctively modern manifestations of spiritual life are based on the realization of the dependence of objective values upon personal being-oneself translucent in the advocacy or acceptance of such values. What is traditionally described as grace is experienced by modern man in the rare moments when it is given to him to be himself (*Existenz*) and to encounter adequately such being-oneself in others (communication)" (Hennig, "Karl Jaspers' Attitude towards History," 567).

49. Based on a variety of Jaspers's writings, Eugene Thomas Long comments: "Jaspers rejects what he calls the orthodox view of revelation for three basic reasons. First, he does not wish to locate Transcendence in an observable object in the world. . . . Second, Jaspers maintains that orthodoxy arrests what is beyond the limits of comprehension. . . . Third, Jaspers rejects orthodoxy's claim to an exclusive revelation. . . . Jaspers does not mean that one must make a synthesis of all religions in the manner of the Enlightenment. But he does mean that one should concentrate on the *pro-me* of revelation, the becoming of God as the absolute in my particular historical experience. On this basis one can make claims to truth only in oneself and cannot create from this a universally

valid truth. . . . Revelation in this sense does not refer to something that can be definitely known but to that which can be apprehended only indirectly through the world. Thus it cannot refer to something that happened once and for all in some particular period of time. The Being of Transcendence must be at any time or place newly and freely grasped. In my individual historicity, I experience the presence of Being as that which I have always known, but which can never be bound to a worldly form" (Long, *Jaspers and Bultmann*, 32–33; cf. 43–46 for Jaspers's reflections on Jesus, in which Jesus becomes an ideal philosopher).

50. See Paul Ricoeur, "The Relation of Jaspers' Philosophy to Religion," trans. Forrest W. Williams, in *The Philosophy of Karl Jaspers*, ed. Paul Arthur Schilpp (La Salle, IL: Open Court, 1957), 611–42. Ricoeur allows for religious authority in a manner that goes beyond Jaspers, but, in accord with the traditional Protestant critique of the Catholic Church, he agrees with Jaspers's fundamental critique. He states, "The original authority of the Scriptures and of the Church is none other than the authority of the *witness*. The witness constrains no one. He shows the truth which has authority, but which is not the authority of a group of men. To be sure, this authority conferred on the witness necessarily comes into conflict with the authority of the truth according to science and according to the philosopher. . . . But this polarity does not take on the character of mutual exclusion until clerical violence perverts the non-coercive authority of the Word. . . . It is the power of man over man in the ecclesiastical community which maintains this *guilt* of a violent Truth. The clerical passion follows the history of the Church and churches like a shadow" (640–41).

51. See Hoffman, "Basic Concepts of Jaspers' Philosophy," 103, where he notes that Jaspers affirms "the historicity of truth itself, as opposed to every pretension of its universality, timelessness or totality. If, for Jaspers, a thought is philosophically true to the degree to which its thinking furthers communication, it must be clear that for him discursive thought can never arrive at a universally valid concept of Being, but only at *one* view of Being among others. The historicity of truth stands for an epistemological limitation, as well as for a personal dimension in the acquisition of knowledge. The truth of a thought is, for Jaspers, inseparable from the thinker, whose temporal situation and biography will determine the intensity and profundity of his insight into Being."

52. Jaspers, much like Heidegger, warns against arriving at an ontology: "Every word of existential elucidation that is not taken for an appeal but for a statement of being—which it is only in its most literal sense—constitutes a *temptation* to such abuse. Stripped of the element of appealing, of calling for their translation into real Existenz, the signs of existential elucidation can be talked about in terms of *applying* it, as if something were or were not so. A consummate doctrine, indeed the very rudiment, of an ontology of Existenz would have the same meaning. The result is the specific sophistry that accompanies all existential philosophizing. We take our worst falls when we seem nearest to the core" (*Philosophy*, 2:376).

53. As Jaspers later says, truth "is made unconditional by a choice" (*Philosophy*, 2:362). He makes the same point at more length: "Objective truth is one for all men; and regarding the reasons for it, from a standpoint, it is always particular. Existential truth is different. Because I cannot step out of the truth that is the possibility of my Existenz, because I cannot contemplate it from outside, I cannot say, 'There are several truths'; for multiplicity applies only to the outward appearance of visible forms, of thoughts and

dogmas that can be stated. The truth of Existenz is not manifold, because it cannot be seen as manifold from outside, and not established as extent. Nor can I say, 'I myself am the sole truth,' for I am not without the others to whom I relate. The unconditionality in my Existenz is not universally valid; it is an unconditionality that can never be identically transferred" (2:362). Drawing upon Jaspers, Heidegger, Sartre, and others, Piotr Mróz comments: "Let us recall once again that it is the possibility structure of both *Dasein* and *pour-soi*, the structure of freedom identified with nothingness (all our choices cannot refer to any moral authorities, respected norms, established values unless it is we who choose them, thus making them valid!) that 'forces us' to transcend both ourselves and the world." Mróz, "What Does It Mean to Be an Existentialist Today?," in *Phenomenology and Existentialism in the Twentieth Century. Book One: New Waves of Philosophical Inspirations*, ed. A.-T. Tymieniecka (Hanover, NH: Springer, 2009), 134.

54. See Stephen J. Plant, "'In the Sphere of the Familiar': Heidegger and Bonhoeffer," in *Bonhoeffer's Intellectual Formation*, ed. Peter Frick (Tübingen: Mohr Siebeck, 2008), 301–27. Plant remarks that Bonhoeffer likely read *Being and Time* soon after its publication, due to the influence of "Hans-Christoph von Hase, a theologian and Bonhoeffer's cousin, [who was] a student at Marburg" at this time ("'Sphere of the Familiar,'" 314). For the argument that Heidegger serves as one of Bonhoeffer's central dialogue partners with respect to ethics, see Yinya Liu's "From Response to Responsibility: A Study of the Other and Language in the Ethical Structure of Responsibility in the Writings of Bonhoeffer and Levinas," PhD Diss., National University of Ireland (Maynooth), 2010.

55. Heidegger, *Being and Time*, 258.

56. Barry Harvey, *Taking Hold of the Real: Dietrich Bonhoeffer and the Profound Worldliness of Christianity* (Eugene, OR: Cascade, 2015), 297. Harvey has in view Bonhoeffer's account of "responsibility" in his *Ethics*.

57. For discussion of the strong influence of Luther on Bonhoeffer's view of conscience, see Wolf Krötke, "Dietrich Bonhoeffer and Martin Luther," trans. Peter Frick, in *Bonhoeffer's Intellectual Formation: Theology and Philosophy in His Thought*, ed. Peter Frick (Tübingen: Mohr Siebeck, 2008), 65–67. See also, however, Jacob Phillips, "My Enemy's Enemy Is My Friend: Martin Luther and Joseph Ratzinger on the Bi-Dimensionality of Conscience," *Heythrop Journal* 61 (2020): 317–26.

58. Dietrich Bonhoeffer, *Act and Being: Transcendental Philosophy and Ontology in Systematic Theology*, ed. Wayne Whitson Floyd Jr., trans. H. Martin Rumscheidt, vol. 2 of *Dietrich Bonhoeffer Works* (Minneapolis: Fortress, 1996), 67, 71. Hereafter, page references from this work will be given in parentheses in the text. Bonhoeffer goes on to say: "From the perspective of the problem of act and being, it would seem that here a genuine coordination of the two has been reached. The priority of being turned out to be the priority of spirit-being in which the spirit does not annihilate being, but 'is' and understands it. This solution, though reminiscent of Hegel, is fundamentally different from Hegel's theory, in that being is Dasein, 'being in the world', existing in temporality. Thus, pure consciousness in Husserl's sense does not dominate; neither does the material a priori in Scheler's sense. Heidegger has succeeded in forcing together act and being in the concept of Dasein; both what Dasein itself decides, and the fact that it is itself determined, are brought into one here. . . . Dasein is neither a discontinuous succession of individual acts nor the continuity of a being that transcends time. Dasein is constant decision-making and, in every instance, already being determined" (71).

While admiring Heidegger's insight (and adopting it into his own account of conscience and the Christian moral life), Bonhoeffer notes that the problem is that "Heidegger's philosophy is a consciously atheistic philosophy of finitude," leaving no room for God or divine revelation (72). He concludes that Heidegger's understanding of Dasein cannot be adopted by Christians without reworking it. For analysis of *Act and Being* in relation to Heidegger and to Bonhoeffer's later works, see Nicholas Byle, "Divine Temporality: Bonhoeffer's Theological Appropriation of Heidegger's Existential Analytic of Dasein," PhD Diss., University of South Florida, 2016; cf. Byle, "Heidegger's Adam and Bonhoeffer's Christ: Evaluating Bonhoeffer's Appraisals of Heidegger," *Dietrich Bonhoeffer Jahrbuch* 5 (2011/2012): 99–119.

59. Bonhoeffer rejects pondering a pre-fall Adam understood as a sinless human individual who then committed the first sin. For Bonhoeffer, no "retreat to sinless being" is possible (*Act and Being*, 145).

60. See also Bonhoeffer's point that "all ontological definitions remain bound to the revelation in Christ; they are appropriate only in the concretions of being-the-sinner and being-justified" (*Act and Being*, 152–53).

61. Dietrich Bonhoeffer, *Creation and Fall; Temptation: Two Biblical Studies*, trans. John C. Fletcher (New York: Touchstone, 1997), 91.

62. Bonhoeffer, *Creation and Fall;Temptation*, 92.

63. For discussion, see Jacob Phillips, "Joseph Ratzinger and Dietrich Bonhoeffer on Heteronomy and Conscience during the Third Reich," in *Joseph Ratzinger and the Healing of the Reformation-Era Divisions*, ed. Emery de Gaál and Matthew Levering (Steubenville, OH: Emmaus Academic, 2019), 281–96.

64. Dietrich Bonhoeffer, *Ethics*, ed. Eberhard Bethge, trans. Neville Horton Smith (New York: Macmillan, 1965), 242. Hereafter, page references from this work will be given in parentheses in the text. I have also consulted the more recent English edition of his *Ethics*, ed. Clifford J. Green, trans. Reinhard Krauss, Charles C. West, and Douglas W. Stott, vol. 6 of *Dietrich Bonhoeffer Works* (Minneapolis: Fortress, 2005).

65. For the argument that Bonhoeffer changed his mind about "vicarious representative action" or "bearing guilt" after reading Barth's *Church Dogmatics* 2.2, see Matthew Puffer, "Election in Bonhoeffer's *Ethics*: Discerning a Late Revision," *International Journal of Systematic Theology* 14 (2012): 255–76.

66. As he continues: "The call of Christ alone, when it is responsibly obeyed in the calling, prevails over the compromise [of a divided conscience, split between diverse duties] and over the conscience which this compromise has rendered insecure" (Bonhoeffer, *Ethics*, ed. Bethge, 257). Again, he states, "Such a departure can be undertaken only after a serious weighing up of the vocational duty which is directly given, of the dangers of interference in the responsibility of others, and finally of the totality of the question which is involved; when this is done I shall be guided in the one direction or the other by a free responsibility towards the call of Jesus Christ. Responsibility in one's calling obeys only the call of Christ. There is a wrong and a right restriction and there is a wrong and a right extension of responsibility: there is an enthusiastic breaking-down of all limits, and there is a legalistic setting-up of limits" (258).

67. Karl Barth, *Church Dogmatics*, vol. 3, bk. 2, *The Doctrine of Creation*, trans. Harold Knight, G. W. Bromiley, J. K. S. Reid, and R. H. Fuller, ed. G. W. Bromiley and

T. F. Torrance (Peabody, MA: Hendrickson, 2010), 119. For discussion, see David R. Law, "Jaspers and Theology," *Heythrop Journal* 46 (2005): 334–51.

68. See Bernd Jaspert, ed., *Karl Barth-Rudolf Bultmann: Letters, 1922–1966*, trans. G. W. Bromiley (Grand Rapids, MI: Eerdmans, 1981); Heinrich Barth, "Ontologie und Idealismus," *Zwischen den Zeiten* 7 (1929): 511–40; Heinrich Barth, "Philosophie, Theologie und Existenzproblem," *Zwischen den Zeiten* 10 (1932): 99–124. See also the helpful discussion in Baring, *Converts to the Real*, 214–17. On Barth and Bultmann, see also John R. Williams, "Heidegger and the Theologians," *Heythrop Journal* 12 (1971): 263. For Bultmann's response to somewhat similar criticisms, from a philosophical perspective, put forward by Jaspers, see Williams, "Heidegger and the Theologians," 267–69, surveying Karl Jaspers and Rudolf Bultmann's *Myth and Christianity: An Inquiry into the Possibility of Religion without Myth* (New York: Noonday, 1958). Baring astutely observes: "In their criticism of Heidegger's 'authenticity' and its related 'mineness' (*Jemeinigkeit*), many Protestant theologians sought to reassert, against Heidegger, the importance of the 'non-self'—of God, but also of other humans. That is, they sought to radicalize the intersubjective aspects of Heidegger's analytic to challenge his ontology" (*Converts to the Real*, 218).

69. Karl Barth, *Church Dogmatics*, vol. 3, bk. 3, *The Doctrine of Creation*, trans. G. W. Bromiley and R. J. Ehrlich, ed. G. W. Bromiley and T. F. Torrance (Edinburgh: T&T Clark, 1960), 334–49. To my mind, Barth is correct when he states that, for Heidegger, "nothing is not a dreadful, horrible, dark abyss but something fruitful and salutary and radiant. In face of Heidegger's nothing, acceptance and not exclusion is demanded" (*Church Dogmatics*, III.3:347). For discussion, see Wolfe, *Heidegger and Theology*, 154–57; and Williams, "Heidegger and the Theologians," 263; as well as the criticisms of Heidegger lodged by Hans Jonas, "Heidegger and Theology," *Review of Metaphysics* 18 (1964): 207–33. See also Renée van Riessen, "On the Creation and Possession of Time: Barth's Critique of Augustine and Heidegger in *CD* I/2, §14," *Zeitschrift Für Dialektische Theologie*, Supplement Series 4 (2010): 6–20; and Timothy Stanley, *Protestant Metaphysics after Karl Barth and Martin Heidegger* (Eugene, OR: Wipf & Stock, 2010), which supposes a "theological turn" in Heidegger's thought (237). For Stanley, a crucial link between Heidegger and Barth—with regard to their questioning of classical metaphysics—is found in Martin Luther and in Luther's twentieth-century reception. He states, "by returning to the Protestant theology which influenced Heidegger's understanding of onto-theology in the first place, we can uncover alternative strategies and lost insights. . . . It is vitally important to recover the ontological nuance in Luther's thought, but so too, the manner in which other prominent Protestant theologians such as Barth reappropriated Luther in response to their own theological and philosophical problematics" (*Protestant Metaphysics*, 239). Stanley rejects Heidegger's reading of Luther as radically antimetaphysical, a reading that was current among Luther scholars in early twentieth-century Germany and that is picked up by Pope Benedict XVI in his Regensburg Lecture. In Stanley's view, Barth separates himself from this (Heideggerian) reading by "work[ing] out a theologically grounded notion of ontological difference through his explication of Anselm's *Proslogion* 2–4. It was this theological ontology which offers one of the most thoroughgoing alternatives to Heidegger's thought" (*Protestant Metaphysics*, 244; cf. 246). I am not persuaded by Barth's theological ontology, but Stanley's work is quite helpful.

70. Baring, *Converts to the Real*, 221.

71. John Webster, "'The Great Disruption': Word of God and Moral Consciousness in Barth's Münster *Ethics*," in *Barth's Moral Theology: Human Action in Barth's Thought* (Grand Rapids, MI: Eerdmans, 1998), 50.

72. My survey cannot claim to be a full overview of Barth's ethics. For further discussion, see for example Gerald P. McKenny, "Ethics," in *The Oxford Handbook of Karl Barth*, ed. Paul Dafydd Jones and Paul T. Nimmo (Oxford: Oxford University Press, 2019), 482–95; McKenny, *The Analogy of Grace: Karl Barth's Moral Theology* (Oxford: Oxford University Press, 2010); Paul T. Nimmo, *Being in Action: The Theological Shape of Barth's Ethical Vision* (London: T&T Clark, 2007); Matthew Rose, *Ethics with Barth* (Aldershot: Ashgate, 2010); Nigel Biggar, *The Hastening That Waits: Karl Barth's Ethics* (Oxford: Oxford University Press, 1993). Elsewhere, McKenny aptly points out that, against Kant's notion of conscience, "answerability to an other external to oneself is . . . central to Barth's theological ethics. For Barth, God decides on our conduct, measuring it by the criterion of electing grace and questioning it as to its fulfilment of this criterion. It follows that our conduct, and we in our conduct, constitute a continuous reply (*Antwort*) to the Word of God as command. . . . The decision of God regarding our conduct gives our conduct the character of a reply or response to the question posed to us by the command of God as the witness to, or expression of, God's decision on us and our conduct. . . . This alterity that pertains between the command of God and the subject governs Barth's conception of conscience. Etymologically, conscience involves a co-knowledge (*conscientes*, *suneidotēs*) of the command of God. But to know the command of God through conscience in this way would erase the alterity between the command of God and the knowing subject. Barth therefore identifies conscience as an eschatological, rather than an anthropological, concept; the Word of God that commands us is the promise that we *will* become co-knowers with God. . . . Barth thus combines the alterity of Kant with the participation in the law of God of Aquinas—now understood eschatologically." McKenny, "Responsibility," in *The Oxford Handbook of Theological Ethics*, ed. Gilbert Meilaender and William Werpehowski (Oxford: Oxford University Press, 2005), 247–48.

73. At this time, Barth in his own (later) view was still too much "an advocate of the doctrine of the orders of creation." See Dietrich Braun, "Editor's Preface," in Karl Barth, *Ethics*, ed. Dietrich Braun, trans. G. W. Bromiley (New York: Seabury, 1981), vii.

74. Karl Barth, *Ethics*, ed. Dietrich Braun, trans. G. W. Bromiley (New York: Seabury, 1981), 475. Hereafter, page references from this work will be given in parentheses in the text.

75. Webster emphasizes that Barth is undertaking a "striking displacement of conscience with its assumptions of competence" ("'Great Disruption,'" 51).

76. Webster comments, "God's command is judgement. . . . Once again, the disturbance is felt most keenly in the area of moral anthropology. Judgement means that I *am* by virtue of God's decision; I do not posit myself or even condemn myself, but take my self-knowledge from the divine act of justification in which I come to be" ("'Great Disruption,'" 51).

77. Here he differs from the nineteenth-century Protestant liberal theologian Albrecht Ritschl's Über das Gewissen: Ein Vortrag (Bonn: A. Marcus, 1876). For Barth's critique of Ritschl more broadly, see Christophe Chalamet, "Barth and Liberal Prot-

estantism," in *The Oxford Handbook of Karl Barth*, ed. Paul Dafydd Jones and Paul T. Nimmo (Oxford: Oxford University Press, 2019), 140–42. Chalamet is aware also of continuities between Ritschl and Barth, namely, their "sharp rejection of five errors found in Protestant theology: (a) mysticism, especially mysticism of a kind which grounds faith's certainty in a subjective conversion experience, which flees worldly reality and the Christian community's responsibility in it, and which often goes hand-in-hand with (b) a tendency to focus on the individual; (c) metaphysics and natural theology, or any God-talk not grounded in scriptural interpretation and the divine revelation to which Scripture bears witness; (d) an undervaluation of the Old Testament in Schleiermacher's thought ... and (e) theology that is done neither from within the church nor for the sake of the church. . . . More anecdotally, it may be noted that Ritschl enjoyed mocking the 'liberal theology' (*freisinnige Theologie*) of his time" ("Barth and Liberal Protestantism," 141).

78. Barth adds, "Proclaiming the absolute future, conscience proclaims the relativity of everything present. Directing us to the former, it detaches us unavoidably from the latter. In its true and final point, where it is totally itself, it is a revolutionary principle" (Barth, *Ethics*, 487).

79. The active waiting upon God that Barth associates here with conscience is another critique of Ritschl's perspective. Barth explains, "The Pietist, in antithesis not to the original Protestant but to Ritschl's view of him, could be the one who can never forget that as a real hearer of the Word, beyond his standing in creatureliness and beyond his standing in the justification of the sinner, in comforted despair, he must also wait for God, and live his life in this waiting, this supremely active waiting, if he is to be a doer of the Word or its existential hearer. Pietism has the possibility of being obedience to the command in the specific form of obedience to the command of promise" (*Ethics*, 490).

80. Karl Barth, *Church Dogmatics*, vol. 2, bk. 2, *The Doctrine of God*, trans. G. W. Bromiley, J. C. Campbell, Iain Wilson, J. Strathearn McNab, Harold Knight, and R. A. Stewart, ed. G. W. Bromiley and T. F. Torrance (Peabody, MA: Hendrickson, 2010), 665. Hereafter, page references from this work will be given in parentheses in the text.

81. McKenny, *Analogy of Grace*, ix. As McKenny says, this means that Barth certainly does not "begin with a human moral subject who is capable of at least a partial grasp by reason of a created moral order which is more perfectly known with the aid of historical revelation and who is naturally yet imperfectly oriented to a good which is more fully attained with the assistance of grace" (ix). McKenny goes on to offer a very helpful summary of Barth's ethics: "These claims would seem to bring ethics to an end, but Barth insists that it is only with these claims that ethics in its proper form can truly begin. There are negative and positive aspects of both claims. Negatively, the presumption that we are like God, sitting in judgment of good and evil and supposing that the cause of the good rests on us, leads to great moral evils and destroys the moral solidarity of human beings. By contrast, when we know that we stand under a divine judgment which we ourselves are in no position to pronounce, we exist in right relationships to God and to our fellow human beings. Positively, the command of God as God's judgment summons us to participate in the divine knowledge of good and evil as those who hear this judgment (which is always spoken through a fellow human being) and confirm it with our free decision. Negatively, the claim that, in Jesus Christ, God accomplishes the good in our place means that grace radically interrupts our moral striving. Positively,

this claim means that the good confronts us from the site of its fulfillment, and that in turn means that it confronts us not as something that it is up to us to do, to bring about, or to become, but as a reality in which we already stand and which therefore addresses us as that which we are now at last free to do and to be, saying 'You may' rather than 'You must'" (ix).

82. Here it is important to note that for Barth (as in his *Ethics*) "God's commanding can only be this individual, concrete and specific commanding. We must divest ourselves of the fixed idea that only a universally valid rule can be a command. We must realise that in reality a rule of this kind is not a command. We must be open to the realisation that the biblical witness to God's ruling is this: to attest God as the Father, or Lord, who in the process of the revelation and embodiment of His grace, *hic et nunc*, orders or forbids His child, or servant, something quite specific, and in such a way that there can be no question of an appraisal or judgment by man of what is required (which would be legitimate and necessary if the command consisted in a universally binding rule), but the question put to man can be only that of his hearing and obeying" (*Church Dogmatics*, 2.2:673).

83. Barth emphasizes, "The objection is obviously futile that God has not really given, and does not and will not give, His command with such wholeness, clarity and definiteness that it only remains for us to be obedient or disobedient, and not to try to discover what the divine command really is; that we cannot be unequivocally responsible to it simply because it has not been unequivocally given to us. This objection is futile because it tries to evade the objective fact that God—God in His Word, the God who has sacrificed Himself for us in His Son and who in His Son is King of kings—is present to the world and each individual, and confronts him in the smallest of his steps and thoughts as his Commander and Judge. Because God has given us Himself, and constituted Himself our Lord, He has also given us His command. Because He is ours and we are His, He gives us His command. Because He will not cease to be ours, as we cannot cease to be His, He will not cease to give us His command. We are able to hear it, as surely as we belong to Him and to no one else. The question cannot be whether He speaks, but only whether we hear. And this means that we are already faced again by the question of our obedience or disobedience, our faith or ungodliness" (*Church Dogmatics*, 2.2:669–70).

84. Karl Barth, *Church Dogmatics*, vol. 3, bk 4, *The Doctrine of Creation*, trans. A. T. Mackay, T. H. L. Parker, Harold Knight, H. A. Kennedy, and J. Marks, ed. G. W. Bromiley and T. F. Torrance (Peabody, MA: Hendrickson, 2010), 4. Hereafter, page references from this work will be given in parentheses in the text.

85. For a very helpful discussion of Barth on casuistry, see McKenny, *Analogy of Grace*, 238–45, including his critique of Biggar, *Hastening That Waits*, 7–45.

86. On this latter point, see the agreement of Ambroise Gardeil, OP (writing before Barth): "The secret of this outlook will not be found in the manuals of asceticism or of casuistry that strive to predict every possible case and to provide lines of appropriate conduct corresponding to them. Such a book has its use, for it renders its services by furnishing authoritative models for resolving problems. However, given that, concretely speaking, no equivalent case exists, onsite adaptation remains the proper task of good personal government. Suggestions, orientations—yes, as many as you can desire! However, such casuistry cannot, in the end, furnish wholly polished-off solutions which are

practical on all points and imperative, applicable straightaway to every single concrete case. There is no prudence that is written on paper. In order to govern oneself well, a tactical maneuver is needed, one that is utterly versatile because it develops on the essentially moving terrain of human contingencies." Gardeil, *La vraie vie chrétienne*, ed. H.-D. Gardeil (Paris: Desclée, 1935), 116.

87. Much as he does in *Church Dogmatics* 2.2, Barth notes that God's commands can never be universalized, and he argues that this point applies even to the Decalogue.

88. Here Barth calls into question the ethics of Emil Brunner's book *The Divine Imperative*, which is similar to Barth's ethics in rejecting casuistry in favor of God's free concrete command at each moment and in insisting upon the constancy of God, but which in Barth's view exaggerates our knowledge of the order of creation and the order of human corporate life under God's rule. Barth rejects appeal to "natural law" and insists that the commanding God whose constancy can be depended upon can only be known in "His Word revealed in Jesus Christ" (*Church Dogmatics*, 4.4:21). Barth notes that his own position is much more in accord with Bonhoeffer's notion of divine "mandates," although even here Barth raises significant questions. Barth concludes that we must seek "to learn from the Word of God what is to be done. But we do not acquire this knowledge simply by considering the specifically ethical sayings of Scripture relevant to those spheres, and their previous 'deposit' in our own consciousness. A radical and comprehensive consideration of the Word of God to which these words of Scripture bear witness must be attempted. . . . Hidden in their being, both God and man are revealed in their manner, not in themselves, not directly, nor on the basis of a human ability or accomplishment, but in the Word of God, in Jesus Christ. Without ceasing to be a mystery, they are an open mystery in Him" (23–24). See Emil Brunner, *The Divine Imperative: A Study in Christian Ethics*, trans. Olive Wyon (London: James Clarke, 2002).

89. I note that Barth also engages conscience in *Church Dogmatics*, vol. 4, bk. 1, *The Doctrine of Reconciliation*, trans. G. W. Bromiley, ed. G. W. Bromiley and T. F. Torrance (Edinburgh: T&T Clark, 1956). Randall C. Zachman explains the concerns that Barth raises in 4.1: "By creating a Word of God called Law independent of the one Word of God Jesus Christ, Luther and Calvin began the collapse of the Word of God into Scripture that was accelerated in the period of Protestant orthodoxy, which Barth is convinced leads directly to the replacement of the one Word of God with reason or human consciousness. . . . When Luther and Calvin sought to derive the knowledge of sin from a Word of God in Scripture divorced from Jesus Christ, they necessarily had to combine this Word with a capacity of the human sinner, especially the conscience, which has a prior knowledge of God via its knowledge of good and evil which the Word of God can activate. Once this combination is allowed to stand—the Word of God in Scripture and the conscience of the sinner—an inevitable dynamic is set in motion that will lead from the 'and' to the 'only,' leading to the point that theology will seek to derive the entirety of human sin from the self-communing of human reason or consciousness." Zachman, "Barth and Reformation Theology," in *The Oxford Handbook of Karl Barth*, ed. Paul Dafydd Jones and Paul T. Nimmo (Oxford: Oxford University Press, 2019), 113.

90. See Fergus Kerr, OP, *Twentieth-Century Catholic Theologians* (Oxford: Blackwell, 2007).

91. See Hue Woodson, *Heideggerian Theologies: The Pathmarks of John Macquarrie, Rudolf Bultmann, Paul Tillich, and Karl Rahner* (Eugene, OR: Wipf & Stock,

2018), 129. See also Thomas Sheehan, *Karl Rahner: The Philosophical Foundations* (Athens: Ohio University Press, 1987). Drawing upon Sheehan and Johann Baptist Metz, Woodson adds further details about the relationship of Rahner's theology to Heidegger's philosophy: "Though the chief task of [Rahner's] *Geist in Welt* is to provide an interpretative study of Thomas Aquinas' metaphysics and epistemology, Rahner focuses that analysis, at least in part, through Heideggerian existentialism, rather than Maréchal's Thomism. . . . *Geist in Welt* has major Heideggerian influences, particularly from Heidegger's *Sein und Zeit* and *Kant und das Problem der Metaphysik*. From these works of Heidegger, Rahner's *Geist in Welt* attempts to, through an analysis of Aquinas, 'ground transcendental epistemology in a new reading of human being influenced by Heidegger.' Rahner's 'new reading,' as it is, ultimately develops from Rahner having located an intersectionality between Heidegger's concept of *Dasein* and Aquinas' concept of the dynamism of the human mind" (*Heideggerian Theologies*, 145). See also Thomas F. O'Meara, OP, "Heidegger and His Origins: Theological Perspectives," *Theological Studies* 47 (1986): 205–26. O'Meara remarks appreciatively, "Theologians from Troeltsch to Tillich and Rahner agree that the Judeo-Christian tradition is not, ultimately, about Israel or Jesus but about an underlying presence whose unperceived dynamic expresses itself as grace in human lives" ("Heidegger and His Origins," 223). Philosophically, see the concerns raised about Rahner's approach—in light of Heidegger—by Thomas Joseph White, OP, *Wisdom in the Face of Modernity: A Study in Thomistic Natural Theology*, 2nd ed. (Ave Maria, FL: Sapientia, 2016), especially chapter 6.

92. Woodson, *Heideggerian Theologies*, 141. Woodson argues that "'grace' is what turns Rahner's theology into an 'existential theology,' especially as a means of positioning humanity to God, and God to humanity" (142). Peter Joseph Fritz has argued against "the conventional view of both Rahner and Heidegger under the rubric of 'existentialism'" (Fritz, *Karl Rahner's Theological Aesthetics*, 146). I am using the term loosely, since it is clear that thinkers such as Heidegger, Jaspers, Bonhoeffer, Barth, and Rahner—despite each advocating an "existentialist ethics" with some significant common threads—differ from each other on many points. Fritz dissents sharply from the judgment of O'Meara noted above: "Rahner's 'negative anthropology' and his relativizing of concrete humanisms might seem to turn Christianity into an engine of indeterminacy and an advocate of relativism. He does not intend this. Like Heidegger, Rahner deems himself privy to a humanism more concrete and more effective than the modern ones surrounding him. Heidegger finds his 'humanism' in *Dasein*'s thrownness into the truth of being. Rahner locates it in the person of Jesus Christ and the people of Christ's Church. Heidegger invokes the 'mystery of being' so as to clear space for human existence's entrance into the home being prepared for it. Rahner invokes the 'intractable mystery of God' to imply that *we* do not create our humanism. Christianity does not construct a particular humanism. God does" (151). Fritz's Rahner here sounds Barthian notes. For further background to Rahner, see Peter Joseph Fritz, *Freedom Made Manifest: Rahner's Fundamental Option and Theological Aesthetics* (Washington, DC: Catholic University of America Press, 2019); as well as Peter Eicher, *Die anthropologische Wende* (Freiburg: Universitätsverlag Freiburg, 1970).

93. Vincent Holzer, "Karl Rahner—Genèse et aspects d'une théologie," *Recherches de Science Religieuse* 108 (2020): 444. See also Klaus Vechtel, SJ, "Karl Rahner: Ses sources

et ses lieux théologiques," trans. Robert Kremer, *Recherches de Science Religieuse* 108 (2020): 395–96.

94. Karl Rahner, SJ, "The Concept of Existential Philosophy in Heidegger," trans. Andrew Tallon, *Philosophy Today* 13 (1969): 126–37; originally published as "Introduction au concept de philosophie existentiale chez Heidegger," trans. R. Celle, *Recherches de Science Religieuse* 30 (1940): 152–71 (the published version mistakenly ascribed this text to Hugo Rahner). In a brief bibliography attached to the end of his essay, Rahner draws attention to Delp's book (cited below) as well as to von Balthasar's treatment of Heidegger in volume 3 of his *Apokalypse der deutschen Seele* (Salzburg: Pustet, 1938). See also Rahner, *Hearer of the Word*, trans. Joseph Donceel, SJ (New York: Crossroad, 1994). For further discussion, see Robert Masson, "Rahner and Heidegger: Being, Hearing, and God," *Thomist* 37 (1973): 455–88. For other essays from this period by German Catholic scholars on Heidegger's thought, see Caspar Nink, SJ, "Grundbegriffe der Philosophie Martin Heideggers," *Philosophisches Jahrbuch* 45 (1932): 129–58; Theodor Droege, CSsR, "Die Existenz-Philosophie Martin Heideggers," *Divus Thomas* 16 (1938): 265–94, 371–92; August Brunner, SJ, "Die Entwertung des Seins in der Existenzialphilosophie," *Scholastik* 12 (1937): 233–38; Brunner, "Ursprung und Grundzüge der Existenzialphilosophie," *Scholastik* 13 (1938): 173–205; and J. B. Lotz, SJ, "Immanenz und Transzendenz heute: Zur inneren Struktur der Problematik unserer Tage," *Scholastik* 13 (1938): 161–72. See also the later study by Joseph Möller, *Existenzialphilosophie und katholische Theologie* (Baden-Baden: Kunst und Wissenschaft, 1952); as well as the recent survey provided by Emilio Brito, SJ, "La reception de la pensée de Heidegger dans la théologie catholique," *Nouvelle Revue Théologique* 119 (1997): 352–73. Brito, whose focus is metaphysics, discusses Rahner's essay, translated into English in 1969; Brito also mentions (among many other texts) Hans Urs von Balthasar's "Heideggers Philosophie vom Standpunkt des Katholizismus," *Stimmen der Zeit* 137 (1940): 1–8; and Johann Baptist Metz's "Heidegger und das Problem der Metaphysik," *Scholastik* 28 (1953): 1–22.

95. See the summary of Rahner's essay offered by Williams, "Heidegger and the Theologians," 259.

96. James Collins, "The German Neoscholastic Approach to Heidegger," *Modern Schoolman* 21 (1944): 143–52. Collins suggests that the Catholic critique of Husserl's phenomenology (insofar as Husserl remained committed to transcendental idealism) contributed to the emergence of existentialism. He concludes, "No other philosophical school in Germany has been able to extract so much sound doctrine from existentialism as has Scholasticism, nor to offer so penetrating a criticism of its deficiencies. It is this approach that we should imitate in our own country and in terms of our own philosophical environment" (152).

97. Alfred Delp, SJ, *Gesammelte Schriften*, vol. 4, ed. Roman Bleistein (Frankfurt: Knecht, 1984), 326. See also Philip Endean, SJ, "'A Symbol Perfected in Death': Rahner's Theology and Alfred Delp (1907–1945)," *The Way* 43 (2004): 67–82.

98. Graham, *Josef Fuchs on Natural Law*, 8.

99. Graham, *Josef Fuchs on Natural Law*, 9; see Hans Wulf, SJ, "Gesetz und Liebe in der Ordnung des Heils," *Geist und Leben* 22 (1949): 356–67. As Gallagher says, "Michel's position, at least as summarized by Wulf, might well have been the sort of theology Pius XII had in mind in his addresses on situation ethics. Michel at best minimalized the role of moral rules and viewed the teaching church as more of a danger than an asset

to Christian living" (*Time Past, Time Future*, 229). For Fuchs's criticisms of Michel in 1955, defending natural law against "extreme situation-ethics" (with which he also associates Emil Brunner and Karl Barth), see Josef Fuchs, SJ, *Natural Law: A Theological Investigation*, trans. Helmut Reckter, SJ, and John A. Dowling (New York: Sheed and Ward, 1965), 135–38.

100. See Karl Rahner, SJ, "The Individual in the Church," in *Nature and Grace*, trans. Dinah Wharton (New York: Sheed and Ward, 1964), 9–38; originally published as "Der Einzelne in der Kirche," *Stimmen der Zeit* 39 (1946–47): 260–76. Graham describes Hirschmann's contribution: "Another Jesuit, Hans Hirschmann, praised situationism's emphasis on attending to concrete circumstances and questioned the assumption prevalent in Roman Catholic moral theology that universal norms can adequately capture all the morally relevant factors in concrete situations. For Hirschmann, moral awareness requires not only attending to moral norms, but a keen understanding of local conditions, the network of social relations affected by moral decisions, and changing historical situations" (Graham, *Josef Fuchs on Natural Law*, 9, discussing Hans Hirschmann, SJ, "Im Spiegel der Zeit," *Geist und Leben* 25 [1951]: 300–4). In "Existential Ethics: A Thomistic Appraisal," *Thomist* 27 (1963): 496–98, William A. Wallace, OP, quotes from Rahner's *Gefahren im heutigen Katholizismus* (Einsiedeln: Benzinger, 1950), 16–17: "Though there cannot be, nor ought there to be, an individual ethics in which the individual and his rights contravene the general norms of morality, there is an individual ethics and an individual morality which obliges the individual in a way that is uniquely his, and nevertheless cannot be reckoned as a mere 'case,' a mere instance of the universal. . . . This private sphere is not in any way one of private choice and freedom, but stands univocally under the morally obliging and holy will of God, and freely so, directly willing the incommunicable and singular unity of the individual person. . . . Therefore there must also be in man an organ which recognizes this individually obliging norm. When we call this conscience, we must distinguish between two functions of conscience: one which compares the *general* norms of ethics and moral theology with man's subjective knowledge and applies it to his 'case,' and another whereby the individual hears the unique call of God which is valid only for him and is never completely deducible from general norms. There must therefore be a 'technique,' or better a *technē*, an 'art' in the sense of the ancients, for perceiving these imperatives of strict individual ethics, which is to be clearly distinguished from the 'theory,' the *epistēmē* of moral philosophy and theology with their generally valid norms. If we seek a traditional name for this, we would call it the charismatic art of 'discernment of spirits,' a concept which in later centuries has been generally misunderstood, because this distinction, either explicitly or by tacit agreement, has been restricted to the casuistic technique for applying theoretical norms to the individual 'case.' In its proper nature, however, it is something quite different, namely, the ability to discern the unique call of God for the individual as such." See Rahner's "Der Appell an das Gewissen: Situationsethik und Sündenmystik," *Wort und Wahrheit* 4 (1949): 721–34. For a critique of Rahner's essay for not going far enough, see Walter Dirks, "How Can I Know What God Wants of Me?," trans. Sally S. Cunneen, *Cross Currents* 5 (1955): 76–92. By the early 1960s Rahner had come to agree with Dirks. See also Rahner, "Some Thoughts on a Good Intention," in *Theology of the Spiritual Life*, trans. Karl-H. Kruger and Boniface Kruger, vol. 3 of *Theological Investigations* (New York: Seabury, 1967), 105–28.

101. Rahner, "Individual in the Church," 23. Rahner adds: "Not as if this sphere were not also Christian, that is, conformed to Christ and superformed by grace; on the contrary. Not as if this sphere were a sphere of private arbitrary choices and of freedom from moral obligation to God; not as if, for this sphere, laws could not be formulated" (23).

102. The notion of choosing a fundamental existential stance or "fundamental option" has connections to scholastic understandings of the "first act of freedom." Developing the texts of *ST* I-II q. 89, a. 6 and q. 109, a. 3, as well as *De veritate*, q. 14, a. 2, Jacques Maritain describes this concept in his essay "The Immanent Dialectic of the First Act of Freedom," in his book *The Range of Reason* (New York: Scribner's Sons, 1952), 66–85. Maritain notes that this "first act of freedom" is "any *first or primal* free act, any free act through which a new basic direction is imposed on my life. Such an act goes down to the sources of my moral life; through it I take hold of myself so as to project myself in a spray of ulterior actions which may be indefinite" (66). In this first act of freedom, Maritain argues, a person implicitly knows God "as ultimate end of his existence," though this knowledge "is a purely practical, non-conceptual and non-conscious knowledge of God, which can co-exist with a theoretical ignorance of God" (70). See also Maritain, *An Introduction to the Basic Problems of Moral Philosophy*, trans. Cornelia N. Borgerhoff (New York: Magi, 1990), 132–41. For a view dependent upon Maritain, see Michel Labourdette, *Cours de théologie morale*, vol. 1, *Morale fondamentale* (Paris: Parole et Silence, 2010), 492–94. For parallel views that can be harmonized with Maritain's, see Réginald Garrigou-Lagrange, OP, *De revelatione per ecclesiam catholicam propositam* (Rome: Desclée de Socii, 1950), 313–14, 392, 395–96, 501–503; Édouard Hugon, OP, *Hors de l'église pas de salut*, 2nd ed. (Paris: Tequi, 1914), 105 (and the whole of chapter 4). Rahner's view has a different orientation, given his understanding of the supernatural existential, which simply requires an awakening to the self.

103. See Heidegger, "Letter on 'Humanism,'" 270–71. Rahner was familiar with this text; as Fritz remarks, "Rahner's negative disposition toward humanism accords largely with Heidegger's rejection of humanism in his 'Letter on Humanism.' Rahner's rejection of humanism is unlike Heidegger's, though, because it refers the human person to God's infinite incomprehensibility instead of being's finite evasiveness" (*Karl Rahner's Theological Aesthetics*, 146). See also Bresnahan, "Rahner's Ethics," 40: "[Rahner] criticizes pre-Kantian Scholastics because their conception of nature was excessively objective. By that Rahner means that human nature was treated as if it were not decidedly different from what it meant by nature in intrahuman entities (such as animals). 'Nature' is 'essence' considered precisely in relation to characteristic activity of the being. The older conception treated human nature in an excessively 'cosmocentric' way, as if it were but another kind of static determinant of activities and as if there were not a decisive difference in the way nature is related to conscious self-possession (knowing) and self-disposal (freedom) uniquely characteristic of man as 'subject.'"

104. Karl Rahner, SJ, "Principles and Prescriptions," in *The Dynamic Element in the Church*, trans. W. J. O'Hara (New York: Herder and Herder, 1964), 14; originally published as "Prinzipien und Imperative," *Wort und Wahrheit* 12 (1957): 325–39.

105. Rahner, "Principles and Prescriptions," 16.

106. Rahner, "Principles and Prescriptions," 23.

107. John Gallagher comments, "The material will of God to which the individual must respond is not a deduction from a universal norm, but rather an individual or ex-

istential norm unique to the person to whom it is addressed. Rahner's formal existential ethic focuses on the coming-to-be of the unique, individual person" (*Time Past, Time Future*, 209). He adds that "Rahner's ethic, theology of grace, and theory of the person were developed in explicit opposition to neo-Thomist theology" (209).

108. Rahner, "Principles and Prescriptions," 30.

109. Rahner, "Principles and Prescriptions," 30.

110. Rahner, "Principles and Prescriptions," 35.

111. Rahner, "Principles and Prescriptions," 38.

112. Karl Rahner, SJ, "On the Question of a Formal Existential Ethics," in *Man in the Church*, trans. Karl-H. Kruger, vol. 2 of *Theological Investigations* (Baltimore, MD: Helicon, 1963), 219; originally published as "Über die Frage einer formalen Existentialethik," in *Schriften zur Theologie*, vol. 2 (Einsiedeln: Benziger, 1955). Hereafter, page references from this work will be given in parentheses in the text.

113. Louis Monden, SJ, speaks similarly, in 1960, of "an almost universal, but all too well justified, *discontent* with the usual *textbook morality*. It is charged that this morality is negatively protective, fostering infantilism instead of stimulating adult self-reliance; that it depersonalizes the human situation of the individual into abstract casuistry." Monden, *Sin, Liberty and Law*, trans. Joseph Donceel, SJ (New York: Sheed and Ward, 1965), 84. As a result, he notes, in actual Catholic life (encountered by confessors) people often start "from the unstated premise that something which is very difficult loses its obligatory character when existentially it is no longer felt to be feasible or acceptable" (85).

114. Conscience is doing prudence's work here.

115. For further reflection, see Karl Rahner, SJ, "The Dignity and Freedom of Man," in *Man in the Church*, trans. Karl-H. Kruger, vol. 2 of *Theological Investigations* (Baltimore, MD: Helicon, 1963), 235–63 (an essay originally delivered in 1952); and Rahner, "The Theological Concept of Concupiscentia," in *God, Christ, Mary and Grace*, trans. Cornelius Ernst, OP, vol. 1 of *Theological Investigations* (London: Darton, Longman & Todd, 1961), 360–62. See also Maritain's "First Act of Freedom," noted above.

116. This problem is noted with concern by William Wallace. Wallace also comments: "Instead of the emphasis being on prudence, however, as in the Thomist solution to the problem of ethical individuality, this art is now identified as the art of discerning spirits, following the teaching of the *Spiritual Exercises* of St. Ignatius Loyola. Thus Father Rahner's moral theology becomes a mixture of casuistry, with conscience looking to universal and essentialist norms and applying them to individual cases, and a type of mysticism, with conscience harkening to the movements of the Holy Spirit and discerning God's 'pointing gestures' as these successively establish its moral imperatives. . . . They must be subjectively experienced, can only be known to the one experiencing them, and nonetheless constitute ultimate norms for the actions of the individual" (Wallace, "Existential Ethics," 510–12). Wallace is aware that Rahner is drawing not only upon existentialism but also upon phenomenology (e.g., Max Scheler).

117. See also the background in Josef Römelt, CSsR, *Personales Gottesverständnis in heutiger Moraltheologie auf dem Hintergrund der Theologie von Karl Rahner und Hans Urs von Balthasar* (Innsbruck: Tyrolia, 1988). See Hans Urs von Balthasar's 1946 *Wahrheit der Welt*, repurposed with a new introduction as *Theo-Logic: Theological Logical Theory*, vol. 1, *Truth of the World*, trans. Adrian J. Walker (San Francisco: Ignatius,

2000), 105–6: "Existence is ultimately inseparable from the sphere of essences. To probe the intimate character of an individual substance, to pose the question of its uniqueness and personality, is to inquire into its essence and its existence at once. . . . The degree to which the two poles condition and include each other has been shown by existentialist philosophy's (unsuccessful) attempt to plumb the sphere of existence independently of essence."

118. Karl Rahner, SJ, "Guilt—Responsibility—Punishment within the View of Catholic Theology," in *Concerning Vatican Council II*, trans. Karl-H. and Boniface Kruger, vol. 6 of *Theological Investigations* (London: Darton, Longman & Todd, 1969), 200.

119. Rahner, "Guilt—Responsibility—Punishment," 203. See also his account of grace, the supernatural existential, and anonymous Christianity.

120. Rahner, "Guilt—Responsibility—Punishment," 203.

121. Rahner, "Guilt—Responsibility—Punishment," 203. For further development of this viewpoint, see also other essays by Rahner from the same time period: Rahner, "Theology of Freedom," in *Concerning Vatican Council II*, trans. Karl-H. Kruger and Boniface Kruger, vol. 6 of *Theological Investigations* (London: Darton, Longman & Todd, 1969), 178–96; Rahner, "The 'Commandment' of Love in Relation to the Other Commandments," in *Later Writings*, trans. Karl-H. Kruger, vol. 5 of *Theological Investigations* (New York: Crossroad, 1966), 439–59. See also Monden, *Sin, Liberty and Law*, 30–31 (cf. 33–35): "Not every choice involves the kind of freedom man has. . . . The choice in human activity becomes a really free choice only from the fact that it comes from a much deeper root than ordinary actions. That deeper source, too, is some kind of choice, not with respect to specific objects but with respect to the totality of existence, its meaning and its direction. . . . The choice among the many objects offers an infinite number of possibilities; the fundamental option is made between a 'yes' and a 'no' in which man, as a spirit, unconditionally commits or refuses himself. That option always amounts to letting oneself go: either yielding to a 'becoming,' to a growing towards a more perfect self-realization, or falling back on an already acquired self-possession, rejecting the advance in self-realization and the new risks." See also Josef Fuchs, SJ, "Good Acts and Good Persons," in *Considering "Veritatis Splendor,"* ed. John Wilkins (Cleveland, OH: Pilgrim, 1994), 23: "The theory of a 'fundamental option' goes back mainly to the development by the late Karl Rahner, S. J., of ideas borrowed from Jacques Maritain and Joseph Maréchal, S. J. Rahner's preferred term was not in fact 'fundamental option' but 'the human person's disposition of his self as a whole.'"

122. Rahner, "Guilt—Responsibility—Punishment," 203.

123. Rahner, "Guilt—Responsibility—Punishment," 204. For the issues involved here, see Pope John Paul II, *Veritatis Splendor* (Vatican City: Libreria Editrice Vaticana, 1993), §§65–70, http://www.vatican.va/content/john-paul-ii/en/encyclicals/documents/hf_jp-ii_enc_06081993_veritatis-splendor.html.

124. Rahner, "Guilt—Responsibility—Punishment," 210. See also Rahner's 1963 "Justified and Sinner at the Same Time," in *Concerning Vatican Council II*, trans. Karl-H. Kruger and Boniface Kruger, vol. 6 of *Theological Investigations* (London: Darton, Longman & Todd, 1969), 218–30, and, in the same volume, his 1965 "Reflections on the Unity of the Love of Neighbour and the Love of God," 231–49. In "Justified and Sinner at the Same Time," Rahner urges: "It cannot be denied, however, that it is a onesidedness in Catholic moral theology and confessional practice to regard each of the individual events of

our moral activity on their own, almost in an atomised fashion. We often overlook in this way the total structure of our moral position, our ultimate attitude towards God, and our basic religious condition. . . . The one whole man lives out of a basic outlook which is either directed toward God or turned away from Him" (226). The framework for this insight is not God's neutrality, but rather the reality of God's "favour and grace" by which God liberates us and makes us his own, despite the fact that "of ourselves we would always turn away from God if God's grace did not anticipate us" (228). When we confess that we are turned away from God, we find that in fact, precisely from within this confession, "God fills our hands with his glory and makes our heart overflow with love and faith. Anyone who confesses that of himself he is a sinner, experiences precisely in this that grace of God which really and truly makes him a saint and a just man" (230). For his postconciliar view of the fundamental option and of the interior depths of conscience, see Karl Rahner, SJ, *Foundations of Christian Faith: An Introduction to the Idea of Christianity*, trans. William V. Dych (New York: Crossroad, 1993), 93–106, originally published in German in 1976.

125. Karl Rahner, SJ, *The Shape of the Church to Come*, trans. Edward Quinn (New York: Seabury Press, 1974), 67; the original German version appeared as *Strukturwandel der Kirche als Aufgabe und Chance* (Freiburg im Breisgau: Herder, 1972). Hereafter, page references from this work will be given in parentheses in the text. For discussion of this work in the context of the German Synod of 1969–75, see Roman A. Siebenrock, "Obéissance ecclésiale comme engagement et protestation: La théologie de Karl Rahner comme 'théologie attentive aux signes du temps présent,'" trans. Robert Kremer, *Recherches de Science Religieuse* 108 (2020): 414–17. I am not attempting to describe Rahner's moral theology as a whole. For efforts to do so, see James F. Bresnahan, "An Ethics of Faith," in *A World of Grace: An Introduction to the Themes and Foundations of Karl Rahner's Theology*, ed. Leo J. O'Donovan (Washington, DC: Georgetown University Press, 1995), 169–84; and Brian Linnane, "Ethics," in *The Cambridge Companion to Karl Rahner*, ed. Declan Marmion and Mary E. Hines (Cambridge: Cambridge University Press, 2005), 158–73.

126. Clearly (though implicitly) Rahner has *Humanae Vitae* in view, but not only *Humanae Vitae*.

127. Linnane comments: "Submitting to the dictates of objective morality—even the moral teaching of the Catholic Church—without reference to personal conscience is, in Rahner's view, 'nothing but a higher kind of dog training' that is demeaning of God and of the individual person. . . . Because Rahner views the moral teaching of the Catholic Church to be fundamentally sound, it will be an unusual occurrence that a person with a well-formed conscience will diverge from this teaching" ("Ethics," 169). I think it is an exaggeration to say that Rahner considers Catholic moral teaching to be "fundamentally sound." Although he emphasizes Rahner's "deeply ecclesial" perspective in which the teaching church "plays a vital role," Linnane grants that "Rahner raises important questions about the ability of any source of moral wisdom to adequately generate detailed, universally binding norms in a context of greatly accelerated social, economic, and cultural change. In light of these circumstances, it is not impossible for such detailed and specific teachings to be 'simply erroneous.' Overly specific solutions to particular moral issues ought to be avoided therefore in favor of general ethical guidance based upon fundamental principles" (171). For a better path forward, see Servais Pinckaers,

OP, "A Historical Perspective on Intrinsically Evil Acts," trans. Mary Thomas Noble, OP, with Craig Steven Titus, in *The Pinckaers Reader: Renewing Thomistic Moral Theology*, ed. John Berkman and Craig Steven Titus (Washington, DC: Catholic University of America Press, 2005), 185–235.

128. See also Rahner's "Some Thoughts on a Good Intention"; as well as Rahner, "The Experiment with Man: Theological Observations on Man's Self-Manipulation," in *Writings of 1965–1967*, trans. Graham Harrison, vol. 9 of *Theological Investigations* (New York: Herder and Herder, 1972), 213: "In an anthropology based on a really Christian philosophy, a man's free action—which, in affecting the world, determines himself too—must not be imagined as an external epiphenomenon sustained on the surface of a substantial essence which itself remains untouched, but becomes part of the innermost determination of this essence itself. In contradistinction to 'things' which are always complete and which are moved from one mode of completion to another and thus are at the same time always in a final state and yet never ultimate, man begins his existence as the being who is radically open and incomplete. When his essence *is* complete it is as he himself has freely created it." Bresnahan sums up Rahner's position well: "In Rahner's critical natural law, a corrective dialectic between empirically observed (objective) phenomena and systematic reflection on the conscious (subjective) conditions of possibility which ground all such objective experiences lies at the center of epistemology. Though this can only be stated here without full exposition of reasons, the dialectic in both ontology and the critical natural law based on it has to be understood to be a constantly developing task. Normative content that results from this dialectical process must be explicitly recognized to be time conditioned and culture related, potentially incomplete and partially inadequate—and, therefore, for another time and culture than that in which it has been elaborated, possibly misleading" (Bresnahan, "Rahner's Ethics," 42).

129. One sees the shift from his perspective of the 1940s and 1950s—although it is clearly anticipated in the earlier essays. In addition to essays noted above, see Rahner's "Bemerkungen über das Naturgesetz und seine Erkennbarkeit," *Orientierung* 19 (1955): 239–43, although his later position comes closer to the existentialism that he criticizes in this essay. Linda Hogan argues: "Karl Rahner's theological anthropology . . . relied on the premise that one could not speak of human beings in terms of immutable essences. His model was based on identifying the material, biological and spiritual dimensions of the person, each of which highlights its uniqueness. As a result he argued that a transhistorical and universal concept of human nature is inappropriate." Hogan, *Confronting the Truth: Conscience in the Catholic Tradition* (New York: Paulist, 2000), 103. With Bresnahan, I hold that Rahner's notion of the transcendental structures of human spirit does in fact entail a stable concept of human nature, if only in the domain of spirit (and, as spirit, allowing for constant evolution). Bresnahan maintains that Rahner consistently rejects "existentialism's affirmation that man has unlimited potentialities because he has no permanent essence constituting conditions of possibility limiting freedom as self-creation, that the only limits are historical in the sense of factually but contingently and not necessarily present at a particular moment of history and culture in the existence of an individual or human grouping" ("Rahner's Ethics," 49n33). For the fundamental historicity of human nature (so that "human nature" cannot be spoken of abstracted from particular acting persons), see also Rudolf Bultmann, "The Historicity of Man and Faith," in *Existence and Faith: Shorter Writings of Rudolf Bultmann*, ed. and

trans. Schubert M. Ogden (New York: The World Publishing Company, 1966), 92–102. For a scholastic account of how our knowledge of the natural law can grow (without overturning the positive content of the law), see Jacques Maritain, *La loi naturelle ou loi non écrite*, ed. Georges Brazzola (Fribourg: Éditions Universitaires, 1986), 155–200.

130. As Rahner says approvingly a bit later: "By proclaiming such imperatives the Church is not teaching any eternal truths; she is not setting up any dogmas nor issuing any laws in the proper sense of the term. In this respect she appeals more to the expertise, to the capacity for critical discrimination, of the Christian conscience whose verdict theoretically cannot be completely nullified; she makes appeals which certainly leave decisions to the Christian conscience of the individual and of particular groups, but are nevertheless relevant to the formation of that conscience. . . . However little these imperatives can be derived purely theoretically from general principles alone, they must be seen clearly to emerge from the innermost centre of a committed Christian conscience, they must be put forward with prophetic force and therefore presuppose also office-holders who are capable of doing this, without having to cover themselves pedantically by referring to the paragraphs of Denzinger" (*Shape of the Church*, 78–80).

131. Karl Rahner, SJ, "Conscience," in *Humane Society and the Church of Tomorrow*, trans. Joseph Donceel, SJ, vol. 22 of *Theological Investigations* (New York: Crossroad, 1991), 4; the original German version appeared as "Vom irrenden Gewissen: Über Freiheit und Würde menschlicher Entscheidung," *Orientierung* 47 (1983): 246–50. Hereafter, page references from this work will be given in parentheses in the text. Discussing this essay, Reinhard Hütter observes that, for Rahner, "Conscience signifies the subject's transcendental experience of freedom and responsibility in relation to God." Hütter, *John Henry Newman on Truth and Its Counterfeits: A Guide for Our Times* (Washington, DC: Catholic University of America Press, 2020), 84. Hütter finds Rahner's position to be deeply flawed: "Rahner's account endangers if not makes principally inconceivable the very possibility of an erroneous conscience. If different by intention, there seems to be in place in this essay a rather striking and disturbing *de facto* identity between Rahner's construal of conscience as transcendental subjectivity and any philosophically sophisticated account of the counterfeit of conscience reviewed above. Without the supposition of *synderesis* and the correlated phenomenon of the erroneous conscience, there is the grave danger that 'autonomy' and 'creativity' become—if not actually intended by Rahner, nevertheless arguably entailed in his construal of conscience—identical with 'self-determination' and 'sovereignty'" (*Newman on Truth*, 85).

132. My book could be lengthened by reflection upon the influence of Maurice Blondel and Joseph Maréchal here. Blondel argues, "All the mystery of life comes from this superficial disagreement between apparent desires and the sincere aspiration of the primitive willing. . . . To will all that we will, in full sincerity of heart, is to place the action and the being of God within ourselves." Blondel, *Action (1893): Essay on a Critique of Life and a Science of Practice*, trans. Oliva Blanchette (Notre Dame: University of Notre Dame Press, 1984), 445. For discussion of Blondel's later work in light of the relationship of nature and grace, see Ryan A. Longton, "A Reconsideration of Maurice Blondel and the 'Natural' Desire," *Heythrop Journal* 56 (2015): 919–30.

133. Here Rahner is referring to transcendental proofs of God's existence that were developed by Blondel and Maréchal earlier in the twentieth century. See also Woodson, *Heideggerian Theologies*, 147–54, focusing on Rahner's understanding of nature and

grace. Woodson draws upon Jack A. Bonsor, *Rahner, Heidegger, and Truth: Karl Rahner's Notion of Christian Truth: The Influence of Heidegger* (Lanham, MD: University Press of America, 1987).

134. It will be clear that, although Rahner does not seem to go as far as Fuchs, the practical import of their respective positions will be the same. Commenting on Rahner's "Some Thoughts on a Good Intention," Gallagher draws the link to Fuchs's postconciliar approach: "Rahner does not say, nor does he suggest, that a good intention can make an objectively evil act good. But what happens when one begins to question, as proponents of situation ethics had already done, whether there were in fact no intrinsically evil acts? In such a case the object, end, and circumstances might be viewed as co-equal determinants of the morality of a specific act. And, if indeed one can accept that position, then one has embraced one of the key tenets of proportionalism" (Gallagher, *Time Past, Time Future*, 233).

135. John Gallagher concludes, "One could do what Rahner did, in essence reinterpret every Christian doctrine, because it was always done within a Thomistic framework"—by which Gallagher means a framework understandable to those who, like Rahner, had received a Jesuit scholastic education under the influence of Maréchal (*Time Past, Time Future*, 153). Gallagher adds with regard to Rahner: "His is a metaphysics of knowledge, not of being. He differs from Kant in that he contends that the mind can know the world of objective reality, but the world of objective reality is a fluctuating, historical world about which specific predictions are at best risky. What is important, therefore, is to make as clear as possible the conditions under which human knowing and doing occur; what becomes important is a theological anthropology which can depict the *a priori* and to the extent possible the *a posteriori* conditions under which human life is lived" (156).

136. For further background, see Jochen Sautenmeister, "Josef Fuchs (1912–2005)," in *Christliche Ethik im Porträt: Leben und Werk bedeutender Moraltheologen*, ed. Konrad Hilpert (Freiburg im Breisgau: Herder, 2012), 759–90.

137. See Josef Fuchs, SJ, *Theologia Moralis Generalis*, rev. ed. (Rome: Gregorian University Press, 1963). For discussion of this work, see Gallagher, *Time Past, Time Future*, 176–78. Gallagher considers that Fuchs's manual sought "to reconcile the insights of Tillmann and Häring with those of neo-Thomist theology and moral theory" (176). Characteristically, given his own anti-Thomist perspective (and, in my view, his philosophical confusion), Gallagher complains: "There was one significant vestige of neo-Thomist theology which Fuchs retained. The notion of a metaphysical finality impelling persons to God as their final end remained a tenet of his theology" (177).

138. Graham, *Josef Fuchs on Natural Law*, 2. See also Josef Fuchs, SJ, *De Castitate et Ordine Sexuali: Conspectus Praelectionum Theologiae Moralis ad Usum Auditorium*, 2nd ed. (Rome: Editrice Università Gregoriana, 1960); and Fuchs, *Situation und Entscheidung: Grundfragen christlicher Situationsethik* (Frankfurt: Knecht, 1952).

139. Discussing Fuchs's *Theologia Moralis Generalis*, Gallagher appreciatively remarks upon Fuchs's emphasis on "Esse hominis personalis" and "Esse in Christo" (*Time Past, Time Future*, 178). Gallagher states, "Clearly with Häring and Fuchs . . . the notion of person was in the process of replacing human nature as the basis of objective moral norms" (179).

140. Graham, *Josef Fuchs on Natural Law*, 22.

141. Graham faults the preconciliar Fuchs for never systematically articulating the

contents of metaphysical human nature and for thereby avoiding the question of how natural law's principles are non-arbitrarily derived. Graham states regarding Fuchs's preconciliar work that "Fuchs's restricted notion of historicity as particularity or situatedness allows him to forge a deceptively unproblematic wedding between metaphysics and historicity, between universal human nature and the human person conditioned by historical circumstances, and between absolute natural law and relative natural law" (*Josef Fuchs on Natural Law*, 23).

142. Graham, *Josef Fuchs on Natural Law*, 2.

143. Pierre Teilhard de Chardin, SJ, *The Phenomenon of Man*, trans. Bernard Wall (New York: HarperCollins, 2008), 248. Teilhard adds that "the human group is in fact turning, by planetary arrangement and convergence of all elemental terrestrial reflections, towards a second critical pole of reflection of a collective and higher order; towards a point beyond which . . . we can see nothing directly, but a point through which we can nevertheless prognosticate the contact between thought, born of involution upon itself of the stuff of the universe, and that transcendent focus we call Omega, the principle which at one and the same time makes this involution irreversible and moves and gathers it in" (*Phenomenon of Man*, 307). For the explicit influence of Teilhard's thought on Rahner, see Rahner's 1967 "Immanent and Transcendent Consummation of the World," in *Writings of 1965–67*, trans. David Bourke, vol. 10 of *Theological Investigations* (New York: Seabury, 1973), 273–89; as well as Rahner's 1961 "Christology within an Evolutionary View of the World," in *Later Writings*, trans. Karl-H. Kruger, vol. 5 of *Theological Investigations* (Baltimore: Helicon, 1966), 157–92. In the latter essay, Rahner makes clear that without being "dependent on" or "obligated to" Teilhard, his conclusions are fundamentally the same as Teilhard's ("Christology within an Evolutionary View," 159–60). Rahner goes on to affirm: "The cosmos evolves . . . in a really essential self-transcendence towards the spirit, the person and freedom. In that moment in which spirit and freedom have been attained in the cosmos, the history of the cosmos receives its structures and its interpretation from the spirit and from freedom and not from matter, in so far as the latter is still in a pre-spiritual way the otherness of the spirit as such" (185; cf. "Immanent and Transcendent Consummation," 288). For discussion see Denis Edwards, "Teilhard's Vision as Agenda for Rahner's Christology," *Pacifica* 23 (2010): 233–45; Thomas F. O'Meara, OP, *God in the World: A Guide to Karl Rahner's Theology* (Collegeville, MN: Liturgical Press, 2007), 91n12; and Karl Lehmann, "He Simply Was Unique," in *Encounters with Karl Rahner: Remembrances of Rahner by Those Who Knew Him*, ed. and trans. Andreas R. Batlogg and Melvin E. Michalski, translation ed. Barbara G. Turner (Milwaukee, WI: Marquette University Press, 2009), 111–34.

144. Thus, in a book published originally in 1960, Monden sharply separates natural law from "the physical or biological concept of 'nature'" (*Sin, Liberty and Law*, 88), and he defines natural law as "a *dynamic existing reality*, an ordering of man towards his self-perfection and his self-realization, through all the concrete situations of his life and in intersubjective dialog with his fellow man and with God. . . . It is precisely the law of evolution, as it appears, for instance, in Teilhard's vision, that an increasing complexity of structures goes along with an increasing interiorization of consciousness, and that this development does not proceed in a steady way but shows, at definite thresholds, sudden total modifications of aspect, situation or disposition. . . . It is possible that in evolving humanity some implications of the natural law may rise to full consciousness

only gradually, or that moral intuition in its full purity may detach itself only in a very gradual way from certain representations or projections in which it was caught. It is even possible that, on reaching certain thresholds, the growing moral awareness may show wholly new aspects and forms" (89–90).

145. Jacques Maritain, *The Peasant of the Garonne: An Old Layman Questions Himself about the Present Time*, trans. Michael Cuddihy and Elizabeth Hughes (Eugene, OR: Wipf & Stock, 2011), 120, 122.

146. Graham, *Josef Fuchs on Natural Law*, 28. As does Rahner, Fuchs in the 1950s contends that this emphasis on personal call does not undermine the universal moral norms. Graham's next sentence therefore states: "As Fuchs explains, this response never stands in contradiction to the demands of universal moral norms; indeed, God's purposes in the supernatural sphere are to strengthen the moral agent's resolve, to offer added insight, and to help the agent overcome her or his subjective weaknesses so the agent can act in accordance with universal moral norms" (28). See Josef Fuchs, SJ, "Situationsethik," *Seelsorgehilfe* 4 (1952): 245–55, 273–78; Fuchs, "Morale théologique et morale de situation," *Nouvelle Revue Théologique* 76 (1954): 1073–85; Fuchs, "Éthique objective et éthique de situation," *Nouvelle Revue Théologique* 78 (1956): 798–818. Graham comments, "the Vatican regarded Fuchs's writings on situation ethics as so tolerant and congenial that it imposed punitive measures on him: Fuchs was forbidden to teach fundamental moral theology to priesthood candidates in the Gregorian University for one year, although he retained the privilege of instructing licentiate and doctoral candidates during this time" (Graham, *Josef Fuchs on Natural Law*, 8). See also the discussion of Fuchs's preconciliar viewpoint in Gallagher, *Time Past, Time Future*, 233–35. For more radical positions, embracing situation ethics more fully, see Richard Egenter, "Kasuistik als christliche Situationsethik," *Münchener Theologische Zeitschrift* 1 (1950): 54–65; and Ernst Michel, *Der Partner Gottes: Weisungen zum christlichen Selbtverstandnis* (Heidelberg: Lambert Schneider, 1946). For background from the 1920s, ranging broadly, see Ulrich Bröckling, *Katholische Intellektuelle in der Weimarer Republik: Zeitkritik und Gesellschaftstheorie bei Walter Dirks, Romano Guardini, Carl Schmitt, Ernst Michel und Heinrich Mertens* (Munich: Wilhelm Fink, 1993).

147. James F. Keenan, SJ, "Champion of Conscience," *America*, April 4, 2005, americamagazine.org/issue/526/other-things/champion-conscience. Keenan's essay is a laudatory obituary for Fuchs. See also Josef Fuchs, SJ, "Moral Theology according to Vatican II," in *Human Values and Christian Morality* (Dublin: Gill and Macmillan, 1970), 1–55.

148. Josef Fuchs, SJ, "The Absoluteness of Behavioral Moral Norms," in *Personal Responsibility and Christian Morality*, trans. William Cleves et al. (Washington, DC: Georgetown University Press, 1983), 116.

149. Graham comments: "It is revealing to note the significant differences Fuchs displays in his pre- and postconversion writings when assessing the validity of moral norms in terms of his breadth of interest, the ability to question critically, and the components of his Roman Catholic natural law tradition that he simply presumes as true and indisputable. In his postconversion work Fuchs offers a panoramic, far-ranging, comprehensive, and thorough treatment of moral norms. Most of his attention focuses on epistemological issues, in other words, the role of reason in the formulation of moral norms and the inability of human reason to foresee all the possible circumstances in

which moral norms are applied. But Fuchs also considers the implications of historicity (at this point Fuchs had embraced a more sophisticated understanding of 'historical consciousness'), diverse cultural backgrounds, and newly emergent conceptions of theological anthropology on the validity of moral norms, as well as the competency of the magisterium in formulating moral norms. . . . Standing in stark contrast to this is Fuchs's limited scope and the dearth of direct analysis he offers on the issue of universal moral norms in his preconversion period" (Graham, *Josef Fuchs on Natural Law*, 25–26).

150. Fuchs, "Behavioral Moral Norms," 124.

151. Fuchs states: "For even that which essentially constitutes man, that which therefore belongs unalterably to his nature, as also his permanent structures, is basically mutable. Mutability belongs to man's immutable essence; irrevocably, man is man (tautology!). To be sure, a priori, some essential elements of man's nature can be identified: body-soul unity, personality, accountability, interpersonality; while one cannot say with equal a priori validity, respecting other components of existential man, whether they belong necessarily and unchangeably to human nature. But even these a priori and inalienable elements of man's nature subsist in it in variable modes" ("Behavioral Moral Norms," 126).

152. Fuchs, "Behavioral Moral Norms," 126–27. For criticism of the *preconciliar* viewpoint of Fuchs on human historicity, see Norbert J. Rigali, "The Uniqueness and Distinctiveness of Christian Morality and Ethics," in *Moral Theology: Challenges for the Future; Essays in Honor of Richard A. McCormick*, ed. Charles E. Curran (New York: Paulist, 1990), 74–93. See also, for the opposite perspective on universal moral norms, Herbert McCabe, OP, "The Validity of Absolutes," in *Situationism and the New Morality*, ed. Robert L. Cunningham (New York: Meredith, 1970), 66–78. McCabe remarks, "Are there some things that you must never under any circumstances do? I think it is possible to formulate such prohibitions" (68). Particularly with English-speaking "situation" ethicists in view, such as Joseph Fletcher, he notes that "the New Moralists seem to hold that 'loving' can be used to differentiate between kinds of behavior, and is therefore descriptive, but also that there is no possible piece of behavior which might not [in some circumstance] be called 'loving.' I think it is possible for them to hold this only because they believe that the adjective 'loving' is descriptive not of bodily behavior as such but of something else that accompanies it. I think, in fact, that the New Morality only becomes plausible on a dualistic view of man according to which moral values attach to events in an 'interior' invisible life which runs alongside a man's public physical life" (73–74).

153. Fuchs, "Behavioral Moral Norms," 128.

154. See Fuchs, "Behavioral Moral Norms," 130–32. He adds with regard to the cultural component: "One might point out, perhaps, that in many cases a given self-concept and a given viewpoint and form of a reality—e.g., marriage in, let us say, a certain African tribe—may not in themselves correspond in all respects to *recta ratio*. Then, of course, the question arises whether another form of marriage, presupposing another culture, may legitimately be imposed upon men belonging to an endemic culture—by missionaries, for instance—provided the indigenous culture itself has not changed by a rather gradual process, and provided it admits of a 'human' form of marriage. But might it not be assumed also that on the basis of dissimilar experiences, a heterogeneous self-concept and varying options and evaluations on the part of man (humanity) projecting himself into his future in a human fashion—*secundum rectam rationem*—are entirely

possible, and that these options and evaluations within the chosen system postulate varied forms of behavior?" ("Behavioral Moral Norms," 132).

155. Fuchs, "Behavioral Moral Norms," 133. He makes use also of a distinction between the "moral" and the "pre-moral," with the latter being ontic or physical evil but not moral wickedness. Thus, "killing is the realization of an evil, but it is not always a moral evil" (135; cf. 136–39, emphasizing the determinative character of intention and circumstances). He argues that the phrase "intrinsically evil" can be applied, but only from within a concrete situation: "Every action that is objectively—*secundum rectam rationem*—not justified in the concrete human situation (according to [Edward] Schillebeeckx, the sole norm and only adequate norm of conduct) is *intrinsece malum* and therefore absolutely to be avoided" (142).

156. Fuchs, "Behavioral Moral Norms," 145.

157. See also, in the same volume, Fuchs's "Morality as the Shaping of the Future of Man," in *Personal Responsibility and Christian Morality*, trans. William Cleves et al. (Washington, DC: Georgetown University Press, 1983), 183–84: "It could be that sometimes we find ourselves faced with certain situations which require us to test the projects-norms which we have formulated: the latter no longer seem to be those which correspond to the reality which we face in today's circumstances. Thus, they seem to be norms which perhaps no longer guarantee the *humanum* in the modern world. . . . Specialists ought to be men who have developed a global vision of mankind and who thus keep alive within themselves fundamental principles for human action which is truly worthy of this designation. They ought to be men who have an idea of the dignity of mankind as a whole, and of the individual, as well as of the role of society and humanity. Only in this way will they be capable of shaping projects which are humanly valid." Again in the same volume, see Fuchs's "*Epikeia* Applied to Natural Law?," 185–99, for discussion of his view that natural law, insofar as it consists in humanly articulated norms, cannot be universalizable without losing touch with reality. Fuchs draws attention to Bernard Häring, CSsR, "Dynamism and Continuity in a Personalistic Approach to Natural Law," in *Norm and Context in Christian Ethics*, ed. Gene H. Outka and Paul Ramsey (New York: SMC-Canterbury, 1968), 199–218.

158. Josef Fuchs, SJ, "Vocation and Hope: Conciliar Orientations for a Christian Morality," in *Personal Responsibility and Christian Morality*, trans. William Cleves et al. (Washington, DC: Georgetown University Press, 1983), 45.

159. Fuchs, "Vocation and Hope," 45.

160. See a related study also published in 1971, Alfons Auer's *Autonome Moral und christlicher Glaube* (Darmstadt: WBG, 2016); and see Éric Gaziaux, *Morale de la foi et morale autonome: Confrontation entre P. Delhaye et J. Fuchs* (Leuven: Peeters, 1995).

161. Josef Fuchs, SJ, "The Question Addressed to Conscience," in *Personal Responsibility and Christian Morality*, trans. William Cleves et al. (Washington, DC: Georgetown University Press, 1983), 216. Hereafter, page references from this work will be given in parentheses in the text. See also Fuchs's "Conscience and Conscientious Fidelity," in *Moral Theology: Challenges for the Future; Essays in Honor of Richard A. McCormick*, ed. Charles E. Curran (New York: Paulist, 1990), 108–24, which focuses mainly on the relationship of a believer's conscience to the church's magisterium. In his description of conscience in this essay, Fuchs strives to emphasize that conscience is not merely subjective. Rather, its judgment involves "the work of the personal subject in conscience

with the aim of finding a creative and objectively justified word in the situational conscience. This is anything but a pure 'subjectivity' that would be improper for an organ; but it is also anything but a pure listening to an 'objective' oracle in conscience" (Fuchs, "Conscience and Conscientious Fidelity," 117). For Fuchs, moral norms, too, are neither purely subjective nor purely objective, and therefore they can neither be dismissed nor given an absolute character. Against the view that "God's commandment, the ethical norms and the solutions of the ethical natural law are somehow and somewhere objectively 'present,'" he argues that "since God himself has not given them to us directly . . . such ethical normative statements in human society exist only thanks to human ethical knowledge 'in conscience.' They are neither 'invented' nor 'created,' but experienced and recognized 'creatively'—although in the (merely) created human participation in God's own wisdom. . . . It follows that the adoption or rejection of ethical claims or prohibitions always takes place via the responsible, decision-making function of the personal conscience" (118).

162. Here the echo of Bultmann (and Rahner) is notable. For Fuchs's version of the "fundamental option," see Fuchs, "Basic Freedom and Morality," in his *Human Values and Christian Morality* (Dublin: Gill and Macmillan, 1970), 92–111. James Keenan, in his published dissertation completed under Fuchs's direction, *Goodness and Rightness in Thomas Aquinas's "Summa theologiae"* (Washington, DC: Georgetown University Press, 1992), 143, argues that "charity [is] singularly the description of moral goodness. . . . [A]lthough some contemporary moral theologians have contributed greatly to develop the notion of fundamental option, that notion only provides a conceptual understanding of the moral person pre- or a-thematically. Charity, on the other hand, provides a description for thematic or categorial description. Whereas fundamental option describes our abiding condition as either good or bad, charity as striving describes our daily living as good when we strive and bad when we fail to strive. Thus, charity rescues fundamental option from the recesses of the human person." In my view, this position is inadequate. Consider someone who, striving to reduce his gravely vicious habit, cuts it down to once a week from five times a week. The person has moved in the right direction but has not yet arrived at "charity" or "good daily living." See also Keenan, "Distinguishing Charity as Goodness and Prudence as Rightness: A Key to Thomas's *Secunda pars*," *Thomist* 56 (1992): 407–26. For responses to Keenan's proposal regarding Aquinas, see Michael S. Sherwin, OP, *By Knowledge and By Love: Charity and Knowledge in the Moral Theology of St. Thomas Aquinas* (Washington, DC: Catholic University of America Press, 2005); and, more recently, Ryan J. Brady, "Aquinas the Voluntarist? An Investigation of the Claims of James Keenan, S. J.," *Nova et Vetera* 18 (2020): 853–73. See also, for Fuchs's distinction between "goodness" (core intention and striving) and "rightness" (particular acts), Christopher Kaczor, *Proportionalism and the Natural Law Tradition* (Washington, DC: Catholic University of America Press, 2002), 10, drawing upon Fuchs, *Christian Ethics in a Secular Arena*, trans. Bernard Hoose and Brian McNeil (Washington, DC: Georgetown University Press, 1984), 81.

163. This is something like a blending of conscience, prudence, and reflective knowledge all together.

164. Graham, while supporting Fuchs's general approach, nonetheless raises a telling issue: "Fuchs's readers are left in the dark concerning how to adjudicate between conflicting values, how to sort relevant from irrelevant information, how analogies are to

be drawn and paradigms utilized, and how to prioritize values" (Graham, *Josef Fuchs on Natural Law*, 186). Fuchs appeals to conscience and self-actualization, but this is hardly likely to be sufficient. In Graham's view, Fuchs's consequentialist approach does in fact succeed because it provides the best possible basis for understanding which actions will support human flourishing, but I think that the problem here is that Fuchs, by sharply historicizing human nature and rejecting the grounding of practical reason in eternal and divine law, has eviscerated the very notion of "human flourishing." See also Josef Fuchs, SJ, "Christian Faith and the Disposing of Human Life," *Theological Studies* 46 (1985): 664–84, where Fuchs reflects upon euthanasia and concludes: "the Christian faith gives birth to particular attitudes without determining an unambiguous ethics concerning the disposing of human life"—in other words, there is no universal moral norm against euthanasia (684).

165. He gives the examples of slavery and of the position of women in society, which biblical and medieval authors did not understand as we do. He notes, too, the difficulty of determining what is required concretely in every case for the exercise of chastity.

166. For an aspect of Fuchs's approach that I cannot treat here, see Justin M. Anderson, "Is It Better to Die Excommunicated Than Act against One's Conscience? What Aquinas Famously (Never) Said on Conscience and Church Authority," *Ephemerides Theologicae Lovanienses* 95 (2019): 567–93. As Anderson shows, the claim that, according to Aquinas, Catholics should choose excommunication rather than act against conscience was first put forward in 1958 by Josef Rudin, SJ. This claim is based upon an inaccurate paraphrase of a statement made by Aquinas in his *Commentary on the Sentences*. Unfortunately, the misreading of Aquinas on this point has been adopted by many scholars. See also Keenan, *Moral Wisdom: Lessons and Texts from the Catholic Tradition*, 3rd ed. (Lanham, MD: Rowman & Littlefield, 2006), 28–29n6, cited in Anderson, "Better to Die Excommunicated?," 582–83n45.

167. For further background, see Josef Römelt, CSsR, "Bernhard Häring (1912–1998)," in *Christliche Ethik im Porträt: Leben und Werk bedeutender Moraltheologen*, ed. Konrad Hilpert (Freiburg im Breisgau: Herder, 2012), 705–28.

168. See Raphael Gallagher, CSsR, "Interpreting Thomas Aquinas," 376. See also John Gallagher's claim, "The publication of *The Law of Christ* was a watershed in the history of moral theology. From the date of its publication (1954) a process was set in motion that would result in the gradual removal of the neo-Thomist manuals of moral theology from the seminaries of Europe and the United States" (*Time Past, Time Future*, 169). Häring's doctoral work focused on Max Scheler and Rudolf Otto, employing their concepts of the good and the holy to reflect upon the relationship of freedom and grace: see Häring, *Das Heilige und das Gute* (Krailling: Erich Wewel, 1950).

169. See Charles E. Curran, *The Development of Moral Theology: Five Strands* (Washington, DC: Georgetown University Press, 2013), 26. See also Curran's laudatory obituary for Häring, "Bernard Häring: A Moral Theologian Whose Soul Matched His Scholarship," *National Catholic Reporter*, July 17, 1998, natcath.org/NCR_Online/archives2/1998c/071798/071898h.htm.

170. See the essays in Augustin Schmied, CSsR, and Josef Römelt, CSsR, eds., *50 Jahre "Das Gesetz Christi": Der Beitrag Bernhard Härings zur Erneuerung der Moraltheologie* (Münster: LIT, 2005); and see also the reflections on these essays offered by Martin McKeever, CSsR, "The 50th Anniversary of *The Law of Christ*: Bernhard

Häring's Contribution to the Renewal of Moral Theology," *Studia Moralia* 44 (2006): 233–50.

171. See Gallagher, *Time Past, Time Future*, 171–74. Gallagher explains Häring's use of "value": "In addition to basic value [knowledge of God], Häring also spoke of types of values and particular values. Types of values referred to a set of particular or specific values which shared a more general or generic value. Types of values were associated with Häring's theory of the virtues. Charity, justice or chastity, for instance, were instances of types of values. Particular values referred to the specific values realized in concrete human acts—the avoidance of scandal, feeding the hungry, appropriate sexual behavior. . . . Häring's introduction of the notion of value as the primary concept in his moral theory made it possible for him not just to relate the choice of particular moral values to the order of goods, but also to identify such choices as essential elements within the Christian response to the divine summons and invitation" (173–75). Nonetheless, Gallagher admits that Häring's *The Law of Christ* is "quite traditional" in its casuistic positions (175).

172. Karol Wojtyła's work in philosophical ethics was also influenced significantly by Roman Ingarden, as well as, in certain respects, by Jacques Maritain. For an introduction to Wojtyła's philosophy, see Miguel Acosta and Adrian J. Reimers, *Karol Wojtyła's Personalist Philosophy: Understanding "Person & Act"* (Washington, DC: Catholic University of America Press, 2016). For background to the perspective and influence of Max Scheler, see Baring, *Converts to the Real*, 134–47, 244–48. Baring notes that Catholic scholars appreciative of Scheler generally "valorized Scheler's sensitivity to religious experience while bolstering his metaphysical claims with a more robust appeal to reason" (248).

173. Bernard Häring, CSsR, *The Law of Christ: Moral Theology for Priests and Laity*, vol. 1, *General Moral Theology*, trans. Edwin G. Kaiser, CPPS. (Westminster, MD: The Newman Press, 1963), vii. John Gallagher emphasizes Tillmann's influence, despite the notable differences between Tillmann's approach and Häring's: "Although not the exegete that Tillmann had been, Häring strove in his writing to be responsible primarily to the scriptures. The theological themes he developed were those found in scripture. He did not turn to dogmatic theology for signs of what was theologically relevant; the relationship between nature and grace, body and soul, philosophy and theology were not his organizing categories. Rather the central theological themes of moral theology, he proposed, were the invitation of Christ, the human response, and conversion" (*Time Past, Time Future*, 170). Missing here is Häring's commitment to the centrality of conscience.

174. Häring, *The Law of Christ*, 1:xi.

175. Servais Pinckaers, OP, *The Sources of Christian Ethics*, trans. Mary Thomas Noble, OP (Washington, DC: Catholic University of America Press, 1995), 301.

176. Häring, *The Law of Christ*, 1:23.

177. Häring, *The Law of Christ*, 1:29.

178. Häring, *The Law of Christ*, 1:26–27. Häring does not end up at the same place as Pinckaers on the Sermon on the Mount, however. In 1967, shortly after the end of the Council, Häring published "The Normative Value of the Sermon on the Mount" in *Catholic Biblical Quarterly* 29, no. 3 (1967): 375–85. Häring describes Jesus's commandments in the Sermon on the Mount as "goal commandments" and as "an ethic of attitude" ("Normative Value," 76). He argues that Jesus's words in the Sermon in

no way support "a pastoral rigorism which requires from all indiscriminately what is psychologically impossible for many" (77). In *The Law of Christ*, Häring contrasts the Decalogue negatively with "the Sermon on the Mount, the new law of the kingdom of God promulgated by Christ, the law of disinterested and unbounded love, humility, and love of the cross"; he adds that the Sermon "determines the ideals and goals toward which we must strive (purposive precepts)" (1:403). For his part, Pinckaers rejects any "explanation that places the Sermon on the Mount in the category of an imaginary ideal rather than a concrete reality where the action is. The perception of ourselves as unable to follow a moral teaching makes the teaching quite ineffective. We will soon abandon an ideal too far beyond us. . . . The exterior dimension, in the sense of concrete action in our neighbor's behalf, is as essential to the Sermon on the Mount as the interior dimension, in the sense of the 'heart' and the 'hidden place' where only the Father sees us. The teaching of the Sermon cannot be turned into a morality of sentiment or intention, any more than it can be considered as a purely formal morality consisting exclusively of universal principles" (Pinckaers, *Sources of Christian Ethics*, 137–38).

179. Häring, *The Law of Christ*, 1:42.

180. Häring, *The Law of Christ*, 1:506.

181. Häring, *The Law of Christ*, 1:149.

182. Häring, *The Law of Christ*, 1:135, 140, 143.

183. For Häring's vision of the Council itself, see his *The Johannine Council* (New York: Herder and Herder, 1963); for Häring's contributions to the Council, see the laudatory study by Hill, "Bernard Häring and the Second Vatican Council." For Häring's eulogy for Rahner (who died in 1984), see Häring, "Karl Rahner—His Personality and His Work," *The Furrow* 35, no. 5 (1984): 301–5. Häring rightly remarks (by contrast to those who do not include Rahner in the ranks of moral theologians), "In his numerous writings . . . , he is never confined to one discipline in a narrow sense. On the contrary, starting with dogmatic theology as his appointed discipline he built bridges to moral and pastoral theology" ("Karl Rahner," 303).

184. See Bernard Häring, CSsR, *Free and Faithful in Christ: Moral Theology for Clergy and Laity*, vol. 1, *General Moral Theology* (New York: Crossroad, 1984). Hereafter, page references from this work will be given in parentheses in the text. Häring states that *Free and Faithful in Christ* is not a revision or new edition of his preconciliar three-volume *The Law of Christ*. For scholarly reflection on Häring's moral theology, see Kathleen A. Cahalan, *Formed in the Image of Christ: The Sacramental-Moral Theology of Bernard Häring, C.Ss.R.* (Collegeville, MN: Liturgical Press, 2004); and Felix Bak, "Bernard Häring's Interpretation of Cardinal Newman's Treatise on Conscience," *Ephemerides Theologicae Lovanienses* 49 (1973): 124–59. Robert J. Smith has compared Häring's understanding of conscience—to which he devotes a chapter—to the accounts of conscience found in Thomas Aquinas and Germain Grisez. Smith argues that "Häring's understanding of the nature and function of conscience is in line with the tradition as it is articulated by Thomas Aquinas. . . . Conscience is primary in the making of personal moral decisions and is inviolable once those decisions are made." Smith, *Conscience and Catholicism: The Nature and Function of Conscience in Contemporary Roman Catholic Moral Theology* (Lanham, MD: University Press of America, 1998), 103. I think, however, that the view that conscience is "primary in the making of personal moral decisions" conflates conscience with prudence (and also leaves out charity). For

the point that Smith has misunderstood Aquinas on conscience, see Anderson, "Better to Die Excommunicated?," 583–84.

185. For further explanation of the "reciprocity of consciences," see Häring, *Free and Faithful in Christ*, 265–84.

186. Häring notes a debt to James Gustafson's *Can Ethics Be Christian?* (Chicago: University of Chicago Press, 1975) and Gustafson's *Christ and the Moral Life* (New York: Harper & Row, 1968), although Rahner and Fuchs are also crucial for Häring. In an extensive discussion of dispositions in *Christ and the Moral Life*, Gustafson proposes: "What is given us in Jesus' teaching, as part of the whole revelation, is the evocation and beckoning to a basic attitude, or basic disposition. We are called to an attitude of obedience, of trust, of love. We are to be disposed toward God in obedience and to obey him in our relations to others. We are to be disposed toward God in love, and in turn to be affirmative toward others in love since God has loved us. What do the teachings of Jesus make clear to men in faith? They are to be obedient, to be loving, to have a basic disposition in accord with the gift of God in Jesus Christ. What ought I to do? I ought to have a basic purpose or intention in accord with Jesus' teaching, for his teaching is in accord with God's purpose and intention for man revealed in the gospel. The teachings give us the *telos*, the ultimate end of God's will and law. They give us the basic direction for our new life in Christ. They are not so important for their moral details, for the specific rules and precepts, but for the direction and way that they show Christians to go. Our own intentions and direction of life ought to be in accord with the basic direction of Jesus' teaching" (194). The last few sentences here fit well with Hastings Rashdall's approach, as with Häring's own understanding of the Sermon on the Mount. See Häring, "Normative Value"; as well as Jeffrey Siker's chapter "Bernard Häring: The Freedom of His Responsive Love," in *Scripture and Ethics: Twentieth-Century Portraits* (Oxford: Oxford University Press, 1996), 59–79.

187. Thus Häring states, "Jesus does not follow the rules of the priestly tradition in his interpretation of the Bible. His use of the Old Testament is creative. His teaching about the Sabbath and the law, his opposition to meaningless traditions that hinder freedom for God, and especially his protest against a religion that would attribute such pettiness to God, is in itself manifestation of God's gratuitous freedom, an undeserved gift of himself" (*Free and Faithful in Christ*, 117). The last sentence here could stand as a description of how Häring conceives of his own work, but it obviously cannot stand as an accurate description of Jesus's own relationship to Judaism. Häring comments in a similar vein that Jesus "died his redemptive death because of his battle against the powers, and especially against the abuse of power in organized religion" (137).

188. Louis Monden argues in 1960, drawing upon the work of Piet Schoonenberg, SJ: "Possibly Fr. Schoonenberg has discovered the right middle position through the distinction he makes between 'mortal sin' and 'sin unto death.' The biblical expression 'sin unto death' (1 Jn. 5.16ff.)—which he rightly equates with the Johannine 'anomia' (injustice or wickedness, 1 Jn. 3.4) and the 'sin against the Holy Spirit' of the gospel (Mk. 3.28ff. and par.)—is interpreted by him as *final impenitence*, the final choice which occurs in the act of dying. It is the last, the final sin. One who commits it is dead before God; he died, morally speaking, in sin, even if biologically he may survive for a while. By definition, however, this total commitment cannot be discovered in the course of this life, and if one puts as a condition for a mortal sin committed during life that absolute,

conscious and total rejection of God, it is quite evident that man is unable to commit a real mortal sin. However, in the sense in which Schoonenberg understands *mortal sin*—as a rejection of God within a still provisional but important choice, deriving from a central option—it does occur, not as frequently as a rigid moral catalog would make us accept, but still as something which remains within the normal possibilities of free human choice" (Monden, *Sin, Liberty and Law*, 37–38). For Monden the key is not "mortal sin" on the moral level—doing a bad thing—but rather the conscious and free rejection of God on the religious level (which may be somewhat present in a "mortal sin" on the moral level, but really is about a free choice of one's fundamental option, a radical and decisive "sin unto death"). Monden also speaks about the slow and gradual "rhythm of organic growth" in the moral life, meaning that one must account for the "law of gradualness" in moving toward goodness (41). He concludes, much like the later Häring: "The real meaning of the symptom the sinful action is can be discovered only when we can go down to the root of the decisions and, as it were, *coincide with the basic option* which embodies itself in that action, so that from that perspective we can measure the resistances and determinisms this option has met on its road to realization" (42). There are important truths here and yet, also, an inadequate anthropology that underestimates particular actions.

189. He cites various passages from Pauline and non-Pauline letters, including Titus 1:15–16; Heb. 9:14; Heb. 13:18; 2 Tim. 1:3; 1 Cor. 4:4; and 1 Cor. 10:25–29.

190. As an example, Häring gives Aquinas's view that a person cannot profess faith in Christ *against* his or her sincere conscience without this profession being a sin—but if a person came to believe in sincere conscience that he or she must leave the church, this, too, would be a sin, implying personal culpability for failure to form conscience adequately.

191. He cites Rom. 3:31 and 14:23, along with 1 Tim. 1:5, 1:19, 3:9, and 4:2.

192. Linda Hogan observes more broadly, "Vatican II encouraged moral theologians to continue the process of renewal, already begun by theologians like Rahner, Doms and Häring. . . . [Yet] the documents of the Council themselves give out contradictory messages. As a result it is often hard to discern precisely what the Council has mandated. My suggestion is that where ambiguities exist these should be interpreted in light of the spirit and objective of the Council. In relation to moral theology this means a determination to develop a paradigm dominated by the concerns of persons rather than laws" (Hogan, *Confronting the Truth*, 118). See also Josef Fuchs, SJ, "A Harmonization of the Conciliar Statements on Christian Moral Theology," in *Vatican II: Assessment and Perspectives*, ed. Rene Latourelle, SJ (Mahwah, NJ: Paulist, 1989), 479–500; and Fuchs, "Moral Theology according to Vatican II," in *Human Values and Christian Morality*, 1–55.

193. Häring praises "the prophetic ministry of dissent within the Church," which, he argues, was what led to the development of the teaching of *Dignitatis Humanae*; those who dissented from the church's teaching against religious freedom eventually were shown to be right (*Free and Faithful in Christ*, 280).

194. He adds, "Only where and when this reciprocity of consciences comes to its full bearing will magisterial interventions and the ongoing research of theologians strengthen the teaching authority of the Church. . . . The magisterium of the Church, in all its forms and on all levels, is authentic and faithful to Christ when the overriding

concern is not for submission but for honesty, sincerity and responsibility" (Häring, *Free and Faithful in Christ*, 283–84). See also his remarks in his final book, *My Hope for the Church: Critical Encouragement for the Twenty-First Century*, trans. Peter Heinegg (Liguori, MO: Liguori, 1999), 93, 136, published in German in 1997: "In my interpretation, in the last years of the pontificate of Karol Wojtyla an old model has largely run itself into the ground, thus paving the way for a turnaround that is in the offing. . . . The protagonists of partial restoration [of the 'old model' of Catholic morality] have been and are two highly gifted men, Karol Wojtyla and Joseph Ratzinger. Both have made masterful use of the modern media. In many ways they are men of unusual energy and talent. Both experienced the Council as participants and effectively promoted certain measures there. Behind them stood (and stand) many pious believing Catholics, people for whom obedience and tightly structured order are the foundational values of the Church. Not a few such men and women were moved to accept the Council in principle, though only in a modified version, thanks to the restrictive interpretation of it by these two leading figures. . . . I admire the courage, but not the wisdom, of the pope in his unlimited zeal for the controlled and controlling application of his doctrines and decisions. No doubt he is following his conscience. Of course, that conscience is shaped by a specific tradition and mode of thinking." In Häring's view, John Paul II and Benedict XVI were all about obedience and control—thereby setting themselves in opposition to Vatican II—and he thinks the same about theologians who uphold the moral teachings of *Humanae Vitae* and *Veritatis Splendor*.

195. Häring comments (implicitly with his side of contemporary debates in view), "Great Christians, totally dedicated to the Church and to the dignity of consciences, were frequently considered less faithful to the Church because their explanation of formulations of doctrine and laws was less rigoristic and less adequate for complete control. Their intentions could not be understood by those who were only concerned for the upholding of traditions, of order and discipline in a sometimes self-defensive Church" (*Free and Faithful in Christ*, 287–88).

196. After the Council, Ratzinger raised some questions in commenting upon *Gaudium et Spes* §16's discussion of conscience. He suggests that the paragraph is too optimistic about the power of conscience. See Joseph Ratzinger, "The Dignity of the Human Person," in *Pastoral Constitution on the Church in the Modern World*, ed. Herbert Vorgrimler, vol. 5 of *Commentary on the Documents of Vatican II* (New York: Herder & Herder, 1969), 134–36. For criticism of Ratzinger as a retrograde, unwilling to appreciate the new perspective of the Council, see David E. DeCosse, "The Primacy of Conscience, Vatican II, and Pope Francis: The Opportunity to Renew a Tradition," in *From Vatican II to Pope Francis: Charting a Catholic Future*, ed. Paul Crowley, SJ (Maryknoll, NY: Orbis, 2014), 156–69. See also Gallagher, "Interpreting Thomas Aquinas," 377: "Already in 1969, Joseph Ratzinger saw the potential problems with regard to a slippery-slope interpretation of *Gaudium et Spes* 16, which is a central text with regard to the understanding of conscience (and in the formulation of which, incidentally, some Redemptorists had a key role). Ratzinger fears that the precise relationship between the will and reason could be broken in a way that would lead to what would come to be called the 'creative conscience.' Should this happen, one is, indeed, faced with the possibility of truth having a double status: truth would contradict truth, which is a clearly silly position." Gallagher adds, "The heart of the problem is the theological definition of moral truth in the

particular circumstances in which one is faced with the practical decision of following the truth as a matter that has consequences for one's salvation. Unless this problem is satisfactorily resolved, the inheritors of the casuist tradition will be unclear as to whether the *formulation* of truth is one question and the *experience* of truth quite another" (377). See William McDonough, "'New Terrain' and a 'Stumbling Block' in Redemptorist Contributions to *Gaudium et Spes*," *Studia Moralia* 35 (1997): 9–48.

197. Joseph Ratzinger, "Conscience in Time," trans. W. J. O'Hara, in *Joseph Ratzinger in* Communio, vol. 2, *Anthropology and Culture*, ed. David L. Schindler and Nicholas J. Healy (Grand Rapids, MI: Eerdmans, 2013), 17.

198. Ratzinger, "Conscience in Time," 19.

199. Ratzinger, "Conscience in Time," 21.

200. Ratzinger, "Conscience in Time," 22.

201. Joseph Ratzinger, "Conscience and Truth," in *Crisis of Conscience*, ed. John M. Haas (New York: Crossroad, 1996), 1.

202. Ratzinger traces this view to the late-eighteenth-century German philosopher J. G. Fichte, who deemed conscience to be infallible, as the highest authority whose decisions cannot be challenged by other humans.

203. Ratzinger, "Conscience and Truth," 4.

204. Ratzinger, "Conscience and Truth," 6.

205. Ratzinger, "Conscience and Truth," 7.

206. Ratzinger, "Conscience and Truth," 10. Here Ratzinger takes up the language of the early Barth, no doubt shared by many other German thinkers. Ratzinger does not mention Barth.

207. Reinhard Hütter has evaluated Ratzinger's proposal to replace the term "synderesis" with "anamnesis" (see Hütter, *John Henry Newman*, 86–88). He rightly finds Ratzinger's proposal unnecessary, since the change in terms does not really add clarity. For Hütter, the question is "which word would be preferable for pragmatic, prudential, or pedagogical reasons to signify the innate *habitus* of the first principle and precept of practical reason. If one is committed to maintaining the distinction between a natural *habitus* on the ontological level of conscience (*synderesis*) and its reduction to act (*conscientia*), as then-Cardinal Ratzinger himself seems to suggest, the introduction of the concept of *anamnesis* might in the end only complicate the fundamental distinction between the *habitus* and its actualization. In light of the potential misunderstanding of *anamnesis* as an innate *actus*, it seems preferable to keep the initially unfamiliar, but now received technical term *synderesis*" (88).

208. Ratzinger, "Conscience and Truth," 14.

209. Ratzinger, "Conscience and Truth," 14.

210. Ratzinger, "Conscience and Truth," 15.

211. Ratzinger, "Conscience and Truth," 15. For further connections between conscience and memory—for the purpose of showing how both conscience and memory must be simultaneously trusted and questioned—see G. E. M. Anscombe's essay "Authority in Morals," in *Faith in a Hard Ground: Essays on Religion, Philosophy and Ethics by G. E. M. Anscombe*, ed. Mary Geach and Luke Gormally (Exeter: Imprint Academic, 2008), 92–100, especially 96–97.

212. Ratzinger, "Conscience and Truth," 16.

213. Ratzinger, "Conscience and Truth," 18.

214. Ratzinger, "Conscience and Truth," 18. See also Joseph Ratzinger, "Bishops, Theologians, and Morality," in *On Conscience: Two Essays by Joseph Ratzinger*, ed. John M. Haas (San Francisco: Ignatius, 2007), 43–75, 80–82. Ratzinger argues in this 1984 essay, "The Church professes herself the advocate of the reason of creation and practices what she means when she says, 'I believe in God, the Creator of Heaven and Earth.' There is a reason for being, and when man separates himself from it totally and recognizes the reason only of what he himself has made, then he abandons what is precisely moral in the strict sense. . . . In the last analysis, the language of being, the language of nature, is identical with the language of conscience. But in order to hear that language, it is necessary, as with all language, to practice it" (67). He makes a connection here to Christ: "Through contact with God, depending on how perceptive the conscience is, this primitive human knowledge becomes a real vehicle of communication with truth by means of the communion it shares with the conscience of the saints and with the knowledge of Jesus Christ" (69). Earlier in the essay he agrees with Robert Spaemann that "conscience is an organ, not an oracle" and not, in every individual judgment, "the voice of God"; although conscience does signify "in some way the voice of God within us" since it connects us with God's law (59–61). He sums up his position as follows: "Man is in himself a being who has an organ of internal knowledge about good and evil. But for it to become what it is, it needs the help of others. Conscience requires formation and education. It can become stunted, it can be stamped out, it can be falsified so that it can only speak in a stunted or distorted way. The silence of conscience can become a deadly sickness for an entire civilization" (62; cf. 51). See also Robert Spaemann, *Moralische Grundbegriffe* (Munich: Beck, 1982), 73–84.

215. Timothy Gorringe, "Barth and Politics," in *The Oxford Handbook of Karl Barth*, ed. Paul Dafydd Jones and Paul T. Nimmo (Oxford: Oxford University Press, 2019), 181.

216. Richard A. McCormick, SJ, "Moral Theology since Vatican II: Clarity or Chaos?," in *The Critical Calling: Reflections on Moral Dilemmas since Vatican II* (Washington, DC: Georgetown University Press, 1989), 21.

217. For a summary of McCormick's own perspective and a recognition of his derivativeness, see Gallagher, *Time Past, Time Future*, 214–17. See also the work of present-day exponents (to greater or lesser degrees) of conscience-centered morality, including Julio L. Martinez, SJ, *Consciencia, discernimiento y verdad* (Madrid: BAC, 2019); Alain Thomasset, SJ, *Interpréter et agir: Jalons pour une éthique chrétienne* (Paris: Cerf, 2011); Thomasset, "La conscience morale et les questions posées par les documents récents du magistère romain," *Revue d'Éthique et de Théologie Morale*, no. 293 (2017): 25–42; Karl-Wilhelm Merks, *Theologische Fundamentalethik* (Freiburg: Herder, 2020); and Maurizio Chiodi, *Amore, dono e giustizia: Teologia e filosofia sulla traccia del pensiero di Paul Ricoeur* (Milan: Glossa, 2011); Chiodi, *Teologia morale fondamentale*, vol. 1 (Brescia: Queriniana, 2018); and Chiodi, *Norma, coscienza e discernimento: Testo e contest del capitol VIII di "Amoris Laetitia"* (Cinsiello Balsamo: Edizione San Paolo, 2018). Chiodi is indebted to Ricoeur's view of conscience, which I discussed above in relation to Heidegger. Thomasset, too, pays significant attention to Ricoeur's "ethic of responsibility." Chapter 7 of *Interpréter et agir* bears the title, "La conscience, la liberté et la loi: Le jugement moral en situation." In this chapter, Thomasset rehearses the probabilist controversies and draws upon the magisterial documents of Vatican II and Pope John Paul II, as well as such works as Xavier Thévenot, *Repères éthiques pour un monde nouveau*

(Paris: Salvator, 1982); Paul Valadier, Éloge de la conscience (Paris: Esprit, 1994); and Théodule Rey-Mermet, *Conscience et liberté* (Paris: Nouvelle Cité, 1990). The Thomasset affirms universal principles as well as particular moral norms, while observing that conscience must take account of "the *singular* and unique situation in which I find myself" (*Interpréter et agir*, 282), in which there will be tensions that cannot be resolved by the application of a moral law. He states: "the conscience is the conductor, the *referee*, which seeks to humanize life, evaluates the goods in play, and finally decides what is best in a given situation" (283). Thomasset's twenty-eight-page chapter on conscience is followed by a thirty-three-page chapter on the virtues, with three pages devoted to the theological and moral virtues. See also, for the impact of Ricoeur, Thomas Kopfensteiner's essay "The Metaphorical Structure of Normativity," *Theological Studies* 58 (1997): 331–46.

218. Twenty-first-century moral theologians who share McCormick's conscience-centered perspective generally see no need to combine it with proportionalism or consequentialism (or with "autonomous ethics"); instead they focus upon responsible freedom and upon combatting structural sins. See James F. Keenan, SJ, *A History of Catholic Moral Theology in the Twentieth Century: From Confessing Sins to Liberating Consciences* (New York: Continuum, 2010), 158, 181. Keenan comments: "Proportionalism was basically a transitional phase in Catholic theological ethics. In trying to establish a method for moral judgment as an alternative to the moral manuals, proportionalism was simply the logic of the moral manuals without the overriding absolute moral norms" (*Catholic Moral Theology*, 158).

219. McCormick, "Moral Theology since Vatican II," 21. Hereafter, page references from this work will be given in parentheses in the text.

220. Richard A. McCormick, SJ, "Fundamental Freedom Revisited," in *The Critical Calling: Reflections on Moral Dilemmas since Vatican II* (Washington, DC: Georgetown University Press, 1989), 188.

221. McCormick, "Fundamental Freedom Revisited," 173. As McCormick notes, this transcendental anthropology is Rahner's, and "a rich literature has developed around this anthropology. Furthermore, it is all but taken for granted in most theological circles. This can be seen in its use by such authors as Josef Fuchs, Bernard Häring, George Lobo, Franz Böckle, Timothy O'Connell, Bruno Schüller and a host of others" (174). He also examines the postconciliar conscience-centered work of George Lobo, SJ, *Guide to Christian Living* (Westminster, MD: Christian Classics, 1984). See also such writings as Franz Böckle, *Fundamental Concepts of Moral Theology* (New York: Paulist, 1968); Bruno Schüller, SJ, *Gesetz und Freiheit* (Düsseldorf: Patmos, 1966); and Schüller, *Wholly Human: Essays on the Theory and Language of Morality*, trans. Peter Heinegg (Washington, DC: Georgetown University Press, 1986).

222. According to McCormick, the person who is God-oriented in his or her fundamental option is gradually unfolding in Christlike discipleship, through the Spirit's power, even if at present the person is committing grave sins—so long as the fundamental option remains in place. For McCormick, this is a tremendously liberating moral vision that allows for continual conversion without demanding perfection (or even the stopping of sin) yet. McCormick argues that the fundamental option cannot be altered by actions that the culture does not regard as gravely sinful. In modern culture, this takes care of culpability for almost all sexual sins, just as in other cultures it takes care of other prevalent sins. For example, I note that in cultures where the physical abuse

of wives is not considered serious—or the owning of slaves is not considered serious—these actions could be freely done without changing one's fundamental option at all, even if the mature and fully converted person will presumably come to avoid them. The key is whether in a particular action one has made, at the core of one's freedom, a fully conscious decision to reject God and to choose the creature over God. If not, then one remains in union with Christ. Thus, McCormick agrees that there can be "*sins* that destroy charity," but it is hard to do ("Fundamental Freedom Revisited," 180). The problem with McCormick's approach—which echoes that of Fuchs and Häring—consists not in the notion of continual conversion, the growth in the Christian moral life, or the possibility of invincible ignorance in certain cultures regarding grave sins. Rather, the problem lies deeper, in the critique of accessible and authoritative natural and divine law—a critique that in fact turns conscience into subjective sovereignty—as well as in the loss of the virtues, the reduction of the moral life to the dynamisms of transcendental freedom, and the separation of Christian moral theology from scriptural teaching.

223. Rahner, "Conscience," 12.

224. Fuchs, "Question Addressed to Conscience," 225.

225. Graham, *Josef Fuchs on Natural Law*, 148. I note the concerns of Russell Hittinger: "Fuchs contends: 'When in fact, nature-creation does speak to us, it tells us only what it is and how it functions on its own. In other words, the Creator shows us what is divinely willed to exist, and how it functions, but not how the Creator wills the human being qua person to use this existing reality.' Fuchs goes on to assert: 'Neither the Hebrew Bible nor the New Testament produces statements that are independent of culture and thus universal and valid for all time; nor can these statements be given by the church or its magisterium. Rather, it is the task of human beings—of the various persons who have been given the requisite intellectual capacity—to investigate what can and must count as a conviction about these responsibilities.' In other words, God creates, but he gives no operating instructions. . . . While God creates, he does not govern the human mind. The human mind is a merely natural light, to which there corresponds a merely natural jurisdiction over ethics. In its work of discovering moral norms, the mind discovers the contextual proportions of good and evil, case by case as it were. Although Fuchs struggles to avoid the implication, it would seem that a general statute of positive law could never concretely bind human conscience, because it could never adequately measure the proportions of good and evil across cases and contexts. . . . For the older tradition, there is a clear distinction between the mind's *discovering* or discerning a norm and the being or *cause* of the norm. The human mind can go on to make new rules because it is first ruled. This, in essence, is the doctrine of participation as applied to natural law. Natural law designates for Fuchs, however, the human power to make moral judgments, not any moral norm regulating that power—at least no norm extrinsic to the operations of the mind." Hittinger, *The First Grace: Rediscovering the Natural Law in a Post-Christian World* (Wilmington, DE: ISI, 2003), 22–24, citing Fuchs, *Moral Demands and Personal Obligations*, trans. Brian McNeil (Washington, DC: Georgetown University Press, 1993), 55, 100.

226. Robert Barron, *Letter to a Suffering Church: A Bishop Speaks on the Sexual Abuse Crisis* (Park Ridge, IL: Word on Fire, 2019), 88.

227. Barron, *Letter to a Suffering Church*, 92.

228. See also Jacques Maritain's previously unpublished 1949 lectures, *La loi na-*

turelle ou loi non écrite. For a misleading attack upon Maritain's natural law teaching, see John R. T. Lamont, "Conscience, Freedom, Rights: Idols of the Enlightenment Religion," *Thomist* 73 (2009): 227–29.

229. See Hannah Arendt, *The Human Condition*, 2nd ed. (Chicago: University of Chicago Press, 2018); Alasdair MacIntyre, *Dependent Rational Animals: Why Human Beings Need the Virtues* (Chicago: Open Court, 1999). See also more recent books such as Pierre Manent, *Natural Law and Human Rights: Toward a Recovery of Practical Reason*, trans. Ralph C. Hancock (Notre Dame: University of Notre Dame Press, 2020); Hadley Arkes, *Constitutional Illusions and Anchoring Truths: The Touchstone of the Natural Law* (Cambridge: Cambridge University Press, 2010); and Paulinus Ikechukwu Odozor, CSSp, *Morality Truly Christian, Truly African: Foundational, Methodological, and Theological Considerations* (Notre Dame: University of Notre Dame Press, 2014). I note that the late Lúcás Chan, SJ's *Biblical Ethics in the 21st Century: Developments, Emerging Consensus, and Future Directions* (New York: Paulist, 2013) is moving in the right direction, though in an introductory way that does not enable him to go deeply into either biblical ethics or virtue ethics. In addition, see the essays collected in John Berkman and William C. Mattison III, eds., *Searching for a Universal Ethic: Multidisciplinary, Ecumenical, and Interfaith Responses to the Catholic Natural Law Tradition* (Grand Rapids, MI: Eerdmans, 2014). For a brief sketch of the debate about natural law since the 1950s—much too brief, but still instructive regarding the current situation—see Éric Gaziaux, "La loi naturelle: Quelques repères historiques et interrogations contemporaines," *Revue d'Éthique et de Théologie Morale*, no. 293 (2017): 53–66.

230. Pope Benedict XVI, "Address of His Holiness Benedict XVI to Members of the International Theological Commission," October 5, 2007, available at www.vatican.va.

231. Ratzinger, "Conscience and Truth," 17.

232. Ratzinger, "Conscience and Truth," 17.

233. Peter Casarella, "Culture and Conscience in the Thought of Joseph Ratzinger/Pope Benedict XVI," in *Explorations in the Theology of Benedict XVI*, ed. John C. Cavadini (Notre Dame: University of Notre Dame Press, 2012), 82.

Conclusion

1. See Romanus Cessario, OP, *Introduction to Moral Theology* (Washington, DC: Catholic University of America Press, 2001), 204–5.

2. Exponents of Christian versions of these philosophies sometimes assumed themselves to be at odds with Thomism, but in fact this is not the case—so long as philosophical realism about God and human nature is retained, as, unfortunately, it often was not. See, for example, Alasdair MacIntyre, *Edith Stein: A Philosophical Prologue, 1913–1922* (Lanham, MD: Rowman & Littlefield, 2006), especially chapter 17; Thomas Petri, OP, *Aquinas and the Theology of the Body: The Thomistic Foundations of John Paul II's Anthropology* (Washington, DC: Catholic University of America Press, 2016); and Robert Spaemann, *Persons: The Difference between "Someone" and "Something,"* trans. Oliver O'Donovan (Oxford: Oxford University Press, 2006). See also the early existentialist and personalist Christian moral theology of Louis Janssens in *Personne et société: Théories actuelles et essai doctrinal* (Gembloux: Duculot, 1939), although Janssens's reading of

Aquinas was mistaken in significant ways and he was led to adopt a proportionalist moral position, allied with the postconciliar conscience-centered morality of Fuchs and Häring. For Janssens's lengthiest treatment of conscience, see his 1965 book *Freedom of Conscience and Religious Freedom*, trans. Brother Lorenzo, CFX (Staten Island, NY: Alba House, 1965). See Dolores L. Christie, *Adequately Considered: An American Perspective on Louis Janssens' Personalist Morals* (Louvain: Peeters, 1990); as well as the later Janssens, "Personalism in Moral Theology," in *Moral Theology: Challenges for the Future; Essays in Honor of Richard A. McCormick*, ed. Charles E. Curran (New York: Paulist, 1990), 94–107.

3. Edward Baring, *Converts to the Real: Catholicism and the Making of Continental Philosophy* (Cambridge, MA: Harvard University Press, 2019), 164. Baring comments insightfully: "Maritain hoped to affirm the wonder of existing reality, which had attracted [Gabriel] Marcel, without succumbing to what he saw as Marcel's irrationalism. Being, for Maritain, was a mystery, infinitely rich and ripe with new insights. But it was still open to human understanding" (164).

4. See also, more broadly, Baring, *Converts to the Real*, 152, with reference to the soirée that Gabriel Marcel hosted regularly beginning in May 1932 and whose first session was devoted to Jaspers's *Philosophy*: "First in Paris and later elsewhere in Europe, non-Thomist [Catholic] thinkers came to articulate their relationship to Catholic orthodoxy by drawing on the work of the German Karl Jaspers and declaring themselves existentialists." Baring describes the spread of existential Thomism: "Maritain's work was translated widely, with partisans in Germany, Italy, and Poland, while [Etienne] Gilson's *Thomism* book was read across Europe and the Americas. In particular, the Odzrodzenie (Renaissance) group in Lublin, Poland, led by Stefan Wyszynski, helped bring Maritain and Gilson's ideas to Eastern Europe, where a decade later they would be picked up by Karol Wojtyla" (171). He adds: "To explain the proliferation of existential Thomism in this period, however, it is not necessary to appeal to the influence of Gilson and Maritain. Existential philosophy responded to broader trends within neo-scholasticism, and in the 1930s there were many articles across Europe independently presenting Thomism in this way. In the Netherlands in 1936 the Jesuit Henricus Robbers argued that Thomism was a philosophy 'of reality, of being. If any vision has the right to the name existential [*existentieel*], it is the Aristotelian-Thomistic.' For the same reason, the German Redemptorist Theodor Droege felt able to claim in the 1938 edition of *Divus Thomas* that Aquinas's *Summa theologica* was 'the best ideal of a Catholic *Existenzphilosophie*.' In Italy, several commentators, including Cornelio Fabro, made a similar argument" (171; second set of brackets in the original). In this passage, Baring cites Henricus Robbers, SJ, "De Beteekenis van het Neo-Thomisme voor het hedendaagsche katholieke denkleven," *Synthese* 1 (1936): 377–82; and Theodor Droege, CSsR, "Die Existenz-Philosophie Martin Heideggers," *Divus Thomas* 16 (1938): 265–94, 371–92, respectively.

5. David F. Kelly, "Karl Rahner and Genetic Engineering: The Use of Theological Principles in Moral Analysis," *Philosophy and Theology* 9 (1995): 178, with reference to Ronald Modras, "Implications of Rahner's Anthropology for Fundamental Moral Theology," *Horizons* 12 (1984): 70–90. Kelly notes that by contrast to Rahner's early-1960s "On the Question of a Formal Existential Ethics"—which already focused on the person's existential situation—his 1977 "On Bad Arguments in Moral Theology," originally published in a festschrift for Bernard Häring, is "more ready . . . to argue against a

facile acceptance of universal norms," though Rahner is consistent in emphasizing "the historicity of moral principles, and their grounding in existential human experience" ("Karl Rahner and Genetic Engineering," 179). See Karl Rahner, SJ, "On the Question of a Formal Existential Ethics," in *Man in the Church*, trans. Karl-H. Kruger, vol. 2 of *Theological Investigations* (Baltimore, MD: Helicon, 1963); and Rahner, "On Bad Arguments in Moral Theology," in *God and Revelation*, trans. Edward Quinn, vol. 18 of *Theological Investigations* (New York: Crossroad, 1983), 74–85.

6. For a recent example of this approach, see Jochen Sautenmeister, *Identität und Authentizität. Studien zur normativen Logik personaler Orientierung* (Freiburg im Breisgau: Herder, 2013).

7. John Mahoney, SJ, *The Making of Moral Theology: A Study of the Roman Catholic Tradition* (Oxford: Oxford University Press, 1987), 309. For discussion, arguing that Mahoney was concerned not only with deconstructing the Catholic past (manualism) but also with "promoting the relevance of the Holy Spirit for moral theology," see James F. Keenan, SJ, *A History of Catholic Moral Theology in the Twentieth Century: From Confessing Sins to Liberating Consciences* (New York: Continuum, 2010), 50–51; as well as Keenan, "John Mahoney's *The Making of Moral Theology*," in *The Oxford Handbook of Theological Ethics*, ed. Gilbert Meilaender and William Werpehowski (Oxford: Oxford University Press, 2005), 503–19. For background, see Mahoney's *Seeking the Spirit: Essays in Moral and Pastoral Theology* (London: Sheed and Ward, 1981).

8. Mahoney, *Making of Moral Theology*, 340.

9. Mahoney, *Making of Moral Theology*, 341, citing *Gaudium et Spes* §16. See also John Mahoney, SJ, "Conscience, Discernment and Prophecy in Moral Decision Making," in *Riding Time Like a River: The Catholic Moral Tradition since Vatican II*, ed. William O'Brien (Washington, DC: Georgetown University Press, 1993), 81–97.

10. John A. Gallagher, in his chapter from *Time Past, Time Future* entitled "The Impact of Moral Theology on Post Vatican II Theological Developments," examines solely Bernard Häring, Karl Rahner, Bruno Schüller, Josef Fuchs, Richard McCormick, and Charles Curran. This demonstrates my point about the dominance of this strand of postconciliar Catholic moral theology. But Gallagher also argues, unpersuasively in my view: "Although there are affinities in Curran's writings to the positions taken by Häring, and in Fuchs and McCormick to the theology of Rahner, these authors do not in any way constitute a new school of Catholic theology. On the contrary, they exemplify the plurality of theologies which form the contemporary Catholic environment." Gallagher, *Time Past, Time Future: An Historical Study of Catholic Moral Theology* (Mahwah, NJ: Paulist, 1990), 203.

11. For his work in biblical ethics and virtue theory, see, for example, James F. Keenan, SJ, *Virtue Ethics* (New York: Sheed and Ward, 1996); and Daniel J. Harrington, SJ, and James F. Keenan, SJ, *Paul and Virtue Ethics: Building Bridges between New Testament Studies and Moral Theology* (Lanham, MD: Rowman & Littlefield, 2010). For the full scope of Keenan's project, see Keenan, ed., *Catholic Theological Ethics Past, Present, and Future: The Trento Conference* (Maryknoll, NY: Orbis, 2011). For discussion, see David Cloutier, "Catholic Moral Theology: Piecing Together a Discipline in Pieces," *Modern Theology* 29 (2013): 381–90.

12. See, for example, Maurizio Chiodi, *Teologia morale fondamentale*, vol. 1 (Brescia: Queriniana, 2018).

13. See Servais Pinckaers, OP, "An Encyclical for the Future: *Veritatis splendor*," in *"Veritatis Splendor" and the Renewal of Moral Theology*, ed. J. A. Di Noia, OP, and Romanus Cessario, OP (Chicago: Scepter, 1999), 11–71; and Pinckaers, "Scripture and the Renewal of Moral Theology: The *Catechism* and *Veritatis Splendor*," trans. Mary Thomas Noble, OP, in *The Pinckaers Reader: Renewing Thomistic Moral Theology*, ed. John Berkman and Craig Steven Titus (Washington, DC: Catholic University of America Press, 2005), 46–63. See also Michael Dauphinais, "The Splendor and Gift of the Christian Moral Life: *Veritatis Splendor* at Twenty-Five," *Nova et Vetera* 16 (2018): 1261–312.

14. Keenan, *History of Catholic Moral Theology*, 128. Keenan's position echoes that of Mary Elsbernd, "The Reinterpretation of *Gaudium et Spes* in *Veritatis Splendor*," *Horizons* 29, no. 2 (2002): 225–39. Along these lines, see also Bernard Häring, CSsR, "A Distrust that Wounds," in *Considering "Veritatis Splendor*," ed. John Wilkins (Cleveland, OH: Pilgrim, 1994), 9–13; and Häring, *My Hope for the Church: Critical Encouragement for the Twenty-First Century*, trans. Peter Heinegg (Liguori, MO: Liguori, 1999). For discussion of conscience according to *Gaudium et Spes*, various ecclesiastical responses to *Humanae Vitae*, the *Catechism of the Catholic Church*, and various encyclicals of Pope John Paul II, see Luc-Thomas Somme, OP, "La conscience morale à Vatican II et dans le Magistère postérieur," *Revue Thomiste* 110 (2010): 217–40. Somme argues that *Veritatis Splendor* upholds the teaching of *Gaudium et Spes* §16 while taking a different tone that wards off misreadings of the conciliar text.

15. Bernard Häring, *Free and Faithful in Christ*, vol. 1, *General Moral Theology* (New York: Crossroad, 1984), 292.

16. Häring, *Free and Faithful in Christ*, 293.

17. James F. Keenan, SJ, "Redeeming Conscience," *Theological Studies* 76 (2015): 146. Keenan directs attention to Klaus Demmer, MSC, *Living the Truth: A Theory of Action*, trans. Brian McNeil (Washington, DC: Georgetown University Press, 2010), in which Demmer argues: "Norms concern segments of our varied lives, and they make orientation a realistic possibility. At the same time, they create a freedom that must be respected—but that brings about a 'surplus' that goes beyond what can be foreseen by norms. . . . Persons accept existing norms and make them their own; at the same time, they keep these norms in motion. A person who grows into an ethical personality in the course of his life history brings with him a 'surplus' of insight and freedom that leaves its traces upon the customary understanding of norms. This is done with respect and tolerance, for what is born of higher insight and freedom can in turn lead only to higher insight and freedom" (39–40). See also Demmer, *Shaping the Moral Life: An Approach to Moral Theology*, ed. James F. Keenan, SJ, trans. Roberto Dell'Oro (Washington, DC: Georgetown University Press, 2000), especially its third chapter, "The Decisive Factor: Toward a Theology of Conscience." Here Demmer remarks about the probabilist system that its purpose "was simply to provide help in the decision-making process without pretending to question the objectivity of moral norms" (18–19). While defending the existence of moral norms, he adds: "A purely legalistic conscience that concentrates on the fulfillment of norms cannot suffice. Indeed, a notion of morality defined by the pure observance of preformulated norms would entirely miss the present challenge. Such a paradigm is too short-sighted; it cannot possibly grasp the fullness of reality, with all its surprises. On the contrary, the individual should become able to recognize the meaning of a norm. What is needed is intelligent obedience and the gift of discernment" (20).

18. Keenan, "Redeeming Conscience," 130.

19. Keenan, "Redeeming Conscience," 131. I note that in its 2014 *"Sensus fidei* in the Life of the Church,"* available at www.vatican.va, the International Theological Commission does not mention conscience—and for good reason. See also Robert Spaemann, "Conscience and Responsibility in Christian Ethics," in *Crisis of Conscience: Philosophers and Theologians Analyze Our Growing Inability to Discern Right from Wrong,* ed. John M. Haas (New York: Crossroad, 1996), 129; and Janet E. Smith, "The *Sensus fidelium* and *Humanae Vitae,"* in *Why "Humanae Vitae" Is Still Right,* ed. Janet E. Smith (San Francisco: Ignatius, 2018), 264–94.

20. Keenan, "Redeeming Conscience," 131.

21. Keenan, "Redeeming Conscience," 131–33. See also H. Richard Niebuhr's reflections on the "social understanding of *conscience"* in his *The Responsible Self: An Essay in Christian Moral Philosophy* (Louisville, KY: Westminster John Knox, 1999), 71–79 (quotation from 76).

22. Keenan, "Redeeming Conscience," 135, 140. Keenan argues that conscience in Europe has made this leap, whereas Americans have been stuck with individualistic conscience that has failed to own up to "our history of slavery and our national willfulness to accommodate oppressive racism" (135). The result, he imagines, is that large sectors of Americans condone racism: "With diminished capacity the Christian conscience has accommodated a racism that now engenders a paralysis as we face critical immigration issues" (135). The contrast between Europe and the United States here is simplistic, but the main point is to critique American ("conservative") consciences—supposedly by contrast to European consciences—as "blind, weak, and self-centered" and thus in need of "redeeming" (136). See also Rahner's "logic of existential decision," "sustained by a responsibility before God and before man's dignity in justice and love" (*Shape of the Church to Come,* 69).

23. Margaret A. Farley, RSM, *Just Love: A Framework for Christian Sexual Ethics* (New York: Continuum, 2006), 195. See also Mark Graham, *Josef Fuchs on Natural Law* (Washington, DC: Georgetown University Press, 2002), 211; Gerard Mannion, "Magisterium, Margaret Farley, and the Ecclesial Role of Feminist Moral Theology: Discerning the *Ecclesia Discens* Today," in *Feminist Catholic Theological Ethics,* ed. Linda Hogan and A. E. Orobator (Maryknoll, NY: Orbis, 2014), 77–92; as well as the essays in Maura A. Ryan and Brian F. Linnane, eds., *A Just and True Love: Feminism at the Frontiers of Theological Ethics; Essays in Honor of Margaret A. Farley* (Notre Dame: University of Notre Dame Press, 2007).

24. Keenan, *History of Catholic Moral Theology,* 222.

25. Keenan, *History of Catholic Moral Theology,* 178.

26. For Mahoney, the doctrine of evolution not only does away with the notion that Christ's cross redeems us from sin—because there is no original sin or fallen "concupiscence" to be redeemed from—but also frees human sexuality to move beyond male-female marital relationships to what he euphemistically calls "other forms of relationships between the sexes that express and are influenced by their mutual interest and attraction." Mahoney, *Christianity in Evolution: An Exploration* (Washington, DC: Georgetown University Press, 2011), 150. See also Stephen J. Pope, *Human Evolution and Christian Ethics* (Cambridge: Cambridge University Press, 2007).

27. Rahner, *Shape of the Church to Come,* 65.

28. Rahner, *Shape of the Church to Come*, 65. For discussion, see James F. Bresnahan, "Rahner's Ethics: Critical Natural Law in Relation to Contemporary Ethical Methodology," *Journal of Religion* 56 (1976): 39–40: "[Rahner's] metaphysical answer to the question of the normatively human treats what traditional Thomism calls 'constitutive principles of being'—such as 'essence' or 'nature' in natural law—differently than do the larger number of exponents of that tradition. It is the self-conscious 'spirit in the world,' the self-disposing 'person in the world,' or subjectivity, in a Kantian sense, that one seeks to subject to explanatory understanding by talk of 'constitutive principles of being.' While such a project, therefore, continues to employ traditional metaphysical categories, it claims that these have a fuller, explicitly subjective, meaning because Kant's critical method has been pushed beyond Kant's own use of it. To locate the conditions of possibility of the content (*Begriff*) of object-oriented thinking and willing was not sufficient; the completion of Kant's 'turn to the subject' is found by asking after the conditions of possibility of object-oriented thinking and the deciding activity of a self or subject precisely as performance (*Vollzug*). This founds a metaphysics which is also explicitly an anthropology—thus, in a sense, derived from Heidegger, an 'ontology.'" Rahner distinguishes between "ontic" and "ontological" (the latter being transcendental metaphysics, the former being traditional metaphysics). See also Karl Rahner, SJ, "Reflections on Methodology in Theology," in *Confrontations 1*, trans. David Bourke, vol. 11 of *Theological Investigations* (New York: Seabury, 1974), 87–89.

29. Rahner, *Shape of the Church to Come*, 65. According to many thinkers today, such as Susannah Cornwall in her *Controversies in Queer Theology*, it is axiomatic that "gender must be seen as provisional or fluid." Cornwall, *Controversies in Queer Theology* (London: SCM, 2011), 236.

30. James F. Keenan, SJ, "Natural Law Debates and the Forces of Nature," in *Contemplating the Future of Moral Theology: Essays in Honor of Brian V. Johnstone, C.Ss.R.*, ed. Robert C. Koerpel and Vimal Tirimanna, CSsR (Eugene, OR: Pickwick, 2017), 72. Keenan is drawing upon Bernard Lonergan, SJ, "Transition from a Classicist World View to Historical Mindedness," in *A Second Collection*, ed. William Ryan and Bernard Tyrrell (Philadelphia: Westminster, 1975), 1–9. Keenan details his position: "Historical-minded theologians look at the world and at truth as constantly emerging. They argue that we are learning more, not only about the world, but about ourselves. As subjects we are affected by history: we become hopefully the people whom we are called to become. . . . Contrary to their detractors, historicists do not argue that truth is constructed or manufactured; rather truth is 'discovered' in history by historical persons. Our grasp on truth is evolving and we need to update or modify our understandings of it. Truth has its objectivity, but it is only gradually grasped by us in our judgment over time, through experience, and with maturity. Our grasp of truth, then, is always open to reform" ("Natural Law Debates," 74).

31. Harrington and Keenan, *Paul and Virtue Ethics*, 67. This section comes from chapter 6, which was written by Keenan.

32. Harrington and Keenan, *Paul and Virtue Ethics*, 70.

33. Harrington and Keenan, *Paul and Virtue Ethics*, 70.

34. James F. Keenan, SJ, "To Follow and to Form over Time: A Phenomenology of Conscience," in *Conscience and Catholicism: Rights, Responsibilities, and Institutional Responses*, ed. David E. DeCosse and Kristin E. Heyer (Maryknoll, NY: Orbis, 2015), 2.

35. Keenan, "To Follow and to Form," 12.

36. For the view that this renewal of conscience was a great achievement of the Council, see Michael G. Lawler and Todd A. Salzman, "*Gaudium et Spes* and *Dignitatis Humanae* on Conscience: A Forgotten Concept of Vatican II?," *Louvain Studies* 40 (2017): 153–69. I disagree with Lawler and Salzman that "the emphasis in *Gaudium et Spes* (and *Dignitatis Humanae*) is on the authority and dignity of conscience, not on the authority and dignity of the norm" (159). This opposition is unhelpful, and it indicates the need for locating conscience more firmly within a virtue framework. Drawing upon Häring and Fuchs, Lawler and Salzman state: "Church doctrine is at the service of women and men in their sincere conscience search for goodness, truth, and Christian wholeness; conscience is not at the service of doctrine" (161). Solemn doctrine, however, includes authoritative moral doctrine that forms Christian conscience rather than first being judged by Christian conscience—a point that need not cause problems for rightly understood religious freedom or dialogue with the world.

37. Among contemporary Catholics, see also Pierre Manent, *Natural Law and Human Rights: Toward a Recovery of Practical Reason*, trans. Ralph C. Hancock (Notre Dame: University of Notre Dame Press, 2020). In Manent's view, Machiavelli and Luther, despite their massive differences, agree on the following: "Since the *nature* of the human being or of the Christian cannot really be improved or made more perfect, we can only dare radically to change the *condition* of the human being or of the Christian, and this by a supremely audacious gesture that removes them from their practical condition or lifts them above it" (41). For Manent as for Hütter, it is necessary to return to an acceptation of conscience in light of natural law and virtuous practical reason. For Manent, this means recovering not so much a sense of eternal law (though Manent broadly affirms Aquinas's approach to law, including eternal law), but of human nature, practical reason ordered to the common good, and command and obedience in light of the "archic" character of action (see 99, 106–13, 119–29). Manent adds that the legalization of homosexual marriage—rejecting marriage's grounding in "the natural difference of sexes or the natural difference of generations"—constitutes a decisive rejection of both nature and law as "the rule and measure of action" (123).

38. Reinhard Hütter, *Bound to Be Free: Evangelical Catholic Engagements in Ecclesiology, Ethics, and Ecumenism* (Grand Rapids, MI: Eerdmans, 2004), 149.

39. Hütter, *Bound to Be Free*, 150.

40. Reinhard Hütter, *Dust Bound for Heaven: Explorations in the Theology of Thomas Aquinas* (Grand Rapids, MI: Eerdmans, 2012), 77.

41. Hütter, *Dust Bound for Heaven*, 93.

42. Reinhard Hütter, *Bound for Beatitude: A Thomistic Study in Eschatology and Ethics* (Washington, DC: Catholic University of America Press, 2019).

43. Hütter, *Bound for Beatitude*, 27. See also the reflections of Michel Nodé-Langlois, "Science et conscience," *Revue Thomiste* 111 (2011): 583–616. Nodé-Langlois engages Kant, Nietzsche, and Heidegger at length.

44. Hütter, *Bound for Beatitude*, 150. Hütter's discussion of grace-integralism, grace-extrinsicism, and the varieties of the "postmetaphysical exception" (145), including postliberalism and nihilism, makes for necessary reading.

45. Hütter, *Bound for Beatitude*, 153.

46. Hütter, *Bound for Beatitude*, 153.

47. See also Mark McGovern, "Synderesis: A Key to Understanding Natural Law in Aquinas," in *Freedom, Virtue, and the Common Good*, ed. Curtis L. Hancock and Anthony O. Simon (Mishawaka, IN: American Maritain Association, 1995), 104–24.

48. Hütter, *Bound for Beatitude*, 162. Gerald P. McKenny describes something similar when, after a brief but accurate summary of Aquinas on conscience, he turns to Kant: "In Kant, then, the reason which conscience commands has ceased to be reason which participates in the law of a God who exists apart from the subject. In terms which Karl Barth applied to a parallel development in the transition from the Protestant Reformers to orthodoxy and rationalism, accountability to God is on the way to becoming a dramatization and (with the demise of Kant's notion of God as a rational moral idea) mythologization of our relation to a law that is really within ourselves. . . . Standing at the end of this process, Paul Ricoeur can refer to conscience as 'surely the most internalized expression of the responding self' (Ricoeur 1995: 271). At this point the modern subject reigns, and the very notion of answerability is threatened." McKenny, "Responsibility," in *The Oxford Handbook of Theological Ethics*, ed. Gilbert Meilaender and William Werpehowski (Oxford: Oxford University Press, 2005), 246; citing Ricoeur, "The Summoned Subject in the School of the Narratives of the Prophetic Vocation," in *Figuring the Sacred* (Minneapolis: Fortress, 1995), 271. For McKenny, Hütter's argument in favor of returning to Aquinas on conscience (and prudence) would inevitably be mistaken because Aquinas, living as he did prior to Kantian subjectivity, lacked the understanding of what we mean today by "responsibility." Instead, McKenny favors the positions of Bonhoeffer and Barth, on the grounds that in their ethics the concept of "responsibility" serves "to limit the ambitions and self-assertion of the modern moral subject" ("Responsibility," 252).

49. Hütter is aware of the response that this claim will elicit. Bresnahan names the response well when, in 1976, he argues from a Rahnerian perspective that what is needed for true "natural law" is "a striving after ever greater opening out of one's own viewpoint to the moral exigencies experienced by contemporary human beings. Today, an effort at responsible decision means encountering moral dilemma repeatedly and in unexpected forms within a perceptibly evolving world" ("Rahner's Ethics," 43). This is Keenan's position as well, as we saw. Hütter rejects it on the grounds that it does not conform with what conscience actually is (in the light of synderesis) and that it inevitably reduces to sovereign subjectivity, obstructing the divine moral commandments given in Scripture and tradition. I note that Bresnahan still speaks of "God's sovereign Word" and "the special categories elaborated by authoritative Christian doctrinal tradition and the theology which has surrounded it" ("Rahner's Ethics," 44).

50. Hütter, *Bound for Beatitude*, 169.

51. Hütter, *Bound for Beatitude*, 169–70.

52. Hütter, *Bound for Beatitude*, 172. See also Friedrich Nietzsche's "'Guilt,' 'Bad Conscience,' and the Like," in *On the Genealogy of Morals*, trans. Walter Kaufmann and R. J. Hollingdale (New York: Vintage, 1989), 57–96. Published with *Ecce Homo*, ed. and trans. Walter Kaufmann. Hütter sums up Nietzsche's essay: "This is the counterfeit of conscience pursued with consistency. As the best form of defense is attack, it is a given that Nietzsche should identify the residual evidence of theonomic conscience as bad conscience and should attempt to discard it by way of a naturalist genealogy" (Hütter, *John Henry Newman*, 28).

53. Hütter, *Bound for Beatitude*, 172. On this point, Hütter cites Alasdair MacIntyre's *Three Rival Versions of Moral Enquiry: Encyclopaedia, Genealogy, and Tradition* (Notre Dame: University of Notre Dame Press, 1990), 194. Hütter is well aware of the various moral theories that have sought to replace theocentric, teleological ethics. None of them has borne the test of time well. He remarks, "Modern deontology, consequentialism, and contractarianism are moral theories that emerge in the wake of the anthropocentric turn. As the history of modernity has demonstrated, these moral theories turned out to be utterly unfit to contain the power of subjective sovereignty that the anthropocentric turn unleashed. Aquinas's metaphysics of the good with its special emphasis on *synderesis*, natural law, and the virtue of prudence advances a compelling account of why this is the case and thereby offers a powerful analytic device that allows us accurately to gauge the profoundly problematic implications of the anthropocentric turn for moral theory and especially for the moral life" (*Bound for Beatitude*, 173). Note that Hütter is not here romanticizing an earlier period in the history of moral action. He is well aware that humans in every generation have been sinners. The answer to this problem, he points out, is not a moral theory but rather is Christ himself, acting through his Spirit (although a good moral theory can help).

54. Hütter, *Bound for Beatitude*, 174.

55. Hütter, *Bound for Beatitude*, 174. As Hütter observes, it follows that (because of who Christ is and what he does, not least in sending forth the Spirit) faith, hope, and charity are thereby necessary for prudence and conscience to be effective. Hütter has also examined conscience in *John Henry Newman*. According to Newman, conscience communicates to us moral truth; obedience to conscience is not a matter of freeing us from doing something but rather a matter of doing precisely the duty (in accord with moral truth) that conscience commands. For Newman, as Hütter says, "any proper understanding of conscience must first and foremost articulate the *theonomic nature of conscience*, that is, its grounding in the divine law. Conscience is not simply a human faculty. It is constituted by the eternal law, the divine wisdom communicated to the human intellect" (*John Henry Newman*, 24–25). Newman draws upon Augustine and Aquinas—specifically their understanding of eternal law, natural law, and conscience— to elucidate his own viewpoint.

56. Elsewhere Keenan, with his coauthor Peter Black, CSsR, makes the point that given that "we moral theologians look for moral truth in the person, we need to see ourselves as constitutively related as well. In particular we are related to all in the Church, especially to those who have developed, in their service to the magisterium, a metaphysics of morals that looks too much like the premises of the moral manuals. As ministers of reconciliation, we moral theologians must recall our ecclesial vocation in which we do not at all compromise our search for moral truth, but where we invite into professional dialogue those colleagues who have left our enterprise. Now in the jubilee of reconciliation, we can only understand well the nature of moral truth if we engage those others, trained with us, who look more for consistency with previous teachings than to the critical tradition itself. By making the effort to be reconciled with them, we might better understand indeed how relational the human being is and can be." Black and Keenan, "The Evolving Self-Understanding of the Moral Theologian: 1900–2000," *Studia Moralia* 39 (2001): 325–26. For Keenan and Black, the scholars who were "trained with us" but have "left our enterprise"—who are overly indebted to "the premises of the moral manuals"

and who have thereby shown themselves (despite their assertion of orthodoxy) to be, as the manualists were, "less traditional, less orthodox and less theological" (324)—are the moral theologians who contributed to or affirmed Pope John Paul II's *Veritatis Splendor*, such as Pinckaers. It is clear that, in seeking reconciliation, Keenan and Black feel free to lodge sharp criticisms. These criticisms are demonstrably inaccurate.

57. Jean-Pascal Gay, *Morales in conflit: Théologie et polémique au Grand Siècle (1640–1700)* (Paris: Cerf, 2011), 844.

58. Hütter, *John Henry Newman*, 84.

59. Hütter, *John Henry Newman*, 84.

60. Hütter, *John Henry Newman*, 84.

61. Of course, the solution is not to ignore conscience altogether. Conscience merits the important role that it has in the New Testament, integrated with Christian prudence and located within the whole Christian moral organism. See, for example, the discussion of conscience in N. T. Wright's *After You Believe: Why Christian Character Matters* (New York: HarperCollins, 2010), 159–64. In the context of the book, Wright makes clear that Paul integrates conscience within the Christian virtuous organism. As Wright says, Christians "were modeling a different way of life, a different kind of virtue, outflanking those on offer elsewhere but still with the recognizable classical shape: a clear perception of a goal (*telos*) up ahead, giving rise to fresh, chosen, and worked-at habits of heart, mind, and life" (168). In his reflection on conscience, Wright emphasizes both its valuable place and the necessity that it be formed: "Supposing, for instance, the man guilty of incest in 1 Corinthians 5 had declared that his conscience had told him to do it? (This is, sadly, not uncommon. I recently heard of a clergyman who excused his affair with a married parishioner by explaining that he felt Jesus very close to him when he was engaging in the illicit relationship.) But Paul clearly regards moral self-knowledge as a vital element in the formation of overall moral character. It is, in other words, part of the equipment which sustains the Christian in anticipating in the present time the moral character that will be completed in the future. And, tellingly, conscience is something shared in principle by all people—Jew, Gentile, and Christian alike. It is part of the universal human makeup, subject to the same problems that we find in other aspects of human life but nevertheless to be respected, appealed to, and ultimately brought in line with the gospel" (164).

62. In addition to works cited above, see, for example, Clodovis Boff and George V. Pixley, *The Bible, the Church, and the Poor* (Maryknoll, NY: Orbis, 1990). See also the discussion in Yiu Sing Lúcás Chan, SJ, *Biblical Ethics in the 21st Century: Developments, Emerging Consensus, and Future Directions*, foreword by James F. Keenan, SJ (New York: Paulist, 2013), 37–46.

63. John Webster, "God and Conscience," in *The Doctrine of God and Theological Ethics*, ed. Alan J. Torrance and Michael Banner (London: T&T Clark International, 2006), 147. The quotation is from Paul Lehmann, *Ethics in a Christian Context* (London: SCM, 1963). Relying solely on virtue theory can have reductive results, because one loses contact with the eternal law and with the first principles of practical reason known in synderesis, thereby turning the notion of moral truth into a totalitarian ideology to be feared. See André Comte-Sponville, *A Small Treatise on the Great Virtues: The Uses of Philosophy in Everyday Life*, trans. Catherine Temerson (New York: Metropolitan, 2001), 167–70.

64. Webster, "God and Conscience," 147.

65. Webster, "God and Conscience," 147.

66. Webster, "God and Conscience," 147. See also Fergus Kerr, OP's helpful "Doctrine of God and Theological Ethics according to Thomas Aquinas," in *The Doctrine of God and Theological Ethics*, ed. Alan J. Torrance and Michael Banner (London: T&T Clark International, 2006), 71–84, arguing that the larger moral landscape is defined by beatitude. For further discussion, see William A. Wallace, OP, *The Role of Demonstration in Moral Theology: A Study of Methodology in St. Thomas Aquinas* (Washington, DC: Thomist, 1962), 143–62.

Bibliography

Acosta, Miguel, and Adrian J. Reimers. *Karol Wojtyła's Personalist Philosophy: Understanding "Person & Act."* Washington, DC: Catholic University of America Press, 2016.

Aertnys, Joseph, and C. A. Damen. *Theologia moralis secundum doctrinam S. Alfonsi de Ligorio Doctoris Ecclesiae.* 16th ed. Turin: Marietti, 1950.

Althaus, Paul. *The Ethics of Martin Luther.* Translated by Robert C. Schultz. Minneapolis: Fortress, 2007.

Anderson, Justin M. "Is It Better to Die Excommunicated Than Act against One's Conscience? What Aquinas Famously (Never) Said on Conscience and Church Authority." *Ephemerides Theologicae Lovanienses* 95 (2019): 567–93.

Angier, Tom. "Quaestiones Disputatae de Pinckaers." *Journal of Moral Theology* 8, Special Issue 2 (2019): 166–87.

Annas, Julia. *The Morality of Happiness.* Oxford: Oxford University Press, 1993.

Anscombe, G. E. M. *Faith in a Hard Ground: Essays on Religion, Philosophy and Ethics by G. E. M. Anscombe.* Edited by Mary Geach and Luke Gormally. Exeter: Imprint Academic, 2008.

———. *Human Life, Action and Ethics: Essays by G. E. M. Anscombe.* Edited by Mary Geach and Luke Gormally. Exeter: Imprint Academic, 2005.

Anselm of Canterbury. *Proslogion.* In *A New, Interpretive Translation of St. Anselm's Monologion and Proslogion.* Minneapolis: Arthur J. Banning, 1986.

Aquinas, Thomas. *Summa theologiae.* Translated by the Fathers of the English Dominican Province. Westminster, MD: Christian Classics, 1981.

———. *Truth.* Vol. 2, *Questions X-XX.* Translated by James V. McGlynn, SJ. Indianapolis, IN: Hackett, 1994.

Arendt, Hannah. *The Human Condition.* 2nd ed. Chicago: University of Chicago Press, 2018.

———. "Karl Jaspers: A Laudatio." In *Men in Dark Times*, 71–80. New York: Harcourt Brace & Co., 1968.

———. "Karl Jaspers: Citizen of the World?" In *Men in Dark Times*, 81–94. New York: Harcourt Brace & Co., 1968.

Arintero, Juan G., OP. *The Mystical Evolution in the Development and Vitality of the Church.* 2 vols. Translated by Jordan Aumann. St. Louis, MO: B. Herder, 1949–51.

Arkes, Hadley. *Constitutional Illusions and Anchoring Truths: The Touchstone of the Natural Law.* Cambridge: Cambridge University Press, 2010.

Ash, Christopher. *Pure Joy: Rediscover Your Conscience.* Downers Grove, IL: InterVarsity, 2012.

Aubert, Jean-Marie. "Morale et Casuistique." *Recherches de Science Religieuse* 68 (1980): 167–204.

Aubert, Roger. *La théologie catholique au milieu du XXe siècle.* Tournai: Casterman, 1953.

Auer, Alfons. *Autonome Moral und christlicher Glaube.* Darmstadt: WBG, 2016.

Bak, Felix. "Bernard Häring's Interpretation of Cardinal Newman's Treatise on Conscience." *Ephemerides Theologicae Lovanienses* 49 (1973): 124–59.

Balthasar, Hans Urs von. *Apokalypse der deutschen Seele.* Salzburg: Pustet, 1938.

———. "Heideggers Philosophie vom Standpunkt des Katholizismus." *Stimmen der Zeit* 137 (1940): 1–8.

———. *Theo-Logic: Theological Logical Theory.* Vol. 1, *Truth of the World*, translated by Adrian J. Walker. San Francisco: Ignatius, 2000.

Baring, Edward. *Converts to the Real: Catholicism and the Making of Continental Philosophy.* Cambridge, MA: Harvard University Press, 2019.

Barron, Robert. *Letter to a Suffering Church: A Bishop Speaks on the Sexual Abuse Crisis.* Park Ridge, IL: Word on Fire, 2019.

Barth, Heinrich. "Ontologie und Idealismus." *Zwischen den Zeiten* 7 (1929): 511–40.

———. "Philosophie, Theologie und Existenzproblem." *Zwischen den Zeiten* 10 (1932): 99–124.

Barth, Karl. *Church Dogmatics.* Vol. 2, bk. 2, *The Doctrine of God*, translated by G. W. Bromiley, J. C. Campbell, Iain Wilson, J. Strathearn McNab, Harold Knight, and R. A. Stewart. Edited by G. W. Bromiley and T. F. Torrance. Peabody, MA: Hendrickson, 2010.

———. *Church Dogmatics.* Vol. 3, bk. 2, *The Doctrine of Creation*, translated by Harold Knight, G. W. Bromiley, J. K. S. Reid, and R. H. Fuller. Edited by G. W. Bromiley and T. F. Torrance. Peabody, MA: Hendrickson, 2010.

——. *Church Dogmatics*. Vol. 3, bk. 3, *The Doctrine of Creation*, translated by G. W. Bromiley and R. J. Ehrlich. Edited by G. W. Bromiley and T. F. Torrance. Edinburgh: T&T Clark, 1960.

——. *Church Dogmatics*. Vol. 3, bk. 4, *The Doctrine of Creation*, translated by A. T. Mackay, T. H. L. Parker, Harold Knight, H. A. Kennedy, and J. Marks. Edited by G. W. Bromiley and T. F. Torrance. Peabody, MA: Hendrickson, 2010.

——. *Church Dogmatics*. Vol. 4, bk. 1, *The Doctrine of Reconciliation*, translated by G. W. Bromiley. Edited by G. W. Bromiley and T. F. Torrance. Edinburgh: T&T Clark, 1956.

——. *Ethics*. Edited by Dietrich Braun. Translated by G. W. Bromiley. New York: Seabury, 1981.

Bauerschmidt, Frederick Christian. "Doctrine: Knowing and Doing." In *The Morally Divided Body: Ethical Disagreement and the Disunity of the Church*, edited by Michael Root and James J. Buckley, 25–42. Eugene, OR: Cascade, 2012.

Beaudouin, Réginald, OP. *Tractatus de Conscientia*. Edited by Ambroise Gardeil, OP. Tournai: Desclée, 1911.

Beauvoir, Simone de. *The Ethics of Ambiguity*. Translated by Bernard Frechtman. New York: Philosophical Library, 1948.

Belmans, Théo G., OPraem. "Au croisement des chemins en morale fondamentale." *Revue Thomiste* 89 (1989): 246–78.

——. "Le 'jugement prudentiel' chez saint Thomas: Réponse à R. McInerny." *Revue Thomiste* 91 (1991): 414–20.

Benedict XVI, Pope. "Address of His Holiness Benedict XVI to Members of the International Theological Commission." October 5, 2007. Vatican.va.

Berkman, John, and William C. Mattison III, eds. *Searching for a Universal Ethic: Multidisciplinary, Ecumenical, and Interfaith Responses to the Catholic Natural Law Tradition*. Grand Rapids, MI: Eerdmans, 2014.

Besong, Brian. "Reappraising the Manual Tradition." *American Catholic Philosophical Quarterly* 89 (2015): 557–84.

Best, Ernest. *Second Corinthians*. Louisville, KY: Westminster John Knox, 1987.

Betz, John R. "Translator's Introduction." In Przywara, *Analogia Entis*, 1–115.

Biggar, Nigel. *The Hastening That Waits: Karl Barth's Ethics*. Oxford: Oxford University Press, 1993.

Black, Peter, CSsR, and James F. Keenan, SJ. "The Evolving Self-Understanding of the Moral Theologian: 1900–2000." *Studia Moralia* 39 (2001): 291–327.

Blondel, Maurice. *Action (1893): Essay on a Critique of Life and a Science of*

Practice. Translated by Oliva Blanchette. Notre Dame: University of Notre Dame Press, 1984.

Böckle, Franz. *Fundamental Concepts of Moral Theology.* New York: Paulist, 1968.

Boff, Clodovis, and George V. Pixley. *The Bible, the Church, and the Poor.* Maryknoll, NY: Orbis, 1990.

Bonhoeffer, Dietrich. *Act and Being: Transcendental Philosophy and Ontology in Systematic Theology.* Edited by Wayne Whitson Floyd Jr. Translated by H. Martin Rumscheidt. Vol. 2 of *Dietrich Bonhoeffer Works.* Minneapolis: Fortress, 1996.

———. *Creation and Fall; Temptation: Two Biblical Studies.* Translated by John C. Fletcher. New York: Touchstone, 1997.

———. *Ethics.* Edited by Clifford J. Green. Translated by Reinhard Krauss, Charles C. West, and Douglas W. Stott. Vol. 6 of *Dietrich Bonhoeffer Works.* Minneapolis: Fortress, 2005.

———. *Ethics.* Edited by Eberhard Bethge. Translated by Neville Horton Smith. New York: Macmillan, 1965.

Bonsor, Jack A. *Rahner, Heidegger, and Truth: Karl Rahner's Notion of Christian Truth; The Influence of Heidegger.* Lanham, MD: University Press of America, 1987.

Brady, Ryan J. "Aquinas the Voluntarist? An Investigation of the Claims of James Keenan, S. J." *Nova et Vetera* 18 (2020): 853–73.

Braun, Dietrich. "Editor's Preface." In Karl Barth, *Ethics,* edited by Dietrich Braun, translated by G. W. Bromiley, vii–ix. New York: Seabury, 1981.

Brencio, Francesca. "Heidegger, Catholicism and the History of Being." *Journal of the British Society for Phenomenology* 51, no. 2 (2020): 137–50.

Bresnahan, James F. "An Ethics of Faith." In *A World of Grace: An Introduction to the Themes and Foundations of Karl Rahner's Theology,* edited by Leo J. O'Donovan, 169–84. Washington, DC: Georgetown University Press, 1995.

———. "Rahner's Ethics: Critical Natural Law in Relation to Contemporary Ethical Methodology." *Journal of Religion* 56 (1976): 36–60.

Bretzke, James, SJ. *A Morally Complex World: Engaging Contemporary Moral Theology.* Collegeville, MN: Liturgical Press, 2004.

Brito, Emilio, SJ. "La reception de la pensée de Heidegger dans la théologie catholique." *Nouvelle Revue Théologique* 119 (1997): 352–73.

Bröckling, Ulrich. *Katholische Intellektuelle in der Weimarer Republik: Zeitkritik und Gesellschaftstheorie bei Walter Dirks, Romano Guardini, Carl*

Schmitt, Ernst Michel und Heinrich Mertens. Munich: Wilhelm Fink, 1993.

Brunner, August, SJ. "Die Entwertung des Seins in der Existenzialphilosophie." *Scholastik* 12 (1937): 233–38.

———. "Ursprung und Grundzüge der Existenzialphilosophie." *Scholastik* 13 (1938): 173–205.

Brunner, Emil. *The Divine Imperative: A Study in Christian Ethics.* Translated by Olive Wyon. London: James Clarke, 2002.

Bullivant, Stephen. "Newman and Modernism: The *Pascendi* Crisis and Its Wider Significance." *New Blackfriars* 92 (2011): 189–208.

Bultmann, Rudolf. "The Historicity of Man and Faith." In *Existence and Faith: Shorter Writings of Rudolf Bultmann,* edited and translated by Schubert M. Ogden, 92–110. New York: The World Publishing Company, 1966.

———. "New Testament and Mythology." In *Kerygma and Myth: A Theological Debate,* edited by Hans W. Bartsch, 1–44. New York: Harper & Row, 1961.

———. *Theology of the New Testament.* 2 vols. Translated by Kendrick Grobel. Waco, TX: Baylor University Press, 2007.

Byle, Nicholas. "Divine Temporality: Bonhoeffer's Theological Appropriation of Heidegger's Existential Analytic of Dasein." PhD diss., University of South Florida, 2016.

———. "Heidegger's Adam and Bonhoeffer's Christ: Evaluating Bonhoeffer's Appraisals of Heidegger." *Dietrich Bonhoeffer Jahrbuch* 5 (2011/2012): 99–119.

Byrne, Brendan, SJ. *Romans.* Collegeville, MN: Liturgical Press, 1996.

Cahalan, Kathleen A. *Formed in the Image of Christ: The Sacramental-Moral Theology of Bernard Häring, C.Ss.R.* Collegeville, MN: Liturgical Press, 2004.

Callahan, Sidney. *In Good Conscience: Reason and Emotion in Moral Decision-Making.* San Francisco: HarperSanFrancisco, 1991.

Campenhausen, Hans von. *Die Bergründung kirchlicher Entscheidungen beim Apostel Paulus: Zur Grundlegung des Kirchenrechts.* Heidelberg: Carl Winter, 1957.

Caputo, John D. *Demythologizing Heidegger.* Bloomington: Indiana University Press, 1993.

Carpentier, René, SJ. "Conscience." In *Dictionnaire de spiritualité: Ascétique et mystique, doctrine et histoire,* vol. 2, bk. 2, 1547–75. Paris: Beauchesne, 1949–53.

Casarella, Peter. "Culture and Conscience in the Thought of Joseph Ratzinger/ Pope Benedict XVI." In *Explorations in the Theology of Benedict XVI*, edited by John C. Cavadini, 63–86. Notre Dame: University of Notre Dame Press, 2012.

Catechism of the Catholic Church, 2nd ed. Vatican City: Libreria Editrice Vaticana, 1997.

Cessario, Romanus, OP. *Introduction to Moral Theology*. Washington, DC: Catholic University of America Press, 2001.

———. *The Moral Virtues and Theological Ethics*. Notre Dame: University of Notre Dame Press, 1991.

———. "Religion and the Gifts of the Holy Spirit." *Nova et Vetera* 15 (2017): 983–98.

Chalamet, Christophe. "Barth and Liberal Protestantism." In *The Oxford Handbook of Karl Barth*, edited by Paul Dafydd Jones and Paul T. Nimmo, 132–46. Oxford: Oxford University Press, 2019.

Chan, Yiu Sing Lúcás, SJ. *Biblical Ethics in the 21st Century: Developments, Emerging Consensus, and Future Directions*. Foreword by James F. Keenan, SJ. New York: Paulist, 2013.

Chan, Yiu Sing Lúcás, SJ, James F. Keenan, SJ, and Ronaldo Zacharias, eds. *The Bible and Catholic Theological Ethics*. Maryknoll, NY: Orbis, 2017.

Chiodi, Maurizio. *Amore, dono e giustizia: Teologia e filosofia sulla traccia del pensiero di Paul Ricoeur*. Milan: Glossa, 2011.

———. *Norma, coscienza e discernimento: Testo e contesto del capitolo VIII di "Amoris Laetitia."* Cinisello Balsamo: Edizioni San Paolo, 2018.

———. *Teologia morale fondamentale*. Vol. 1. Brescia: Queriniana, 2018.

Christie, Dolores L. *Adequately Considered: An American Perspective on Louis Janssens' Personalist Morals*. Louvain: Peeters, 1990.

Churchland, Patricia S. *Conscience: The Origins of Moral Intuition*. New York: W. W. Norton, 2019.

Clark, Patrick. "Servais Pinckaers's Retrieval of Martyrdom as the Culmination of the Christian Life." *Josephinum Journal of Theology* 17 (2010): 1–27.

Cloutier, David. "Catholic Moral Theology: Piecing Together a Discipline in Pieces." *Modern Theology* 29 (2013): 381–90.

Colish, Marcia L. *Faith, Fiction, and Force in Medieval Baptismal Debates*. Washington, DC: Catholic University of America Press, 2014.

Collins, James. "The German Neoscholastic Approach to Heidegger." *Modern Schoolman* 21 (1944): 143–52.

Comte-Sponville, André. *A Small Treatise on the Great Virtues: The Uses of*

Philosophy in Everyday Life. Translated by Catherine Temerson. New York: Metropolitan, 2001.

Congar, Yves, OP. "St. Paul's Casuistry." In *A Gospel Priesthood*, 49–73. Translated by P. J. Hepburne-Scott. New York: Herder and Herder, 1967.

Conn, Walter. *Christian Conversion: A Developmental Interpretation of Autonomy and Surrender*. New York: Paulist, 1986.

———. *Conscience: Development and Self-Transcendence*. Birmingham, AL: Religious Education, 1981.

Cornwall, Susannah. *Controversies in Queer Theology*. London: SCM, 2011.

Corvez, Maurice. *L'être et la conscience morale*. Paris: Béatrice-Nauwelaerts, 1968.

Cox, Kathryn Lilla. *Water Shaping Stone: Faith, Relationships, and Conscience Formation*. Collegeville, MN: Liturgical Press, 2015.

Creveld, Martin van. *Conscience: A Biography*. London: Reaktion, 2015.

Cronin, Michael. *The Science of Ethics*. Vol. 1, *General Ethics*. New York: Benziger, 1909.

Crotty, Nicholas. "Conscience and Conflict." *Theological Studies* 32 (1971): 208–32.

Cuddeback, John. "Law, Pinckaers, and the Definition of Christian Ethics." *Nova et Vetera* 7 (2009): 301–26.

Cuddy, Cajetan, OP. "St. Thomas Aquinas on Conscience." In *Christianity and the Laws of Conscience: An Introduction*, edited by Helen M. Alvaré and Jeffrey B. Hammond. Cambridge: Cambridge University Press, forthcoming.

Curran, Charles, E. "Bernard Häring: A Moral Theologian Whose Soul Matched His Scholarship." *National Catholic Reporter*, July 17, 1998. https://natcath.org/NCR_Online/archives2/1998c/071798/071898h.htm.

———. *Catholic Moral Theology in the United States: A History*. Washington, DC: Georgetown University Press, 2008.

———, ed. *Conscience*. Mahwah, NJ: Paulist, 2004.

———. *The Development of Moral Theology: Five Strands*. Washington, DC: Georgetown University Press, 2013.

Damen, C. A. "S. Alfonsus Doctor Prudentiae." *Rassegna di Morale e Diritto* 5–6 (1939–40): 1–27.

D'Arcy, Eric. *Conscience and Its Right to Freedom*. New York: Sheed and Ward, 1961.

Dastur, Francoise. "Conscience: The Most Intimate Alterity." In *Heidegger and Practical Philosophy*, edited by F. Raffoul and D. Pettigrew, 87–98. Albany: State University of New York Press, 2002.

Dauphinais, Michael. "The Splendor and Gift of the Christian Moral Life: *Veritatis Splendor* at Twenty-Five." *Nova et Vetera* 16 (2018): 1261–312.

DeCosse, David E. "The Primacy of Conscience, Vatican II, and Pope Francis: The Opportunity to Renew a Tradition." In *From Vatican II to Pope Francis: Charting a Catholic Future*, edited by Paul Crowley, SJ, 156–69. Maryknoll, NY: Orbis, 2014.

DeCosse, David E., and Kristin E. Heyer. "Introduction." In *Conscience and Catholicism: Rights, Responsibilities, and Institutional Responses*, edited by David E. DeCosse and Kristin E. Heyer, xv-xxiii. Maryknoll, NY: Orbis, 2015.

De Franceschi, Sylvio Hermann. "La défense doctrinale du système thomiste de la mystique étendue: Le P. Réginald Garrigou-Lagrange et la construction d'une école dominicaine de spiritualité." *Revue des Sciences Philosophiques et Théologiques* 103 (2019): 113–43.

De Haan, Daniel D. "Moral Perception and the Function of the *Vis Cogitativa* in Thomas Aquinas's Doctrine of Antecedent and Consequent Passions." *Documenti e Studi sulla Traditione Filosofica Medievale* 25 (2014): 289–330.

———. "Perception and the Vis Cogitativa: A Thomistic Analysis of Aspectual, Actional, and Affectional Percepts." *American Catholic Philosophical Quarterly* 88, no. 3 (2014): 397–437.

Delhaye, Philippe. *The Christian Conscience*. Translated by Charles Underhill Quinn. New York: Desclée, 1968. Originally published as *La conscience morale du chrétien* (Tournai: Desclée, 1964).

———. "La théologie morale d'hier et d'aujourd'hui." *Revue des Sciences Religieuses* 27 (1953): 112–30.

Delp, Alfred, SJ. *Gesammelte Schriften*. Vol. 4, edited by Roman Bleistein. Frankfurt: Knecht, 1984.

———. *Tragische Existenz: Zur Philosophie Martin Heideggers*. Freiburg: Herder, 1935.

Deman, Thomas, OP. *Aux origines de la théologie morale*. Paris: Vrin, 1951.

———. "Probabilisme." In *Dictionnaire de théologie catholique*, vol. 13, cols. 417–619. Paris: Librairie Letouzey et Ané, 1936.

Demmer, Klaus, MSC. "Erwägungen über den Segen der Kasuistik." *Gregorianum* 63 (1982): 133–40.

———. *Living the Truth: A Theory of Action*. Translated by Brian McNeil. Washington, DC: Georgetown University Press, 2010.

———. *Shaping the Moral Life: An Approach to Moral Theology*. Edited by

James F. Keenan, SJ. Translated by Roberto Dell'Oro. Washington, DC: Georgetown University Press, 2000.

Dennison, William D. *The Young Bultmann: Context for His Understanding of God, 1884–1925.* New York: Peter Lang, 2008.

Dirks, Walter. "How Can I Know What God Wants of Me?" Translated by Sally S. Cunneen. *Cross Currents* 5 (1955): 76–92.

Doherty, Reginald G., OP. *The Judgments of Conscience and Prudence in the Doctrine of St. Thomas Aquinas.* River Forest, IL: The Aquinas Library, 1961.

Droege, Theodor, CSsR. "Die Existenz-Philosophie Martin Heideggers." *Divus Thomas* 16 (1938): 265–94, 371–92.

Duffé, Bruno-Marie, ed. *La conscience morale: Questions pour aujourd'hui.* Lyon: Profac, 1994.

Dupré, Louis. "Situation Ethics and Objective Morality." In *Situationism and the New Morality*, edited by Robert L. Cunningham, 90–102. New York: Meredith, 1970. Originally published in *Theological Studies* 28 (1967): 245–57.

Ebeling, Gerhard. *Theologie und Verkündigung: Ein Gespräch mit Rudolf Bultmann.* Tübingen: J. C. B. Mohr, 1962.

Edwards, Denis. "Teilhard's Vision as Agenda for Rahner's Christology." *Pacifica* 23 (2010): 233–45.

Egenter, Richard. "Kasuistik als christliche Situationsethik." *Münchener Theologische Zeitschrift* 1 (1950): 54–65.

Eicher, Peter. *Die anthropologische Wende.* Freiburg: Universitätsverlag Freiburg, 1970.

Elders, Leo J., SVD. *The Ethics of St. Thomas Aquinas: Happiness, Natural Law and the Virtues.* Washington, DC: Catholic University of America Press, 2019.

Elsbernd, Mary. "The Reinterpretation of *Gaudium et Spes* in *Veritatis Splendor*." *Horizons* 29, no. 2 (2002): 225–39.

Endean, Philip, SJ. "'A Symbol Perfected in Death': Rahner's Theology and Alfred Delp (1907–1945)." *The Way* 43 (2004): 67–82.

Fagothey, Austin, SJ. *Right and Reason: Ethics in Theory and Practice*, 2nd ed. Charlotte, NC: TAN, 2000.

Farley, Margaret A., RSM. *Just Love: A Framework for Christian Sexual Ethics.* New York: Continuum, 2006.

Flannery, Kevin L., SJ. *Christian and Moral Action.* Arlington, VA: The Institute for the Psychological Sciences, 2012.

Fleming, Julia. *Defending Probabilism: The Moral Theology of Juan Caramuel.* Washington, DC: Georgetown University Press, 2006.

Francis, Pope. *Amoris Laetitia.* Frederick, MD: The Word Among Us, 2016.

Franke, William. "Existentialism: An Atheistic or a Christian Philosophy?" In *Phenomenology and Existentialism in the Twentieth Century. Book One: New Waves of Philosophical Inspirations*, edited by A.-T. Tymieniecka, 371–94. Dordrecht: Springer, 2009.

Fritz, Peter Joseph. *Freedom Made Manifest: Rahner's Fundamental Option and Theological Aesthetics.* Washington, DC: Catholic University of America Press, 2019.

———. *Karl Rahner's Theological Aesthetics.* Washington, DC: Catholic University of America Press, 2014.

Fuchs, Josef, SJ. "The Absoluteness of Behavioral Moral Norms." In *Personal Responsibility and Christian Morality*, translated by William Cleves et al., 115–52. Washington, DC: Georgetown University Press, 1983.

———. "Basic Freedom and Morality." In *Human Values and Christian Morality*, 92–111. Dublin: Gill and Macmillan, 1970.

———. *Christian Ethics in a Secular Arena.* Translated by Bernard Hoose and Brian McNeil. Washington, DC: Georgetown University Press, 1984.

———. "Christian Faith and the Disposing of Human Life." *Theological Studies* 46 (1985): 664–84.

———. "Conscience and Conscientious Fidelity." In *Moral Theology: Challenges for the Future; Essays in Honor of Richard A. McCormick*, edited by Charles E. Curran, 108–24. New York: Paulist, 1990.

———. *De Castitate et Ordine Sexuali: Conspectus Praelectionum Theologiae Moralis ad Usum Auditorium*, 2nd ed. Rome: Editrice Università Gregoriana, 1960.

———. *"Epikeia* Applied to Natural Law?" In *Personal Responsibility and Christian Morality*, translated by William Cleves et al., 185–99. Washington, DC: Georgetown University Press, 1983.

———. "Éthique objective et éthique de situation." *Nouvelle Revue Théologique* 78 (1956): 798–818.

———. "Good Acts and Good Persons." In *Considering "Veritatis Splendor,"* edited by John Wilkins, 23–24. Cleveland, OH: Pilgrim, 1994.

———. "A Harmonization of the Conciliar Statements on Christian Moral Theology." In *Vatican II: Assessment and Perspectives*, edited by Rene Latourelle, SJ, 479–500. Mahwah, NJ: Paulist, 1989.

———. *Moral Demands and Personal Obligations.* Translated by Brian McNeil. Washington, DC: Georgetown University Press, 1993.

———. "Morale théologique et morale de situation." *Nouvelle Revue Théologique* 76 (1954): 1073–85.

———. "Morality as the Shaping of the Future of Man." In *Personal Responsibility and Christian Morality*, translated by William Cleves et al., 176–84. Washington, DC: Georgetown University Press, 1983.

———. "Moral Theology according to Vatican II." In *Human Values and Christian Morality*, 1–55. Dublin: Gill and Macmillan, 1970.

———. *Natural Law: A Theological Investigation*. Translated by Helmut Reckter, SJ, and John A. Dowling. New York: Sheed and Ward, 1965.

———. "The Question Addressed to Conscience." In *Personal Responsibility and Christian Morality*, translated by William Cleves et al., 216–28. Washington, DC: Georgetown University Press, 1983.

———. "Situationsethik." *Seelsorgehilfe* 4 (1952): 245–55, 273–78.

———. *Situation und Entscheidung: Grundfragen christlicher Situationsethik*. Frankfurt: Knecht, 1952.

———. *Theologia Moralis Generalis*. Rev. ed. Rome: Gregorian University Press, 1963.

———. "Vocation and Hope: Conciliar Orientations for a Christian Morality." In *Personal Responsibility and Christian Morality*, translated by William Cleves et al., 32–49. Washington, DC: Georgetown University Press, 1983.

Gallagher, John A. *Time Past, Time Future: An Historical Study of Catholic Moral Theology*. Mahwah, NJ: Paulist, 1990.

Gallagher, Raphael, CSsR. "L'actualité de la théologie morale de saint Alphonse de Liguori." *Revue d'Éthique et de Théologie Morale* 268 (2012): 35–57.

———. "Bernard Häring's *The Law of Christ*: Reassessing Its Contribution to the Renewal of Moral Theology in Its Era." *Studia Moralia* 44 (2006): 317–51.

———. "Interpreting Thomas Aquinas: Aspects of the Redemptorist and Jesuit Schools in the Twentieth Century." In *The Ethics of Aquinas*, edited by Stephen J. Pope, 374–84. Washington, DC: Georgetown University Press, 2002.

Gardeil, Ambroise, OP. "La certitude probable." *Revue des Sciences Philosophiques et Théologiques* 5 (1911): 237–66, 441–85.

———. "La topicité." *Revue des Sciences Philosophiques et Théologiques* 5 (1911): 750–57.

———. *La vraie vie chrétienne*. Edited by H.-D. Gardeil. Paris: Desclée, 1935.

Garrigou-Lagrange, Réginald, OP. "De conscientia secundum principia sancti Thomae. Supplementum quaestionis XIX et XX." In *De beatitudine de actibus humanis et habitibus: Commentarius in Summam theologicam S. Thomae Ia–IIa qq. 1-54,* 373–96. Turin: Berutti, 1951.

———. *De revelatione per ecclesiam catholicam propositam.* Rome: Desclée de Socii, 1950.

———. *The Order of Things: The Realism of the Principle of Finality.* Translated by Matthew K. Minerd. Steubenville, OH: Emmaus Academic, 2020.

———. "Remarks Concerning the Metaphysical Character of St. Thomas's Moral Theology, in Particular as It Is Related to Prudence and Conscience." Translated by Matthew K. Minerd. *Nova et Vetera* 17, no. 1 (2019): 245–70. Originally published as "Du charactère métaphysique de la théologie morale de saint Thomas, en particulier dans ses rapports avec la prudence et la conscience." *Revue Thomiste* 30 (1925): 341–55.

———. *The Three Ages of the Interior Life.* 2 vols. Translated by M. Timothea Doyle. St. Louis, MO: Herder, 1948.

Gay, Jean-Pascal. *Morales in conflit: Théologie et polémique au Grand Siècle (1640–1700).* Paris: Cerf, 2011.

Gaziaux, Éric. "Les conflits de la conscience dans la tradition catholique: Retour sur l'histoire et les différentes écoles." *Revue d'Éthique et de Théologie Morale,* no. 293 (2017): 11–24.

———. "La loi naturelle: Quelques repères historiques et interrogations contemporaines." *Revue d'Éthique et de Théologie Morale,* no. 293 (2017): 53–66.

———. *Morale de la foi et morale autonome: Confrontation entre P. Delhaye et J. Fuchs.* Leuven: Peeters, 1995.

———. "Philippe Delhaye (1912–1990)." In *Christliche Ethik im Porträt: Leben und Werk bedeutender Moraltheologen,* edited by Konrad Hilpert, 729–58. Freiburg im Breisgau: Herder, 2012.

Gilleman, Gérard, SJ. *The Primacy of Charity in Moral Theology.* Translated by William F. Ryan, SJ, and André Vachon, SJ. Westminster, MD: Newman, 1959. Originally published as *Le primat de la charité en théologie morale.* Paris: Desclée, 1954.

Gillon, Louis-Bertrand, OP. *Christo e la teologia morale.* Rome: Edizioni Romae Mame, 1961.

———. "L'imitation du Christ et la morale de saint Thomas." *Angelicum* 36 (1959): 263–86.

Gonzales, Philip John Paul. *Reimagining the "Analogia Entis": The Future of Erich Przywara's Christian Vision.* Grand Rapids, MI: Eerdmans, 2019.

Gorman, Michael J. *Cruciformity: Paul's Narrative Spirituality of the Cross.* Grand Rapids, MI: Eerdmans, 2001.

Gorringe, Timothy. "Barth and Politics." In *The Oxford Handbook of Karl Barth,* edited by Paul Dafydd Jones and Paul T. Nimmo, 178–92. Oxford: Oxford University Press, 2019.

Graham, Mark E. *Josef Fuchs on Natural Law.* Washington, DC: Georgetown University Press, 2002.

Guardini, Romano. *Das Gute, das Gewissen und die Sammlung.* Mainz: Matthias-Grünewald, 1929.

———. *The Virtues: On Forms of Moral Life.* New York: Regnery, 1967.

Gula, Richard M., SS. *Moral Discernment.* New York: Paulist, 1997.

Gustafson, James. *Can Ethics Be Christian?* Chicago: University of Chicago Press, 1975.

———. *Christ and the Moral Life.* New York: Harper & Row, 1968.

Haas, John M., ed. *Crisis of Conscience.* New York: Crossroad, 1996.

Hansen, Charlotte. "Newman, Conscience and Authority." *New Blackfriars* 92 (2011): 209–23.

Harakas, Stanley Samuel. *Toward Transfigured Life: The* Theoria *of Eastern Orthodox Ethics.* Minneapolis: Light and Life, 1983.

Hare, Robert D. *Without Conscience: The Disturbing World of the Psychopaths.* New York: Guilford, 1993.

Häring, Bernard, CSsR. "A Distrust that Wounds." In *Considering "Veritatis Splendor,"* edited by John Wilkins, 9–13. Cleveland, OH: Pilgrim, 1994.

———. "Dynamism and Continuity in a Personalistic Approach to Natural Law." In *Norm and Context in Christian Ethics,* edited by Gene H. Outka and Paul Ramsey, 199–218. New York: SMC-Canterbury, 1968.

———. *Free and Faithful in Christ: Moral Theology for Clergy and Laity.* Vol. 1, *General Moral Theology.* New York: Crossroad, 1984.

———. *Free and Faithful in Christ: Moral Theology for Clergy and Laity.* Vol. 3, *Light to the World.* New York: Crossroad, 1981.

———. *Das Heilige und das Gute.* Krailling: Erich Wewel, 1950.

———. *The Johannine Council.* New York: Herder and Herder, 1963.

———. "Karl Rahner—His Personality and His Work." *The Furrow* 35, no. 5 (1984): 301–5.

———. *The Law of Christ.* 3 vols. Translated by Edwin G. Kaiser, CPPS. Westminster, MD: Newman, 1961–66.

———. *My Hope for the Church: Critical Encouragement for the Twenty-First Century.* Translated by Peter Heinegg. Liguori, MO: Liguori, 1999. Originally published in German (1997).

———. "The Normative Value of the Sermon on the Mount." *Catholic Biblical Quarterly* 29, no. 3 (1967): 375–85.

Harmignie, Pierre. "Review of Emile Mersch, S. J., *L'obligation morale principe de liberté.*" *Revue Néo-scholastique de Philosophie* 29 (1927): 353–57.

Harnack, Adolf von. *What Is Christianity?* Translated by Thomas Bailey Saunders. New York: Harper & Brothers, 1957.

Harrington, Daniel J., SJ, and James F. Keenan, SJ. *Paul and Virtue Ethics: Building Bridges between New Testament Studies and Moral Theology.* Lanham, MD: Rowman & Littlefield, 2010.

Harvey, Barry. *Taking Hold of the Real: Dietrich Bonhoeffer and the Profound Worldliness of Christianity.* Eugene, OR: Cascade, 2015.

Hays, Richard B. *First Corinthians.* Louisville, KY: Westminster John Knox, 1997.

———. *The Moral Vision of the New Testament: Community, Cross, New Creation; A Contemporary Introduction to New Testament Ethics.* New York: HarperCollins, 1996.

Healy, Gerald W., SJ. "Recent Moral Theology." *Philippine Studies* 9 (1961): 311–32.

Heidegger, Martin. *Being and Time.* Translated from the 7th German edition (1953) by Joan Stambaugh. Translation revised by Dennis J. Schmidt. Albany: State University of New York Press, 2010.

———. "Letter on 'Humanism.'" Translated by Frank A. Capuzzi. In *Pathmarks*, edited by William McNeill, 239–76. Cambridge: Cambridge University Press, 1998.

Henderson, Ian. *Myth in the New Testament.* London: SCM, 1952.

Hennig, John. "Karl Jaspers' Attitude towards History." In *The Philosophy of Karl Jaspers*, edited by Paul Arthur Schilpp, 565–91. La Salle, IL: Open Court, 1957.

Herrmann, Friedrich-Wilhelm von, and Francesco Alfieri. *Martin Heidegger: La verità sui "Quaderni neri."* Brescia: Morcelliana, 2016.

Hibbs, Thomas S. *Virtue's Splendor: Wisdom, Prudence, and the Human Good.* New York: Fordham University Press, 2001.

Higgins, Thomas J., SJ. *Man as Man: The Science and Art of Ethics.* Milwaukee, WI: Bruce, 1949.

Hildebrand, Dietrich von. *The Encyclical "Humanae Vitae": A Sign of Contradiction.* Translated by Damian Fedoryka and John Crosby. Chicago: Franciscan Herald, 1969. Republished as *Love, Marriage, and the Catholic Conscience.* Manchester, NH: Sophia Institute, 1998.

Hildebrand, Dietrich von, and Alice Jourdain. *True Morality and Its Counterfeits.* New York: David McKay, 1955.

Hill, Brennan R. "Bernard Häring and the Second Vatican Council." *Horizons* 33 (2006): 78–100.

Hirschmann, Hans, SJ. "Im Spiegel der Zeit." *Geist und Leben* 25 (1951): 300–4.

Hittinger, Russell. *The First Grace: Rediscovering the Natural Law in a Post-Christian World.* Wilmington, DE: ISI, 2003.

Hoffman, Kurt. "The Basic Concepts of Jaspers' Philosophy." In *The Philosophy of Karl Jaspers*, edited by Paul Arthur Schilpp, 95–113. La Salle, IL: Open Court, 1957.

Hoffmann, Tobias. "Conscience and Synderesis." In *The Oxford Handbook of Aquinas*, edited by Brian Davies and Eleonore Stump, 255–64. Oxford: Oxford University Press, 2008.

Hogan, Linda. *Confronting the Truth: Conscience in the Catholic Tradition.* New York: Paulist, 2000.

Holzer, Vincent. "Karl Rahner—Genèse et aspects d'une théologie." *Recherches de Science Religieuse* 108 (2020): 425–49.

Höver, Gerhard, and Andrea Schaeffer. "Fritz Tillmann (1873–1953)." In *Christliche Ethik im Porträt: Leben und Werk bedeutender Moraltheologen*, edited by Konrad Hilpert, 599–624. Freiburg im Breisgau: Herder, 2012.

Hughes, Gerald J. "Conscience." In *The Cambridge Companion to John Henry Newman*, edited by Ian Ker and Terrence Merrigan, 189–220. Cambridge: Cambridge University Press, 2009.

Hugon, Édouard, OP. *Hors de l'église pas de salut*, 2nd ed. Paris: Tequi, 1914.

Hursthouse, Rosalind. *Virtue Ethics.* Oxford: Oxford University Press, 1999.

Hurtubise, Pierre. *La casuistique dans tous ses états: De Martin Azpilcueta à Alphonse de Liguori.* Ottawa: Novalis, 2005.

Hütter, Reinhard. *Bound for Beatitude: A Thomistic Study in Eschatology and Ethics.* Washington, DC: Catholic University of America Press, 2019.

———. *Bound to Be Free: Evangelical Catholic Engagements in Ecclesiology, Ethics, and Ecumenism.* Grand Rapids, MI: Eerdmans, 2004.

———. *Dust Bound for Heaven: Explorations in the Theology of Thomas Aquinas.* Grand Rapids, MI: Eerdmans, 2012.

———. *John Henry Newman on Truth and Its Counterfeits: A Guide for Our Times.* Washington, DC: Catholic University of America Press, 2020.

International Theological Commission of the Catholic Church. "In Search of a Universal Ethic: A New Look at the Natural Law." 2009. Vatican.va.

———. "*Sensus fidei* in the Life of the Church." 2014. Vatican.va.

Inwood, Michael. *Heidegger: A Very Short Introduction.* Oxford: Oxford University Press, 1997.

Janssens, Louis. *Freedom of Conscience and Religious Freedom.* Translated by Brother Lorenzo, CFX. Staten Island, NY: Alba House, 1965.

———. "Personalism in Moral Theology." In *Moral Theology: Challenges for the Future; Essays in Honor of Richard A. McCormick,* edited by Charles E. Curran, 94–107. New York: Paulist, 1990.

———. *Personne et société: Théories actuelles et essai doctrinal.* Gembloux: Duculot, 1939.

Jaspers, Karl. "Philosophical Autobiography." In *The Philosophy of Karl Jaspers,* edited by Paul Arthur Schilpp, 3–94. La Salle, IL: Open Court, 1957.

———. *Philosophy.* Vol. 2. Translated by E. B. Ashton. Chicago: University of Chicago Press, 1970.

———. *The Question of German Guilt.* Translated by E. B. Ashton. New York: Doubleday, 1947.

———. *Reason and Existenz: Five Lectures.* Translated by William Earle. New York: Noonday, 1955.

Jaspers, Karl, and Rudolf Bultmann. *Myth and Christianity: An Inquiry into the Possibility of Religion without Myth.* New York: Noonday, 1958.

Jaspert, Bernd, ed. *Karl Barth-Rudolf Bultmann: Letters, 1922–1966.* Translated by G. W. Bromiley. Grand Rapids, MI: Eerdmans, 1981.

John Paul II, Pope. *Veritatis Splendor.* Vatican City: Libreria Editrice Vaticana, 1993. http://www.vatican.va/content/john-paul-ii/en/encyclicals/documents/hf_jp-ii_enc_06081993_veritatis-splendor.html.

Jonas, Hans. "Heidegger and Theology." *Review of Metaphysics* 18 (1964): 207–33.

Jonsen, Albert R., and Stephen Toulmin. *The Abuse of Casuistry: A History of Moral Reasoning.* Berkeley: University of California Press, 1988.

Journet, Charles. *The Church of the Word Incarnate.* London: Sheed and Ward, 1955.

Kaczor, Christopher. *Proportionalism and the Natural Law Tradition.* Washington, DC: Catholic University of America Press, 2002.

Kaufmann, Fritz. "Karl Jaspers and a Philosophy of Communication." In *The Philosophy of Karl Jaspers,* edited by Paul Arthur Schilpp, 210–95. La Salle, IL: Open Court, 1957.

Kazim, Emre. *Kant on Conscience: A Unified Approach to Moral Self-Consciousness.* Leiden: Brill, 2017.

Keenan, James F., SJ. "Bernard Häring's Influence on American Catholic Moral Theology." *Journal of Moral Theology* 1 (2012): 23–42.

———, ed. *Catholic Theological Ethics Past, Present, and Future: The Trento Conference.* Maryknoll, NY: Orbis, 2011.

———. "Champion of Conscience." *America*, April 4, 2005. https://www.ameri-camagazine.org/issue/526/other-things/champion-conscience.

———. "Distinguishing Charity as Goodness and Prudence as Rightness: A Key to Thomas's *Secunda pars*." *Thomist* 56 (1992): 407–26.

———. *Goodness and Rightness in Thomas Aquinas's "Summa theologiae."* Washington, DC: Georgetown University Press, 1992.

———. *A History of Catholic Moral Theology in the Twentieth Century: From Confessing Sins to Liberating Consciences.* New York: Continuum, 2010.

———. "John Mahoney's *The Making of Moral Theology*." In *The Oxford Handbook of Theological Ethics*, edited by Gilbert Meilaender and William Werpehowski, 503–19. Oxford: Oxford University Press, 2005.

———. *Moral Wisdom: Lessons and Texts from the Catholic Tradition*, 3rd ed. Lanham, MD: Rowman & Littlefield, 2006.

———. "Natural Law Debates and the Forces of Nature." In *Contemplating the Future of Moral Theology: Essays in Honor of Brian V. Johnstone, C.Ss.R.*, edited by Robert C. Koerpel and Vimal Tirimanna, CSsR, 71–87. Eugene, OR: Pickwick, 2017.

———. "Redeeming Conscience." *Theological Studies* 76 (2015): 129–47.

———. "To Follow and to Form over Time: A Phenomenology of Conscience." In *Conscience and Catholicism: Rights, Responsibilities, and Institutional Responses*, edited by David E. DeCosse and Kristin E. Heyer, 1–15. Maryknoll, NY: Orbis, 2015.

———. *Virtue Ethics.* New York: Sheed and Ward, 1996.

Keenan, James F., SJ, and Thomas A. Shannon. "Contexts of Casuistry: Historical and Contemporary." In Keenan and Shannon, *The Context of Casuistry*, 221–31.

———, eds. *The Context of Casuistry.* Washington, DC: Georgetown University Press, 1995.

Kelly, David F. "Karl Rahner and Genetic Engineering: The Use of Theological Principles in Moral Analysis." *Philosophy and Theology* 9 (1995): 177–200.

Kerr, Fergus, OP. "Doctrine of God and Theological Ethics according to Thomas Aquinas." In *The Doctrine of God and Theological Ethics*, edited by Alan J. Torrance and Michael Banner, 71–84. London: T&T Clark International, 2006.

———. *Twentieth-Century Catholic Theologians.* Oxford: Blackwell, 2007.

Kerr, Gaven. *Aquinas and the Metaphysics of Creation.* Oxford: Oxford University Press, 2019.

Khuory-Hélou, Dominique. "Servais Pinckaers et le renouveau de la théologie morale." PhD diss., Universidad de Navarra, 2009.

Kim, Andrew. *An Introduction to Catholic Ethics since Vatican II.* Cambridge: Cambridge University Press, 2015.

Kirwan, Jon. *An Avant-garde Theological Generation: The* Nouvelle Théologie *and the French Crisis of Modernity.* Oxford: Oxford University Press, 2018.

Klubertanz, George. *The Discursive Power: Sources and Doctrine of the* Vis cogitativa *according to St. Thomas Aquinas.* St. Louis, MO: The Modern Schoolman, 1952.

Koch, Antony. *A Handbook of Moral Theology.* Edited by Arthur Preuss. Vol. 1, *Introduction: Morality, Its Subject, Norm, and Object.* St. Louis, MO: Herder, 1918.

Koonz, Claudia. *The Nazi Conscience.* Cambridge, MA: Harvard University Press, 2003.

Kopfensteiner, Thomas. "The Metaphorical Structure of Normativity." *Theological Studies* 58 (1997): 331–46.

———. "Science, Metaphor and Moral Casuistry." In Keenan and Shannon, *The Context of Casuistry,* 207–20.

Krötke, Wolf. "Dietrich Bonhoeffer and Martin Luther." Translated by Peter Frick. In *Bonhoeffer's Intellectual Formation: Theology and Philosophy in His Thought,* edited by Peter Frick, 53–82. Tübingen: Mohr Siebeck, 2008.

Kunz, Hans. "Critique of Jaspers' Concept of 'Transcendence.'" In *The Philosophy of Karl Jaspers,* edited by Paul Arthur Schilpp, 499–522. La Salle, IL: Open Court, 1957.

Labourdette, Michel, OP. *Les actes humains.* Vol. 2 of *"Grand cours" de théologie morale.* Latin passages translated by a Benedictine of l'Abbaye Notre-Dame du Pesquié. Paris: Parole et Silence, 2016.

———. "Connaissance pratique et savoir morale." *Revue Thomiste* 48 (1948): 142–79.

———. *Cours de théologie morale.* Vol. 1, *Morale fondamentale.* Paris: Parole et Silence, 2010.

———. *Foi catholique et problèmes modernes.* Tournai: Desclée & Cie, 1953.

———. "Théologie morale." *Revue Thomiste* 50 (1950): 192–230.

Lamont, John R. T. "Conscience, Freedom, Rights: Idols of the Enlightenment Religion." *Thomist* 73 (2009): 169–239.

Langston, Douglas C. *Conscience and Other Virtues: From Bonaventure to MacIntyre.* University Park: Pennsylvania State University Press, 2001.

Lavelle, Louis. *De l'acte.* Paris: Aubier, 1937.

———. *Le moi et son destin.* Paris: Aubier, 1936.

Law, David R. "Jaspers and Theology." *Heythrop Journal* 46 (2005): 334–51.

Lawler, Michael G., and Todd A. Salzman. "*Gaudium et Spes* and *Dignitatis Humanae* on Conscience: A Forgotten Concept of Vatican II?" *Louvain Studies* 40 (2017): 153–69.

Leclercq, Jacques. *L'enseignment de la morale chrétienne.* Paris: Vitrail, 1949.

Leclercq, Vincent, AA. "Le *Primat de la charité* de Gilleman et la *Conscience* de Carpentier: Le renouveau théologal de la vie morale." *Studia Moralia* 44 (2006): 353–75.

Lehmann, Karl. "He Simply Was Unique." In *Encounters with Karl Rahner: Remembrances of Rahner by Those Who Knew Him,* edited and translated by Andreas R. Batlogg and Melvin E. Michalski, translation edited by Barbara G. Turner, 111–34. Milwaukee, WI: Marquette University Press, 2009.

Lehmann, Paul. *Ethics in a Christian Context.* London: SCM, 1963.

Leites, Edmund, ed. *Conscience and Casuistry in Early Modern Europe.* Cambridge: Cambridge University Press, 1988.

Le Senne, René. *Obstacle et valeur.* Paris: Aubier, 1934.

———. *Traité de morale générale.* 3rd ed. Paris: Presses Universitaires de France, 1949.

Levering, Matthew. *Aquinas's Eschatological Ethics and the Virtue of Temperance.* Notre Dame: University of Notre Dame Press, 2019.

———. *Biblical Natural Law: A Theocentric and Teleological Approach.* Oxford: Oxford University Press, 2008.

———. *Engaging the Doctrine of Marriage: Human Marriage as the Image and Sacrament of the Marriage of God and Creation.* Eugene, OR: Cascade, 2020.

———. *Engaging the Doctrine of Revelation: The Mediation of the Gospel through Church and Scripture.* Grand Rapids, MI: Baker Academic, 2014.

———. *The Indissolubility of Marriage: "Amoris Laetitia" in Context.* San Francisco: Ignatius, 2019.

———. "Supplementing Pinckaers: The Old Testament in Aquinas's Ethics." In *Reading Sacred Scripture with Thomas Aquinas: Hermeneutical Tools, Theological Questions and New Perspectives,* edited by Piotr Roszak and Jörgen Vijgen, 349–73. Turnhout: Brepols, 2015.

Levinas, Emmanuel. *Difficult Freedom: Essays on Judaism.* Translated by S. Hand. Baltimore, MD: Johns Hopkins University Press, 1997.

Lienkamp, Andreas. "Theodor Steinbüchel (1888–1949)." In *Christliche Ethik im Porträt: Leben und Werk bedeutender Moraltheologen,* edited by Konrad Hilpert, 659–78. Freiburg im Breisgau: Herder, 2012.

Lightfoot, J. B. "Dissertation [or Appendix] II: St. Paul and Seneca." In *Saint Paul's Epistle to the Philippians: A Revised Text with Introduction, Notes and Dissertations*, 270–332. 12th ed. Peabody, MA: Hendrickson, 1995.

Liguori, Alphonsus de. *Moral Theology*. Vol. 1, *Books I-III: On Conscience, Law, Sin and the Theological Virtues*. Translated by Ryan Grant. Post Falls, ID: Mediatrix, 2006.

———. *Theologia Moralis*. Vol. 1. Edited by *Léonard. Gaudé*. Rome: Typographia Vaticana, 1905.

Linnane, Brian. "Ethics." In *The Cambridge Companion to Karl Rahner*, edited by Declan Marmion and Mary E. Hines, 158–73. Cambridge: Cambridge University Press, 2005.

Liu, Yinya. "From Response to Responsibility: A Study of the Other and Language in the Ethical Structure of Responsibility in the Writings of Bonhoeffer and Levinas." PhD diss., National University of Ireland (Maynooth), 2010.

Lobo, George, SJ. *Guide to Christian Living*. Westminster, MD: Christian Classics, 1984.

Lonergan, Bernard, SJ. "Transition from a Classicist World View to Historical Mindedness." In *A Second Collection*, edited by William Ryan and Bernard Tyrrell, 1–9. Philadelphia: Westminster, 1975.

Long, Eugene Thomas. *Jaspers and Bultmann: A Dialogue between Philosophy and Theology in the Existentialist Tradition*. Durham, NC: Duke University Press, 1968.

Longton, Ryan A. "A Reconsideration of Maurice Blondel and the 'Natural' Desire." *Heythrop Journal* 56 (2015): 919–30.

Lotz, J. B., SJ. "Immanenz und Transzendenz heute: Zur inneren Struktur der Problematik unserer Tage." *Scholastik* 13 (1938): 161–72.

MacArthur, John. *The Vanishing Conscience*. Dallas, TX: Word, 1994.

MacIntyre, Alasdair. *Dependent Rational Animals: Why Human Beings Need the Virtues*. Chicago: Open Court, 1999.

———. *Edith Stein: A Philosophical Prologue, 1913–1922*. Lanham, MD: Rowman & Littlefield, 2006.

———. "Preface." In Pinckaers, *Morality*, vii–viii.

———. *Three Rival Versions of Moral Enquiry: Encyclopaedia, Genealogy, and Tradition*. Notre Dame: University of Notre Dame Press, 1990.

Maher, Anthony M. *The Forgotten Jesuit of Catholic Modernism: George Tyrrell's Prophetic Theology*. Minneapolis: Fortress, 2018.

Mahoney, John, SJ. *Christianity in Evolution: An Exploration*. Washington, DC: Georgetown University Press, 2011.

———. "Conscience, Discernment and Prophecy in Moral Decision Making." In *Riding Time Like a River: The Catholic Moral Tradition since Vatican II*, edited by William O'Brien, 81–97. Washington, DC: Georgetown University Press, 1993.

———. *The Making of Moral Theology: A Study of the Roman Catholic Tradition*. Oxford: Oxford University Press, 1987.

———. *Seeking the Spirit: Essays in Moral and Pastoral Theology*. London: Sheed and Ward, 1981.

Mandonnet, Pierre, OP. "Le décret d'Innocent XI et le Probabilisme." *Revue Thomiste* 9 (1901): 460–81, 520–39, 652–73; 10 (1902): 676–98.

———. "De la valeur des theories sur la probabilité morale." *Revue Thomiste* 10 (1902): 314–35.

———. "La position du Probabilisme dans l'Eglise catholique." *Revue Thomiste* 10 (1902): 5–20.

Manent, Pierre. *Natural Law and Human Rights: Toward a Recovery of Practical Reason*. Translated by Ralph C. Hancock. Notre Dame: University of Notre Dame Press, 2020.

Mannion, Gerard. "Magisterium, Margaret Farley, and the Ecclesial Role of Feminist Moral Theology: Discerning the *Ecclesia Discens* Today." In *Feminist Catholic Theological Ethics*, edited by Linda Hogan and A. E. Orobator, 77–92. Maryknoll, NY: Orbis, 2014.

Marinelli, Anthony J. *Conscience and Catholic Faith: Love and Fidelity*. Mahwah, NJ: Paulist, 1991.

Maritain, Jacques. *Bergsonian Philosophy and Thomism*. Translated by Mabel L. Andison and J. Gordon Andison. New York: The Philosophical Library, 1955.

———. *Existence and the Existent: An Essay on Christian Existentialism*. Translated by Lewis Galantiere and Gerald B. Phelan. Garden City, NY: Doubleday, 1956.

———. "The Immanent Dialectic of the First Act of Freedom." In *The Range of Reason*, 66–85. New York: Scribner's Sons, 1952.

———. *An Introduction to the Basic Problems of Moral Philosophy*. Translated by Ornelia N. Borgerhoff. New York: Magi, 1990.

———. *La loi naturelle ou loi non écrite*. Edited by Georges Brazzola. Fribourg: Éditions Universitaires, 1986.

———. *The Peasant of the Garonne: An Old Layman Questions Himself about the Present Time*. Translated by Michael Cuddihy and Elizabeth Hughes. Eugene, OR: Wipf & Stock, 2011.

Marshall, L. H. *The Challenge of New Testament Ethics.* London: Macmillan, 1946.

Masson, Robert. "Rahner and Heidegger: Being, Hearing, and God." *Thomist* 37 (1973): 455–88.

Matera, Frank J. *New Testament Ethics: The Legacies of Jesus and Paul.* Louisville, KY: Westminster John Knox, 1996.

———. *II Corinthians: A Commentary.* Louisville, KY: Westminster John Knox, 2003.

Mattison, William C., III. "Beatitude and Beatitudes in the *Summa theologiae* of St. Thomas Aquinas." *Josephinum Journal of Theology* 17 (2010): 233–49.

———. *Introducing Moral Theology: True Happiness and the Virtues.* Grand Rapids, MI: Brazos, 2008.

———. *The Sermon on the Mount and Moral Theology: A Virtue Perspective.* Cambridge: Cambridge University Press, 2017.

McCabe, Herbert, OP. "The Validity of Absolutes." In *Situationism and the New Morality*, edited by Robert L. Cunningham, 66–78. New York: Meredith, 1970.

McCarthy, David Matzo, and James Donahue, CR. *Moral Vision: Seeing the World with Love and Justice.* Grand Rapids, MI: Eerdmans, 2018.

McCormick, Richard A., SJ. "Fundamental Freedom Revisited." In *The Critical Calling: Reflections on Moral Dilemmas since Vatican II*, 171–90. Washington, DC: Georgetown University Press, 1989.

———. "Moral Theology since Vatican II: Clarity or Chaos?" In *The Critical Calling: Reflections on Moral Dilemmas since Vatican II*, 3–24. Washington, DC: Georgetown University Press, 1989.

McDonough, William. "'New Terrain' and a 'Stumbling Block' in Redemptorist Contributions to *Gaudium et Spes*." *Studia Moralia* 35 (1997): 9–48.

McGinn, Bernard. *Thomas Aquinas's "Summa theologiae": A Biography.* Princeton, NJ: Princeton University Press, 2014.

McGovern, Mark. "Synderesis: A Key to Understanding Natural Law in Aquinas." In *Freedom, Virtue, and the Common Good*, edited by Curtis L. Hancock and Anthony O. Simon, 103–24. Mishawaka, IN: American Maritain Association, 1995.

McInerny, Daniel. *The Difficult Good: A Thomistic Approach to Moral Conflict and Human Happiness.* New York: Fordham University Press, 2006.

McInerny, Ralph. *Aquinas on Human Action: A Theory of Practice.* Washington, DC: Catholic University of America Press, 1992.

———. "The Right Deed for the Wrong Reason: Comments on Theo Belmans."

In *Aquinas on Human Action: A Theory of Practice*, 220–39. Washington, DC: Catholic University of America Press, 1992.

McKeever, Martin, CSsR. "The 50th Anniversary of *The Law of Christ*: Bernhard Häring's Contribution to the Renewal of Moral Theology." *Studia Moralia* 44 (2006): 233–50.

McKenny, Gerald P. *The Analogy of Grace: Karl Barth's Moral Theology.* Oxford: Oxford University Press, 2010.

———. "Ethics." In *The Oxford Handbook of Karl Barth*, edited by Paul Dafydd Jones and Paul T. Nimmo, 482–95. Oxford: Oxford University Press, 2019.

———. "Responsibility." In *The Oxford Handbook of Theological Ethics*, edited by Gilbert Meilaender and William Werpehowski, 237–53. Oxford: Oxford University Press, 2005.

Melina, Livio. *Sharing in Christ's Virtues: For a Renewal of Moral Theology in Light of "Veritatis Splendor."* Translated by William E. May. Washington, DC: Catholic University of America Press, 2001.

Merkelbach, Benoît-Henri, OP. *Summa Theologiae Moralis.* 3 vols. Paris: Desclée de Brouwer, 1931–40.

———. "Where Should We Place the Treatise on Conscience in Moral Theology?" Translated by Matthew K. Minerd. *Nova et Vetera* 18, no. 3 (2020): 1017–37.

Merks, Karl-Wilhelm. *Theologische Fundamentalethik.* Freiburg: Herder, 2020.

Mersch, Emile, SJ. *Morality and the Mystical Body.* Translated by Daniel F. Ryan, SJ. New York: P. J. Kennedy & Sons, 1939.

———. *L'obligation moral principe de liberté: Étude de philosophie morale.* Paris: Alcan, 1927.

Metz, Johann Baptist. "Heidegger und das Problem der Metaphysik." *Scholastik* 28 (1953): 1–22.

Michalson, Carl, ed. *Christianity and the Existentialists.* New York: Scribner's Sons, 1956.

Michel, Ernst. *Der Partner Gottes: Weisungen zum christlichen Selbtverstandnis.* Heidelberg: Lambert Schneider, 1946.

Milhaven, John Giles, SJ. "Objective Moral Evaluation of Circumstances." *Theological Studies* 32 (1971): 407–30.

———. *Toward a New Catholic Morality.* Garden City, NY: Doubleday, 1970.

Milhaven, John Giles, SJ, and David J. Casey, SJ. "Introduction to the Theological Background of the New Morality." *Theological Studies* 28 (1967): 213–44.

Miron, Ronny. "The Guilt Which We Are: On Ontological Approach to Jaspers'

Idea of Guilt." In *Phenomenology and Existentialism in the Twentieth Century. Book Three: Heralding the New Enlightenment*, edited by A.-T. Tymieniecka, 229–51. Hanover, NH: Springer, 2010.

Mitchell, Andrew J., and Peter Trawny, eds. *Heidegger's Black Notebooks: Responses to Anti-Semitism*. New York: Columbia University Press, 2017.

Modras, Ronald. "Implications of Rahner's Anthropology for Fundamental Moral Theology." *Horizons* 12 (1984): 70–90.

Möller, Joseph. *Existenzialphilosophie und katholische Theologie*. Baden-Baden: Kunst und Wissenschaft, 1952.

Monden, Louis, SJ. *Sin, Liberty and Law*. Translated by Joseph Donceel, SJ. New York: Sheed and Ward, 1965.

Moore, Kenneth A., OCarm. "Situational Ethics." *American Ecclesiastical Review* 135 (1956): 29–38.

Morrow, Maria C. *Sin in the Sixties: Catholics and Confession, 1955–1975*. Washington, DC: Catholic University of America Press, 2016.

Mróz, Piotr. "What Does It Mean to Be an Existentialist Today?" In *Phenomenology and Existentialism in the Twentieth Century. Book One: New Waves of Philosophical Inspirations*, edited by A.-T. Tymieniecka, 127–43. Hanover, NH: Springer, 2009.

Naselli, Andrew David, and J. D. Crowley. *Conscience: What It Is, How to Train It, and Loving Those Who Differ*. Wheaton, IL: Crossway, 2016.

Nethöfel, Wolfgang. *Moraltheologie nach dem Konzil: Personen, Programme, Positionem*. Göttingen: Vandenhoeck & Ruprecht, 1987.

Neufeld, Karl Heinz, SJ. *Die Brüder Rahner: Eine Biographie*. Freiburg im Breisgau: Herder, 1994.

Newman, Jeremiah. "The Ethics of Existentialism." *Irish Ecclesiastical Record* 77 (1952): 321–32, 421–31.

Newman, John Henry. "Letter to the Duke of Norfolk." In *Certain Difficulties Felt by Anglicans in Catholic Teaching*, vol. 2, 171–378. London: Longmans Green, 1885.

Niebuhr, H. Richard. *The Responsible Self: An Essay in Christian Moral Philosophy*. Louisville, KY: Westminster John Knox, 1999.

Nietzsche, Friedrich. "'Guilt,' 'Bad Conscience,' and the Like." In *On the Genealogy of Morals*, translated by Walter Kaufmann and R. J. Hollingdale, 57–96. Published with *Ecce Homo*, edited and translated by Walter Kaufmann. New York: Vintage, 1989.

Nimmo, Paul T. *Being in Action: The Theological Shape of Barth's Ethical Vision*. London: T&T Clark, 2007.

Nink, Caspar, SJ. "Grundbegriffe der Philosophie Martin Heideggers." *Philosophisches Jahrbuch* 45 (1932): 129–58.

Noble, Henri-Dominique, OP. *La conscience morale.* Paris: Lethielleux, 1923.

———. *Le discernment de la conscience.* Paris: Lethielleux, 1934.

Nodé-Langlois, Michel. "Science et conscience." *Revue Thomiste* 111 (2011): 583–616.

Noonan, Pius Mary, OSB. "*Auriga et Genetrix*: Le role de la prudence dans le jugement de la conscience (I)." *Revue Thomiste* 114 (2014): 355–77.

———. "*Auriga et Genetrix*: Le role de la prudence dans le jugement de la conscience (II)." *Revue Thomiste* 114 (2014): 531–68.

Nykänen, Hannes. "Heidegger's Conscience." *Nordic Journal of Philosophy* 6 (2005): 40–65.

O'Connell, Timothy. *Principles for a Catholic Morality.* Rev. ed. San Francisco: Harper & Row, 1990.

Odozor, Paulinus Ikechukwu, CSSp. *Morality Truly Christian, Truly African: Foundational, Methodological, and Theological Considerations.* Notre Dame: University of Notre Dame Press, 2014.

Ojakangas, Mika. *The Voice of Conscience: A Political Genealogy of Western Ethical Experience.* London: Bloomsbury, 2013.

Oliveira, Carlos-Josephat Pinto de, OP. "La prudence, concept clé de la morale du P. Labourdette." *Revue Thomiste* 92 (1992): 267–92.

O'Meara, Thomas F., OP. *God in the World: A Guide to Karl Rahner's Theology.* Collegeville, MN: Liturgical Press, 2007.

———. "Heidegger and His Origins: Theological Perspectives." *Theological Studies* 47 (1986): 205–26.

———. "Interpreting Thomas Aquinas: Aspects of the Dominican School of Moral Theology in the Twentieth Century." In *The Ethics of Aquinas*, edited by Stephen J. Pope, 355–73. Washington, DC: Georgetown University Press, 2002.

O'Regan, Cyril. "Heidegger and Christian Wisdom." In *Christian Wisdom Meets Modernity*, edited by Kenneth Oakes, 37–58. London: Bloomsbury, 2016.

Overberg, Kenneth R., SJ. *Conscience in Conflict: How to Make Moral Choices*, 3rd ed. Cincinnati, OH: St. Anthony Messenger, 2006.

Owen, H. P. *Revelation and Existence: A Study in the Theology of Rudolf Bultmann.* Cardiff: University of Wales Press, 1957.

Pareyson, Luigi. *La filosofia dell'esistenza e Carlo Jaspers.* Naples: Loffredo, 1940.

———. *Studi sull'esistenzialismo.* Florence: Sansoni, 1943.

Patrick, Anne E. *Liberating Conscience: Feminist Explorations in Catholic Moral Theology.* New York: Continuum, 1997.

Paul VI, Pope. *Humanae Vitae.* San Francisco: Ignatius, 2011.

Peghaire, Julien. "A Forgotten Sense: The Cogitative according to St. Thomas Aquinas." *The Modern Schoolman* 20 (1943): 123–40, 210–29.

Pennington, Jonathan T. *The Sermon on the Mount and Human Flourishing: A Theological Commentary.* Grand Rapids, MI: Baker Academic, 2017.

Petri, Thomas, OP. *Aquinas and the Theology of the Body: The Thomistic Foundations of John Paul II's Anthropology.* Washington, DC: Catholic University of America Press, 2016.

Phillips, Jacob. "Joseph Ratzinger and Dietrich Bonhoeffer on Heteronomy and Conscience during the Third Reich." In *Joseph Ratzinger and the Healing of the Reformation-Era Divisions*, edited by Emery de Gaál and Matthew Levering, 281–96. Steubenville, OH: Emmaus Academic, 2019.

———. "My Enemy's Enemy Is My Friend: Martin Luther and Joseph Ratzinger on the Bi-Dimensionality of Conscience." *Heythrop Journal* 61 (2020): 317–26.

Pieper, Josef. *The Four Cardinal Virtues.* Translated by Richard Winston and Clara Winston et al. Notre Dame: University of Notre Dame Press, 1966.

Pierce, C. A. *Conscience in the New Testament.* Chicago: Alec R. Allenson, 1955.

Pinckaers, Servais, OP. "Conscience and Christian Tradition." Translated by Mary Thomas Noble, OP. In *The Pinckaers Reader: Renewing Thomistic Moral Theology*, edited by John Berkman and Craig Steven Titus, 321–41. Washington, DC: Catholic University of America Press, 2005.

———. "Conscience and the Virtue of Prudence." Translated by Mary Thomas Noble, OP. In *The Pinckaers Reader: Renewing Thomistic Moral Theology*, edited by John Berkman and Craig Steven Titus, 342–55. Washington, DC: Catholic University of America Press, 2005.

———. "Dominican Moral Theology in the 20th Century." Translated by Mary Thomas Noble, OP. In *The Pinckaers Reader: Renewing Thomistic Moral Theology*, edited by John Berkman and Craig Steven Titus, 73–89. Washington, DC: Catholic University of America Press, 2005.

———. "An Encyclical for the Future: *Veritatis Splendor.*" In *"Veritatis Splendor" and the Renewal of Moral Theology*, edited by J. A. Di Noia, OP, and Romanus Cessario, OP, 11–71. Chicago: Scepter, 1999.

———. "A Historical Perspective on Intrinsically Evil Acts." Translated by Mary Thomas Noble, OP, with Craig Steven Titus. In *The Pinckaers Reader: Renewing Thomistic Moral Theology*, edited by John Berkman and Craig

Steven Titus, 185–235. Washington, DC: Catholic University of America Press, 2005.

———. *Morality: The Catholic View*. Translated by Michael Sherwin, OP. South Bend, IN: St. Augustine's Press, 2001.

———. *Le renouveau de la morale: Études pour une morale fidèle à ses sources et à sa mission présente*. Paris: Casterman, 1964.

———. "Scripture and the Renewal of Moral Theology: The *Catechism* and *Veritatis Splendor*." Translated by Mary Thomas Noble, OP. In *The Pinckaers Reader: Renewing Thomistic Moral Theology*, edited by John Berkman and Craig Steven Titus, 44–63. Washington, DC: Catholic University of America Press, 2005.

———. *The Sources of Christian Ethics*. Translated by Mary Thomas Noble, OP. Washington, DC: Catholic University of America Press, 1995.

———. *The Spirituality of Martyrdom: To the Limits of Love*. Translated by Patrick M. Clark and Annie Hounsokou. Washington, DC: Catholic University of America Press, 2016.

Pius X, Pope. *Pascendi Dominici Gregis. Acta Sanctae Sedis* 40 (1907). Vatican. va.

Pius XII, Pope. "Address to the World Federation of Catholic Young Women." *Catholic Documents* 8 (1952): 15–20.

———. "The Christian Conscience as an Object of Education." *Catholic Documents* 8 (1952): 1–7.

———. *Humani Generis. Acta Apostolicae Sedis* 42 (1950): 561-78. Vatican.va.

Plant, Stephen J. "'In the Sphere of the Familiar': Heidegger and Bonhoeffer." In *Bonhoeffer's Intellectual Formation*, edited by Peter Frick, 301–27. Tübingen: Mohr Siebeck, 2008.

Pope, Stephen J. *Human Evolution and Christian Ethics*. Cambridge: Cambridge University Press, 2007.

Potts, Timothy C. *Conscience in Medieval Philosophy*. Cambridge: Cambridge University Press, 1980.

Prümmer, Dominic M., OP. *Handbook of Moral Theology*. Translated by Gerald W. Shelton. Harrison, NY: Roman Catholic Books, 1957.

Przywara, Erich, SJ. "Alter und Neuer Katholizismus." In *Katholische Krise*, edited by Berhard Gertz, 167–90. Düsseldorf: Patmos, 1967.

———. *Analogia Entis: Metaphysics; Original Structure and Universal Rhythm*. Translated by John R. Betz and David Bentley Hart. Grand Rapids, MI: Eerdmans, 2014.

———. *Christliche Existenz*. Leipzig: Hegner, 1934.

———. "Sein im Scheitern—Sein im Aufgang." *Stimmen der Zeit* 123 (1932): 152–61.

Puffer, Matthew. "Election in Bonhoeffer's *Ethics*: Discerning a Late Revision." *International Journal of Systematic Theology* 14 (2012): 255–76.

Rahner, Karl, SJ. "Der Appell an das Gewissen: Situationsethik und Sünden-mystik." *Wort und Wahrheit* 4 (1949): 721–34.

———. "Bemerkungen über das Naturgesetz und seine Erkennbarkeit." *Orientierung* 19 (1955): 239–43.

———. "Christology within an Evolutionary View of the World." In *Later Writings*, translated by Karl-H. Kruger, 157–92. Vol. 5 of *Theological Investigations*. Baltimore, MD: Helicon, 1966.

———. "The 'Commandment' of Love in Relation to the Other Commandments." In *Later Writings*, translated by Karl-H. Kruger, 439–59. Vol. 5 of *Theological Investigations*. New York: Crossroad, 1966.

———. "The Concept of Existential Philosophy in Heidegger." Translated by Andrew Tallon. *Philosophy Today* 13 (1969): 126–37. Originally published as "Introduction au concept de philosophie existentiale chez Heidegger." Translated by. R. Celle. *Recherches de Science Religieuse* 30 (1940): 152–71.

———. "Conscience." In *Humane Society and the Church of Tomorrow*, translated by Joseph Donceel, SJ, 3–13. Vol. 22 of *Theological Investigations*. New York: Crossroad, 1991. Originally published as "Vom irrenden Gewissen: Über Freiheit und Würde menschlicher Entscheidung." *Orientierung* 47 (1983): 246–50.

———. "The Dignity and Freedom of Man." In *Man in the Church*, translated by Karl-H. Kruger, 235–63. Vol. 2 of *Theological Investigations*. Baltimore, MD: Helicon, 1963.

———. "The Experiment with Man: Theological Observations on Man's Self-Manipulation." In *Writings of 1965–1967*, translated by Graham Harrison, 205–24. Vol. 9 of *Theological Investigations*. New York: Herder and Herder, 1972.

———. *Foundations of Christian Faith: An Introduction to the Idea of Christianity.* Translated by William V. Dych. New York: Crossroad, 1993.

———. *Gefahren im heutigen Katholizismus.* Einsiedeln: Benzinger, 1950.

———. "Guilt—Responsibility—Punishment within the View of Catholic Theology." In *Concerning Vatican Council II*, translated by Karl-H. Kruger and Boniface Kruger, 197–217. Vol. 6 of *Theological Investigations*. London: Darton, Longman & Todd, 1969.

———. *Hearer of the Word*. Translated by Joseph Donceel, SJ. New York: Cross-road, 1994.

———. "Immanent and Transcendent Consummation of the World." In *Writings of 1965-67*, translated by David Bourke, 273–89. Vol. 10 of *Theological Investigations*. New York: Seabury, 1973.

———. "The Individual in the Church." In *Nature and Grace*, translated by Dinah Wharton, 9–38. New York: Sheed and Ward, 1964. Originally published as "Der Einzelne in der Kirche." *Stimmen der Zeit* 39 (1946–47): 260–76.

———. "Justified and Sinner at the Same Time." In *Concerning Vatican Council II*, translated by Karl-H. Kruger and Boniface Kruger, 218–30. Vol. 6 of *Theological Investigations*. London: Darton, Longman & Todd, 1969.

———. "On Bad Arguments in Moral Theology." In *God and Revelation*, translated by Edward Quinn, 74–85. Vol. 18 of *Theological Investigations*. New York: Crossroad, 1983.

———. "On the Question of a Formal Existential Ethics." In *Man in the Church*, translated by Karl-H. Kruger, 217–34. Vol. 2 of *Theological Investigations*. Baltimore, MD: Helicon, 1963. Originally published as "Über die Frage einer formalen Existentialethik." In *Schriften zur Theologie*. Vol. 2. (Einsiedeln: Benziger, 1955).

———. "Principles and Prescriptions." In *The Dynamic Element in the Church*, translated by W. J. O'Hara, 13–41. New York: Herder and Herder, 1964. Originally published as "Prinzipien und Imperative." *Wort und Wahrheit* 12 (1957): 325–39.

———. "Reflections on Methodology in Theology." In *Confrontations 1*, translated by David Bourke, 68–114. Vol. 11 of *Theological Investigations*. New York: Seabury, 1974.

———. "Reflections on the Unity of the Love of Neighbour and the Love of God." In *Concerning Vatican Council II*, translated by Karl-H. Kruger and Boniface Kruger, 231–49. Vol. 6 of *Theological Investigations*. London: Darton, Longman & Todd, 1969.

———. *The Shape of the Church to Come*. Translated by Edward Quinn. New York: Seabury, 1974. Originally published as *Strukturwandel der Kirche als Aufgabe und Chance* (Freiburg im Breisgau: Herder, 1972).

———. "Some Thoughts on a Good Intention." In *Theology of the Spiritual Life*, translated by Karl-H. Kruger and Boniface Kruger, 105–28. Vol. 3 of *Theological Investigations*. New York: Seabury, 1967.

———. "The Theological Concept of *Concupiscentia*." In *God, Christ, Mary and Grace*, translated by Cornelius Ernst, 347–82. Vol. 1 of *Theological Investigations*. London: Darton, Longman & Todd, 1961.

———. "Theology of Freedom." In *Concerning Vatican Council II*, translated by Karl-H. Kruger and Boniface Kruger, 178–96. Vol. 6 of *Theological Investigations*. London: Darton, Longman & Todd, 1969.

Ramage, Matthew J. *The Experiment of Faith: Pope Benedict XVI on Living the Theological Virtues in a Secular Age*. Washington, DC: Catholic University of America Press, 2020.

Rambert, Paul. "L'articulation entre la loi éternelle et la loi naturelle dans les manuels thomistes d'avant Vatican II." *Revue Thomiste* 113 (2013): 47–82.

———. "Conscience et loi naturelle dans les manuels d'avant Vatican II." *Revue Thomiste* 119 (2019): 397–448.

———. "La loi comme ordination rationis dans les manuels d'avant Vatican II." *Revue Thomiste* 109 (2009): 531–88.

Rashdall, Hastings. *Conscience and Christ: Six Lectures on Christian Ethics*. London: Duckworth, 1916.

Ratzinger, Joseph. "Bishops, Theologians, and Morality." In *On Conscience: Two Essays by Joseph Ratzinger*, edited by John M. Haas, 43–75, 80–82. San Francisco: Ignatius, 2007.

———. "Conscience and Truth." In *Crisis of Conscience*, edited by John M. Haas, 1–20. New York: Crossroad, 1996.

———. "Conscience in Time." Translated by W. J. O'Hara. In *Anthropology and Culture*, edited by David L. Schindler and Nicholas J. Healy, 17–27. Vol. 2 of *Joseph Ratzinger in* Communio. Grand Rapids, MI: Eerdmans, 2013.

———. "The Dignity of the Human Person." In *Pastoral Constitution on the Church in the Modern World*, edited by Herbert Vorgrimler, 134–36. Vol. 5 of *Commentary on the Documents of Vatican II*. New York: Herder & Herder, 1969.

———. *Milestones: Memoirs 1927–1977*. Translated by Erasmo Leiva-Merikakis. San Francisco: Ignatius, 1998.

———. *Salt of the Earth: Christianity and the Catholic Church at the End of the Millennium: An Interview with Peter Seewald*. Translated by Adrian Walker. San Francisco: Ignatius, 1997.

Reinhardt, Nicole. "How Individual Was Conscience in the Early-Modern Period? Observations on the Development of Catholic Moral Theology." *Religion* 45 (2015): 409–28.

Rey-Mermet, Théodule. *Conscience et liberté*. Paris: Nouvelle Cité, 1990.

Rhonheimer, Martin. *The Perspective of Morality: Philosophical Foundations of Thomistic Virtue Ethics*. Translated by Gerald Malsbury. Washington, DC: Catholic University of America Press, 2011.

Ricoeur, Paul. *Oneself as Another.* Translated by Kathleen Blamey. Chicago: University of Chicago Press, 1995.

———. "The Relation of Jaspers' Philosophy to Religion." Translated by Forrest W. Williams. In *The Philosophy of Karl Jaspers*, edited by Paul Arthur Schilpp, 611–42. La Salle, IL: Open Court, 1957.

———. "The Summoned Subject in the School of the Narratives of the Prophetic Vocation." In *Figuring the Sacred*, 262–75. Minneapolis: Fortress, 1995.

Riessen, Renée van. "On the Creation and Possession of Time: Barth's Critique of Augustine and Heidegger in *CD* I/2, §14." *Zeitschrift Für Dialektische Theologie*, Supplement Series 4 (2010): 6–20.

Rigali, Norbert J. "The Uniqueness and Distinctiveness of Christian Morality and Ethics." In *Moral Theology: Challenges for the Future; Essays in Honor of Richard A. McCormick*, edited by Charles E. Curran, 74–93. New York: Paulist, 1990.

Ritschl, Albrecht. Über das Gewissen*: Ein Vortrag.* Bonn: A. Marcus, 1876.

Robbers, Henricus, SJ. "De Beteekenis van het Neo-Thomisme voor het hedendaagsche katholieke denkleven." *Synthese* 1 (1936): 377–82.

Robinson, Daniel N., Gladys M. Sweeney, and Richard Gill, LC, eds. *Human Nature and Its Wholeness: A Roman Catholic Perspective.* Washington, DC: Catholic University of America Press, 2006.

Römelt, Josef, CSsR. "Bernhard Häring (1912–1998)." In *Christliche Ethik im Porträt: Leben und Werk bedeutender Moraltheologen*, edited by Konrad Hilpert, 705–28. Freiburg im Breisgau: Herder, 2012.

———. *Personales Gottesverständnis in heutiger Moraltheologie auf dem Hintergrund der Theologie von Karl Rahner und Hans Urs von Balthasar.* Innsbruck: Tyrolia, 1988.

Rose, Matthew. *Ethics with Barth.* Aldershot: Ashgate, 2010.

Russell, Daniel C., ed. *The Cambridge Companion to Virtue Ethics.* Cambridge: Cambridge University Press, 2013.

Ryan, Maura A., and Brian F. Linnane, eds. *A Just and True Love: Feminism at the Frontiers of Theological Ethics; Essays in Honor of Margaret A. Farley.* Notre Dame: University of Notre Dame Press, 2007.

Rziha, John. *Perfecting Human Actions: St. Thomas Aquinas on Human Participation in Eternal Law.* Washington, DC: Catholic University of America Press, 2009.

Safranski, Rüdiger. *Martin Heidegger: Between Good and Evil.* Translated by Ewald Osers. Cambridge, MA: Harvard University Press, 1998.

Sartre, Jean-Paul. *Being and Nothingness: A Phenomenological Essay on Ontology.* Translated by Hazel E. Barnes. New York: Philosophical Library, 1956.

———. *Existentialism Is a Humanism*. Translated by Carol Macomber. New Haven, CT: Yale University Press, 2007.

Sautenmeister, Jochen. *Identität und Authentizität: Studien zur normativen Logik personaler Orientierung*. Freiburg im Breisgau: Herder, 2013.

———. "Josef Fuchs (1912–2005)." In *Christliche Ethik im Porträt: Leben und Werk bedeutender Moraltheologen*, edited by Konrad Hilpert, 759–90. Freiburg im Breisgau: Herder, 2012.

Scheler, Max. *Formalism in Ethics and Non-Formal Ethics of Values: A New Attempt toward the Foundation of an Ethical Personalism*. Translated from the 5th rev. ed. (1966) by Manfred S. Frings and Roger L. Funk. Evanston, IL: Northwestern University Press, 1973.

Schilpp, Paul Arthur, ed. *The Philosophy of Karl Jaspers*. La Salle, IL: Open Court, 1957.

Schmied, Augustin, CSsR, and Joseph Römelt, CSsR, eds. *50 Jahre "Das Gesetz Christi": Der Beitrag Bernhard Härings zur Erneuerung der Moraltheologie*. Münster: LIT, 2005.

Schnackenburg, Rudolf. *The Moral Teaching of the New Testament*. Translated by J. Holland-Smith and W. J. O'Hara. New York: Herder and Herder, 1965.

Schockenhoff, Eberhard. "Pater Bernard Häring als Wegbereiter einer konziliaren Moraltheologie." In *50 Jahre "Das Gesetz Christi": Der Beitrag Bernhard Härings zur Erneuerung der Moraltheologie*, edited by Augustin Schmied, CSsR, and Josef Römelt, CSsR, 43–68. Münster: LIT, 2005.

———. *Wie Gewiss ist das Gewissen? Eine ethische Orientierung*. Freiburg: Herder, 2003.

Schockenhoff, Eberhard, and Christiane Florin. *Gewissen—eine Gebrauchsanweisung*. Freiburg: Herder, 2009.

Schuessler, Rudolf. *The Debate on Probable Opinions in the Scholastic Tradition*. Leiden: Brill, 2019.

———. *Moral im Zweifel*. Vol. 2, *Die Herausforderung des Probabilismus*. Paderborn: Mentis Verlag, 2006.

———. "Scholastic Social Epistemology in the Baroque Era." *American Catholic Philosophical Quarterly* 93 (2019): 335–60.

Schüller, Bruno, SJ. *Gesetz und Freiheit*. Düsseldorf: Patmos, 1966.

———. *Wholly Human: Essays on the Theory and Language of Morality*. Translated by Peter Heinegg. Washington, DC: Georgetown University Press, 1986.

Schultenover, David G., SJ. *George Tyrrell: In Search of Catholicism*. Shepherdstown: Patmos, 1981.

Schüssler, Ingeborg. "Conscience et vérité: L'interpretation existentiale de la conscience chez Martin Heidegger (Être et Temps §§54–62)." *Revista Portuguesa de Filosofia* 59 (2003): 1051–78.

Schweiker, William. *Responsibility and Christian Ethics.* Cambridge: Cambridge University Press, 1995.

Seewald, Peter. *Benedict XVI: A Life.* Vol. 1, *Youth in Nazi Germany to the Second Vatican Council, 1927–1965.* London: Bloomsbury, 2020.

Sheehan, Thomas. *Karl Rahner: The Philosophical Foundations.* Athens: Ohio University Press, 1987.

Sherwin, Michael S., OP. *By Knowledge and By Love: Charity and Knowledge in the Moral Theology of St. Thomas Aquinas.* Washington, DC: Catholic University of America Press, 2005.

Sherwin, Michael S., OP, and Craig Steven Titus, eds. *Renouveler toutes choses en Christ: Vers un renouveau thomiste de la théologie morale.* Fribourg: Fribourg University Press, 2009.

Siebenrock, Roman A. "Obéissance ecclésiale comme engagement et protestation: La théologie de Karl Rahner comme 'théologie attentive aux signes du temps present.'" Translated by Robert Kremer. *Recherches de Science Religieuse* 108 (2020): 405–23.

Siker, Jeffrey. "Bernard Häring: The Freedom of His Responsive Love." In *Scripture and Ethics: Twentieth-Century Portraits,* 59–79. Oxford: Oxford University Press, 1996.

Simon, Yves. *Freedom of Choice.* Translated and edited by Peter Wolff. New York: Fordham University Press, 1969.

Smith, Janet E. "The *Sensus fidelium* and *Humanae Vitae.*" In *Why "Humanae Vitae" Is Still Right,* edited by Janet E. Smith, 264–94. San Francisco: Ignatius, 2018.

Smith, Robert J. *Conscience and Catholicism: The Nature and Function of Conscience in Contemporary Roman Catholic Moral Theology.* Lanham, MD: University Press of America, 1998.

Somme, Luc-Thomas, OP. "La conscience morale à Vatican II et dans le Magistère postérieur." *Revue Thomiste* 110 (2010): 217–40.

Sorabji, Richard. *Moral Conscience through the Ages: Fifth Century BCE to the Present.* Chicago: University of Chicago Press, 2014.

Spaemann, Robert. "Conscience and Responsibility in Christian Ethics." In *Crisis of Conscience: Philosophers and Theologians Analyze Our Growing Inability to Discern Right from Wrong,* edited by John M. Haas, 111–34. New York: Crossroad, 1996.

———. *Moralische Grundbegriffe.* Munich: Beck, 1982.

———. *Persons: The Difference between "Someone" and "Something."* Translated by Oliver O'Donovan. Oxford: Oxford University Press, 2006.

Spicq, Ceslas, OP. "La conscience dans le Nouveau Testament." *Revue Biblique* 47 (1938): 50–80.

———. *Les épitres pastorales.* Paris: Gabalda, 1947.

Stanley, Timothy. *Protestant Metaphysics after Karl Barth and Martin Heidegger.* Eugene, OR: Wipf & Stock, 2010.

Staten, John C. *Conscience and the Reality of God: An Essay on the Experiential Foundations of Religious Knowledge.* Berlin: Mouton de Gruyter, 1988.

Steinbüchel, Theodor. *Existenzialismus und christliches Ethos.* Heidelberg: F. H. Kerle, 1948.

———. *Religion und Moral: Im Lichte personaler christlicher Existenz.* Frankfurt am Main: Josef Knecht, 1951.

Stelzenberger, Johannes. *"Conscientia" bei Augustinus: Studie zur Geschichte der Moraltheologie.* Paderborn: Ferdinand Schöningh, 1959.

———. *Lehrbuch der Moraltheologie: Die Sittlichkeitslehre der Konigherrschaft Gottes.* Paderborn: Ferdinand Schöningh, 1953.

———. *Syneidesis bei Origenes: Studie zur Geschichte der Moraltheologie.* Paderborn: Ferdinand Schöningh, 1963.

———. *Syneidesis im Neuen Testament.* Paderborn: Ferdinand Schöningh, 1961.

Strohm, Paul. *Conscience: A Very Short Introduction.* Oxford: Oxford University Press, 2011.

Sullivan, Ezra, OP. *Habits and Holiness: Ethics, Theology, and Biological Psychology.* Washington, DC: Catholic University of America Press, 2021.

Swanton, Christine. *Virtue Ethics: A Pluralistic View.* Oxford: Oxford University Press, 2005.

Szmyd, Jan. "Post-Modernism and the Ethics of Conscience: Various 'Interpretations' of the Morality of the Post-Modern World. Role of A. T. Tymieniecka's Phenomenology of Life." In *Phenomenology and Existentialism in the Twentieth Century*, bk. 3, *Heralding the New Enlightenment*, edited by A.-T. Tymieniecka, 111–22. Dordrecht: Springer, 2010.

Tanner, Kathryn. "A Theological Case for Human Responsibility in Moral Choice." *Journal of Religion* 73 (1993): 592–612.

Teilhard de Chardin, Pierre, SJ. *The Phenomenon of Man.* Translated by Bernard Wall. New York: HarperCollins, 2008.

Theiner, Johann. *Die Entwicklung der Moraltheologie zur eigenständigen Disziplin.* Regensburg: Friedrich Pustet, 1970.

Theobald, Christoph, SJ. "Karl Rahner—La puissance d'engendrement d'une pensée." *Recherches de Science Religieuse* 108 (2020): 451–81.

Thévenot, Xavier. *Repères éthiques pour un monde nouveau*. Paris: Salvator, 1982.

Thils, Gustav. *Tendances actuelles en théologie morale*. Gembloux: J. Duclot, 1940.

Thomasset, Alain, SJ. "La conscience morale et les questions posées par les documents récents du magistère romain." *Revue d'Éthique et de Théologie Morale*, no. 293 (2017): 25–42.

———. *Interpréter et agir: Jalons pour une éthique chrétienne*. Paris: Cerf, 2011.

Thornhill, Chris, and Ronny Miron. "Karl Jaspers." In *Stanford Encyclopedia of Philosophy*, edited by Edward N. Zalta. Stanford University, 1997-. Article published June 5, 2006; last modified July 17, 2018. https://plato.stanford.edu/archives/spr2020/entries/jaspers/.

Thyssen, Johannes. "The Concept of 'Foundering' in Jaspers' Philosophy." In *The Philosophy of Karl Jaspers*, edited by Paul Arthur Schilpp, 297–335. La Salle, IL: Open Court, 1957.

Tillmann, Fritz. *The Master Calls: A Handbook of Christian Living*. Translated by Gregory Roettger, OSB. Baltimore, MD: Helicon, 1960. Originally published as *Der Meister ruft: Die katholische Sittenlehre gemeinverständlich dargestellt* (Düsseldorf: Patmos, 1948).

———. *Die Idee der Nachfolge Christi*. Vol. 3 of *Handbuch der katholischen Sittenlehre*. Düsseldorf: L. Schwann, 1934.

———. *Der Verwirklichung der Nachfolge Christi*. Vol. 2 of *Handbuch der katholischen Sittenlehre*. Düsseldorf: L. Schwann, 1934.

Timpe, Kevin, and Craig A. Boyd, eds. *Virtues and Their Vices*. Oxford: Oxford University Press, 2014.

Titus, Craig Steven. "Servais Pinckaers and the Renewal of Catholic Moral Theology." *Journal of Moral Theology* 1 (2012): 43–68.

Torrell, Jean-Pierre, OP. *Saint Thomas Aquinas*. Vol. 2, *Spiritual Master*. Translated by Robert Royal. Washington, DC: Catholic University of America Press, 2003.

Troeltsch, Ernst. *The Christian Faith: Based on Lectures Delivered at the University of Heidelberg in 1912 and 1913*. Edited by Gertrud von le Fort. Translated by Garrett E. Paul. Minneapolis: Fortress, 1991.

Turner, Denys. *Thomas Aquinas: A Portrait*. New Haven, CT: Yale University Press, 2013.

Turrini, Miriam. *La coscienza e le leggi: Morale e diritto nei testi per la confessione della prima età moderna*. Bologna: Il Mulino, 1991.

Tutino, Stefania. *Uncertainty in Post-Reformation Catholicism: A History of Probabilism*. Oxford: Oxford University Press, 2018.

Tyrrell, George. *Essays on Faith and Immortality.* Edited by M. D. Petre. New York: Longmans, Green & Co., 1914.

———. *Through Scylla and Charybdis; or, The Old Theology and the New.* London: Longmans, Green, and Co., 1907.

Valadier, Paul. *Éloge de la conscience.* Paris: Esprit, 1994.

———. *Rigorisme contre liberté morale: Les Provinciales; Actualité d'une polémique antijésuite.* Brussels: Lessius, 2013.

Van Buren, John. *The Young Heidegger: Rumor of the Hidden King.* Bloomington: Indiana University Press, 1994.

Van Hove, Brian, SJ. "Looking Back at *Humani Generis.*" *Homiletic and Pastoral Review.* December 23, 2013. https://www.hprweb.com/2013/12/looking-back-at-humani-generis/.

Vatican Council II. *Gaudium et Spes.* In *The Conciliar and Postconciliar Documents,* rev. ed., edited by Austin Flannery, 903–1001. Vol. 1 of *Vatican Council II: Constitutions, Decrees, Declarations.* Northport, NY: Costello, 1996.

———. *Optatam Totius.* In *The Conciliar and Postconciliar Documents,* rev. ed., edited by Austin Flannery, 707–24. Vol. 1 of *Vatican Council II: Constitutions, Decrees, Declarations.* Northport, NY: Costello, 1996.

———. *Unitatis Redintegratio.* In *The Conciliar and Postconciliar Documents,* rev. ed., edited by Austin Flannery, 452–70. Vol. 1 of *Vatican Council II: Constitutions, Decrees, Declarations.* Northport, NY: Costello, 1996.

Vechtel, Klaus, SJ. "Karl Rahner: Ses sources et ses lieux théologiques." Translated by Robert Kremer. *Recherches de Science Religieuse* 108 (2020): 387–404.

Vereecke, Louis. "La conscience selon saint Alphonse Liguori." *Studia Moralia* 21 (1983): 259–73.

Vermeersch, Arthur, SJ. "Soixante ans de théologie morale." *Nouvelle Revue de Théologie* 56 (1929): 863–84.

Wahl, Jean. "Notes on Some Relations of Jaspers to Kierkegaard and Heidegger." Translated by Forrest W. Williams. In *The Philosophy of Karl Jaspers,* edited by Paul Arthur Schilpp, 393–406. La Salle, IL: Open Court, 1957.

Wallace, William A., OP. "Existential Ethics: A Thomistic Appraisal." *Thomist* 27 (1963): 493–515.

———. *The Role of Demonstration in Moral Theology: A Study of Methodology in St. Thomas Aquinas.* Washington, DC: Thomist, 1962.

Wassmer, Thomas, SJ. *Christian Ethics for Today.* Milwaukee, WI: Bruce, 1969.

———. "Contemporary Situational Morality and the Catholic Christian." In

To Be a Man, edited by George Devine, 93–106. Englewood Cliffs, NJ: Prentice Hall, 1969.

————. "Is Intrinsic Evil a Viable Term?" *Chicago Studies* 5 (1966): 307–14.

Webster, John. "God and Conscience." In *The Doctrine of God and Theological Ethics*, edited by Alan J. Torrance and Michael Banner, 147–65. London: T&T Clark International, 2006.

————. "'The Great Disruption': Word of God and Moral Consciousness in Barth's Münster *Ethics*." In *Barth's Moral Theology: Human Action in Barth's Thought*, 41–64. Grand Rapids, MI: Eerdmans, 1998.

White, Thomas Joseph, OP. *The Incarnate Lord: A Thomistic Study in Christology*. Washington, DC: Catholic University of America Press, 2015.

————. *Wisdom in the Face of Modernity: A Study in Thomistic Natural Theology*. 2nd ed. Ave Maria, FL: Sapientia, 2016.

Williams, John R. "Heidegger and the Theologians." *Heythrop Journal* 12 (1971): 258–80.

Winkler, Rafael. "Alterity and the Call of Conscience: Heidegger, Levinas, and Ricoeur." *International Journal of Philosophical Studies* 24 (2016): 219–33.

Wolfe, Judith. *Heidegger and Theology*. London: Bloomsbury, 2014.

Woodson, Hue. *Heideggerian Theologies: The Pathmarks of John Macquarrie, Rudolf Bultmann, Paul Tillich, and Karl Rahner*. Eugene, OR: Wipf & Stock, 2018.

Wright, N. T. *After You Believe: Why Christian Character Matters*. New York: HarperCollins, 2010.

Wulf, Hans, SJ. "Gesetz und Liebe in der Ordnung des Heils." *Geist und Leben* 22 (1949): 356–67.

Zachman, Randall C. "Barth and Reformation Theology." In *The Oxford Handbook of Karl Barth*, edited by Paul Dafydd Jones and Paul T. Nimmo, 101–15. Oxford: Oxford University Press, 2019.

Zuijdwegt, Geertjan, and Terrence Merrigan. "Conscience." In *The Oxford Handbook of John Henry Newman*, edited by Frederick D. Aquino and Benjamin J. King, 434–53. Oxford: Oxford University Press, 2018.

Zukowski, Edward. "The Good Conscience of Nazi Doctors." *The Annual of the Society of Christian Ethics* 14 (1994): 53–82.

Index